Teaching Critical Thinking in Psychology

Teaching Critical Thinking in Psychology

A Handbook of Best Practices

Edited by
Dana S. Dunn, Jane S. Halonen,
and Randolph A. Smith

A John Wiley & Sons, Ltd., Publication

This edition first published 2008
© 2008 Blackwell Publishing Ltd

Blackwell Publishing was acquired by John Wiley & Sons in February 2007. Blackwell's publishing program has been merged with Wiley's global Scientific, Technical, and Medical business to form Wiley-Blackwell.

Registered Office
John Wiley & Sons Ltd, The Atrium, Southern Gate, Chichester, West Sussex, PO19 8SQ, United Kingdom

Editorial Offices
350 Main Street, Malden, MA 02148-5020, USA
9600 Garsington Road, Oxford, OX4 2DQ, UK
The Atrium, Southern Gate, Chichester, West Sussex, PO19 8SQ, UK

For details of our global editorial offices, for customer services, and for information about how to apply for permission to reuse the copyright material in this book please see our website at www.wiley.com/wiley-blackwell.

The right of Dana S. Dunn, Jane S. Halonen, and Randolph A. Smith to be identified as the authors of the editorial material in this work has been asserted in accordance with the Copyright, Designs and Patents Act 1988.

Library of Congress Cataloging-in-Publication Data

Teaching critical thinking in psychology : a handbook of best practices / edited by Dana S. Dunn, Jane S. Halonen, and Randolph A. Smith.
    p. cm.
    Includes bibliographical references and indexes.
    ISBN 978-1-4051-7402-2 (pbk. : alk. paper) – ISBN 978-1-4051-7403-9 (hardcover : alk. paper)
1. Critical thinking–Study and teaching. 2. Thought and thinking–Study and teaching. 3. Psychology–Study and teaching. I. Dunn, Dana S. II. Halonen, Jane S. III. Smith, Randolph A., 1951-

    BF441.T35 2008
    150.71–dc22

                                2008011373

A catalogue record for this book is available from the British Library.

Set in 10.5/12.5pt Adobe Garamond by SPi Publisher Services, Pondicherry, India
Printed in Singapore by Markono Print Media Pte Ltd

1   2008

In memory of my grandmother, Yvonne Harman, ever a critical thinker. DSD

In honor of my amazing colleagues at Alverno College who helped me find such satisfaction in the mystery of teaching critical thinking. JSH

To my parents—Anna and Hugh—and my mentors—Phil, Dick, Eric, and Mrs. Flowers—who encouraged my early efforts at critical thinking. RAS

Contents

Contents

Contents

List of Contributors

Jeffrey Andre, James Madison University – andrejt@jmu.edu
Kevin J. Apple, James Madison University – applekj@jmu.edu
Suzanne C. Baker, James Madison University – bakers@jmu.edu
Kenneth E. Barron, James Madison University – barronke@jmu.edu
Bernard C. Beins, Ithaca College – beins@ithaca.edu
Ronald W. Belter, University of West Florida – rbelter@uwf.edu
Deborah S. Briihl, Valdosta State University – dbriihl@valdosta.edu
William Buskist, Auburn University – buskiwf@auburn.edu
David W. Carroll, University of Wisconsin-Superior – dcarroll@uwsuper.edu
Maria Darcy, Private practice, Orlando, FL – drmariadarcy@cfl.rr.com
Beth Dietz-Uhler, Miami University – uhlerbd@muohio.edu
Bryan J. Dik, Colorado State University – Bryan.dik@ColoState.edu
Dana S. Dunn, Moravian College – dunn@moravian.edu
Laird R. O. Edman, Northwestern College – ledman@nwciowa.edu
Alisha L. Francis, Northwest Missouri State University – ALISHAF@nwmissouri.edu
Marin Gillis, University of Nevada School of Medicine – mgillis@medicine.nevada.edu
Dana Gross, St. Olaf College – grossd@stolaf.edu
Jane S. Halonen, University of West Florida – jhalonen@uwf.edu
Diane F. Halpern, Claremont McKenna College – diane.halpern@
    claremontmckenna.edu
Elizabeth Yost Hammer, Xavier University of Louisiana – eyhammer@xula.edu
Richard D. Harvey, Saint Louis University – harveyr@slu.edu
Jeffrey D. Holmes, Ithaca College – jholmes@ithaca.edu
Jessica G. Irons, James Madison University – ironsjg@jmu.edu
Kiersten A. Jarvis, University of North Florida – kiersten.jarvis@unf.edu
Allen H. Keniston, University of Wisconsin-Eau Claire – kenistah@uwec.edu
Trina C. Kershaw, University of Massachusetts Dartmouth – tkershaw@umassd.edu

Katherine Kipp, Gainesville College-Oconee Campus – kkipp@gsc.edu

James H. Korn, Saint Louis University – kornjh@earthlink.net

Janet E. Kuebli, Saint Louis University – kueblije@slu.edu

Nina Lamson, Gainesville College–Oconee Campus – nlamson@gsc.edu

Sherri B. Lantinga, Dordt College – lantinga@dordt.edu

Natalie Kerr Lawrence, James Madison University – lawrennk@jmu.edu

Lawrence Benjamin Lewis, Loyola University of New Orleans – lewis@loyno.edu

Scott O. Lilienfeld, Emory University – slilien@emory.edu

Jordan P. Lippman, University of Illinois at Chicago – jlippman@uic.edu

Jeffrey M. Lohr, University of Arkansas – jlohr@uark.edu

Sherrie L. Mahurin, George Fox University – slmahurin@comcast.net

Joseph A. Mayo, Gordon College – joe _m@gdn.edu

Susan L. O'Donnell, George Fox University – sodonnell@georgefox.edu

Stellan Ohlsson, University of Illinois at Chicago – stellan@uic.edu

Bunmi O. Olatunji, Vanderbilt University – olubunmi.o.olatunji@vanderbilt.edu

Blaine F. Peden, University of Wisconsin-Eau Claire – pedenbf@uwec.edu

James W. Pellegrino, University of Illinois at Chicago – pellejw@uic.edu

Monica J. Reis-Bergan, James Madison University – reisbemj@jmu.edu

Bryan K. Saville, James Madison University – savillbk@jmu.edu

Sherry L. Serdikoff, James Madison University – serdiksl@jmu.edu

Paul C. Smith, Alverno College – paul.smith@alverno.edu

Randolph A. Smith, Lamar University – randolph.smith@lamar.edu

Stacie M. Spencer, Massachusetts College of Pharmacy and Health Sciences – stacie. spencer@mcphs.edu

Claudia J. Stanny, University of West Florida – cstanny@uwf.edu

Andrew P. Tix, Normandale Community College – andrew.tix@normandale.edu

Kris Vasquez, Alverno College – kris.vasquez@alverno.edu

Carole Wade, Dominican University of California – cwade2@sbcglobal.net

Rebecca Wenrich Wheeler, Southeast Raleigh Magnet High School – rwheeler1@ wcpss.net

Todd J. Wilkinson, University of Minnesota – wilk0159@umn.edu

Tracy E. Zinn, James Madison University – zinnte@jmu.edu

About the Editors

Dana S. Dunn, a social psychologist, is professor of psychology and director of the Learning in Common Curriculum at Moravian College, Bethlehem, PA. He received his PhD from the University of Virginia, having graduated previously with a BA in psychology from Carnegie Mellon University. A Fellow of the American Psychological Association, Dunn is active in the Society for the Teaching of Psychology, and served as the Chair of Moravian's Department of Psychology from 1995 to 2001. He writes frequently about his areas of research interest: the teaching of psychology, social psychology, and rehabilitation psychology. Dunn is the author of five previous books—*The Practical Researcher: A Student Guide to Conducting Psychological Research, Statistics and Data Analysis for the Behavioral Sciences, A Short Guide to Writing about Psychology, Research Methods for Social Psychology,* and *Psychology Applied to Modern Life* (with Wayne Weiten, Margaret Lloyd, and Elizabeth Y. Hammer)—and the coeditor of three others—*Measuring Up: Educational Assessment Challenges and Practices for Psychology* (with Chandra M. Mehrotra and Jane S. Halonen), *Best Practices for Teaching Introduction to Psychology* (with Stephen L. Chew), and *Best Practices for Teaching Statistics and Research Methods in the Behavioral Sciences* (with Randolph Smith and Bernard C. Beins).

Jane S. Halonen, a clinical psychologist by training, is Dean of Arts and Sciences at the University of West Florida. Jane began her career at Alverno College, an institution widely recognized as a leader in higher education assessment. She served as Director of the School of Psychology at James Madison University from 1998 to 2002. She received her bachelor's degree from Butler University and her advanced degrees from the University of Wisconsin-Milwaukee. A Fellow of the American Psychological Association's Division 2 (Teaching), she has served as both president of the division and associate editor of its journal, *Teaching of Psychology*. Named an Eminent Woman in Psychology by the APA in 2002, her service contributions to the teaching community have been recognized by Division 2, which named its Early Career Achievement award in her honor. The award is given annually to the most compelling national candidate in the first five years of an academic career. Jane has been an academic consultant to universities on critical thinking and faculty development as well as a department reviewer for nearly two dozen psychology departments. She served on the steering committees of both the St. Mary's Conference and the Psychology Partnerships Project, both national forums to address quality in undergraduate programs. She has been involved with every project undertaken by the American Psychological Association to help establish student performance standards since the initial project on high school student learning outcomes. She has authored and collaborated on a variety of publications, including *Your Guide to College Success,* a first year experience textbook coauthored with John Santrock, which is going into its seventh edition. She codirects the annual international Improving University Teaching Conference with Peter Seldin. Jane is completing her final year as Chief Reader in managing the Advanced Placement Psychology Reading.

Randolph A. Smith is currently Professor and Chair of the Department of Psychology at Lamar University. He taught at Kennesaw State University from 2003 to 2007; prior to that time, he spent 26 years at Ouachita Baptist University (Arkadelphia, AR). Randy is a Fellow of the American Psychological Association (Divisions 1 and 2) and has filled a variety of positions within the Society for the Teaching of Psychology. Currently, he is editor of *Teaching of Psychology,* a post he has held since 1997. He is coauthor (with Steve Davis) of a research methods textbook (*The Psychologist as Detective: An Introduction to Conducting Research in Psychology*) and a combined statistics/research methods text (*An Introduction to Statistics and Research Methods: Becoming a Psychological Detective*). In addition, he has authored a critical thinking book (*Challenging Your Preconceptions: Thinking Critically About Psychology*) and has edited the Instructor's Manual for Wayne Weiten's introductory psychology text. Randy has more than 50 publications, including books, journal articles, and book chapters. In addition, he has given over 100 presentations and has supervised almost 150 undergraduate conference presentations. Randy's interests and research revolve around the scholarship of teaching of psychology. He was a cofounder of the Southwestern Conference for Teachers of Psychology and the Arkansas Symposium for Psychology Students, a student research conference that has existed for more than 20 years. He was a participant in the St. Mary's Conference in 1991 and on the Steering Committee for the Psychology Partnerships Project in 1999. Randy is also a member of the American Psychological Society, Psi Chi, and the Southwestern Psychological Association (where he served as President in 1990–91). He earned his bachelor's degree from the University of Houston and his doctorate from Texas Tech University.

Foreword

Diane F. Halpern

Everyone wants to do it—help their students become better thinkers—but it is always difficult to know where or how to start. All professors believe they have been teaching critical thinking. As one miffed professor once asked me, "What kind of thinking do you think I have been teaching all these years—noncritical thinking?" Actually, I didn't want to answer that question because I was afraid that he was doing just that. Not deliberately of course, but without a clear idea of what critical thinking is, it is easy to teach as you were taught, following a long and well-meaning lineage of professors who are teaching for a time that no longer exists. Our knowledge is constantly being revised and new skills are needed to replace old ones. What do our students need to know and be able to do, and how can we help them know it and do it?

Before we answer this question, let's think about the current and future lives of our students and today's college students in general. According to several different surveys, college students spend many hours every day Facebooking, e-mailing, and IMing (instant messaging for those of you whose lives are not a constant blur of technology-mediated communication). They are rarely disconnected. They walk to class talking with invisible others via small wires that hang from their ears, and sing along with music that is piped directly into their ears. Many of today's college students spend the equivalent of one workday every week playing online games, some of which are so intricate that they make any assignment we could think up look like child's play. Many of our students work while going to school, with close to one-fifth working full-time while they are racking up debts the size of a mortgage. Surveys conducted as a creative class project devised by Michael Wesch, an assistant professor of cultural anthropology at Kansas State University, found that college students spend much of their time multitasking. How else could they create more online hours in a real, not virtually real, day? The students who collected the data chronicle the lives of many students who rarely come to class, do not buy the books we assign, or if they do buy them, do only half of the assigned readings. Of course, our students are more diverse than ever before, and any summary statistic fails to capture the essential essence of their busy lives.

Our students are likely to change jobs six times, working at jobs that do not exist today. They expect to find any fact with no more than three clicks of a mouse, but much of what they retrieve is of questionable quality, and I sincerely hope they are stopping to question it. It has been estimated that there is more information in a weekday edition of *The New York Times* than an average person living in the 17th century would encounter in a lifetime. We are awash with information, which creates the real danger of having all of the answers and still not knowing what they mean. Our students will need to solve the problems that we created, including pollution, terrorism, racism, poverty, nuclear weapons, obesity, and loneliness, just to name a few.

It is against this background of our students' current and future lives that I return to the question of what our students need to know and be able to do and how we can help them know it and know how to do it. Given the reliance on the Internet for information ranging from finding a date, engaging in online gaming, finding research from university libraries, making health decisions, and investing in an array of options that guarantee quick riches, the ability to recognize credible evidence is critical. The need is great and the task is large—how can we help our students become better thinkers?

Help is on the way. Dana Dunn, Jane Halonen, and Randy Smith have put together this collection of short gems that provide guideposts for faculty who need some help in knowing what to do to enhance their students' critical thinking skills. Each of the chapters provides an activity or new way of thinking about thinking for anyone who is thinking about the how-tos and what-to-dos in their classes this afternoon or later on in this semester. There are short activities that do not sacrifice standard course content in exchange for improving the process of thinking about that content. In addition, there are numerous tips on assessing growth in critical thinking, and overviews that discuss skills, dispositions, and the activities to develop them. Looking through the listing of chapters is like opening a new box of chocolates. They all look enticing. You can take a bite out of one, and if it is not to your liking you can put it back in the box and go on and find just the ones you like best. There are some great ideas and lots to think about. There is surely something to enhance critical thinking skills for everyone and every class. I enjoyed reading the varied chapters and cannot wait to try out some of the ideas in my own classes. You will too.

Diane F. Halpern, Claremont McKenna College

Preface

Critical thinking is not one activity; rather, the term refers to a collection of thinking skills that advance intellectual focus, motivation, and engagement with new ideas (Halonen & Gray, 2000). These thinking skills include the ability to recognize patterns; to solve problems in practical, creative, or scientific ways; to engage in psychological reasoning; and to adopt different perspectives when evaluating ideas or issues. Teaching students to think critically in or outside the classroom improves their abilities to observe, infer, question, decide, develop new ideas, and analyze arguments.

The goal of teaching critical thinking to psychology students is to refine their abilities to describe, predict, explain, and control behavior. Teachers need relevant tools and classroom strategies for enhancing students' critical thinking abilities in psychology. Our handbook contains a variety of scholarly perspectives aimed at teaching faculty how to teach critical thinking to students regardless of the course level or content area in psychology. As well as asking our authors to provide strategies and ideas for improving critical thinking pedagogy in the discipline, we asked them to discuss how to assess critical thinking within the context covered in their contributions.

This edited handbook is a scholarly yet pedagogically practical attempt to teach critical thinking skills in the context of the discipline of psychology. Our authors provide a showcase for best practices for teaching critical thinking issues in psychology courses taught at four-year colleges and universities, two-year colleges, and high schools. The chapters and short reports in this book grew out of professional presentations delivered at the September 30–October 1, 2005 conference, *Engaging Minds: Best Practices in Teaching Critical Thinking Across the Psychology Curriculum*, which was held in Atlanta, GA. The conference was sponsored by the Society for the Teaching of Psychology (STP), the National Institute on the Teaching of Psychology (NIToP), and the Kennesaw State University Center for Excellence in Teaching and Learning (CETL).

What's new about teaching critical thinking? The chapters and reports herein reveal innovations on various pedagogical fronts, including:

1 *New materials and perspectives.* The book offers novel, nontraditional approaches to teaching critical thinking, including strategies, tactics, diversity issues, service learning, and the use of case studies.

2 *New course delivery formats.* Faculty can create online course materials to foster critical thinking within a diverse student audience.

3 *A focus on assessment.* Authors place specific emphasis on how to both teach and assess critical thinking in the classroom. Discussion also focuses on issues of wider program assessment.

4 *Critical thinking in course contexts.* Contributors discuss ways to use critical thinking in the psychology classroom from the introductory psychology course into mid and upper level course offerings, including statistics and research methods courses, cognitive psychology, and capstone offerings.

5 *Developmental perspectives on critical thinking.* Students' stages of social and intellectual development—their "readiness"—for learning different types of critical thinking are explored.

6 *Teaching critical thinking through student-generated research.* Critical thinking has a purpose, especially the practice of creating, conducting, and evaluating empirical research in psychology.

7 *Critical thinking and scientific literacy.* How can critical thinking help our students become more scientifically aware and literate?

8 *Writing and critical thinking.* The role of critical thinking in learning and using APA-style writing, as well as improving writing generally, is considered.

Who will benefit from using this book? This book is aimed at educators—teachers, researchers, and graduate students—who teach critical thinking in psychology or who want to insert critical thinking activities into their teaching of the discipline. The added value found in this handbook is the diversity of approaches to teaching critical thinking found within it.

Dana S. Dunn, Jane S. Halonen,
and Randolph A. Smith

Reference

Halonen, J., & Gray, C. (2000). *The critical thinking companion for introductory psychology* (2nd ed.). New York: Worth.

Acknowledgments

We three have worked on a variety of writing and editing projects together. We enjoy one another's company, whether in person, by phone, or—as is true most of the time—via e-mail. We believe that we balance one another quite well, particularly where good humor and meeting deadlines are concerned. We do know that we could not have finished this work without the good efforts of our authors. We also know that we would not have undertaken this project without the enthusiastic support and sage advice of our Blackwell editor and friend, Chris Cardone. As one of us likes to say: Chris is rare and true. We are also grateful for the good work of Chris's team, Sarah Coleman and Kelly Basner. Without their good work, the project would never have moved forward so quickly or in such an organized fashion. We are grateful to Jenny Roberts and Hannah Rolls for preparing the manuscript for publication.

We also owe a debt of gratitude to Bill Hill and his colleagues at Kennesaw State University's Department of Psychology and the Center for Excellence in Teaching and Learning (CETL). Kennesaw has created a convivial atmosphere where colleagues who are interested in cutting-edge pedagogy in psychology are welcome to contribute and to learn. We also want to thank our colleagues who lead the Society for the Teaching of Psychology who, with the Kennesaw crowd, have conducted the successful "Best Practices" conferences that led to this and previous books. We also want to thank our friends at NIToP, especially Doug Bernstein, for their ongoing support toward improving teaching and learning in psychology.

Dana would like to thank his family—Sarah, Jake, and Hannah—for encouraging him to edit and write. As always, Moravian College provided Dana with the necessary resources to plan and complete this editorial effort. Jane credits her ability to get scholarly work accomplished both to her husband Brian's patience and tolerance and the good-natured support she receives from the University of West Florida to remain active as a scholar despite her role as a dean. Randy thanks the love of his life, Corliss, for 37+ years of support,

Acknowledgments

encouragement, and nurturance in pursuit of his academic goals and dreams. Kennesaw State University and Lamar University both provided resources and assistance to work on this project.

Dana S. Dunn, Bethlehem, PA
Jane S. Halonen, Pensacola, FL
Randolph A. Smith, Beaumont, TX

Chapter 1

Engaging Minds: Introducing Best Practices in Teaching Critical Thinking in Psychology

Dana S. Dunn, Jane S. Halonen, and Randolph A. Smith

Critical thinking is consequential thinking. As teachers, we want our students to both appreciate and exemplify the sort of critical thinking displayed by Dr. John Snow, a mid-19th-century London physician who searched for a pattern in cholera-plagued neighborhoods in the city's center. Using a city map, Snow plotted the addresses of the known dead—around 500 people—as well as the location of all the local public water pumps (cholera is a water-borne bacterial infection). Upon discovering that the majority of deaths occurred near one pump, he had it removed. The epidemic ended when his observation and analysis led to insight and action (Gilbert, 1958; Johnson, 2007; Tufte, 1983).

As teachers of psychology, we want our students to understand that the analysis and evaluation of behavior—thoughts, feelings, and actions—is also complex. We want to spark students' insights and enthusiasm for tough topics, as we expect them to learn and to appreciate that clinical judgments can never be superficial (e.g., Meehl, 1973), for example, or that social behavior is usually more situational or contextual than personality-driven (e.g., Milgram, 2004; Ross & Nisbett, 1991). We want our students to think deeply about the inferential puzzles posed by less dramatic, everyday, yet still fundamentally psychological problems. Why, for example, do people understand conjoint probabilities in statistics classes but ignore them when they are applied in realistic examples? Consider this classic example:

> Linda is 31 years old, single, outspoken, and very bright. She majored in philosophy. As a student, she was deeply concerned with issues of discrimination and social justice, and also participated in anti-nuclear demonstrations.
>
> Which of the following statements is more probable?
>
> Linda is a bank teller.
>
> Linda is a bank teller who is active in the feminist movement. (Tversky & Kahneman, 1984, p. 297)

Unless we are at our inferential best, the second choice seems obvious, even irrefutable. Pause and reflection, however, lead us to conclude that there are more bank tellers than bank tellers with a feminist bent; the probability of A and B cannot be greater than the probability of A or B alone. Examples here range from those developed through the study of decision-making heuristics and biases involved in intuition (e.g., Gilovich, Griffin, & Kahneman, 2002) to persistent belief in sports-related phenomena, such as "streak shooting" and having "hot hands" in basketball (Gilovich, Vallone, & Tversky, 1985; see also, Risen & Gilovich, 2007). Besides these clever, discipline-based examples, of course, psychology teachers hope their students will use critical thinking to plan for the future, to perform well in their careers, and to continue liberal learning throughout their lives. To achieve these desired ends, however, critical thinking needs to be nurtured, and both teachers and students must be weaned from the sort of noncritical thinking that all too routinely appears in the psychology classroom (Halpern, 2007).

We conceived this handbook to be a scholarly yet practical teaching resource for psychology teachers and others interested in enhancing students' critical thinking skills. We challenged our colleagues to craft chapters demonstrating how to improve the quality of thinking that students display in psychology courses and outside the classroom. In short, we asked them to engage the minds of students by sharing their best practices for teaching critical thinking. We believe that they succeeded admirably.

We and the authors believe that that these best practices for critical thinking allow students to see the world, or important aspects of it, anew. Collectively, the contributors provide a vital, analytical, sometimes skeptical, but ever questioning approach to understanding behavior that both enables students to learn from and to actively contribute to the discipline of psychology. We firmly believe—and the chapters and brief reports in this book show— that as teachers become engaged in designing critical thinking activities, their students will respond by becoming more critical thinkers and consumers of psychological knowledge.

A Handbook of Best Practices

This handbook has six parts. The first five contain traditional chapters dealing with the need for teaching critical thinking in psychology, assessment, assimilating critical thinking into key courses in the psychology curriculum, broader implications of critical thinking for the curriculum, and exploring critical thinking outside the classroom. The book's sixth part is innovative, as it contains a thoughtful collection of brief reports on critical thinking and psychology. We now introduce the contents of the six parts in greater detail.

Making a Case for Teaching Critical Thinking in Psychology

Carole Wade opens Part I by making a simple case with which we can all agree: The teaching of critical thinking in the psychology classroom is needed now more than ever. In her open, engaging style, Wade observes that although critical thinking tools are ample and available, the challenge for teachers remains convincing students how vital and helpful these tools are for learning about psychology and life. For example, pointing to various published studies, Wade debunks a variety of scientific myths about behavior that still make the rounds in some therapeutic settings where those practicing the discipline should know better. She then turns to the promise and problems posed by technological advancements—yes, fMRI is a powerful method to study mind and brain, but until researchers know more about precisely what it reveals about behavior, theory and application should be circumspect. Wade closes her contribution by reminding readers that one of the key battles, both in the classroom and our wider culture, is against the relativism that often grips our students, leading to an earnest desire not to argue, debate, or criticize, but to accept or acquiesce. Renewing our efforts in the teaching of critical thinking can help us all combat such banal relativism.

In the second chapter in this section, Natalie Kerr Lawrence, Sherry Serdikoff, Tracy Zinn, and Suzanne Baker bridge the gap lying between faculty and student understanding of what constitutes critical thinking and whether or why it is an important pursuit. These authors share the intriguing results of a survey they conducted at James Madison University, an institution noted for its comprehensive approach to assessing learning outcomes. This effort carries on that tradition nicely, and the authors do an excellent job of linking teacher and student beliefs to the existing critical thinking literature. They then provide a variety of teaching examples aimed at bridging the gap in the classroom between faculty and student beliefs about critical thinking. One important message emerging from this chapter is that the level of students' cognitive development plays a large part in determining how well they understand, learn, and later use critical thinking concepts.

In his chapter, Laird Edman notes that teaching critical thinking as a skills-based approach is inadequate because those skills do not transfer well. Rather, he advocates for a dispositional theory of critical thinking centered in personal epistemology. Taking this approach to developing critical thinking has an important implication for us as teachers: Most of our students will require substantial cognitive reorganization, so we can expect progress to be slow and incremental. According to Edman, we must avoid teaching "facts" to students and, instead, focus on creating disequilibrium for students so that they will make cognitive accommodations.

In the last chapter to put the case for teaching critical thinking to psychology students, William Buskist and Jessica Irons offer a variety of simple strategies they believe promote scientific reasoning. Beyond defining their approach to critical thinking, the authors present general features of the process as well as major qualities that characterize it. They then explore some of the reasons why students avoid doing critical thinking in the classroom without the judicious guidance (and gentle prodding) of committed teachers. As Buskist and Irons nicely demonstrate, with a bit of effort and forethought, faculty can infuse critical thinking into virtually any course within the psychology curriculum.

Assessment Matters

Jane Halonen, a critical thinking scholar and leader in the assessment movement in psychology, opens Part II, which is dedicated to issues of assessment. As most psychologists now know, assessment is not to be feared, as it is hard to argue against a sincere desire to demonstrate whether our teaching and learning is leading to the intended outcome in our students. By discussing her teaching experiences and academic biography, Halonen offers sage and sound advice on how critical thinking activities tied to assessment can enhance what happens in the psychology classroom. Her call for measuring critical thinking is tempered by the reality of classroom dynamics and not the limits of our teaching hopes; earnest attempts are better than worrying about achieving immediate accuracy. Halonen counsels that critical thinking holds the promise to move us all, students as well as faculty and administrators, ahead in the goal of making disciplinary knowledge meaningful in the classroom and in our wider lives.

Halonen's enthusiasm for assessment is channeled into a careful, thoughtful, and well-planned chapter written by Kevin Apple, Sherry Serdikoff, Monica Reis-Bergan, and Kenneth Barron. This second assessment-focused chapter presents a programmatic approach to assessing critical thinking in psychology courses, one aimed at tapping into several components linked to the construct rather than assuming one will suffice. The multimodal approach advanced by the authors hearkens back to sound psychometric practice and looks forward to best classroom practices. True to their James Madison lineage, this group of teacher-scholars advocates that critical thinking should be assessed at multiple points during a psychology student's education, not just once or twice. Their experiences inform readers about how best to improve psychology assessment practices and to avoid predictable pitfalls while doing so.

Stacie Spencer and Marin Gillis close Part II by presenting a process-oriented approach to the study of critical thinking regarding complex psychological topics, such as stress. These authors remind us of the power that language plays in the classroom and daily life, so that teachers must be careful to monitor whether students are using appropriate, empirically based conceptions or, instead, everyday understanding of key constructs. Spencer and Gillis point to the subsequent problem: Language limits lead to context-bound understanding of concepts, which in turn prevent students from being able to properly apply psychological information to new settings or situations. To combat this problem, the authors offer a helpful set of steps teachers can use to help students learn to critically learn, understand, and apply complex ideas.

Integrating Critical Thinking into Critical Psychology Courses

We know that one reason many readers will be interested in this book is to learn how to add critical thinking components into specific courses they teach. The chapters in Part III address this desire very well, beginning with the sage advice of David Carroll, Allen Keniston, and Blaine Peden, who offer counsel to teachers who are not sure of how or where to begin. They offer advice and examples to faculty who want only to add an activity or two, as well as to those who want to overhaul a given course so that critical thinking is embedded throughout it (helpfully, they illustrate their arguments by drawing on exemplar courses examining cognition and the history of psychology). Carroll, Keniston, and Peden conclude by reminding readers of general principles of critical thinking that can inform intellectual experiences throughout the psychology curriculum.

Susan O'Donnell, Alisha Francis, and Sherrie Mahurin advocate using the popular *Taking Sides* book (Slife, 2006) in General Psychology to help students develop their critical thinking skills. They present a list of nine questions that students can use to help them think critically; O'Donnell and Francis have their students use these questions as they read an issue from the *Taking Sides* book. Finally, they provide assessment ideas based on writing.

Joseph Mayo invites teachers to create critical thinking experiences in their classrooms by borrowing concepts from George Kelly's (1955) personal construct theory, one of the most intriguing and underresearched approaches to understanding personality. Following Kelly, Mayo argues that using critical thinking skills, students can learn to act as "personal scientists" in search of understanding in the psychology classroom. By adapting Kelly's repertory grid technique, Mayo teaches students to examine key theories and constructs from different areas of psychology using this creative and evaluative system. He demonstrates that this pedagogical framework improves comprehension of course content and helps to structure a given psychology course (here, life span development and history and systems) in meaningful, accessible, and assessable ways.

Janet E. Kuebli, Richard Harvey, and James Korn provide helpful ideas for infusing critical thinking into social psychology, a capstone course, and a graduate-level Teaching of Psychology course. In addition, they present a critical thinking pedagogical framework that relates academic skills, instructional methodologies, and critical thinking abilities to one another.

The course (or courses) that routinely calls upon critical thinking skills but is often the most daunting to teach—statistics and research methods—is the topic of a chapter written by Bryan Saville, Tracy Zinn, Natalie Lawrence, Kenneth Barron, and Jeffrey Andre. The challenge for teachers, of course, is to keep students interested and learning while reducing their anxiety about skill demands posed by the nature of the topics. The authors wisely note that acquiring a basic, working understanding should not be the goal; rather, students should develop a critical acumen that allows them to become worldly consumers of psychological research as well as everyday scientific information. They provide a variety of thoughtful course approaches and teaching alternatives that can promote student learning in these key topics in the psychology curriculum.

Critical Thinking and the Broader Psychology Curriculum

Critical thinking is not unique to any one class in the psychology curriculum. Ideally, critical thinking should appear throughout the curriculum, a promising idea that authors in Part IV of the book address. The first authors to do so are Dana Dunn and Randolph Smith, who discuss writing, one of the most important skills psychology majors can learn and profit from in and outside the discipline's confines. Dunn and Smith discuss the role critical reading plays in the writing process, suggest some practical writing activities faculty can use in their teaching, and explore the critical thinking-enhancing qualities of the discipline's model for writing, APA style.

Elizabeth Hammer discusses critical thinking qualities associated with the now popular curricular innovation, service learning. Hammer describes her own evolution from merely attaching a service-learning activity in a psychology class to designing service-learning objectives that blend seamlessly with learning psychological concepts and theories.

She recommends specific strategies that optimize student learning through their community contributions and also address the nature of the additional workload that service learning entails from the instructor. Her discussion makes the incorporation of service learning in psychology courses not only easily justified, but an exciting addition that will enhance student engagement in the discipline and community.

Although Jordan Lippman, Trina Kershaw, James Pellegrino, and Stellan Ohlsson write about critical thinking activities that they use in their Cognitive Psychology courses, they also believe that the activities are adaptable to other advanced courses. They advocate having students engage in three processes as they learn to think critically: participation in experiments and reflection on the meaning of the data, analysis of empirical articles and connection to class content, and the cognition in daily life exercise in which students interpret daily life events in light of course concepts.

In the next chapter in this section, Bernard Beins visits the meaning behind the Research Methods course, especially where fostering critical thought and scientific literacy are concerned. Beins argues that the Research Methods course makes a true intellectual contribution by helping students develop a critical stance as well as scientific literacy. Knowing and learning what to believe turns out to be a tricky business, and Beins provides teachers with a terrific set of examples that will help their Research Methods students begin to see the world in more complex terms while simultaneously thinking of ways to experimentally simplify it for empirical study.

Paul Smith and Kris Vasquez close Part IV by discussing the particular challenges that ensue when we ask students to think critically about the values they hold deeply. Smith and Vasquez point out that students can relatively easily move from novice to expert status when coming up with critiques of research design as they make progress through the psychology curriculum, but struggle mightily when we ask them to bring their critical skills to bear on a belief that they have already determined is real or true. Smith and Vasquez offer some tips about how to promote transfer of critical thinking skills from research methods to deeply held values.

Thinking Critically Beyond the Classroom

The single chapter in Part V is devoted to helping students to think critically about their future careers. Deborah S. Briihl, Claudia J. Stanny, Kiersten A. Jarvis, Maria Darcy, and Ronald W. Belter develop profiles of two levels of courses designed to enhance student knowledge about what possibilities await them after the completion of their undergraduate degree. One career course, developed at the University of West Florida, provides an online environment in which students can explore various career options that will facilitate good course choices and other preparation strategies in the courses that remain. In contrast, the senior level career course developed at Valdosta State University emphasizes resume building, interviewing skills, and applicant–job matching to help students make effective decisions at the end of their undergraduate work. The authors conclude the chapter with an analysis of the comparative strengths and weaknesses of both approaches. Their work provides a compelling example of a practical problem—getting their careers launched in psychology— that should profit from well-developed critical thinking abilities in the discipline.

Critical Briefings on Critical Thinking

When we planned this book, we decided that beyond soliciting some authors to submit traditional length chapters, we would also invite others to write brief reports on innovative exercises and classroom activities dealing with critical thinking. The short reports allow casual readers as well as already committed teachers of critical thinking techniques to dip into an offering, quickly learn from the work, and then apply the ideas in their own teaching. Thus we believe that our modest innovation provides readers with serious (and immediately accessible) dividends. Each of our short report authors has crafted critical briefings on timely topics. We will not summarize the ideas contained in these reports here, but we will highlight some of the reviewed topics: Web-based critical thinking modules, teaching students to think like psychologists, introducing controversial issues in class, teaching critical thinking via practical application, and a modular approach to writing research papers. We believe these brief, focused reports make for both good reading and fine pedagogy.

The Rewards of Teaching Critical Thinking

Virtually everyone agrees that teaching critical thinking is a good idea, but as several authors attest, doing so can be hard work. Yet avoiding accepting this responsibility poses perils for us as psychologists and educators (Sternberg, 2007). We want to close this overview chapter by reminding readers that the rewards associated with critical thinking outweigh the demands involved. Where learning is concerned, for example, embedding critical thinking practices in psychology is apt to lead to deeper processing of arguments, ideas, theories, and results. Greater retention may well lead to more frequent application in discipline-related and nondiscipline-related contexts. A less educationally dramatic result is that our classrooms are very likely to become livelier and more welcome places. Just as discussion and small group work have achieved some parity with the traditional lecture method on many campuses in recent years, we believe that critical thinking can also lay siege to established practices that result in less active learning. In the end, we believe one of the best rewards for teaching critical thinking is that at the same time it engages the minds of our students, the necessary preparation for and execution in the classroom serves to rejuvenate our own engagement with the discipline.

References

Gilbert, E. W. (1958). Pioneer maps of health and disease in England. *Geographical Journal, 124,* 172–183.

Gilovich, T., Griffin, D., & Kahneman, D. (Eds.). (2002). *Heuristics and biases: The psychology of intuitive judgment.* New York: Cambridge University Press.

Gilovich, T., Vallone, R., & Tversky, A. (1985). The hot hand in basketball: On the misperception of random sequences. *Cognitive Psychology, 17,* 295–314.

Halpern, D. F. (2007). The nature and nurture of critical thinking. In R. J. Sternberg, H. L. Roediger, III, & D. F. Halpern (Eds.), *Critical thinking in psychology* (pp. 1–14). New York: Cambridge University Press.

Johnson, S. (2007). *The ghost map: The story of London's most terrifying epidemic—and how it changed science, cities, and the modern world.* New York: Riverhead Trade.

Kelly, G. A. (1955). *The psychology of personal constructs* (Vols. 1–2). New York: Norton.

Meehl, P. E. (1973). *Psychodiagnosis: Selected papers.* New York: Norton.

Milgram, S. (2004). *Obedience to authority.* New York: Harper.

Risen, J., & Gilovich, T. (2007). Informal logical fallacies. In R. J. Sternberg, H. L. Roediger, III, & D. F. Halpern (Eds.), *Critical thinking in psychology* (pp. 110–130). New York: Cambridge University Press.

Ross, L., & Nisbett, R. E. (1991). *The person and the situation.* New York: McGraw-Hill.

Slife, B. (Ed.). (2006). *Taking sides: Clashing views on psychological issues* (14th ed.). New York: Dushkin.

Sternberg, R. J. (2007). Critical thinking in psychology: It really is critical. In R. J. Sternberg, H. L. Roediger, III, & D. F. Halpern (Eds.), *Critical thinking in psychology* (pp. 289–296). New York: Cambridge University Press.

Tufte, E. R. (1983). *The visual display of quantitative information.* Cheshire, CT: Graphics Press.

Tversky, A., & Kahneman, D. (1984). Extensional versus intuitive reasoning: The conjunction fallacy in probability judgment. *Psychological Review, 91,* 293–315.

Part I

The Case for Teaching Critical Thinking in Psychology

Chapter 2

Critical Thinking: Needed Now More Than Ever

Carole Wade

Over two decades ago, when I first started to talk and write about critical thinking, people would sometimes tell me that it was a lost cause at worst, a passing fad at best. This reaction always surprised me because I believed that helping students learn to think deeply about things was the main purpose of education, its very heart. Students may know a lot of facts, but if they are unable or unwilling to assess claims and make judgments on the basis of well-supported reasons and evidence rather than emotion or anecdote, can we call them truly educated?

Today it is clear that the critics were wrong: Critical thinking is definitely not yesterday's fad. Just about every psychology textbook now addresses the topic, though they may emphasize somewhat different specific skills and dispositions. Colleges, universities, and high schools around the country now require either a critical thinking course or the integration of critical thinking goals across the curriculum. Two decades ago, critical thinking was mainly the subject of speculation by philosophers and rhetoric professors; today, there is psychological research on the nature of critical thinking and the best ways to teach it. When I searched on PsycINFO for publications with "critical thinking" in the title, I turned up 941 results, and many if not most of those publications appeared to involve empirical research.

That's the good news. The bad news is that getting students to think in a sophisticated manner—to ask questions, define terms, examine evidence, analyze assumptions, avoid emotional reasoning, resist oversimplification, consider alternative interpretations, and tolerate uncertainty—is still an uphill battle. Developments both within and outside our discipline are making our job more important than ever, but also more challenging. I have heard many stories from teachers that inspire me and show how an emphasis on critical thinking can get students' synapses working. But here I'm going to focus on the bad news—the growing barriers to critical thought—and why the efforts of teachers to help students think critically and creatively are needed now more than ever.

Carole Wade

Barriers to Critical Thought in Psychological Practice

First, consider some developments within psychology itself that are working against us. One is the growth of nonscientific approaches to psychological problems. When psychology was established as a formal discipline in the late 1800s, psychologists hoped to replace explanations of behavior based on whim or wishful thinking with explanations based on rigorous standards of evidence and reasoning. Scientific psychology was designed as an antidote to superstition and a way to test the worthiness of one's hunches. It was aimed at helping people, including scientists, overcome what is probably the most entrenched bias in human thinking, the confirmation bias: the tendency to seek and remember information that confirms what we already believe, and to ignore or forget information that challenges our beliefs.

From the beginning, of course, scientific psychology had many pseudoscientific competitors to contend with, ranging from astrology to graphology. In the 20th century, with the growth of technology, we saw the introduction of nonprofessional therapies that added scientific-sounding language: neurolinguistic programming, right-brain training programs, the Transcutaneous Electro-Neural Stimulator, the Brain SuperCharger, the Whole Brain Wave Form Synchro-Energizer. The appeal of such psychobabble is not surprising; people have a great need for easy answers that promise escape from uncertainty and that do not require them to think too hard.

In the past two decades, however, an ominous development has taken place; increasingly, psychobabble has been infiltrating the professional field of psychology itself. People with PhDs are making unsubstantiated and sometimes ludicrous claims that can affect people's lives. This is the result of a worrying trend: the split in the training, methods, and attitudes of scientific psychologists and a growing number of mental-health practitioners (Beutler, 2000; Lilienfeld, Lynn, & Lohr, 2003).

Science and clinical practice have always had a somewhat uneasy relationship, which is why the scientist-practitioner model of training first came into being. Many practitioners are still trained according to this model; indeed, it is thanks in large part to their efforts that we are learning not only why and when therapy is effective, but which therapies are most effective for which problems. But the scientist-practitioner model has been easier to honor in word than in deed. In some free-standing psychology schools around the country, schools unaffiliated with any institution of higher learning, students are now being trained to do therapy with little grounding in methods or research findings. Reviewing the evidence on graduate training in clinical psychology, Donald Peterson (2003) found that the poorer quality programs are turning out increasing numbers of ill-prepared graduates. In the late 1980s, I had the misfortune to teach a course in one such school, and nearly had a rebellion on my hands when I tried to discuss research methods. Most of my students wanted just a grab bag of techniques.

As a result of this trend, a growing number of practitioners have little appreciation for the importance of empirical evidence. Indeed, one survey of 400 clinicians conducted in the 1990s found that the great majority paid little attention to empirical research, stating that they gained their most useful information from clinical work with clients (Elliott &

Morrow-Bradley, 1994). As a result, the scientist-practitioner model has been giving way to the scientist–practitioner gap.

Of course, it is true that therapy is in many ways an art. Science will not necessarily tell you the most effective way to deal with people's complex spiritual, moral, and existential dilemmas. Science will not make you into a discerning and empathic therapist who knows how to forge an alliance with the client, a bond of mutual respect and trust. The detachment and impartiality of the scientist are not always good qualities in a therapist trying to alleviate human suffering.

But a lack of knowledge about basic scientific methods and findings, and about human vulnerability to the confirmation bias, can lead to the practice of incompetent and even fraudulent or harmful therapy. Uncritical thinking about behavior in recent years has led to all sorts of unverified, and in fact, false, claims by therapists. For example:

- that venting negative emotions such as anger can reduce them, when in fact the opposite is true (Bushman, Bonacci, Pedersen, Vasquez, & Miller, 2005; Tavris, 1989);
- that children never lie about or misremember having been sexually abused, when in fact they often do, especially when interrogated by adults who believe the children were molested (Bruck, 2003; Ceci & Bruck, 1995; Garven, Wood, Malpass, & Shaw, 1998);
- that a child's interest in an anatomically realistic doll is a reliable guide to whether the child has been abused, when in fact doll play is unreliable for this purpose (Bruck, Ceci, Francoeur, & Renick, 1995; Hunsley, Lee, & Wood, 2003; Koocher, Goodman, White, & Friedrich, 1995; Wood, Nezworski, Lilienfeld, & Garb, 2003);
- that most abused children grow up to be abusive parents, in a "cycle of abuse," when in fact most do not (Kaufman & Zigler, 1987);
- that people who have experienced a trauma in childhood or adulthood often repress the memory of it, when in fact the usual problem is an inability to *forget* the trauma (Loftus & Ketcham, 1994; McNally, 2003);
- that projective tests are useful in child-custody assessments, when in fact they are not (Emery, Otto, & O'Donohue, 2005);
- that hypnosis is a reliable method for retrieving memories, even those going back to infancy, when in reality it encourages confabulation and false memories (Dinges et al., 1992; Kihlstrom, 1994; Nash, 1987);
- that self-esteem is the root of all social and personal problems, from poor academic performance to drug abuse to juvenile crime, when hundreds of studies show that this notion has no convincing support (Baumeister, Campbell, Krueger, & Vohs, 2003);
- that Critical Incident Stress Debriefing (CISD) can prevent survivors of tragedies and catastrophes from developing posttraumatic stress disorder (PTSD) and other emotional problems, when in fact it is either useless or actually increases the risk of developing PTSD and depression (Gist, Lubin, & Redburn, 1998; Mayou, Ehlers, & Hobbs, 2000; van Emmerik, Kamphuis, Hulsbosch, & Emmelkamp, 2002; van Ommeren, Saxena, & Saraceno, 2005);

- that dissociative identity disorder (multiple personality disorder) is widespread, when it is actually extremely rare, most cases being the probable result of media sensationalism and therapist suggestion (Lilienfeld & Lynn, 2003; Piper & Merskey, 2004; Rieber, 2006).

And this is just a partial list.

Many clinical techniques have become widely used without having first been subjected to the first rule of research: comparison with a control group. And even when good research finds a technique to be useless, seemingly driving a stake through its heart, the technique, vampire-like, may refuse to stay put in its coffin because of a lack of critical thinking on the part of practitioners or their clients. An example is facilitated communication (FC), which involves placing autistic or mentally impaired children in front of a keyboard while an adult places a hand over the child's hand or forearm. Proponents claim that children who have never used words before are, with the help of FC, able to peck out complete sentences. Yet two decades of research have shown that what happens in facilitated communication is what happens when a medium guides a person's hand over a Ouija board to help the person receive "messages" from a "spirit": The person doing the "facilitating" is unconsciously nudging the other person's hand in the desired direction (Mostert, 2001; Wegner, Fuller, & Sparrow, 2003). A recent German review of the literature concluded that FC "has failed to show clinical validity, shows some features of pseudoscience, and bears severe risks of detrimental side effects" (Probst, 2005, p. 43). Nonetheless, FC is still very much in use, and thousands of parents continue to waste their time and money on an unvalidated therapy.

Unreliable and unsubstantiated clinical techniques or assumptions have serious repercussions. If you believe that children always lie, you will fail to investigate their claims, and children will be returned to parents who physically and sexually assault them. If you believe that children *never* lie, you will take some of their fanciful imaginings as truth, and innocent parents and daycare workers will go to jail—as indeed, hundreds have. If you are a client who does not know the most effective treatment for a problem causing you anxiety or unhappiness, you can waste money and time on a therapy that will not help you—and if you are a therapist, you will not be serving your client. Pseudoscientific beliefs about the cycle of abuse have denied some parents custody of their children on the grounds that they will inevitably abuse their own children one day, even when there is no evidence that they would ever do so. Educational policies devoted to improving children's self-esteem take away resources from programs devoted to teaching them how to read, write, and think—skills that build true self-efficacy.

Barriers to Critical Thought in Psychological Science

Lest the reader think I am singling out psychological practice for special scrutiny, let me note that recent developments within scientific psychology also call out for greater critical thought by both teachers and students. I am thinking especially about the biotechnical revolution, and the use of new technologies such as PET scans and fMRI to study that most mysterious and enigmatic of human organs, the brain.

Brain-scanning methods, which every psychology student learns about, have revolutionized medicine and have led to an explosion of research, not only in medicine and cognitive neuroscience but also in many other fields. The number of published studies using functional MRI jumped from just 10 in 1991 to 864 in 2001 (Illes, Kirschen, & Gabrieli, 2003) and thousands of facilities now use fMRI for research and assessment. Researchers are using brain scans to study memory, racial attitudes, moral reasoning, decision making, the anticipation of pain, spiritual meditation, sexual arousal, you name it. They are using scans to compare adolescent and adult brains, and the brains of schizophrenia patients with the brains of mentally healthy people. In the new applied field of neuromarketing, they are even identifying brain areas that are activated while people watch TV commercials or political ads.

So, what's the problem? The answer is that every revolution in science initially evokes uncritical zeal, and this one is no exception. As one team of psychologists who use MRI technology in their research wrote, "Just because you're imaging the brain doesn't mean you can stop using your head" (Cacioppo et al., 2003). And when we use our heads, we find that not all the findings reported in the popular press or even scientific journals are based on good science and critical thinking, no matter how fancy or impressive the tools that produced them.

Some of the problems are methodological. The beautifully colored scans we show our students and that appear all the time in newspapers and magazines and online can convey oversimplified and sometimes misleading impressions (Dumit, 2004). For example, by manipulating the color scales used in PET and MRI scans, researchers can either accentuate or minimize contrasts between two brains. Small contrasts can be made to look dramatic, larger ones to look trivial. An individual's brain can even be made to appear completely different depending on the colors used.

It's not just the colors that are arbitrary. The researcher uses certain algorithms to convert numerical data to a visual representation, and in doing so, sets criteria for deciding where the boundary lies between, say, high neural activity and moderate neural activity. There may be good reasons for setting the criteria at certain points, but for the most part these assignments are arbitrary, and they will influence the results and the graphic image of those results. As William Uttal observes in his provocative book *The New Phrenology: The Limits of Localizing Cognitive Processes in the Brain* (2001), one researcher may draw the line conservatively, and thus obscure evidence of localized activity, whereas another may draw the line more liberally, and thereby produce apparent localizations that are actually mere artifacts.

Other problems with brain scans are conceptual. For example, although brain areas are fairly well defined, the cognitive processes and operations that researchers are attempting to associate with these areas typically are not. You do not have to be a behaviorist to acknowledge that one of psychology's toughest challenges has been to define, to everyone's agreement, just what it is we are trying to study. The definition of an emotion such as happiness, or a mental operation such as remembering a past event, often depends on how a researcher happens to measure the construct in question. Most psychological constructs, once we get beyond simple sensory and motor responses, are denoted by a single word or term but actually cover an intricate and complicated series of operations or processes. How do you establish "where" in the brain happiness is processed if researchers cannot agree on what happiness is in the first place? How do we know where love is found in the brain, when love can mean the romantic infatuation of Romeo and Juliet, the abiding attachment of Prince Charles and Camilla, or the fond bickering of Ma and Pa Kettle?

Even the simple act of looking at something involves attention, sensory encoding, memory, pattern recognition, and interpretation. This makes the physical localization of any mental process a challenge, to say the least. And it helps explain why the simple partition of the brain into a part for this and a part for that keeps falling, well, apart. As Uttal notes, the more complex a psychological process, the less likely it is to be associated uniquely with a circumscribed region of the brain. It is far more likely that it involves the collective interaction of multiple circuits that communicate back and forth in highly complicated and perhaps, in some instances, even unknowable ways.

Even if we could locate discrete centers or brain circuits associated with discrete psychological operations or mental states, we would have to deal with the fact that brain circuitry and structure vary from person to person. Because of genetic differences and because the experiences and sensations of a lifetime are constantly altering the brain's neural networks, each brain is unique. Those nice schematic brain illustrations that you find in every psychology textbook are necessary for teaching purposes, but they are misleading because no such brain actually exists. String musicians have larger than average areas associated with musical production, and the earlier in life they start to play, the larger these areas become (Jancke, Schlaug, & Steinmetz, 1997). Cab drivers tend to have larger than average areas in the hippocampus associated with visual representations of the environment (Maguire et al., 2000). In his acceptance speech for the Nobel Prize, Roger Sperry (1982, p. 1225) put it well: "The individuality inherent in our brain networks makes that of fingerprints or facial features gross and simple by comparison." In brain-scan research, however, such individuality is often ignored. Instead, scans from a number of individuals are averaged or pooled. The result may be an apparently well-demarcated active brain area that does not actually correspond to the pattern of activity in any of the individual brains that were studied.

Perhaps the most important challenge in brain-scan studies has to do with interpreting the results. This is a critical issue for students to understand. At this point in time, brain scans tell us only that *something* is happening at a particular site or sites; despite their precision, they fail to tell us *what* is happening, either mentally or physiologically. If you know that certain parts of the brain are activated when you think hot thoughts of your beloved, what, exactly, does that tell you about love, or sex, or how they are "processed" in the brain? One researcher (cited in Wheeler 1998) drew this analogy: A researcher might scan the brain of gum-chewing volunteers and find out which parts of their brains are active as they chomp away, but that does not mean the researcher has located the brain's "gum-chewing center." Similarly, if a scan shows that a brain area "lights up" when someone is doodling, that does not mean you have found the doodling center.

These examples may seem silly, but analogous errors are sometimes made in neuroscience. A few years back, a prominent researcher reported that he had found where spiritual experiences get processed, and the area promptly got dubbed by reporters as the "God spot." Some writers even speculated that the reason people become atheists or agnostics is that their God spot is less developed than in religious people. Talk about oversimplification!

The truth is that neuroscientists are dealing with correlational data, and if some area is activated during some psychological process, it could mean any number of things: It may be the sole locus of the operation; it may have been disinhibited by some other area that is of equal or greater importance even though that other area is not as active; it may be necessary for the mental operation but not sufficient unless other areas, including areas of lesser activity, are also involved; it may contain neurons that operate less efficiently than do those in other areas, and that therefore must consume more energy; and so on. What this means is that it is hard to know whether the image in a brain scan actually gives us a "picture" of the neurodynamics of the operation in question. All of these caveats fly out the window, however, when the media jump on some finding, especially if it has to do with something that captures the public's imagination, such as sex differences or spiritual experiences.

The issues I have discussed, both methodological and conceptual ones, are not academic. Increasingly, brain scans are being used in ways that those doing the original research may never have anticipated or desired. For instance, brain scans are starting to be introduced as evidence in court cases to argue for diminished responsibility and are being promoted as "lie detectors" in criminal cases; one commercial company has even begun offering a brain-scan test for deception, and the Defense Department and CIA have reportedly invested millions in neuroimaging technologies that might be used in law enforcement or intelligence. But because of the normal variability among people in their brain responses, innocent but highly reactive people may be mislabeled "guilty" by these seemingly scientific tests, just as has happened in the use of the polygraph and other methods that assume the existence of universal biological responses in emotional states.

Thus we need to teach our students to think critically in part so they can separate the wheat from the chaff in our own field of psychology. If they intend to become therapists, they will understand that good therapy and an appreciation of research are not mutually exclusive. If they intend to use the techniques of neuroscience, they will understand that science is not merely a matter of technique; it is rooted in an attitude toward evidence and interpretation—an attitude that requires critical thinking at every stage of the process.

Barriers to Critical Thought in the Culture

There is also a larger picture to consider, for the existence of uncritical thinking within our own field is occurring in a culture that is often distrustful of science and relativistic in its thinking about scientific and nonscientific claims. We hear this distrust and relativism when our students say, "Well, that's just my opinion," as if all opinions were created equal—end of discussion.

Relativism has found expression in the renewed debate about the teaching of creationism, now repackaged as intelligent design, in our public schools, as a counterpoint to evolution. I would certainly never fault a person for having religious faith, and I think a good argument can be made that there is no necessary conflict between evolution and religion as broadly construed. No less a scientist than Francis Collins, Director of the

Human Genome Project, is a Christian who believes that God used the mechanism of evolution to create the world, including human beings. The problem occurs when people misunderstand the meaning of the term *theory* in science, and when they assume that intelligent design and evolution have equal standing as *scientific* theories. Such misunderstandings are common among students.

As Collins (2005) wrote in *Time* magazine, nearly all working biologists, whether religious believers or not, accept that the principles of variation and natural selection explain how multiple species evolved from a common ancestor over very long periods of time, and agree that these processes are sufficient to explain the rich variety of life forms on the planet. Indeed, evolution is the very basis of modern biology, and plays an increasing role in psychological theory as well. The processes of evolution are plain for everyone to see every time a virus or bacterium becomes resistant to a drug, as have flu viruses over just the past five years. Evolution is evident in the adaptive changes that have occurred during the 20th century in many more complex species, such as the peppered moth in England and the rock pocket mouse in Arizona (Nachman, Hoekstra, & D'Agostino, 2003; Young & Musgrave, 2005). And evolution is evident in the recent comparative analyses of human and chimpanzee genomes. In contrast, as Steven Pinker (2005) has observed, the idea of intelligent design runs smack into the inconvenient facts that the retina is installed backward, that the male seminal duct hooks over the ureter like a garden hose snagged on a tree, and that, when we are cold, goose bumps uselessly try to warm us by fluffing up long-gone fur. Nonetheless, because so many people misunderstand what science is, in a 2005 Pew poll, 38% of respondents favored *replacing* evolution with creationism in the science curriculum. As conservative commentator Charles Krauthammer (2005), who is generally sympathetic toward the role of religion in American life, has asked, in an essay lamenting the public confusion of faith with science, "How many times do we have to rerun the Scopes 'monkey trial'?"

Religious ideologies, then, can get in the way of critical thinking about science, including psychological science. And so can political ideologies, so shrill these days on both the right and the left. Because of such ideologies, reactions to psychological findings, especially those that challenge conventional beliefs, such as findings on sexual orientation, gender, abstinence-only sex education, and the emotional effects of abortion, often have little to do with a study's scientific merits. Scientifically literate students need to know this.

Other social trends also decrease the ability (or willingness) of people to think critically. One, as Frank Cioffi (2005) noted in the *Chronicle of Higher Education*, is that the national language of "debate" has become cheapened. Many television programs, and political commentators like Fox News host Bill O'Reilly, whose commentaries contain an average of 8.88 instances of name-calling per minute (as noted in *The Week*, May 18, 2007, p. 16), have reduced public discourse to a verbal food fight, in which the person who shouts the loudest and says the nastiest things wins. Thus it is little wonder that students often fail to understand the very concept of intellectual argumentation, or the value of coming up with counterarguments.

In sum, the scientist–practitioner gap, ideological intrusions into science, relativistic ways of thinking in the culture, uncritical responses to the biotechnical revolution, and other cultural developments have all made the job of the psychology teacher more vital than ever. Of course, each of us can reach only a relatively few students, but collectively we can have some impact on the intellectual and scientific sophistication of a generation. If we can prod students to resist jumping to premature conclusions, to consider the evidence for a claim, to be willing to modify their beliefs in the face of counterevidence, to question received wisdom and to keep questioning until they get better answers, and to tolerate a certain degree of uncertainty—in short, to think critically—we will then have done our jobs well.

References

Baumeister, R. F., Campbell, J. D., Krueger, J. I., & Vohs, K. D. (2003). Does high self-esteem cause better performance, interpersonal success, happiness, or healthier lifestyles? [whole issue]. *Psychological Science in the Public Interest, 4*(1).

Beutler, L. E. (2000). David and Goliath: When empirical and clinical standards of practice meet. *American Psychologist, 55,* 997–1007.

Bruck, M. (2003, May). *Effects of suggestion on the reliability and credibility of children's reports.* Invited address at the annual meeting of the American Psychological Society, Atlanta.

Bruck, M., Ceci, S. J., Francoeur, E., & Renick, A. (1995). Anatomically detailed dolls do not facilitate preschoolers' reports of a pediatric examination involving genital touching. *Journal of Experimental Psychology: Applied, 1,* 95–109.

Bushman, B. J., Bonacci, A. M., Pedersen, W. C., Vasquez, E. A., & Miller, N. (2005). Chewing on it can chew you up: Effects of rumination on triggered displaced aggression. *Journal of Personality and Social Psychology, 88,* 959–983.

Cacioppo, J. T., Berntson, G. G., Lorig, T. S., Norris, C. J., Richett, E., & Nusbaum, H. (2003). Just because you're imaging the brain doesn't mean you can stop using your head: A primer and set of first principles. *Journal of Personality and Social Psychology, 85,* 650–661.

Ceci, S. J., & Bruck, M. (1995). *Jeopardy in the courtroom: A scientific analysis of children's testimony.* Washington, DC: American Psychological Association.

Cioffi, F. (2005, May 20). Argumentation in a culture of discord. *Chronicle of Higher Education, 51,* B6.

Collins, F. (2005, August 7). Can you believe in God and evolution? Compiled by David Van Biema, *Time.* Retrieved May 11, 2007, from www.time.com/time/magazine/article/0,9171,1090921,00.html

Dinges, D. F., Whitehouse, W. G., Orene, E. C., Powell, J. W., Orne, M. T., & Erdelyi, M. H. (1992). Evaluating hypnotic memory enhancement (hypermnesia and reminiscence) using multitrial forced recall. *Journal of Experimental Psychology: Learning, Memory, and Cognition, 18,* 1139–1147.

Dumit, J. (2004). *Picturing personhood: Brain scans and biomedical identity.* Princeton, NJ: Princeton University Press.

Elliot, R., & Morrow-Bradley, C. (1994). Developing a working marriage between psychotherapists and psychotherapy researchers: Identifying shared purposes. In P. F. Talley, H. H. Strupp, & S. F. Butler (Eds.), *Psychotherapy research and practice: Bridging the gap* (pp. 124–142). New York: Basic Books.

Emery, R. E., Otto, R. K., & O'Donohue, W. T. (2005). A critical assessment of child custody evaluations: Limited science and a flawed system. *Psychological Science in the Public Interest, 6,* 1–29.

Garven, S., Wood, J. M., Malpass, R. S., & Shaw, J. S., III. (1998). More than suggestion: The effect of interviewing techniques from the McMartin Preschool case. *Journal of Applied Psychology, 83,* 347–359.

Gist, R., Lubin, B., & Redburn, B. G. (1998). Psychosocial, ecological, and community perspectives on disaster response. *Journal of Personal and Interpersonal Loss, 3,* 25–51.

Hunsley, J., Lee, C. M., & Wood, J. (2003). Controversial and questionable assessment techniques. In S. O. Lilienfeld, S. J. Lynn, & J. M. Lohr (Eds.), *Science and pseudoscience in clinical psychology* (pp. 39–76). New York: Guilford.

Illes, J., Kirschen, M. P., & Gabrieli, J. D. E. (2003). From neuroimaging to neuroethics. *Nature Neuroscience, 6,* 250.

Jancke, L., Schlaug, G., & Steinmetz, H. (1997). Hand skill asymmetry in professional musicians. *Brain and Cognition, 34,* 424–432.

Kaufman, J., & Zigler, E. (1987). Do abused children become abusive parents? *American Journal of Orthopsychiatry, 57(2),* 186–192.

Kihlstrom, J. F. (1994). Hypnosis, delayed recall, and the principles of memory. *International Journal of Clinical and Experimental Hypnosis, 40,* 337–345.

Koocher, G. P., Goodman, G. S., White, C. S., & Friedrich, W. N. (1995). Psychological science and the use of anatomically detailed dolls in child sexual-abuse assessments. *Psychological Bulletin, 118,* 199–222.

Krauthammer, C. (2005, August 1). Let's have no more monkey trials. *Time.* Retrieved March 12, 2008, from www.time.com/time/columnist/krauthammer/article/0,9565,1088869,00.html

Lilienfeld, S. O., & Lynn, S. J. (2003). Dissociative identity disorder: Multiple personalities, multiple controversies. In S. O. Lilienfeld, S. J. Lynn, & J. M. Lohr (Eds.), *Science and pseudoscience in clinical psychology* (pp. 109–142). New York: Guilford.

Lilienfeld, S. O., Lynn, S. J., & Lohr, J. M. (Eds.). (2003). *Science and pseudoscience in clinical psychology.* New York: Guilford.

Loftus, E. F., & Ketcham, K. (1994). *The myth of repressed memory.* New York: St. Martin's Press.

Maguire, E., Gadian, D. G., Johnsrude, I. S., Good, C. D., Ashburner, J., Frackowiak, R. S. J., & Frith, C. D. (2000). Navigation-related structural change in the hippocampi of taxi drivers. *Proceedings of the National Academy of Sciences, 97,* 4398–4403.

Mayou, R. A., Ehlers, A., & Hobbs, M. (2000). Psychological debriefing for road traffic accident victims. *British Journal of Psychiatry, 176,* 589–593.

McNally, R. J. (2003). *Remembering trauma.* Cambridge, MA: Harvard University Press.

Mostert, M. P. (2001). Facilitated communication since 1995: A review of published studies. *Journal of Autism and Developmental Disorders, 31,* 287–313.

Nachman, M. W., Hoekstra, H. E., & D'Agostino, S. L. (2003). The genetic basis of adaptive melanism in pocket mice. *Proceedings of the National Academy of Science, 100,* 5268–5273.

Nash, M. R. (1987). What, if anything, is regressed about hypnotic age regression? A review of the empirical literature. *Psychological Bulletin, 102,* 42–52.

Peterson, D. R. (2003). Unintended consequences: Ventures and misadventures in the education of professional psychologists. *American Psychologist, 58,* 791–800.

Pinker, S. (2005, August 7). Can you believe in God and evolution? Compiled by David Van Biema, *Time.* Retrieved May 11, 2007, from www.time.com/time/magazine/article/0,9171,1090921,00.html

Piper, A., & Merskey, H. (2004). The persistence of folly: A critical examination of dissociative identity disorder. Part I: The excesses of an improbable concept. *Canadian Journal of Psychiatry, 49,* 592–600.

Probst, P. (2005). "Communication unbound—or unfound?"—Ein integratives Literatur-Review zur Wirksamkeit der "Gestützten Kommunikation" ("Facilitated Communication/FC") bei nichtsprechenden autistischen und intelligenzgeminderten Personen. *Zeitschrift für Klinische Psychologie, Psychiatrie und Psychotherapie, 53*, 93–128.

Rieber, R. W. (2006). *The bifurcation of the self.* New York: Springer.

Sperry, R. W. (1982). Some effects of disconnecting the cerebral hemispheres. *Science, 217,* 1223–1226.

Tavris, C. (1989). *Anger: The misunderstood emotion* (rev. ed.). New York: Simon & Schuster/Touchstone.

Utall, W. R. (2001). *The new phrenology: The limits of localizing cognitive processes in the brain.* Cambridge, MA: MIT Press/Bradford Books.

van Emmerik, A. A., Kamphuis, J. H., Hulsbosch, A. M., & Emmelkamp, P. M. G. (2002, September 7). Single session debriefing after psychological trauma: A meta-analysis. *The Lancet, 360,* 766–771.

van Ommeren, M., Saxena, S., & Saraceno, B. (2005, January). Mental and social health during and after acute emergencies: Emerging consensus? *Bulletin of the World Health Organization, 83,* 71–76.

Wegner, D. M., Fuller, V. A., & Sparrlow, B. (2003). Clever hands: Uncontrolled intelligence in facilitated communication. *Journal of Personality and Social Psychology, 85,* 5–19.

Wheeler, D. L. (1998, September 11). Neuroscientists take stock of brain-imaging studies. *Chronicle of Higher Education,* A20–A21.

Wood, J. M., Nezworski, M. T., Lilienfeld, S. O., & Garb, H. N. (2003). *What's wrong with the Rorschach?* San Francisco: Jossey-Bass.

Young, M., & Musgrave, I. (2005, March/April). Moonshine: Why the peppered moth remains an icon of evolution. *Skeptical Inquirer,* 23–28.

Chapter 3

Have We Demystified Critical Thinking?

Natalie Kerr Lawrence, Sherry L. Serdikoff,
Tracy E. Zinn, and Suzanne C. Baker

"Critical thinking scholarship is in a mystified state. No single definition of critical
thinking *is widely accepted" (Halonen, 1995, p. 75)*

Psychology faculty agree that critical thinking instruction is important (Appleby, 2006;
Halpern, 2002), but they cannot agree on a precise definition of critical thinking. Critical
thinking is a "mystified concept" (Minnich, 1990, p. 51), a problem that Halonen (1995)
addressed over a decade ago. In this chapter, we attempt to further demystify the concept
of critical thinking. We begin by looking at student and faculty perceptions of critical
thinking. Building on the work of Halonen (1995) and Halpern (2002, 2003), we then
describe specific activities and techniques designed to address the propensity, cognitive,
and metacognitive components of critical thinking.

Student and Faculty Views of Critical Thinking

Twenty psychology faculty and 170 undergraduate psychology majors completed an
online survey regarding critical thinking and how it is addressed in the classroom. In addition to open-ended questions, we included a forced-choice question, where respondents chose
the best among four different definitions of critical thinking. Students and faculty agreed
that the best definition was that provided by Halonen (1995): "the propensity and skills
to engage in activity with reflective skepticism focused on deciding what to believe or do"
(p. 76). Most students and faculty also agreed that critical thinking was important in
facilitating learning. Not surprisingly, freshmen rated critical thinking as less important
than other participants did. More advanced students and those who had taken a research
methods course were more likely to appreciate the importance of critical thinking.

For faculty, the activities rated most likely to encourage critical thinking were critiquing a journal article, engaging in debates, writing a research paper, submitting discussion

questions for class, and evaluating case studies. Students' top five activities also included critiquing a journal article, engaging in debates, and evaluating case studies. For the most part, students and faculty agreed on which activities were most likely to encourage critical thinking, $r_s(19) = .84$, $p < .01$. Interestingly, students were more likely to say that a class activity "always" or "often" helped develop critical thinking, whereas faculty often reported that the activities "could" encourage critical thinking. Faculty responses acknowledged that the *way* an instructor conducts certain class activities is vital to whether that activity encourages critical thinking.

Our results showed that activities that encourage critical thinking were more likely to occur in higher level classes. To our surprise, we also found a negative correlation between how likely an activity was to encourage critical thinking and how likely instructors were to use it in class, $r_s(19) = -.47$, $p = .03$. This finding may be because activities that encourage critical thinking can be more difficult to design, implement, and grade than other activities. Indeed, instructors may be reluctant to incorporate critical thinking activities into their courses because they perceive the investment to be too costly. In this chapter, we describe specific activities and techniques that instructors can easily incorporate into any psychology course.

Critical Thinking Framework

Halonen (1995) urged faculty to focus on critical thinking skills and proposed a framework to help "demystify" critical thinking. We used Halonen's framework to help identify best practices for fostering critical thinking (see Figure 3.1). The framework includes both the cognitive and propensity elements of critical thinking. Halpern (2002, 2003) presented a similar model for teaching critical thinking skills. Halpern recommended learning activities that:

> (a) explicitly teach the skills of critical thinking, (b) develop the disposition for effortful thinking and learning, (c) direct learning activities in ways that increase the probability of transcontextual transfer (structure training), and (d) make metacognitive monitoring explicit and overt. (Halpern, 2003, p. 14)

Like Halonen's framework, Halpern's model recognized the importance of both cognitive and propensity (i.e., dispositional) factors in critical thinking. In addition, both authors identified metacognition as integral to the development of critical thinking. In the remainder of this chapter, we discuss activities designed to address the propensity, cognitive, and metacognitive components of critical thinking.

Propensity Components

Students who have the skills to think critically do not always use those skills. Like all thinkers, students are "cognitive misers" (Taylor, 1981) who have neither the ability nor the motivation to think critically about every issue. Critical thinking takes effort, and

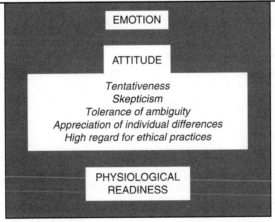

REFINES CRITICAL THINKING

METACOGNITION

The capacity to monitor the quality
of critical thinking process, product,
and changes in the thinker
through developmental self-assessment

COGNITIVE ELEMENTS

FOUNDATION SKILLS	HIGHER LEVEL SKILLS	COMPLEX SKILLS
Describing behavior	Applying concepts, theories • comparing • contrasting • analyzing • predicting	Problem-solving • diagnosis • research design • statistical analysis
Recognizing concepts, theories		
Interpreting behavior	Evaluating theories, behavioral claims • questioning • synthesizing	Theory building
Identifying assumptions	Generating hypotheses	Formal criticism Decision-making
Listening	Challenging	Collaborating

EMOTION

ATTITUDE

Tentativeness
Skepticism
Tolerance of ambiguity
Appreciation of individual differences
High regard for ethical practices

PHYSIOLOGICAL
READINESS

MOTIVATES CRITICAL THINKING

PROPENSITY COMPONENTS

Figure 3.1. Halonen's framework for critical thinking. From "Demystifying Critical Thinking," by J. S. Halonen, 1991, *Teaching of Psychology, 22*, p. 80. Copyright 1995 by Taylor & Francis. Reprinted with permission.

students will exert that effort only when they are sufficiently motivated to do so. What propensity elements motivate students to think critically? Furthermore, how can we as instructors nurture the propensity to think critically?

Before our students can think critically, they need to recognize the attitudes or dispositions of a critical thinker. It is not enough for us to tell them: "Think critically!" We must define the concept for them and provide specific guidelines for how to *do* critical thinking. Wade and Tavris (2002) stated that critical thinkers should (a) ask questions and be willing to wonder, (b) define problems clearly, (c) examine evidence, (d) analyze assumptions and biases, (e) avoid emotional reasoning, (f) avoid oversimplification, (g) consider alternative interpretations, and (h) tolerate uncertainty. These guidelines help to demystify the concept of critical thinking for students.

Students who recognize the attitudes of a critical thinker must also be motivated to adopt them. The literature on attitude change has shown that personal relevance (e.g., Petty & Cacioppo, 1984) and task importance (e.g., Maheswaran & Chaiken, 1991) increase the likelihood that a person will think carefully about an issue. These factors may also increase the likelihood that a person will think *critically*. Thus instructors should attempt to make course material personally relevant. To encourage critical thinking about the research process, have students be a part of the process (as participants, confederates, or experimenters). To encourage critical thinking about conformity, create a situation in which students are likely to conform. You could also have students write a paper in which they apply psychological principles to their lives or to current events. There are scores of other ways in which you can help students understand the personal relevance of psychology. A more difficult task may be getting students to understand why it is important to think critically. The dangers of *not* thinking critically must be apparent. There are many examples of charlatans banking on the poor critical thinking skills of the public, from faith healers to holistic medicine peddlers. These and other everyday examples can help students understand that "critical thinking is not an academic fad; it is an essential skill for living in the information age" (Connor-Greene & Greene, 2002, p. 324).

Emotions can also motivate critical thinking. Indeed, surprise may be one of the most useful tools in critical thinking instruction. Halonen (1995) claimed that "surprise is at the basis of the disequilibrium that triggers the critical-thinking process" (p. 77). We can surprise our students—and trigger critical thinking—by violating their expectations. Sometimes the course content may violate their expectations (consider students' surprise when they learn about Freud's ideas). Other times, instructors may need to employ a surprising strategy or demonstration. One tried and true example is a demonstration of the Barnum effect—the tendency to believe that a personality description is highly accurate even though it is so general that it will apply to almost everyone. Have your students submit a sample of their handwriting and tell them that you will have each sample analyzed by a graphologist. After a few days, give each student a copy of a one-size-fits-all personality description (e.g., see Boyce & Geller, 2002). Ask students to rate the accuracy of the personality description. Many students will demonstrate the Barnum effect. When you reveal the hoax, students will be quite surprised to learn that everyone received the same personality description. This demonstration can motivate students to think critically about the differences between science and pseudoscience (Boyce & Geller, 2002).

Another way to motivate critical thinking is to point out discrepancies between scientific knowledge and students' own naïve psychology (Halonen, 1986). Pointing out discrepancies should be relatively easy to do, especially at the beginning of a course. One way to do this is to give students a test of common misconceptions about psychology (e.g., Taylor & Kowalski, 2004). Many students will learn that some of their deeply held beliefs are inaccurate. This experience creates a discrepancy, and discrepancies stimulate critical thinking. As Halonen (1986) argued, good teachers should exploit discrepancies.

There are many other factors that can increase students' motivation to engage in critical thought (e.g., students' interest in the topic and the instructor's enthusiasm for the course material). These factors warrant attention at all stages of the critical thinker's development. Instructors who want to enhance their students' critical thinking skills must also nurture their "critical spirit" (Passmore, 1967, p. 25).

Foundation Skills

It is important for instructors to consider the cognitive level of their students when developing critical thinking objectives. Although as faculty we are often interested in the more advanced cognitive elements of critical thinking (e.g., generating hypotheses, theory building), it is important that we do not gloss over the foundation skills that students need. Research suggests that we are likely to overestimate the critical thinking abilities of our students (e.g., Chamberlain & Burrough, 1985) as well as the ability of our students to transfer critical thinking skills from one domain to the next (e.g., Granello, 2001). Thus it is important to focus on the foundation skills of critical thinking before moving on to the higher level skills.

It is often the case that students worry more about transcribing everything from the PowerPoint slides than whether they understand those notes. Likewise, instructors may rush through lectures in order to get through the material, without attending to what students are learning. McKeachie (2002) discussed one way of checking for and encouraging student understanding of material—*summary writing*. Writing summaries of lectures or reading material requires increased cognitive activity on the part of students, who must reorganize and synthesize information. It also provides the opportunity for students to put information into their own words, which they will likely remember better than the instructor's words (Davis & Hult, 1997). Research shows that such summary writing can have a substantial impact on learning (Davis & Hult, 1997; Kobayishi, 2006).

There are several ways that you can incorporate summary writing in your classes. One is to announce to students at the beginning of a class that you will be asking for a summary of the main points at the end of the period. Then, at the conclusion of class, allow students 3 to 5 minutes to summarize the lecture's main points. Alternately, you could ask students to write for a brief period on one topic during a pause in your lecture (Davis & Hult, 1997; McKeachie, 2002). Finally, you could ask students to attend to the lecture in order to report the most important thing that they learned from that day's (or week's) discussion (McKeachie, 2002; Zinn, 2003).

McKeachie (2002) gave additional tips on how to use summary writing to shape students into better listeners. For example, at the beginning of the class, ask students to write for 1 minute on what they want to get out of the class meeting or the most interesting topic they read about for that day's lecture. This activity can set the stage for more deliberate and focused attention, thus improving their listening. Alternately, if you are discussing a controversial issue or using a debate in class, you can use the "two-column method" (McKeachie, 2002, p. 47) to summarize different points of view. After taking notes on and participating in a debate or class discussion, students can summarize the points "For" and "Against" each argument. This exercise helps students identify different points of view in addition to basic recognition and listening.

By engaging in summary writing assignments, students can learn to describe and identify concepts, identify alternative points of view, and refine their listening skills. Furthermore, these assignments can encourage metacognition (Halpern, 2002). Self-assessment of foundation skills is as important as that of higher skills, and if you ask students to attend to their abilities on these basic skills, they can better monitor and think about their progress. As Halpern (2002) stated, "students can become better thinkers and learners by developing the habit of monitoring their understanding and judging the quality of their learning" (p. 98). Being able to summarize what they have learned is the first step in this process.

Summary writing is one way of helping develop your students' foundation critical thinking skills; there are many others. For example, have students define key terms in their own words (Stoloff & Rogers, 2004); ask students to distinguish between an inference and a behavior using examples from cartoons or the media (Halonen, 1999); and incorporate media summaries, explanations, and critiques so that students learn to generalize skills to other arenas. Providing time for students to practice these basic skills will result in building a better foundation of good thinking skills.

Higher Level Skills

Once students have the foundation of critical thinking, instructors can focus on developing students' higher level skills. These skills might be most appropriate for intermediate courses, but instructors can also emphasize them in introductory courses. There are many pedagogical tools that instructors can use to develop higher level skills. It is important for instructors to realize that they can employ a specific technique (e.g., writing) to develop skills at any level. The way instructors frame their assignments determines whether the technique will build foundation, higher level, or complex skills.

We can sharpen students' higher level skills by helping them draw connections between psychological knowledge and their everyday lives. One way to do this is to have students keep a journal. Journal writing is a popular assignment in a variety of psychology courses (e.g., Bolin, Khramtsova, & Saarnio, 2005; Connor-Greene, 2000; Graham, 2006; Hettich, 1990). Some instructors ask students to keep a journal in which they write about their personal experiences. These autobiographical journals tend to promote affective outcomes, such as self-knowledge and personal growth (Bolin et al., 2005). Other instructors ask students to make connections between course content and material outside of class, such as film, television, books, and current events. The focus of this type of journal is cognitive rather than affective (see Connor-Greene, 2000).

Journal writing can enhance student learning, and students perceive journal writing as a valuable technique. For example, Connor-Greene (2000) compared the test grades of students who wrote 15, 5, or no journal entries. Both journal groups performed better than the no-journal group, and there was no significant difference between the two journal entry groups. Students who wrote journals also reported that the technique helped improve their understanding and application of the course material.

There are many different ways that instructors can employ this technique in their courses. Students might turn in several entries throughout the semester that are graded and returned with comments and suggestions. If you are concerned about the time it takes to grade all of the entries, you can make the journal an effort-based assignment and grade it on a credit/no credit basis (Bolin et al., 2005).

Instructors can also use media to develop students' higher level skills. Feature films are a popular and effective tool in psychology courses (e.g., Anderson, 1992; Boyatzis, 1994). Students can apply course material to specific films (e.g., identify examples of positive and negative reinforcement in *Liar Liar*, Grazer & Shadyac, 1997) or analyze a film's representation of course material (e.g., have students consider whether Jack Nicholson accurately portrays obsessive-compulsive disorder in *As Good as It Gets*, Ziskin & Brooks, 1997). Students can also find and analyze examples of course material in other "real world" sources (e.g., newspaper or magazine articles, Web sites, comic strips, advertisements, advice columns, television shows, and music videos).

Complex Skills

Complex critical thinking skills include formal criticism, decision making, and collaborating (Halonen, 1995). One way to target these and other critical thinking skills is to use Structured Peer Review Exercises (SPREs). This activity involves having each student (a) read another student's draft of a paper, (b) complete a review form based on the draft, and then (c) discuss the review with the student author. Although suitable for use in any class, this activity is especially useful in classes where written communication is a key objective.

Instructors can schedule SPREs as in-class activities. Ask students to bring a draft of a paper and then pair them with another student. Tell reviewers that their goal is to help the author produce a better final paper. To help with this task, have reviewers complete a Peer Review Form (PRF; Serdikoff, 2006) that lists the required sections of the paper and type of information that should be included in each, along with specific instructions for evaluating the paper. At the end of the review exercise, reviewers should discuss the reviews with the authors.

After the discussion, students give the completed PRFs and drafts to their partners so that they can use the feedback while completing the final paper. The following week, students submit the final paper along with the PRF and the reviewed draft. To increase the probability that students use the feedback provided by this activity, they earn more points when the reviewer's comments prompt changes in the final paper than they earn when comments go unaddressed. Similarly, students earn points based on the quality of the peer reviews they provide.

People often say that the best way to learn something is to teach it to someone else. The SPRE is designed with this notion in mind. Peer reviews can enrich students' learning by allowing them to practice what they have learned while contributing to other students' learning. Reading other students' work helps students attend to the process of writing and develop critical reading skills that are necessary to improve their own writing. The SPRE requires students to engage in collaboration, decision making, and formal criticism, all of which are important complex skills that are part of critical thinking (Halonen, 1995).

Metacognition

Both Halonen (1995) and Halpern (2002) pointed out the importance of metacognitive skills in developing students' critical thinking abilities. Research has shown that metacognitive judgments, typically measured in the form of self-assessment items, are often at odds with more objective measures of knowledge, skills, and abilities (Kruger & Dunning, 1999), a disparity referred to as metacognitive miscalibration. For example, Shaughnessy (1979) measured metacognitive judgments in the form of confidence ratings students supplied for each item on objective examinations in an introductory psychology class. These data showed that examination performance and accuracy of the confidence ratings were positively correlated, indicating that students who had lower levels of achievement showed more metacognitive miscalibration. Sinkavich (1995) used a similar methodology to investigate this phenomenon in students enrolled in an educational psychology class. He found that good students (i.e., those with a final examination grade in the upper 33%) were better able to predict what they did and did not know than poor students (i.e., those with a final examination grade in the lower 33%).

Serdikoff, Farmer, Gilbert, Lunsford, and Noll (2004) examined metacognitive miscalibration with respect to writing APA-style research reports. Students in a research methods course completed four laboratory reports. The students scored their own reports using the same evaluation form as the instructor. Serdikoff et al. then computed miscalibration scores as the difference between the student's self-assessment score and the instructor's score divided by the total points available. They also classified students into three groups based on overall course grade—lowest, middle, and top third of performers.

Figure 3.2 shows the miscalibration scores for the three types of students on each of the four reports. A repeated measures analysis of variance revealed that this interaction was significant, $F(2, 69) = 3.76$, $p = .03$. Levels of miscalibration for the first report were about the same for all students. Miscalibration decreased for the second and third report for all students, but more so for high-level performers than for mid- or low-level performers. For the fourth report, which was a different format (poster vs. paper), both high- and mid-level performers showed about the same level of miscalibration as for report 3, but levels of miscalibration for low-level performers returned to levels similar to report 1.

These data are consistent with Shaughnessy (1979), showing an association between performance and metacognitive miscalibration. Students who earned lower scores on the laboratory reports provided less accurate self-assessments than those who earned higher scores. These data also are consistent with Sinkavich (1995), showing that good students

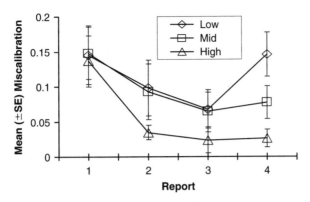

Figure 3.2. Mean (+ SE) miscalibration score for low-, mid-, and high-level performers on each of four laboratory reports.

showed less miscalibration than poor students. In addition, these data suggest that all students *recalibrate* based on feedback – all students showed less miscalibration over the three papers – but high performing students did so more than mid- or low-level students. Furthermore, the data suggest that the benefits of recalibration transferred to the new report format for mid- and high-level students whereas this transfer did not occur for low-level students.

Results such as these underscore the importance of metacognitive skills as a component of critical thinking and performance. They also indicate that some students are better at metacognitive tasks—knowing what they know. Strategies that develop students' abilities to monitor their understanding of the materials and skills they are learning should increase their performance in the class. Angelo and Cross (1993), among others, presented multiple ideas for classroom assessment techniques that can help develop students' metacognitive skills.

Conclusions

It is important to demystify faculty members' and students' conceptions of critical thinking. As instructors who would like to facilitate critical thinking in our students, we can benefit from having a comprehensive conception of critical thinking. First, having an understanding of what critical thinking is, and making its role and importance explicit to our students (Halpern, 2003), can help provide a backdrop on which to design critical thinking activities for a course. Recognizing that critical thinking involves both cognitive skills and propensity elements can help us to design effective class activities that draw on both of these factors (Halonen, 1995). We should also consider the level of our students' cognitive skills when designing activities. Finally, providing students with opportunities to develop their metacognitive skills at all levels can be crucial in developing their critical thinking.

References

Anderson, D. D. (1992). Using feature films as tools for analysis in a psychology and law course. *Teaching of Psychology, 19,* 155–158.

Angelo, T. A., & Cross, K. P. (1993). *Classroom assessment techniques: A handbook for college teachers.* San Francisco: Jossey-Bass.

Appleby, D. (2006). Defining, teaching, and assessing critical thinking in introductory psychology. In D. S. Dunn & S. L. Chew (Eds.), *Best practices for teaching introductory psychology* (pp. 57–69). Mahwah, NJ: Lawrence Erlbaum Associates.

Bolin, A. U., Khramtsova, I., & Saarnio, D. (2005). Using student journals to stimulate authentic learning: Balancing Bloom's cognitive and affective domains. *Teaching of Psychology, 32,* 154–159.

Boyatzis, C. J. (1994). Using feature films to teach social development. *Teaching of Psychology, 21,* 99–100.

Boyce, T. E., & Geller, E. S. (2002). Using the Barnum effect to teach psychological research methods. *Teaching of Psychology, 29,* 316–318.

Chamberlain, K., & Burrough, S. (1985). Techniques for teaching critical reading. *Teaching of Psychology, 12,* 213–215.

Connor-Greene, P. A. (2000). Making connections: Evaluating the effectiveness of journal writing in enhancing student learning. *Teaching of Psychology, 27,* 44–46.

Connor-Greene, P. A., & Greene, D. J. (2002). Science or snake oil? Teaching critical evaluation of "research" reports on the Internet. *Teaching of Psychology, 29,* 321–324.

Davis, M., & Hult, R. E. (1997). Effects of writing summaries as a generative learning activity during note taking. *Teaching of Psychology, 24,* 47–49.

Graham, S. M. (2006). Understanding the applicability of social psychology: The benefits of a semiweekly journal assignment. *Teaching of Psychology, 33,* 54–55.

Granello, D. H. (2001). Promoting cognitive complexity in graduate written work: Using Bloom's taxonomy as a pedagogical tool to improve literature reviews. *Counselor Education and Supervision, 40,* 292–307.

Grazer, B. (Producer), & Shadyac, T. (Director). (1997). *Liar liar* [Motion picture]. United States: Universal Pictures.

Halonen, J. S. (1986). *Teaching critical thinking in psychology.* Milwaukee, WI: Alverno Productions.

Halonen, J. S. (1995). Demystifying critical thinking. *Teaching of Psychology, 22,* 75–81.

Halonen, J. S. (1999). On critical thinking. In B. Perlman, L. I. McCann, & S. H. McFadden (Eds.), *Lessons learned: Practical advice for the teaching of psychology* (pp. 121–125). Washington, DC: American Psychological Society.

Halpern, D. F. (2002). Teaching for critical thinking: A four-part model to enhance thinking skills. In S. F. Davis & W. Buskist (Eds.), *The teaching of psychology: Essays in honor of Wilbert J. McKeachie and Charles L. Brewer* (pp. 91–105). Mahwah, NJ: Lawrence Erlbaum Associates.

Halpern, D. F. (2003). *Thought and knowledge: An introduction to critical thinking* (4th ed.). Mahwah, NJ: Lawrence Erlbaum Associates.

Hettich, P. (1990). Journal writing: Old fare or nouvelle cuisine? *Teaching of Psychology, 17,* 36–39.

Kobayashi, K. (2006). Combined effects of note-taking/-reviewing on learning and the enhancement through interventions: A meta-analytic review. *Educational Psychology, 26,* 459–477.

Kruger, J., & Dunning, D. (1999). Unskilled and unaware of it: How difficulties in recognizing one's own incompetence lead to inflated self-assessments. *Journal of Personality and Social Psychology, 77,* 1121–1134.

Maheswaran, D., & Chaiken, S. (1991). Promoting systematic processing in low motivation settings: Effect of incongruent information on processing and judgment. *Journal of Personality and Social Psychology, 61,* 13–25.

McKeachie, W. J. (2002). *Teaching tips: Strategies, research, and theory for college and university teachers.* Boston, MA: Houghton Mifflin.

Minnich, E. (1990). *Transforming knowledge.* Philadelphia: Temple University Press.

Passmore, J. (1967). *On teaching to be critical.* Boston: Routledge & Kegan Paul.

Petty, R. E., & Cacioppo, J. T. (1984). The effects of involvement on response to argument quantity and quality: Central and peripheral routes to persuasion. *Journal of Personality and Social Psychology, 46,* 69–81.

Serdikoff, S. L. (2006). *Psychological research methods student laboratory manual.* Unpublished manuscript, James Madison University.

Serdikoff, S. L., Farmer, T. A., Gilbert, J. C. Lunsford, M. A., & Noll, N. E. (2004, August). *Relations between students' self-assessments and instructors' assessments of writing.* Poster presented at the annual meeting of the American Psychological Association, Honolulu, HI.

Shaughnessy, J. (1979). Confidence-judgment accuracy as a predictor of test performance. *Journal of Research in Personality, 13,* 505–514.

Sinkavich, F. J. (1995). Performance and metamemory: Do students know what they don't know? *Journal of Instructional Psychology, 22,* 77–87.

Stoloff, M. L., & Rogers, S. (2004). Understanding psychology deeply through thinking, doing, writing. In B. Perlman, L. I. McCann, & S. H. McFadden (Eds.), *Lessons learned: Practical advice for the teaching of psychology* (Vol. 2, pp. 221–229). Washington, DC: American Psychological Society.

Taylor, A. K., & Kowalski, P. (2004). Naïve psychological science: The prevalence, strength, and sources of misconceptions. *The Psychological Record, 54,* 15–25.

Taylor, S. E. (1981). The interface of cognitive and social psychology. In J. H. Harvey (Ed.), *Cognition, social behavior, and the environment* (pp. 189–211). Hillsdale, NJ: Lawrence Erlbaum.

Wade, C., & Tavris, C. (2002). *Invitation to psychology* (3rd ed.). Upper Saddle River, NJ: Prentice Hall.

Zinn, T. E. (2003, February). *Using frequent student feedback to modify and improve course content.* Poster presented at the annual meeting of the Southeastern Teaching of Psychology conference, Kennesaw, GA.

Ziskin, L. (Producer), & Brooks, J. L. (Director). (1997). *As good as it gets* [Motion picture]. United States: TriStar Pictures.

Author Note

Correspondence concerning this article should be addressed to Natalie Kerr Lawrence, Department of Psychology, MSC 7401, James Madison University, Harrisonburg, VA 22807. Electronic mail may be sent to lawrennk@jmu.edu.

Chapter 4

Are They Ready Yet? Developmental Issues in Teaching Thinking

Laird R. O. Edman

The differences among students can be one of the great joys of teaching, but these differences are also probably the most difficult pedagogical problem facing all classroom teachers, regardless of level of instruction. The issue becomes clear to us fairly quickly, usually before the first formal assessment. We can tell by the questions students ask, the answers they give to our questions, and even by the attention they pay and nods of assent they give to what we are doing. Once we give the first test or students hand in their first paper, our intuitions are usually confirmed: some students are with us and some aren't; some students "get it" and some don't; we seem to be teaching some students and missing others.

Our classrooms are filled with students of widely differing cognitive abilities, learning approaches, educational backgrounds, and motivations to learn. The diverse reactions students provide are puzzling. The bimodal nature of our teacher–course evaluations bears this out as we read comments from some students who praise us and others who berate us for the very same teaching approach. Some students claim our course changed their lives while others claim it was a waste of time. And our students' ability to respond to our attempts to nurture critical thinking is at least as multimodal as their disparate performances on our tests and other assignments. Trying to teach students to think like psychologists, rather than simply to memorize what psychologists think, can be a frustrating enterprise. Perhaps we need a clearer idea of what we are trying to accomplish and the developmental issues implicated in those goals.

Definitions and Taxonomies

To teach students to be effective critical thinkers requires one to have a clear conception of critical thinking. The pedagogical need for a clear conception of critical thinking may seem to be obvious, but many faculty, psychology departments, and colleges and universities state that teaching critical thinking is a primary educational goal without ever stipulating what they mean by critical thinking. Of the many definitions of term available, some proscribe normative tenets of good thinking (Fisher & Scriven, 1997; Paul, 1995) and some describe common thinking processes which tend to lead to successful outcomes (Baron & Sternberg, 1987; Edman, 2000; Halpern, 1998). However, most theoretically rigorous definitions of critical thinking present purposeful, self-regulatory judgment that is evidence-based and contextually nuanced as the core of critical thinking (American Philosophical Association, 1990; Edman, 2000; Kurfiss, 1988; Morgan, 1995).

The most common approaches to teaching students to use evidence-based, contextually nuanced judgment often focus on core sets of skills required to make such judgments. These thinking skills usually include the abilities: (a) to interpret texts and other forms of communication, (b) to analyze the issues and arguments presented in those texts, (c) to evaluate those arguments in the light of contextually and methodologically appropriate criteria, (d) to discern the implications of the arguments and presuppositions upon which the arguments are based, and (e) to regulate and evaluate one's own thinking processes while doing this thinking (American Philosophical Association, 1990; Ennis, 1987). Certainly these are essential abilities for our students in a complex, information-rich world. Spelling out these abilities helps instructors and institutions to specify educational goals more clearly for students and better plan pedagogical and assessment strategies for reaching those rather ambitious and elusive goals.

Dispositional Theories

Skills-based approaches to teaching critical thinking now have a long history and literature, but what has become clear through more than 25 years of work on critical thinking theory and pedagogy is that teaching students a set of thinking skills does not seem to be enough (Halpern, 1998; Kuhn, 1999). Students may learn to write an adequate article critique in one class, but fail to use those skills in another. They may learn how to evaluate research methodology in other students' research designs, but completely miss the flaws in their own. They may learn to recognize thinking biases in the classroom, but still use badly flawed reasoning in their own decision making. Too often students think our courses are either about memorizing a great deal of material, or about learning the rules for and playing one more idiosyncratic academic game. Students regularly fail to understand what we are trying to teach them or they fail to transfer and generalize thinking skills across contexts and classes.

The inadequacy of purely skills-based approaches to teaching thinking has led to the development of dispositional theories of critical thinking (Facione & Facione, 1995; Perkins, Jay, & Tishman, 1993). These theories posit that it is not enough for students to learn how to use interpretive or analytic or evaluative thinking skills; students must also learn to value these skills. It is not enough to learn how to find flaws in the arguments and positions with which one already disagrees; good thinking requires one to use those analytic and evaluative skills on one's own thinking, ideologies, and opinions (Paul, 1995). To become good critical thinkers, students must develop several essential thinking dispositions. Although there are many different taxonomies of important thinking dispositions available (Ennis, 1987; Facione & Facione, 1995; Perkins et al., 1993) most lists include traits such as (a) truth-seeking—a desire to know the truth even when it is unpleasant, (b) intellectual curiosity—an interest in learning for learning's sake, (c) intellectual humility—a recognition of one's own limited understanding and information, (d) open-mindedness—a willingness to consider widely divergent views, (e) trust of reason—the confidence that reason works, and (f) intellectual maturity—a tolerance for ambiguity, for withholding judgment, and for the tentative nature of most knowledge.

There is good evidence that these dispositions are tied to a number of positive educational outcomes including the use of critical thinking skills (Halpern, 1998; Hofer & Pintrich, 1997; Klaczynski, 2000; Kuhn & Weinstock, 2002; Sa, Stanovich, & West, 1999). The question is how does one teach these dispositions? Are they even teachable? How malleable are these attitudes? To this point almost all of the work on critical thinking dispositions has been theoretical, and little empirical research exists concerning these dispositions. However, one of the most promising avenues of theory and research related to the critical thinking dispositions is in the area of personal epistemology.

Personal Epistemology

From the perspective of the discipline of philosophy, epistemology concerns the origin, nature, limits, methods, and justification of human knowledge (Hofer, 2002). The study of personal epistemology, on the other hand, refers to how the individual develops conceptions of knowledge—the nature of knowledge, how knowledge is generated, and how one comes to know what one knows. These issues are implicated in how students study, how much and in what ways they value their peers in the classroom, what they expect from faculty, and in their reasons for being in school. Personal epistemology influences comprehension, cognitive processing, conceptual change, and learning (Hofer, 2004a). It may be that differences in personal epistemology are the source of much of faculty frustration in their attempts to teach higher order thinking skills to students. Not only are students at different places in their epistemology from each other, but on the whole they are at a very different place than are faculty. There is often a large disconnection between teachers' assumptions about knowledge and learning and students' assumptions. It is an axiom of educational theory that the most important factor governing what students learn is what they already know. The research on personal epistemology indicates that what students believe about what they know may be more important than what they actually know (Klazynski, 2000; Sa et al., 1999; Schommer-Aikens & Easter, 2006).

Research into personal epistemology began with the work of Perry (1970) and has grown extensively in the past 15 years (Moore, 2002). While research in this area has engaged scholars from a variety of fields, research paradigms, and areas of interest, there are two primary directions epistemology research has taken (Hofer, 2002). The one direction follows the Piagetian paradigm of charting a developmental sequence of cognitive changes; the other approaches personal epistemology as a system of more-or-less independent beliefs on four or five dimensions that may develop asynchronously (Schommer, 1994).

Laird R. O. Edman

Developmental Theories

Perry (1970) pioneered the developmental approach and constructed his influential scheme of epistemological development through questionnaires and interviews with Harvard undergraduates in the 1950s and 1960s. Perry asserted that undergraduate students' personal epistemology could be classified along a continuum of four stages or clusters which could be further subdivided into nine sequential phases. Students in the more naïve stages view knowledge as concrete, absolute, and handed down from authorities (e.g., "We know the universe is 13.7 billion years old because experts say so, and learning means memorizing what the experts say"), whereas students in the more developed stages view knowledge claims as tentative and in need of justification (e.g., "The current state of evidence in several fields indicates the universe is about 13.7 billion years old, but new evidence might be found to challenge that theory. We should accept whatever the best evidence says *for now*"). This important early theory of epistemological development has been revised and developed by a number of researchers using different methods with different populations (Baxter Magolda, 1992; Belenky, Clinchy, Goldberger, & Tarule, 1986; Kuhn, 1999; Kuhn & Weinstock, 2002). While these other theories have important differences in approach, definitions of epistemology, and conclusions, the fundamental outline of Perry's work remains within all of the subsequent epistemological development theories (Hofer & Pintrich, 1997).

Reflective Thinking Model

The most thoroughly researched and perhaps most rigorously empirical developmental theory of personal epistemology is that of King and Kitchener (1994, 2002, 2004). King and Kitchener's reflective judgment model focuses on justification for belief as the key component to discerning someone's epistemological stance. In this approach, students' epistemological development is best understood through their explanations for their answers to difficult issues rather than the actual content of their answers—examining why they believe what they believe, rather than examining what they believe.

King and Kitchener have developed and tested their model using their Reflective Judgment Interview, an hour-long interview through which they observe participants' answers and justifications for their answers to ill-structured problems (problems which cannot be defined with a high degree of completeness nor solved with certainty, e.g., "How can we reconcile conflicting accounts of the origin and diversity of species on the planet?"). The protocols of over 8,000 participants over 25 years in dozens of studies across ages, gender, educational levels, backgrounds, and ethnicities have revealed strong evidence for striking differences in people's underlying assumptions about knowledge, differences that are related to how people make and justify their judgments and which change in a developmental sequence that is related to both age and education (King & Kitchener, 2002, 2004).

Prereflective thinking. King and Kitchener (1994) identified seven stages of reflective thinking organized into three different levels. Stages 1–3, called prereflective thinking, refer to the thinking of those who tend to see knowledge as certain and absolute and who believe single correct answers exist for all questions. For people in stages 1 or 2, something is true or it is false. Beliefs need little or no justification since there is assumed to be an absolute correspondence between what is believed to be true and what exists. Accepted authority figures know the truth, and one learns truth from them. Justification of beliefs is thus primarily a process of repeating what one has been told. Students in these stages see good teachers as those who unambiguously provide material for memorization and then test that memorization. A student who is a prereflective thinker is mystified or angered by being asked to analyze their thinking and justify their opinions. These students find critical thinking exercises and group work to be superfluous. They just want the right answers and a good study guide so they can memorize the correct material for the test. They ask, "Is this going to be on the test?" since anything not tested is unnecessary.

Stage 3 thinkers are a bit more advanced than stage 1 or 2 thinkers, albeit still prereflective. These students understand there may be areas in which knowledge is temporarily uncertain, but all true knowledge is certain. Therefore, in areas in which knowledge is uncertain, everything is "mere opinion." For these students all opinions have equal authority since no one knows the truth (yet). Thus stating one's opinion is justification enough for that opinion, since opinions just happen. They will say, "That's just your opinion!" as reason for discounting something someone says, or "That's just my opinion" as justification for their own view. The idea that opinions have reasons and can be better or worse based upon supporting evidence makes little sense to them; they see no reason for critical thinking. A stage 3 thinker may insist, "Until there is enough clear evidence to convince everyone that evolution is correct, no one knows, and anyone's guess is as good as anyone else's." According to King and Kitchener's (2003, 2004) data, the average high school senior is at stage 2.7 and the average first-year college student is in stage 3 thinking.

Quasi-reflective thinking. Quasi-reflective thinking, stages 4–5, includes the recognition that uncertainty is part of the knowing process. Students in these stages are able to see knowledge as an abstraction, as constructed. This is a major advance in sophistication of thinking. Now beliefs begin to be internally derived, not just accepted from authorities, and evidence is an essential part of the knowing process and is an alternative to dogmatic assertion. There is also awareness of alternative approaches and perspectives, and of contextual issues that dictate differing rules of evidence and different ways of framing issues. In some ways there is a "swing of the pendulum"; students who are prereflective thinkers tend to see knowledge as absolute and certain, while quasi-reflective thinkers may see knowledge as relative and generally unknown and unknowable.

Stage 4 thinkers tend to see knowledge claims as idiosyncratic since all people have their own perspectives and may see evidence differently or have access to different information. Knowing has a strong element of ambiguity, since while beliefs must be justified by giving reasons and using evidence, which reasons and which evidence matter is up to the individual. Such thinkers tend to choose evidence that supports their prereflective beliefs rather than hold those beliefs up to the light of evidence (e.g., young-earth creationism).

Stage 5 thinkers understand that differing opinions may be the result of differing contextual and subjective issues, but that certain contexts do have uniform rules for evidence and judgments can be made. Stage 5 thinkers also understand that absolute truth may never be knowable; only differing interpretations of evidence, events, or issues may be known. Thus beliefs are justified within particular contexts via the rules for inquiry within that context, and specific beliefs are assumed to be related to specific contexts and must be balanced against other interpretations of the available evidence. A stage 5 thinker may assert "I know there is strong evidence for global warming, but other people have evidence arguing against it too. Since different people have different rules of evidence, no one can really say who is right or wrong. It's all just a matter of perspective."

Quasi-reflective thinkers (especially stage 4 thinkers) may see education as a game in which, to get a good grade, one must figure out what each professor "wants." The job of students, then, is to play along and start sounding like the professor, since each person has their own idiosyncratic worldview. Or students may see some disciplines as "scientific" and thus capable of providing clear truth and other disciplines as "subjective" and thus filled only with individualistic interpretations of evidence and "mere" opinion. Students in these stages tend to use a "makes sense" epistemology and have trouble accurately critiquing bad thinking in themselves or others. They are willing to acknowledge bad thinking exists, however, and understand critiques of thinking much better than students in earlier stages. Quasi-reflective thinkers see the need to learn how to be critical thinkers; however, they may latch onto the skills of critical thinking to defend their own prereflective beliefs and to dismantle arguments they find disturbing. Learning how to use their thinking skills to reconsider their own beliefs is very challenging for these students.

Reflective thinking.   Stage 6 and 7 thinkers, reflective thinkers, comfortably and consistently use evidence and reason to support judgments. Context is important to such thinkers and they acknowledge the tentative nature of most conclusions; however, they also recognize that coherence, consistency, and evidence across contexts do allow one to make strong conclusions and committed judgments. Such thinkers are willing to reevaluate conclusions and knowledge claims in the light of new evidence.

Stage 6 thinkers tend to justify beliefs by comparing evidence and opinion from a variety of sources and different perspectives across contexts. Solutions are constructed and evaluated by the weight of the evidence and the usefulness of the solution. Stage 7 thinkers understand even more clearly the probabilistic nature of solutions to ill-structured problems. The adequacy of solutions is evaluated in the light of what is most reasonable or probable using the currently available evidence, perspectives, and tools of inquiry. When new evidence or arguments arise, conclusions must be reevaluated. Beliefs are justified by examining the weight of the evidence; the explanatory power of the various interpretations; contextual, historical, and methodological considerations; the consequences of alternative conclusions; and the way in which these factors interrelate. In understanding the probabilistic nature of the decision process, reflective thinkers acknowledge they may be wrong, yet attempt to reason to conclusions that are the most complete, plausible, and compelling that the context and available evidence allows. A stage 7 thinker may say, "While there is a case to be made against global climate change, the evidence for it seems to cut across many contexts, disciplines, and research paradigms, and the majority of people who have expertise in the appropriate arenas support the theory. Unless stronger evidence arises against the theory, I have to assume it is correct."

The distressing, although perhaps not surprising, news for college and university educators is that while the average college student begins college around stage 3, he or she ends college around stage 4. This may be why the descriptions of stage 6 and 7 thinkers do not sound like many of our students. The research indicates the average doctoral student is between stages 5.5 and 6.2, and stage 7 thinking is fairly rare (King & Kitchener, 2002, 2004). Students tend to move across the stages in fits and starts rather than in a continuous linear fashion. Students also move faster through the lower stages than through the upper stages. In a pattern repeated in seven different longitudinal studies, high school students moved on average 2.5 stages over 10 years; over the same period college students moved on average 1.29 stages, and doctoral students .54 stages (King & Kitchener, 2004). The data indicate students in high school are consistently prereflective thinkers who make decisions on the basis of beliefs that are not open to evaluation, but that in college students shift to quasi-reflective thinking. Students move from "ignorant certainty" to "intelligent confusion" (King & Kitchener, 2004, p. 15).

Most developmental epistemological theorists assert that these stages are complex, more akin to waves than points on a linear process (Baxter Magolda, 2004; Hofer & Pintrich, 1997; King & Kitchener, 2004). People are not "in" a particular stage; it is more the case that people have a typical mode of reasoning but will think across two or three stages. Development is uneven and moves in spurts with overlapping waves of typical thinking. King and Kitchener (2004) found most people tended to use their primary reasoning strategies in two-thirds of the reflective judgment protocols, with the other third of their responses evenly divided between the stage above and stage below their typical thinking stage. However, no individual of the thousands in King and Kitchener's (2004) studies ever had nonadjacent reasoning patterns (e.g., stage 3 and 5 reasoning).

Developmental Gender Differences

Baxter Magolda (1992, 2004), in a longitudinal study that examined, among other issues, gender differences in epistemological development, interviewed 101 men and women annually over the course of what has now been 16+ years. Her work supports the assertion of an identifiable developmental sequence in epistemological beliefs, while positing several gender-related (but not gender-determined) variations in the process. Baxter Magolda identifies a developmental sequence of four ways of knowing in which epistemology is based upon the nature of learning rather than on the nature of knowledge. Like the theories before it, this theory posits a gradual change in students' approach to knowledge and learning, moving from *absolute knowers* for whom knowledge is certain and received from authority figures, to *contextual knowers* for whom knowledge is constructed and evaluated via evidence.

Through the interviews, Baxter Magolda found gender-related differences in the approaches to knowledge and knowing. While men tended to follow masculine patterns and women feminine patterns, men and women were found using each pattern. At the lower levels, the pattern of knowing with masculine connotations tends to focus on mastering and demonstrating knowledge. Debate, challenging and being challenged by others, and using logic in an impersonal and unemotional way are seen as the appropriate forms of learning and demonstrating knowledge. The pattern of knowing with feminine connotations tends to focus on receiving, listening, and recording rather than mastering knowledge. Knowing and learning are seen as interpersonal and discussion-related; uncertainty is to be resolved by personal judgment rather than debate or logic.

At the upper levels of epistemological development the gender differences begin to disappear, although there is some difference between interindividual vs. individualist approaches to knowing. Interindividual approaches (the feminine pattern) tend to focus on connection to others and understanding why others think the way they do before evaluating their thinking. Individual approaches (the masculine pattern) tend to exhibit independent and contextual knowing by evaluating the quality of someone's thinking prior to trying to understanding why they think the way they do.

These gender-related differences are important in thinking about ways to help shepherd students to more sophisticated ways of thinking. Using approaches that call for exclusively masculine-related or feminine-related patterns of thinking may handicap some students. If we want to help students to expand their thinking repertoire, we should look to strategies that support both masculine and feminine patterns of knowing while pushing students to think a step higher than their typical thinking stage (see also Clinchy, 2002).

Independent Belief System Theories

One criticism of developmental stage theories in general is that they tend to oversimplify cognitive development and miss the more subtle nuances found in individual differences. Marlene Schommer (Schommer, 1994; Schommer-Aikens, 2004) has examined personal epistemology not as a unitary belief system that develops synchronously in a uniform pattern for all people, but as a set of relatively independent beliefs that can develop at different rates and in different patterns. Her theory includes a focus on beliefs about both the nature of knowledge and the nature of learning (Schommer-Aikens & Easter, 2006). This approach is currently generating more interest and research than the older unidimensional development theories.

While there are several variations on the nature of independent beliefs (Jehng, Johnson, & Anderson, 1993; Schraw, Bendixen, & Dunkle, 2002; Wood & Kardash, 2002), most theories posit five somewhat autonomous beliefs about knowledge and learning, each of which flows on a continuum from naïve to more sophisticated beliefs (Hofer & Pintrich, 2002). Beliefs about the nature of knowledge include:

1   Beliefs about the *structure of knowledge*: These range from believing that knowledge consists of isolated bits and pieces (which are to be memorized independently), to a more sophisticated understanding that knowledge can be integrated into complex and interrelated concepts. Perhaps this can be illustrated by contrasting the student who thinks learning statistics means memorizing formulae with the student who knows statistics is about understanding logical relationships and the nature of probability and research methodology.

2   Beliefs about the *stability of knowledge*: These range from believing that knowledge is unchanging and eternal (and thus what is true is true, and what is false is false), to a more sophisticated understanding that knowledge is tentative and can change.

Naïve students here are not interested in the history of a problem or the multiple solutions created by different methodologies. They just want to know which solution is the right one.

3   Beliefs about the *source of knowledge*: These range from believing that knowledge comes from omniscient authority (and thus learning means listening and memorizing), to a more sophisticated understanding that knowledge is constructed within communities and contexts using reason and empirical evidence.

Beliefs about the nature of learning include:

1   Beliefs about the *speed of learning*: These can range from immediate or not at all (which means thinking that if you do not understand something right away, there is no use trying to understand it), to a more sophisticated notion that learning is a gradual process that often involves sustained effort. This belief has implications for a student's willingness to persevere on difficult tasks.

2   Beliefs about one's *ability to learn*: These can range from something that is immutable and fixed at birth (one has it, or doesn't—some people are just born smart), to a more sophisticated understanding that one's ability to learn can be improved. This belief may be related to issues of locus of control, rather than to theories of intelligence. For example, naïve students may assume they just "aren't good at math" and thus not put in the necessary work in a statistics class. The poor statistics grade and mediocre understanding that result may confirm their assumptions about their math ability.

These multiple epistemological beliefs lead to asynchronous development possibilities, and thus a more nuanced understanding of how students differ in what they know about knowing is available. For example, it is possible for a student to believe knowledge is highly complex and interwoven, yet also to believe knowledge is eternal and unchanging. The implication of this referent is that to have a better understanding of our students' cognitive developmental needs, we need to consider a more complex model that examines all of these different belief systems.

Pedagogical Implications

Research on these beliefs does support the notion of relatively autonomous belief systems as well as their importance in educational outcomes (Bendixen & Rule, 2004; Hofer, 2004b; Schommer-Aikens, 2004; Schommer-Aikens & Easter, 2006). For example, the more students believe knowledge is simple, the more they think they have achieved understanding when they can recall a list of facts, while more sophisticated thinkers want to see connections and be able to apply their knowledge (Schommer-Aikens, 2004). Students who believe in simple knowledge think less deeply about texts, have poorer text comprehension, and are less likely to use integrative study strategies; students who believe in certain knowledge are more likely to misinterpret tentative information; students who believe in quick learning tend to have poor reading comprehension and lower grade point averages (Hofer & Pintrich, 1997; Klaczynski, 2000; Schommer-Aikens, 2004).

The research on epistemological beliefs is just moving out of the descriptive phase and into the prediction and manipulation phase (Hofer, 2002; Schommer-Aikens, 2004). Newer models are currently being developed and examined that combine developmental theories and the independent belief system approach into a single model (Bendixen & Rule, 2004; Hofer, 2004b; Schommer-Aikens, 2004). However, the primary question for educators is what we do with this information now that we have it. How can knowing about our students' personal epistemology help us teach them how to become better thinkers? One important lesson we can glean from this research is that changes in personal epistemology are slow. Since one's personal epistemology is so heavily implicated in one's ability to value and use critical thinking skills, we can extrapolate that growth in critical thinking ability is similarly slow (King & Kitchener, 2004). Students are probably not going to become great critical thinkers across contexts because of one excellent thinking-based course, a powerful research-methods sequence, or even the opportunity to develop and execute their own research project. Even if education for critical thinking skills is built into an entire program of study, progress may still be slow and incremental. The development of critical thinking requires fairly substantial cognitive reorganization for most of our students and a rather significant pedagogical commitment on our part. Significant success in nurturing critical thinking probably requires long-term strategies that flow across an entire curriculum rather than a few new exercises added to our courses or a critical thinking supplement added to a textbook (not that these are bad things).

There is good news here: Education helps (King & Kitchener, 2002). People who go through college progress faster and farther than those who do not, even when we account for socioeconomic status and IQ. The question is: How can we help our students do better than they are currently doing? Piaget hypothesized that an uncomfortable disequilibrium was required for people to accommodate their existing cognitive schema to new information. Current research suggests that changes in epistemology require similar disequilibrium (Hofer, 2004b; King & Kitchener, 2004). This suggests our educational approach should challenge students' naïve epistemologies and support them as they try out new modes of thinking. One important way to do this is to design our courses so that just memorizing material will not lead to success. Prereflective thinkers too often look to professors simply to provide them with the right answer, even when the instructor is exploring a difficult or problematic issue. When we provide the "right" answer in lieu of teaching the problems and ambiguities of the discipline, we reinforce lower levels of thinking in our students. An important point for us to teach our students is that every declarative sentence in psychology is an answer to a question someone once asked. Teaching students to think like psychologists means teaching them to ask questions and interrogate methodologies for answering the questions.

One thing Perry (1970) discovered, however, is that if the disequilibrium becomes too uncomfortable students will regress to earlier modes of thinking. This implies that if we want our students to grow, they must find our courses to be not only challenging but also safe. It follows that students cannot be forced to become good thinkers by being badgered, dismissed, or ridiculed (Baxter-Magolda, 2004). It appears that students learn best if they can trust their teachers. Dismissing or ridiculing beliefs or ideas that students hold dear probably does not engender the necessary trust.

Perhaps we should model good thinking in front of our students and require them to think in front of us. We should show them the process of our thinking, not just the products of our thinking, to counter the naïve belief that authorities "just know" and that conclusions must come easily or not at all. While there is little research support for this assertion (yet), I believe students need to hear us thinking out loud and the focus of our assignments and assessment should be on the processes of their thinking rather than on the products of their thinking. We should design assignments that allow us to see their thinking, and we should share stories with our students about our own struggles in learning and understanding. If we want students really to understand our discipline as well as grow in the sophistication of their epistemology, it seems to follow that we should help students understand (and critique) how psychologists create knowledge, not just what knowledge psychologists have created.

Metacognition

A focus on metacognition (thinking about thinking) may be an important part of an effective thinking-based pedagogy. Helping students develop better metacognitive strategies has been posited as a key approach for increasing students' critical thinking skills and teaching for transfer across contexts (Halpern, 1998). Metacognitive awareness has also been suggested as an important way to understand personal epistemology—as knowing about knowing (Hofer, 2004b). Critical thinking itself has been defined as "evaluative metacognition" (Edman, 2000), that is, thinking about one's thinking to make that thinking better. Perhaps one of our primary curriculum goals should be to help students to consider how they select and monitor their cognitive strategies; to consider what they know and how they know it; and to grapple with the broader issues of how anyone knows, what knowing means, and what knowledge is within different contexts.

To accomplish this outcome, Halpern (1998) suggests we should foreground the thinking process. We should regularly ask students, "How do you know that?" when they answer questions in class, and "How did so-and-so know that?" when we present theories or conclusions of research. Students can be asked to prioritize information from most to least important in answering a question; to organize the information in several different ways; to list several possible solutions to a problem and define ways to evaluate the solutions; to explore implications and assumptions of questions, methods, and conclusions. Students could also be asked to evaluate their problem-solving processes (Halpern, 1998): How much time is this problem worth? What do we know about this problem already? What is the goal in working on this problem? How will we know when we have solved this problem or come to a conclusion? Helping students to think about their thinking, and then guiding them in their evaluation of that thinking, are keys to helping students grow in their epistemological sophistication and desire to think better. Students can think a full step beyond their typical thinking strategy with support and encouragement and the more sophisticated their thinking becomes, the farther they can go with the thinking scaffolding that good teaching can provide (King & Kitchener, 2004).

Laird R. O. Edman

Finally, perhaps one of the most difficult and important strategies for encouraging metacognitive awareness and more sophisticated thinking in students is making the criteria for good thinking explicit and regularly reinforced in the classroom. I know that far too often my working definition of critical thinking is "Critical thinking is thinking the way I think," and students discern this very quickly. Thus, when my students begin sounding like me in class discussions or in essays, I assume they must be thinking well. Instead of this faulty, and potentially damaging, unreflective approach the appropriate alternative is to make explicit the standards of thinking expected in student discussion and student assignments and to model those standards for the students. Those standards should include the appropriate skills expected, the criteria for judging evidence and reasoning, and the dispositions expected of good thinkers (Bean, 1996; Edman, 1996).

Making the criteria for good thinking explicit and regularly reinforcing and reiterating those standards may also be a key to helping students develop better self-evaluation skills. Almost every definition of critical thinking available includes a "self-regulation" or "self-reflection" component. For students to grow in their thinking and to transfer those thinking skills across contexts they should be able to evaluate their own and other's thinking. Without explicit standards by which to evaluate their thinking, students can only glean the evaluative criteria from instructor comments and peer reactions.

Understanding our students' developmental issues when we teach is basic to good teaching. Faculty are often frustrated by the ways some students reduce complex issues and problems to simple black-and-white terms, and how other students are so enamored by multiple perspectives they cannot take a stand of their own. It is important for us to understand how differently our students think from the kinds of thinking we take for granted. To be effective, our pedagogy should take into account the developmental position and path of the students in the classroom, the fits and starts and regressions of students along that path, and the often painfully slow progress of students developing competence in good thinking. It is part of good teaching to know where our students are, to meet them there, and then to guide them further along the road. I know no greater joy as an educator.

References

American Philosophical Association. (1990). Critical thinking: A statement of expert consensus for purposes of educational assessment and instruction. *The Delphi Report: Research findings and recommendations prepared for the committee on pre-college philosophy.* (ERIC Document Reproduction Service No. ED 315-423).

Baron, J., & Sternberg, R. (1987). *Teaching thinking skills: Theory and practice.* New York: W. H. Freeman & Co.

Baxter Magolda, M. B. (1992). Knowing and reasoning in college: Gender-related patterns in students' intellectual development. San Francisco: Jossey-Bass.

Baxter Magolda, M. B. (2004). Evolution of a constructivist conceptualization of epistemological reflection. *Educational Psychologist, 39,* 31–42.

Bean, J. (1996). *Engaging ideas: The professor's guide to integrating writing, critical thinking, and active learning in the classroom.* San Francisco: Jossey-Bass.

Belenky, M. F., Clinchy, B. M., Goldberger, N., & Tarule, J. (1986). *Women's ways of knowing: The development of self, voice, and mind.* New York: Basic Books.

Bendixen, L., & Rule, D. (2004). An integrative approach to personal epistemology: A guiding model. *Educational Psychologist, 39,* 69–80.

Clinchy, B. M. (2002). Revisiting women's ways of knowing. In B. K. Hofer & P. R. Pintrich (Eds.), *Personal epistemology: The psychology of beliefs about knowledge and knowing* (pp. 63–88). Mahwah, NJ: Erlbaum.

Edman, L. (1996). Teaching teachers to teach thinking. *The National Honors Report, 16,* 8–12.

Edman, L. (2000). Teaching critical thinking in the honors classroom. In L. Clark & C. Fuiks (Eds.), *Teaching and learning in honors* (pp. 45–64). Radford, VA: The National Collegiate Honors Council.

Ennis, R. H. (1987). A taxonomy of critical thinking dispositions and abilities. In J. Baron & R. J. Sternberg (Eds.), *Teaching thinking skills: Theory and practice* (pp. 9–26). New York: W. H. Freeman & Co.

Facione, P. A., & Facione, N. (1995). The disposition toward critical thinking. *The Journal of General Education, 44,* 25–50.

Fisher, A., & Scriven, M. (1997). *Critical thinking: Its definition and assessment.* Point Reyes, CA: Edgepress.

Halpern, D. F. (1998). Teaching critical thinking for transfer across domains. *American Psychologist, 53,* 449–455.

Hofer, B. K. (2002). Personal epistemology as a psychological and educational construct: An introduction. In B. K. Hofer & P. R. Pintrich (Eds.), *Personal epistemology: The psychology of beliefs about knowledge and knowing* (pp. 3–14). Mahwah, NJ: Erlbaum.

Hofer, B. K. (2004a). Introduction: Paradigmatic approaches to personal epistemology. *Educational Psychologist, 39,* 1–3.

Hofer, B. K. (2004b). Epistemological understanding as a metacognitive process: Thinking aloud during online searching. *Educational Psychologist, 39,* 43–55.

Hofer, B. K., & Pintrich, P. R. (1997). The development of epistemological theories: Beliefs about knowledge and knowing and their relation to learning. *Review of Educational Research, 67,* 88–140.

Hofer, B. K., & Pintrich, P. R. (Eds.). (2002). *Personal epistemology: The psychology of beliefs about knowledge and knowing.* Mahwah, NJ: Erlbaum.

Jehng, J. J., Johnson, S. D., & Anderson, R. C. (1993). Schooling and students' epistemological beliefs about learning. *Contemporary Educational Psychology, 18,* 23–35.

King, P. M., & Kitchener, K. S. (1994). *Developing reflective judgment: Understanding and promoting intellectual growth and critical thinking in adolescents and adults.* San Francisco: Jossey-Bass.

King, P. M., & Kitchener, K. S. (2002). The reflective judgment model: Twenty years of research on epistemic cognition. In B. K. Hofer & P. R. Pintrich (Eds.), *Personal epistemology: The psychology of beliefs about knowledge and knowing* (pp. 37–61). Mahwah, NJ: Erlbaum.

King, P. M., & Kitchener, K. S. (2004). Reflective judgment: Theory and research on the development of epistemic assumptions through adulthood. *Educational Psychologist, 39,* 5–18.

Klaczynski, P. A. (2000). Motivated scientific reasoning biases, epistemological beliefs, and theory polarization: A two-process approach to adolescent cognition. *Child Development, 71,* 1347–1366.

Kuhn, D. (1999). A developmental model of critical thinking. *Educational Researcher, 28,* 16–26, 46.

Kuhn, D., & Weinstock, M. (2002). What is epistemological thinking and why does it matter? In B. K. Hofer & P. R. Pintrich (Eds.), *Personal epistemology: The psychology of beliefs about knowledge and knowing* (pp. 121–144). Mahwah, NJ: Erlbaum.

Kurfiss, J. (1988). *Critical thinking: Theory, research, practice, and possibilities*. ASHE-ERIC Higher Education Report No. 2. Washington, DC: Association for the Study of Higher Education.

Moore, W. (2002). Understanding learning in a postmodern world: Reconsidering the Perry scheme of ethical and intellectual development. In B. K. Hofer & P. R. Pintrich (Eds.), *Personal epistemology: The psychology of beliefs about knowledge and knowing* (pp. 17–36). Mahwah, NJ: Erlbaum.

Morgan, W. (1995). "Critical thinking" – What does that mean? Searching for a definition of a crucial intellectual process. *Journal of College Science Teaching, 24,* 336–340.

Paul, R. (1995). *Critical thinking: What every person needs to know to survive in a rapidly changing world* (3rd ed). Santa Rosa, CA: The Critical Thinking Foundation.

Perkins, D. N., Jay, E., & Tishman, S. (1993). Beyond abilities: A dispositional theory of thinking. *Merrill-Palmer Quarterly, 39,* 1–21.

Perry, W. (1970). *Forms of intellectual and ethical development in the college years: A scheme.* New York: Holt, Rinehart.

Sa, W. C., Stanovich, K. E., & West, R. F. (1999). The domain specificity and generality of belief bias: Searching for a generalizable critical thinking skill. *Journal of Educational Psychology, 91,* 497–510.

Schommer, M. (1994). Synthesizing epistemological belief research: Tentative understandings and provocative conclusions. *Educational Psychology Review, 6,* 293–319.

Schommer-Aikens, M. (2004). Explaining the epistemological belief system: Introducing the embedded systemic model and coordinated research approach. *Educational Psychologist, 39,* 19–29.

Schommer-Aikens, M., & Easter, M. (2006). Ways of knowing and epistemological beliefs: Combined effect on academic performance. *Educational Psychology, 26,* 411–423.

Schraw, G., Bendixen, L. D., & Dunkle, M. E. (2002). Development and validation of the epistemic belief inventory (EBI). In B. K. Hofer & P. R. Pintrich (Eds.), *Personal epistemology: The psychology of beliefs about knowledge and knowing* (pp. 261–275). Mahwah, NJ: Erlbaum.

Stanovich, K. E. (1993). Introduction. *Merrill-Palmer Quarterly, 39(1),* i–vi.

Wood, P., & Kardash, C. (2002). Critical elements in the design and analysis of studies of epistemology. In B. K. Hofer & P. R. Pintrich (Eds.), *Personal epistemology: The psychology of beliefs about knowledge and knowing* (pp. 231–260). Mahwah, NJ: Erlbaum.

Author Note

Address all correspondence to Laird R. O. Edman, Ph.D., Northwestern College, 101 7th St. SW, Orange City, IA 54041. E-mail: ledman@nwciowa.edu

Chapter 5

Simple Strategies for Teaching Your Students to Think Critically

William Buskist and Jessica G. Irons

If there is one thing that all college and university teachers want their students to learn, it is to think critically. Teachers who wish to challenge and thereby further develop their students' intellectual skills seldom, if ever, do so by asking them to memorize their textbooks and class notes. To be sure, highly effective teachers realize that the basic facts and figures related to their discipline will change with time, so teaching only these things is far less important than teaching students how to think about them (Buskist, 2004). Thus so-called master teachers use facts and figures in the service of teaching critical thinking skills.

In psychology, these teachers attempt to teach their students to think like scientists—or more specifically psychological scientists—in understanding basic psychological principles and how these principles translate into governing everyday life. However, as Slife, Reber, and Richardson (2005) have warned, psychologists need to be mindful of the assumptions and values embedded within their approach to thinking critically lest they err in their own ability to think critically about critical thinking.

In this chapter, we explore the general characteristics of critical thinking and the key elements involved in the effective teaching of critical thinking. Our goal is to provide some insight into the nature of critical thinking, to examine why students sometimes resist the call to think critically and why teachers may resist asking their students to think critically, and to offer suggestions for how to infuse critical thinking into any psychology course.

What is Critical Thinking?

The past decade has seen no shortage of books and articles on critical thinking. Some of this literature aims at understanding critical thinking from a broad perspective (e.g., Diestler,

2001; Fisher, 2001; Halpern, 2003, Levy, 1997), and other parts of it focus on under-standing critical thinking as it relates specifically to psychology (e.g., Bensley, 1998; Smith, 2002; Stanovich, 2007). Interestingly, as large as the field of critical thinking has become, the literature seems to agree generally about what critical thinking is and the kinds of qualities possessed by people said to be "effective" critical thinkers.

Critical Thinking Defined

Halpern (2003), in the latest edition of her widely read book, *Thought and Knowledge: An Introduction to Critical Thinking*, defines critical thinking as "the use of those cognitive skills or strategies that increase the probability of a desirable outcome ... thinking that is purposeful, reasoned, and goal directed" (p. 6). Compare this definition with three other common definitions of critical thinking:

- "reflective thinking involving the evaluation of evidence relevant to a claim so that a sound conclusion can be drawn from the evidence" (Bensley, 1998, p. 5)
- "the use of specific criteria to evaluate reasoning and make decisions" (Diestler, 2001, p. 2)
- "an active and systematic cognitive strategy to examine, evaluate, understand events, solve problems, and make decisions on the basis of sound reasoning and valid evi-dence" (Levy, 1997, p. 236).

All these definitions highlight both process and outcome. Clearly, the end goal for teach-ing critical thinking is to assist students in making correct judgments based on a careful weighing of available evidence. However, critical thinking is a complex endeavor. It requires students to learn several subtasks along the way that include, among other things, (a) developing a skeptical approach to problem solving and decision making; (b) breaking down problems into their simplest components; (c) searching for evidence that both sup-ports and refutes a given conclusion; and (d) maintaining a vigilant attitude toward their personal biases, assumptions, and values that may interfere with making an objective decision.

To be sure, teachers wishing to teach their students how to develop their critical think-ing skills face no easy task, especially within the confines of a single academic term. How-ever, we have found it useful with our students to start our teaching of critical thinking with the end in mind—the qualities or characteristics that reflect critical thinking. What attitudes and behaviors do we want our students to possess as a result of teaching them about thinking critically?

Qualities of Critical Thinkers

Would you know a critical thinker if you ran into one? After all, critical thinkers do not have "CT" tattooed on their foreheads, they do not wear t-shirts that announce "I'm a

Critical Thinker," and they generally do not provide physical demonstrations of their critical thinking prowess at parties and socials. However, critical thinkers do demonstrate a variety of behaviors and skills that are readily apparent in situations requiring problem solving. For example, the literature (e.g., Bensley, 1998; Diestler, 2001; Fisher, 2001; Halpern, 2003; Levy, 1997) notes that critical thinkers can accurately explain their decisions; consider alternative explanations for any state of affairs; curb their emotional reactions to others' arguments; determine the truth or falsity of assumptions; develop and present reasoned and persuasive arguments; distinguish between primary and secondary sources of information; distinguish credible (e.g., APA) from noncredible sources of information; distinguish evidence from opinion, common sense, anecdotes, and appeals to authority; distinguish opinion from fact; draw inferences; formulate and ask appropriate questions; gather data from multiple sources relevant to a problem to be solved or a decision to be made; identify their preconceptions about important issues; and understand the use and abuses of mathematical and statistical information in decision making.

All of these qualities have relevance to what teachers reveal to students about their particular academic disciplines as well as to how students negotiate problems in everyday life. Surely, if there is one skill that college should teach students, it is how to apply what they learn in their classes to their lives.

Although the list of attitudes and behaviors seems almost intuitive with regard to the picture it paints of the salience of critical thinking to academic and everyday life, students do not exactly beat down faculty doors and demand that they be taught the fundamentals of critical thinking. Indeed, critical thinking is the type of hard work that many college students would rather avoid. In fact, Buskist, Sikorski, Buckley, and Saville (2002) showed that students rate critical thinking near the bottom of those characteristics that they believe are important to effective college and university teaching (fortunately, in contrast, faculty rate critical thinking near the top of their list).

Student Resistance to Learning How to Think Critically

As teachers, it is sometimes easy to attribute deficits in student performance to sheer laziness—a misguided attribution certainly, although some students, like some teachers, are, in fact, lazy. However, students' resistance to investing the time necessary to develop critical thinking skills is likely not solely due to slothfulness. In our interactions with students both at Auburn University and elsewhere, we have found several other student-centered barriers to learning to think critically:

- The outcomes of reasoned decisions do not match their personal preferences. In other words, sometimes students' desire to engage in a particular behavior overpowers their reasoning as to why such behavior may or may not be beneficial.
- Some students are accustomed to being told what to do and when to do it. This point is particularly true for those students who come from backgrounds in which other people (parents, teachers, coaches, and other authority figures) have made

decisions for them. Thus from these students' perspective, there is no apparent reason to think critically when others do all of the thinking for them.

- Having other people make decisions relieves students of responsibility. This reason for failing to think critically is on a par with the notion of just following orders: "Because somebody tells me what to do, and I do it, I should *not* be held accountable for my actions—I was just doing as I was told."

- Some students may think that their judgment is inferior to that of an authority figure. Many students come from backgrounds in which they are instructed to "obey authority," which implies to some extent the notion that "I am not ready to make decisions on my own—I need to look to older, wiser, and more informed people to tell me what to do."

- Many students, particularly freshman and sophomores, think in terms of black and white rather than shades of gray. Perry's (1970) work on the intellectual development of college students substantiates this point—many college students prefer to be told what is true and what is false rather than discovering that information on their own.

- Some students are accustomed to memorizing information rather than thinking about it. Memorizing facts and figures takes time and effort, to be sure, but it does not require the uncertainty that goes with thinking—and that uncertainty can be discomforting to some students.

- Some students may undervalue the consequences of their decisions. These students may have never had to face the genuine consequences of poor decision making before because somebody else has been there to protect them from those consequences (e.g., a student whose parents pay for the financial consequences for his or her arrest for driving under the influence).

- Some students don't have the time to invest in genuine critical thinking. In addition to carrying a full academic load, some students raise families and work in part-time or full-time jobs while working on their degrees. These students often believe that they don't have the time to take classes that require a lot of out-of-class work such as writing papers, preparing presentations, and other assignments that require thoughtful preparation and the integration of knowledge.

- Some students lack the basic topical knowledge needed for critical thinking. They simply do not have the academic background (they lack basic foundational knowledge) to understand, let alone analyze, integrate, and apply the subject matter they currently are "learning."

Part of the difficulty in effectively teaching critical thinking is recognizing that some students enter the classroom not only unprepared, but contraprepared, to learn how to think critically. Nothing in their personal or academic backgrounds has taught them to think critically or be disposed favorably toward learning how to think critically. And for some students, their personal and academic backgrounds have encouraged them *not* to think critically, especially in cases where students have learned to rely on the advice and judgment of others to direct their actions.

Effective teachers understand how the variables that give rise to student resistance to critical thinking impact the learning environment of the classroom (Riggio & Halpern,

2006). Indeed, *effective* teachers act proactively to design classroom environments to overcome these sorts of obstacles.

Teacher Resistance to Teaching Students to Think Critically

Just as students may shy away from the task of thinking critically, teachers may facilitate such avoidance by failing to implement critical thinking as part of their courses. Most college and university teachers aspire to teach their students to think critically, but to do so is no easy task. Developing intellectually challenging activities, problem-based scenarios, and other rigorous assignments is a critical thinking task in its own right. Although many teachers welcome the challenge, there are several reasons why teachers may choose not to teach students to think critically, including the following:

- Academia can be a demanding and time-consuming profession that often requires a delicate balance of teaching, service, and research. When time is scarce, teaching preparation may take a back seat to other, more pressing, obligations.
- Some teachers may forego teaching critical thinking because they cannot easily measure the effects of their teaching efforts to show that it has been effective. As teachers, we often rely on grades as indicators that students have learned and that we have done our jobs. It is not as easy to assess critical thinking skills as typical course content, so that it may not be evident if students are learning the critical thinking skills we try to teach them. Developing ways to assess critical thinking is yet another demanding task to add to teachers' lists of daily chores.
- Because students often resent being urged to think critically and teachers want to be liked by students, some teachers may sacrifice critical thinking in their classes in exchange for popularity.
- Not all teachers are critical thinkers, and these teachers may not feel comfortable enough with their own skills to ask their students to think critically. Holding a master's degree or PhD does not guarantee that one can think critically.
- Many teachers may not know how to teach critical thinking skills, although they value those skills and wish for their students to become critical thinkers.

Despite these student–teacher barriers to teaching critical thinking, teachers can learn to develop classroom environments conducive to critical thinking. In the next section, we outline several simple ways that we have found useful in creating learning environments conducive to enhancing student motivation for learning to think critically.

Effectively Teaching Critical Thinking

One does not just suddenly decide to teach critical thinking during the middle of the academic term and go from there: Teaching critical thinking must be planned in order to be maximally effective. As such, the earlier the planning can begin, the better, which means that teachers may wish to think carefully about how to build critical thinking into their courses long before the academic term starts.

Before the Academic Term Begins

As you start to piece together your syllabus, think about how you will build critical thinking into your course. Choose a textbook and other supportive materials (e.g., print media, video) that reflect the kind of approach to critical thinking that you wish to adopt. Do the text and the other media include built-in critical thinking pedagogy (i.e., exercises that tap students' understanding, analysis, and application of the subject matter)? If so, does it reflect the depth or level of critical thinking you wish your students to acquire? As you review the reading material, look for any particular places that lend themselves especially well to infusing critical thinking and make a note of them. These notes will remind you to look for interesting examples of critical thinking or the lack of critical thinking in your reading of everyday material (e.g., newspapers, magazines).

Research on master teachers has found that students appreciate teachers who tie classroom learning to everyday life (Buskist et al., 2002). Depending on how much advance planning you have done, you should have a good size stock of everyday examples that you can use in the classroom to teach critical thinking. This approach also will enhance your ability to apply psychological principles to everyday life.

Finally, prior to the academic term, you should also be creating a collection of problem-based scenarios for students to solve as they work their way through the course (e.g., Connor-Greene, 2006). These scenarios should be directly relevant to your subject matter and engage students in interesting but challenging problems, dilemmas, even mysteries. You can use these scenarios with individual students or groups of students. We like to combine these approaches by first giving individuals a few minutes to solve a problem and then organizing them into groups of two or three to talk about differences in their individual solutions to the problem. We then bring the whole class together to discuss the scenario and its potential solutions.

Thus, when the academic term begins, you will have done your homework and know full well the kinds of critical thinking exercises available to you in your text and supporting media. You also will have a large handful of compelling scenarios to share with your students as critical thinking activities. Such planning will also compel you to find ways to model critical thinking processes in your teaching, which is a major benefit in honing your teaching skills. From your students' perspective, as the teacher, you become the exemplar par excellence of how to think critically.

The First Week of Class

You should introduce the concept of critical thinking to your students during the first week of class and let them know that a central part of your course will focus on helping them develop their powers of critical thinking. You may safely assume that most students, even many in upper division courses, will not know what critical thinking is or how it might apply to them. Thus, during the first week, we offer a few definitions of critical thinking to our students and share with them a half dozen or so of the key attributes of critical thinkers. We share with them one of our primary goals for the course: We would like them to possess all or at least some of these attributes by the time the academic term ends.

We also stress the importance of critical thinking to making reasonable decisions in college and beyond and we provide one simple example of critical thinking as it relates to the course material. One of our favorite examples in the introductory course is attribution. We pose something like the following scenario to the class: "Suppose you are walking across campus and, being the friendly person that you are, you say 'hi' to a woman who is passing by you. She responds by looking directly at you with a scowl on her face and says nothing to you—to what would you attribute her unkindly response to your friendliness?" Many students react immediately and emotionally to this question and often refer to the woman as a "jerk" or "snob," and go on to refer to the woman's disposition in explaining the potential causes for her behavior. A few students, though, are more thoughtful and note that there may be extenuating circumstances that explain her response—maybe she just received some bad news or is not feeling well at the moment. What this quick exercise does is to get students thinking about alternative explanations for behavior and to understand the role of their own emotions in making judgments about others.

It is one of our favorite examples because (a) it is highly interesting to students, (b) it is a psychological phenomenon in which students regularly (but often unwittingly) engage, (c) the pitfalls of misattributions are clear and compelling, and (d) it is a way for us to tie critical thinking into psychology early in the course.

Throughout the Academic Term

As you work your way through the academic term, follow through on what you have taught students about critical thinking in the first week of class. We have attempted to accomplish this task in two different ways. First, we set aside time each week to do critical thinking exercises, focusing on how it applies to the topic at hand. Each week we give students out-of-class critical thinking assignments, which they complete and turn in. We follow up on these assignments by reviewing them in class. Second, we simply ask students to work through problem-based scenarios in class. Both methods have worked very well for us, although the first method uses less class time. However, the tradeoff is the depth and quality of discussion engendered by the second method.

Regardless of which of these methods (or other methods) you might adopt to teach critical thinking, the key is to be consistent in injecting critical thinking into your class. A little bit of critical thinking here and there will not do—you should attempt to have your students think critically about your subject matter each week. That way, you constantly remind students of the importance of critical thinking in problem solving and decision making. Such consistency also helps students to become accustomed to thinking critically in your class—and it may increase the likelihood that they will apply critical thinking to their lives outside the classroom.

William Buskist & Jessica G. Irons

Summary and Conclusions

We have five main suggestions for teaching critical thinking throughout the academic term:

1 For each and every core topic in your class, provide students with problems to analyze or solve. It doesn't matter whether you ask students to tackle these problems in or out of class—the important thing is that they have the opportunity to think critically about them.

2 Guide students in the development of their critical thinking skills with handouts (either paper or electronic) containing information about critical thinking techniques that you have found particularly effective in your quest to solve problems and make informed decisions (e.g., explain what it means to "consider alternative explanations" or "weigh the evidence" or "determine the truth or falsity of assumptions").

3 Take time in class to apply these methodologies to your subject matter so that you can model effective critical thinking for your students. Your teaching should provide your students the opportunity to see critical thinking in action through a role model—you!

4 You should bring to class some of those great everyday examples of critical thinking (or lack of critical thinking) that you've been collecting since before the academic term started. Make sure the examples are relevant to your subject matter.

5 Give your students plenty of opportunity to practice their developing critical thinking skills, including examinations and other graded assignments. For many students, if you don't test it, they won't study it. Besides, it makes good sense to test students on those key elements of the course that you stress as important—in other words, you should put your money where your mouth is!

The ability of students to think critically—to make sound judgments based on careful weighing of evidence—is one of the most important student learning outcomes for all college and university teachers. College-educated students should, among other things, learn to apply what they learn in their classes to solving problems that they encounter throughout their lives. Unfortunately, the ability to think critically is a complex task that is often impeded by many factors, including students' resistance to learning how to make wise and informed decisions.

You should realize that students do indeed often resist thinking critically and design your classroom learning environment with the goal of overcoming this obstacle. Preparation for teaching critical thinking begins long before the academic term begins and is marked by paying particular attention as to where in the course teachers can infuse critical thinking exercises and teach critical thinking skills. You should collect examples of critical thinking (or not) from everyday life and develop problem-based scenarios for students to solve throughout the academic term. During the first week of classes, unabashedly introduce critical thinking as a primary theme of their course, review the basic tenets of critical thinking and the qualities of effective critical thinkers, and provide examples of how critical thinking is key to making important life decisions.

As the academic term moves along, consistently inject critical thinking into your weekly coverage of your subject matter and give your students plenty of practice in critical thinking through the use of well-crafted exercises, which may be completed in class or assigned as homework. The key to teaching students to become adept at critical thinking is providing them consistent opportunities to practice what they are learning, including critical thinking problems on graded activities such as examinations.

Although students' intellectual abilities vary tremendously, all students should be able to learn to think critically to some degree about the class material as well as about decisions to be made in everyday life. A primary responsibility of college and university teachers is to help students achieve whatever potential they might possess for becoming better thinkers and decision makers. In this chapter, we have outlined a general strategy for meeting this responsibility in any psychology course—from the introductory psychology through the capstone course. Of course, adopting this strategy will not guarantee that your students will become better critical thinkers, but it does increase the likelihood of such an outcome. And that likelihood, after all, is the best that any teacher can hope for—that we increase our students' chances of becoming educated citizens.

References

Bensley, D. A. (1998). *Critical thinking in psychology: A unified skills approach.* Pacific Grove, CA: Brooks/Cole.

Buskist, W. (2004). Ways of the master teacher. *APS Observer, 17*(9), 23–26.

Buskist, W., Sikorski, J., Buckley, T., & Saville, B. K. (2002). Elements of master teaching. In S. F. Davis & W. Buskist (Eds.), *The teaching of psychology: Essays in honor of Wilbert J. McKeachie and Charles L. Brewer* (pp. 27–39). Mahwah, NJ: Erlbaum.

Connor-Greene, P. (2006). Problem-based learning. In W. Buskist & S. F. Davis (Eds.), *Handbook of the teaching of psychology* (pp. 70–77). Malden, MA: Blackwell.

Diestler, S. (2001). *Becoming a critical thinker: A user friendly manual* (3rd ed.). Upper Saddle River, NJ: Prentice-Hall.

Fisher, A. (2001). *Critical thinking: An introduction.* New York: Cambridge University Press.

Halpern, D. F. (2003). *Thought and knowledge: An introduction to critical thinking* (4th ed.). Mahwah, NJ: Erlbaum.

Levy, D. A. (1997). *Tools of critical thinking: Metathoughts for psychology.* Boston: Allyn & Bacon.

Perry, W. G., Jr. (1970). *Forms of intellectual and ethical development in the college years: A scheme.* New York: Holt, Rinehart, and Winston.

Riggio, H. R., & Halpern, D. F. (2006). Understanding human thought: Educating students as critical thinkers. In W. Buskist & S. F. Davis (Eds.), *Handbook of the teaching of psychology* (pp. 78–84). Malden, MA: Blackwell.

Slife, B. D., Reber, J. S., & Richardson, F. C. (2005). Introduction: Thinking critically about critical thinking. In B. D. Slife, J. S. Reber, & F. C. Richardson (Eds.), *Critical thinking about psychology: Hidden assumptions and plausible alternatives* (pp. 3–14). Washington, DC: American Psychological Association.

Smith, R. A. (2002). *Challenging your preconceptions: Thinking critically about psychology* (2nd ed.). Belmont, CA: Wadsworth.

Stanovich, K. E. (2007). *How to think straight about psychology* (8th ed.). Boston: Allyn & Bacon.

Part II
Assessing Critical Thinking

Chapter 6

Measure for Measure: The Challenge of Assessing Critical Thinking

Jane S. Halonen

I am an accidental critical thinking scholar.

As an undergraduate, I was the prototypical student interested in "helping people." I saw research and statistics as hurdles that must be overcome to get to the "good stuff." In fact, my undergraduate advisor recommended, "Jane, you are at least going to have to *pretend* that you like research if you expect to get into graduate school." And so I did, but research was never a comfortable home for me during those formative years.

As I was preparing for a clinical career, it was a great shock to me to discover how much I enjoyed teaching. I learned not to talk about it to my graduate school friends because it would have reinforced my outlier status. However, I thought it was fascinating to see what kinds of improvements I could make over the course of my six discussion sessions per week to enhance student learning. Little did I know I was engaging in the early stages of the scholarship of teaching and learning.

Although I tried the clinical life, I badly missed the classroom so I was thrilled when Alverno College offered me a position in 1981 at a whopping $15,000 per year. I didn't realize when I was hired that I was entering service with a college that would contribute to such dramatic changes in higher education. They long ago abandoned traditional grading in favor of performance assessment. It suited my own ideas about active learning perfectly.

In contrast with truly fine programs that exist today in many psychology graduate programs, mine didn't provide much preparation for what an academic career might entail. At least I like to blame the absence of career preparation to explain why I failed to respond very gracefully when my dean at Alverno, who happened to be a psychologist/historian, offered me an opportunity of a lifetime after I had been teaching for just one year. This episode leads us to the first of several crucial ideas that will enable new faculty members to optimize their critical thinking practices:

Big Idea #1: When your dean or chair asks you to do something, suspend criticality; it could be life-changing.

My academic dean, Austin Doherty, had pulled together a grant-writing team to capture support from the Fund for the Improvement of Postsecondary Education (FIPSE). Their goal was to address the disturbing report *Nation at Risk* (National Commission on Excellence in Education, 1983), which had concluded that colleges and universities were failing in their responsibilities. (If this sounds familiar, a similar theme has been addressed more recently in the higher education bestseller, *Declining by Degrees*, Hersch & Merrow, 2005.) In response to the criticism, Alverno convened four disciplines to discuss and disseminate strategies for the promotion of critical thinking in the classroom. The Dean asked me to select and coordinate a group of 10 psychologists who would come to Milwaukee and debate what strategies and frameworks could shed some light on how best to teach psychology students to think critically about behavior.

Early in the discussions, the specter of critical thinking assessment reared its head. At the outset of the discussion, I recall that one of our members referred to himself jokingly as the "Johnny Appleseed" of critical thinking. He shared that he saw his role as "planting the seed" of critical thinking that would fully flower much later in the student's career. Sadly, he had resigned himself to the idea that he wouldn't be able to observe directly the fruits of his labor. Although I was a relative neophyte in teaching, that comment struck me as unimaginative and perhaps even irresponsible. Why couldn't we develop teaching strategies that would allow us to measure the impact more immediately? Much of my academic writing has been devoted to addressing that question.

My favorite memory from the FIPSE experience still informs my teaching and leads to Big Idea #2. Bruce Henderson from Western Carolina University in an exuberant moment suggested ...

Big Idea #2: Why study psychology? So you won't be a jerk!

I refer to this observation as the *überoutcome* of psychology. If we deconstruct the statement, it reveals a lot about what end states we seek for our students. Avoiding jerk status means, among other things:

- Practicing amiable skepticism
- Seeking evidence to support what we think or believe (Halonen & Gray, 2001)
- Understanding the perspectives of others

- Experiencing the appropriate humility that grows from realizing that you can only have an incomplete handle on reality.

Helping our students not become jerks is a justifiable goal for our activities in the classroom.

One of the controversial aspects of our early FIPSE discussions involved the drive to craft the perfect definition of critical thinking. The philosophers wanted to talk about the attributes of the critical thinker, typically expressed in traits. For example, Paul and Elder's (2002, p. 18) concept of "critical thinking in the deep sense" exemplifies this approach. This "all-or-none" approach makes me uncomfortable because I regularly falter in my ability as a critical thinker. However, I am much more comfortable construing critical thinking as a set of behaviors, leading us to ...

Big Idea #3: We should regard critical thinking as a "state," not a "trait."

A framework that emerged from our FIPSE group (Halonen, 1986) is one that still drives much of the design of the teaching in my own classroom. This model (see Figure 6.1) targets the essential characteristics of how to facilitate critical thinking. The model acknowledges that students do not arrive in psychology classrooms as blank slates with regard to their understanding of behavior. They have a store of facts, beliefs, assumptions, and values that serve as the foundation from which they construct "personal theory" about behavior. As teachers, we present external stimuli that we think and hope will engage students. It is perhaps easiest to get them to engage critically when the external stimulus promotes cognitive disequilibrium, a force described long ago by Jean Piaget as a primary driver of learning. By knocking students cognitively off balance, they will engage in critical thinking to restore their balance.

In the beginning of the student's journey in psychology, the external stimulus needs to be a whopper. For example, in my intro class recently, I introduced something I had heard on the news the morning of my class that I had confidence would be the perfect external stimulus to engage discussion. A morning news team had a spirited discussion about *sagging*, the art of wearing your pants at half-mast without them falling down. One newscaster confidently concluded, "The lower the pants, the lower the IQ." My students were appalled at the audacity of the claim. Not only did we debate the truthfulness of the claim, but it was a good way to begin the important discussion about "correlation is not causation." The conversation was vigorous and laid the groundwork for the develop-mental progression predicted within the model. Challenging the truths promulgated by newscasters in such a personal way should assist students in developing a more critical orientation. According to the FIPSE model, as students improve in their critical thinking skills, the external event that triggers critical thinking can become ever more subtle and nuanced.

This model also launched my personal fascination with the progression of "novice to expert" in the work articulating outcomes in psychology that would follow (see Bosack, McCarthy, Halonen, & Clay, 2004; Halonen et al., 2003, as examples). It is profoundly satisfying to isolate a skill set and describe its evolution from primitive beginnings to

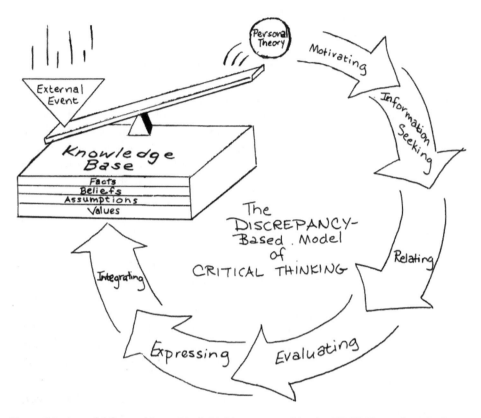

Figure 6.1. A model for teaching critical thinking proposed by the FIPSE Network, in Halonen, J. (Ed.), (1986), *Teaching Critical Thinking in Psychology*, Milwaukee, WI: Alverno College Productions, p. 7.

sophisticated professional performance. Such careful analysis helps me clarify my sometimes unspoken expectations about what I want students to know and do. At the same time, this focus encourages me to be patient with learners who choose to make this disciplinary journey. This observation leads naturally to ...

Big Idea #4: Critical thinking is contextual: Both the discipline and developmental level contribute.

Disciplines define critical thinking in unique and sometimes mystifying ways (Halonen, 1995). And yet there is value in defining critical thinking in generic ways. Consequently, there is practical value added to the curriculum when an institution finds some common language to capture their critical thinking expectations. Common language defining critical thinking across disciplines can foster some important outcomes:

- *A coherent curriculum*: When a faculty articulates a common vision, the elements of the student's program hang together in a logical manner and guide reasonable decisions in curriculum design.

- *Student metacognition*: When we are explicit in our expectations about student learning outcomes, students can develop a much better and richer understanding of the goals we have for them. As a consequence, they should be able to describe themselves in advantageous ways in employment interviews and graduate school competition.
- *Institutional identity*: When we forge a common mission, the activity can facilitate institutional "branding." In the competitive atmosphere of postmodern higher education, a recognizable brand can produce marketing advantages for students looking for an appealing institution that is a good match for their dreams.
- *Accreditation success*: When you must offer evidence of effectiveness that illustrates how you are meeting your institutional vision, a common expectation can produce positive response from accreditors. At University of West Florida's most recent accrediting visit by the Southern Association of College and Universities (SACS), we were pleasantly surprised to find that our coherent assessment proposal engaged the site visitors enthusiastically, well beyond our expectations for the positive collaboration that we had anticipated. Our institutional definition of critical thinking, illustrated in Appendix 1, provides for a generic approach across disciplines that resulted in our accrediting team rooting for our success in implementing the proposed assessment plan.

Big Idea #5: Even within psychology, critical thinking takes multiple forms.

Even within the discipline of psychology, there isn't just one form of critical thinking. A point I tried to make in *The Critical Thinking Companion* (1996; Halonen & Gray, 2001) is that we pursue different kinds of critical thinking objectives across the variety of course experiences we offer, including:

- pattern recognition
- practical problem solving
- creative problem solving
- scientific problem solving
- psychological reasoning
- perspective taking.

And each of those processes has a distinctive developmental path. For example, if we want students to use psychological theory to explain behavior, we have to recognize that novices will not be sophisticated in this skill at the outset. They need practice with basic psychological concepts, recognizing when concepts are appropriate to apply, and then seeing how concepts can be linked to produce more complex predictions in psychological theory. As their expertise grows, their theory skills become more sophisticated, including the ability to criticize existing theory and even invent new theory, If we try to capture how this growth becomes apparent within the psychology curriculum, novice-to-expert progression might look something like the following:

Concept recognition→
    Concept application→
        Theory recognition→

Theory application→
Theory evaluation→
Theory creation

Although I don't think I've published this progression formally anywhere, it grew out of the work I shared with Paul Smith and other colleagues at Alverno College. And it compares favorably with the recent retooling of Bloom's Taxonomy as completed by Anderson and Krathwohl (2001).

However, no matter what the version of critical thinking we have chosen to foster as psychologists, we are still left with the challenge of measuring student progress on that elusive goal. I want to address three general categories that offer some strategy for measurement, starting with …

Big Idea #6: The "aha"s should tell you something, even if not psychometrically robust.

Seeing the lights go on in students' eyes is a powerful and meaningful measure that we should actively track for feedback on how well we are teaching. However, if we get caught up in covering the content of the discipline (Eriksen, 1983), we are much more likely to encourage students to be transcribers and, instead of eyes aglow, you will be treated to a panorama of hair parts as students pretend to scrutinize their papers in the hopes that you won't call on them. Although lit-up eyeballs is an absurd measure for formal accountability, it is an essential one for your own reinforcement as a teacher.

The second general category of measurement is performance assessment, an approach that has captured a lot of my scholarly focus:

Big Idea #7: Performance assessment is proving its viability and value in measuring critical thinking.

Who better than psychologists to come up with reasonable behavioral descriptors for what we think intellectual activity should look like as students move along the continuum from novice to expert? Performance assessment emphasizes specifying the behavioral parameters of what we should expect to see in a student's performance on a cognitive task that we have designed, typically evaluated using a rubric (Trice, 2000). The use of rubrics provides the kind of evidence that makes accreditors happy because the criteria provide a much richer description of what transpires in a class compared to mere grades. However, a few pointers are relevant to optimize the results of performance assessment strategies.

Reward preparation. One of the great frustrations of contemporary college life is how little time students seem to be putting into classroom preparation. I'm almost embarrassed to admit that it has taken me 25 years and the help of some very bright women (Connor-Greene, 2005; Walvoord, 2004) to solve this problem. I have included the convergence of their influence in Appendix 2 to demonstrate the strategy I currently use to motivate students to come to class having read the material and having prepared ideas to explore in class. Students submit a single homework page that requires evidence of critical thinking in each class, whether through applied examples or the generation of questions. Although I designed this strategy to be easy to review and "grade," I have used it long enough to recognize that the quality of questions my students can generate when I hold them accountable for doing so has been one of the most gratifying teaching investments I have made. Although it takes me longer to "grade" their contributions than merely marking the effort as "good faith," as I had intended when I designed the homework pages, the strategy pays off in much more vigorous class discussion fueled by more interesting class questions.

Clarify performance expectations. Answering the question, "What do you want on this project?" is likely to produce more satisfying performance from your students. Building and consistently applying rubrics is not easy—as any advanced placement reader can tell you—but students respond with great focus and confidence when we provide more explicit direction. Appendix 3 contains an exemplar of a rubric I use for a communications project in my intro course.

Require student self-assessment. When students experience the rubric as the basis of their evaluation, they can learn to be good judges of their own performance and personally benefit from having this critical responsibility (Dunn, McEntarffer, & Halonen, 2004). My goal is to have students learn to be self-directing because I won't be able to follow them around with feedback for the rest of their lives. Start simply. Ask beginning students what the best feature of their project or test performance was. Then ask what aspects of performance they would improve upon if they magically had more time. From this introduction to self-critique, students can quickly learn to apply performance criteria that can lead to improved performance.

Pursue perfection (or at least improvement). Accepting performance assessment as a central strategy also means constant tinkering with your standards because student performance provides a feedback loop from which your own skills can be continuously refined.

Obviously the notion of student learning outcomes has become "best practice." Starting with the courageous high school teachers who not only pioneered in this area by developing the *National Standards for Introductory Psychology* (American Psychological Association, 2000), we see educators at every level collaborating to try to establish benchmarks for performance (for a broader discussion of this issue, see Dunn, McCarthy, Baker, Halonen, & Hill, 2007). *The Guidelines for the Undergraduate Psychology Major* (American Psychological Association, 2007) have been approved by the APA and have already been influential for departments across the country dealing with accountability demands. Community college educators embarked on a project to fill in the missing developmental gaps in the *Guidelines* to tie together lower level and advanced work in the major (Puccio, 2006). A group of clinical directors collaborated to produce competence standards for scientifically trained therapists (Bieschke, Fouad, Collins, & Halonen, 2005). This array of activity demonstrates that performance assessment has been embraced across the psychology curriculum from alpha to omega.

Big Idea #8: If you must measure the masses, objective measurement options abound and become richer every year.

You may not have the luxury of being able to address your critical thinking concerns through performance assessment. If you must use objective measures, a variety of psychometrically solid strategies exists, and these are listed in Appendix 4.

Big Idea #9: Many variables should influence your choice of measurement strategy.

Just how do you pick the right kind of measure for gauging your success in helping students to become critical thinkers? Resources, time, expertise, student motivation, and intrinsic enthusiasm for measurement should all influence how a given department or faculty member adopts a specific formal strategy. But one final take-home point remains ...

Big Idea #10: There is no single perfect solution to the challenge of measuring critical thinking.

Whatever measure you choose will be an imperfect representation of what your students can do. Despite imperfection, we should move ahead. Psychology should embrace the

Figure 6.2. A student's view of the risks involved in critical thinking. Taken from Halonen, J. S. (1986). *Teaching critical thinking in psychology* (p. 165). Milwaukee, WI: Alverno College.

opportunity the accountability climate provides for us to become leaders in understanding and measuring critical thinking behavior.

One last thought. I've carried this cartoon (Figure 6.2) with me for 20 years. It was originally rendered by one of my students who asked me to remind anyone who is listening to me talk about critical thinking that students are fragile. Knocking them off balance sometimes knocks the props out and we need to exercise care and planning to elicit their best work.

References

American Psychological Association. (2000). *National standards for the teaching of high school psychology*. Washington, DC: American Psychological Association. Retrieved March 17, 2008, from www.apa.org/ed/natlstandards.html

American Psychological Association. (2007). *APA guidelines for the undergraduate psychology major*. Washington, DC. Retrieved March 17, 2008, from www.apa.org/ed/psymajor_guideline.pdf

Anderson, L. W., & Krathwohl, D. R. (Eds.). (2001). *A taxonomy of learning, teaching, and assessment: A revision of Bloom's Taxonomy of educational objectives*. New York: Longman.

Bieschke, K. J,. Fouad, N. A., Collins, F., & Halonen, J. S. (2005). The scientifically-minded psychologist: Science as a core competency. *Journal of Clinical Psychology, 60,* 713–725.

Bosack, T. N., McCarthy, M. A., Halonen, J. S., & Clay, S. P. (2004). Developing scientific inquiry skills in psychology: Using authentic assessment strategies. In D. S. Dunn, C. M. Mehrotra, & J. S. Halonen (Eds.), *Measuring up: Educational assessment challenges and practices for psychology* (pp. 141–170). Washington, DC: American Psychological Association.

Connor-Greene, P. A. (2005). Fostering meaningful classroom discussion: Student-generated questions, quotations, and talking points. *Teaching of Psychology, 32,* 173–175.

Dunn, D. S., McCarthy, M., Baker, S., Halonen, J. S., & Hill, G. W., III. (2007). Quality benchmarks in undergraduate psychology programs. *American Psychologist, 62,* 650–670.

Dunn, D. S., McEntarffer, R., & Halonen, J. S. (2004). Empowering psychology students through self-assessment. In D. S. Dunn, C. M. Mehrotra, & J. S. Halonen (Eds.), *Measuring up: Educational assessment challenges and practices for psychology* (pp. 171–186). Washington, DC: American Psychological Association.

Ericksen, S. C. (1983). Private measures of good teaching. *Teaching of Psychology, 10,* 133–136.

Halonen, J. S. (Ed.). (1986). *Teaching critical thinking in psychology*. Milwaukee, WI: Alverno Productions.

Halonen, J. S. (1995). Demystifying critical thinking. *Teaching of Psychology, 22,* 75–81.

Halonen, J. S. (1996). *The critical thinking companion for introductory psychology*. New York: Worth.

Halonen, J. S., Bosack, T. N., Clay, S., & McCarthy, M. (with Dunn, D. S., Hill IV, G. W., et al.). (2003). A rubric for authentically learning, teaching, and assessing scientific reasoning in psychology. *Teaching of Psychology, 30,* 196–208.

Halonen, J. S., & Gray, C. (2001). *The critical thinking companion for introductory psychology* (2nd ed.). New York: Worth.

Hersh, R. H., & Merrow, J. (Eds.). (2005). *Declining by degrees: Higher education at risk*. New York: Palgrave Macmillan.

National Commission on Excellence in Education. (1983). *A nation at risk: The imperative for educational reform*. Washington, DC: U.S. Department of Education.

Paul, R. W., & Elder, L. (2002). *Critical thinking: Tools for taking charge of your professional and personal life*. Upper Saddle River, NJ: Prentice Hall.

Puccio, P. (January 2, 2006). *Undergraduate psychology major competencies: Start to finish and everything in-between*. Symposium presented at National Institute for the Teaching of Psychology, St. Petersburg Beach, FL.

Trice, A. (2000). *A handbook of classroom assessment*. New York: Longman.

Walvoord, B. E. (2004). *Assessment clear and simple: A practical guide for institutions, departments, and general education*. San Francisco: Jossey-Bass.

Appendix 1: Generic Rubrics for Possible Critical Thinking Outcomes (University of West Florida Academic Foundations, 2005)

Analysis/Evaluation	Exceeds	Meets	Fails
Applies discipline-based concepts and frameworks			
Asks relevant and helpful questions			
Develops evidence-based arguments			
Applies discipline-based criteria to make informed judgments			
Synthesizes appropriate diverse information sources			
Accurately assesses quality of higher order skill			

Problem Solving	Exceeds	Meets	Fails
Defines problem appropriately			
Develops discipline-based strategies to solve problem			
Provides rationale for selection of most promising strategy			
Successfully applies selected strategy			
Evaluates quality of solution and revises appropriately			

Creativity	Exceeds	Meets	Fails
Describes traditional approaches			
Produces novel response			
Explains unique contribution			
Identifies relevant criteria for evaluating success			
Assesses quality of creative response accurately			

Information Literacy	Exceeds	Meets	Fails
Identifies acceptable types of source material			
Conducts appropriate search strategy			
Uses criteria to determine fitness of source material			
Generates sufficient breadth in selected resources			
Evaluates overall quality of support material			

Appendix 2

Up to Speed Worksheet   Name_____

#1: Research Methods   Value: 5 = solid preparation

10 of 12 counted for max of 50 pts   3 = fair preparation

1/6 of course points   1 = minimal preparation

Show & Tell: *Find an example in the popular press or advertising industry where there is a problematic cause–effect claim. How would you use experimental design to support or disconfirm that claim?*

Your question from chapter:

Talking points from chapter:

Appendix 3

Honors Introductory Psychology   Presenter_____

Presentation Criteria   Topic_____

Reviewer_____

Each of the criteria below should be worth a maximum of 5 points. Use the following scale to make your judgment about quality achieved in each criterion:

5 = excellence   *2 = serious difficulty*

4 = minor difficulty   *1 = minimal effort/achievement*

3 = moderate difficulty   *0 = no achievement*

Add any details in the space below each criterion to justify your conclusion.

Organizes information logically (with focus/precision/proper time limit)   _____

Shows mastery of information; answers questions well   _____

Shows evidence of conducting research   _____

Cites specific experts to support viewpoint   _____

Engages audience through interesting/imaginative content   _____

Relates appropriately to audience level of knowledge   _____

Shows professional delivery (good grammar)   _____

Uses supportive media effectively   _____

Collaborates fairly and effectively (where appropriate)   _____

Judges quality of performance accurately; identifies strength and weakness   _____

Any recommendations for future development?

Appendix 4: Objective Measures of Critical Thinking

Academic Profile (1998)

Higher Education Assessment, Educational Testing Service (ETS), Princeton, NJ 08541

Target: Students at the end of their second year in college, though probably usable at other levels.

Format: A multiple-choice test assessing college-level "reading, writing, critical thinking, and mathematics within the contexts of the humanities, social sciences, and natural sciences." Short form: 36 items in 40 mins; long form: 144 items in 2 hrs 30 mins.

Assessment of Reasoning and Communication (1986)

College Outcome Measures Program, ACT, PO Box 168, Iowa City, IA 52243

Target: Students finishing college, but probably usable with other levels as well.

Format: Open-ended, requiring student to produce three short essays and three short speeches. Yields total subtest score plus part scores in social reasoning, scientific reasoning, and artistic reasoning.

The California Critical Thinking Skills Test: College Level (1990), by Peter Facione

The California Academic Press, 217 LaCruz Ave, Millbrae, CA 94030

Target: Aimed at college students, but probably usable with advanced and gifted high school students.

Format: Multiple-choice, incorporating interpretation, argument analysis and appraisal, deduction, mind bender puzzles, and induction (including rudimentary statistical inference).

Web site: http://www.insightassessment.com/test-cctst.html

The California Critical Thinking Dispositions Inventory (1992) by Peter and N. C. Facione

The California Academic Press, 217 LaCruz Ave., Millbrae, CA 94030

Target: College age, adults, professionals

Format: A multiple-choice attempt to assess critical thinking dispositions. Probably useful for self-appraisal and anonymous information for use in research.

Web site: http://www.insightassessment.com/test-cctdi.html

Cornell Critical Thinking Test, Forms X & Z (1985), by Robert H. Ennis and Jason Millman

Critical Thinking Press and Software, PO Box 448, Pacific Grove, CA 93950

Target: Form X: Grades 4–14; Form Z: College students and adults, but usable with advanced or gifted high school students.

Format: Form X: multiple-choice, sections on induction, credibility, observation, deduction, and assumption identification. Form Z: multiple-choice, sections on induction, credibility, prediction and experimental planning, fallacies (especially equivocation), deduction, definition, and assumption identification.

Web site: http://www.criticalthinking.com/getProductDetails.do?code=c&id=05512

Cambridge Thinking Skills Assessment (1996)

Local Examinations Synd, U Cambridge, Syndicate Building, 1 Hills Road, Cambridge CB1 2EU, UK

Target: Postsecondary students

Format: Two parts: a 30 min 15-item, multiple-choice test of argument assessment; and a 1 hr essay test calling for critical evaluation of an argument and for further argumentation.

Web site: http://tsa.ucles.org.uk/index.html

Critical Thinking Interview (1998), by Gail Hughes and Associates

141 Warwick St. S.E., Mpls., MN 55414 (e-mail: hughe038@tc.umn.edu)

Target: College students and adults

Format: About 30 mins for a one-to-one interview combining displayed knowledge and reasoning on topic of interviewee's choice. Emphasis is on clarity, context, focus, credibility, sources, familiarity with the topic, assumption identification, and appropriate use of such reasoning strategies as generalization, reasoning to the best explanation, deduction, values reasoning, and reasoning by analogy.

Critical Thinking Test (1989)

ACT CAAP Operations (85), PO Box 1688, Iowa City, IA 52243

Target: Students at the end of their second year in college, though probably usable at other levels.

Format: Multiple-choice items based on text readings: identifying conclusions, inconsistency, and loose implications; judging direction of support, strength of reasons, and representativeness of data; making predictions; noticing other alternatives; and hypothesizing about what a person thinks.

Ennis–Weir Critical Thinking Essay Test (1985), by Robert H. Ennis and Eric Weir

Critical Thinking Press and Software, PO Box 448, Pacific Grove CA 93950

Target: General use

Format: Incorporates getting the point, seeing the reasons and assumptions, stating one's point, offering good reasons, seeing other possibilities (including other possible explanations), and responding to and avoiding equivocation, irrelevance, circularity, reversal of an if–then (or other conditional) relationship, overgeneralization, credibility problems, and the use of emotive language to persuade.

Web site: http://faculty.ed.uiuc.edu/rhennis/tewctet/Ennis-Weir_Merged.pdf

ICAT Critical Thinking Essay Test (1996)

The International Center for the Assessment of Thinking, PO Box 220, Dillon Beach, CA 94929

Target: General use

Format: Provides eight criteria (to be shown to students in advance and also to be used for grading by trained graders). Students respond to an editorial (selected by test administrator) by writing an essay summarizing it, identifying its focus, and commenting on its strengths and weaknesses.

Web site: http://www.criticalthinking.org/about/internationalCenter.shtml

Measure of Academic Proficiency and Progress (MAPP)

Educational Testing Service

Target: College but specifically helpful for general education assessment

Format: It allows institutions to measure proficiency in reading, writing, critical thinking, and mathematics; no need for separate tests and multiple administrations. Reading and critical thinking are measured in the context of the humanities, social sciences and natural sciences.

Web site: http://www.ets.org/portal/site/ets/menuitem.1488512ecfd5b8849a77b13bc3921509/?vgnextoid=ff3aaf5e44df4010VgnVCM10000022f95190RCRD&vgnextchannel=f98546f1674f4010VgnVCM10000022f95190RCRD

Reflective Judgment Approach

University of Minnesota

Target: General use

Format: Analysis of faulty logic

The Test of Everyday Reasoning (1998) by Peter Facione

California Academic Press, 217 La Cruz Ave., Millbrae, CA 94030

Target: General use

Format: Derived from The California Critical Thinking Skills Test (listed above), with choices of justifications added. Multiple-choice.

Watson–Glaser Critical Thinking Appraisal (1980) by Goodwin Watson and E M. Glaser

The Psychological Corporation, 555 Academic Court, San Antonio TX 78204

Target: General use

Format: Multiple-choice, sections on induction, assumption identification, deduction, judging whether a conclusion follows beyond a reasonable doubt, and argument evaluation plausibility, reasonableness, and realism of student responses; graded on the basis of the number of responses judged successful (from 0 to 4). Yields total subtest score plus part scores in social reasoning, scientific reasoning, and artistic reasoning.

Web site: http://harcourtassessment.com/haiweb/cultures/en-us/productdetail.htm?pid= 015-8191-013

Adapted from *An Annotated List of Critical Thinking Tests*, prepared by Robert H. Ennis, University of Illinois.
http://www.criticalthinking.net/CTTestList1199.html

Chapter 7

Programmatic Assessment of Critical Thinking

Kevin J. Apple, Sherry L. Serdikoff,
Monica J. Reis-Bergan, and Kenneth E. Barron

Assessing critical thinking is a difficult task because the construct is not easy to define. In our programmatic assessment of critical thinking, we strive to assess different components of this construct. Our approach is similar to the Indian parable of the Blind Men and the Elephant (Saxe, 1878). According to this parable, a group of blind men examined an elephant. Each man touched a different part of the elephant's body and thus had a different impression about the elephant. For example, one of the men touched the long, sharp tusk. This person was convinced the elephant was like a spear. The individual who touched the side of the elephant was convinced that the elephant was like a wall. The individuals who touched the trunk, leg, ear, or tail insisted that the elephant was similar to a snake, tree, fan, or rope, respectively. According to the parable, these blind men argued about the true nature of the elephant. Each man insisted that he was right, without realizing that the other descriptions of the animal were accurate for a different section of the elephant. If the men cooperated with each other and pieced together an image of the elephant based on each other's experiences, they would have created a more accurate image of the elephant.

One lesson from this parable is that multiple measures of a construct are better than a single measure (Campbell & Fiske, 1959). Although critical thinking is difficult to define, we strive to measure it accurately by assessing different components of it. Specifically, we attempt to get an accurate measure by assessing students' abilities at different times with different measures. In this chapter, we will examine how we assess critical thinking at various points during our students' education.

The Assessment Culture at James Madison University

James Madison University (JMU) has a unique assessment culture (Stoloff, Apple, Barron, Reis-Bergan, & Sundre, 2004). As part of University policy, all programs (including non-academic) assess their effectiveness on a yearly basis. In addition to collecting assessment data each year, faculty members use the assessment data to inform departmental decisions. To facilitate systematic assessment, we assess our students at three stages during their academic careers: beginning, middle, and end. The first student assessment occurs before they begin classes as freshmen. Students complete their midcareer assessment during their sophomore/junior year on Assessment Day: a day during mid-February each year when classes are canceled so students can complete their assessments. These first two assessment batteries focus on students' mastery of general education learning objectives. Finally, students complete departmental assessments during their senior year on Assessment Day. The senior-year assessment focuses on students' mastery of the learning objectives for their individual majors.

Assessing Critical Thinking in General Education

Like most U.S. universities, JMU has a core curriculum that all undergraduate students complete regardless of majors, minors, or preprofessional programs. Faculty have arranged the general education curriculum into clusters of courses arranged into five educational themes fundamental to becoming a well-educated student:

- Cluster One: Skills for the 21st Century (3 courses)
- Cluster Two: Arts and Humanities (3 courses)
- Cluster Three: Natural World (3–4 courses)
- Cluster Four: Social and Cultural Processes (2 courses)
- Cluster Five: Individuals in the Human Community (2 courses)

Critical thinking is assessed in both Clusters One and Three. As part of the assessment culture at JMU, we are able to benefit from the data our general education colleagues collect. For Cluster One (Skills for the 21st Century), all students must take one of five courses designed with the explicit purpose of addressing critical thinking. The assessment plan for this set of courses has been evolving. Over the years, faculty members have used various standardized tests, such as the Cornell Critical Thinking Test – Level Z (The Critical Thinking Company, n.d.) with moderate satisfaction. Since 2005, faculty have been using the Comprehensive Test of Critical Thinking (CTCT; James Madison University, Center for Assessment and Research Studies, 2006), developed by Philosophy faculty at JMU who specialize in critical thinking. They designed the test to probe students' understanding of claims, credibility, conclusions, evidence, and argument. The CTCT consists of 55 multiple-choice items that have been linked to Cluster One learning objectives. The Cronbach's alpha for this test was $\alpha = .66$ (Fall, 2005) and $\alpha = .70$ (Spring, 2007). Students completing this test before starting classes ($M = 27.6$, $SD = 5.72$) in the Fall of 2005 scored significantly lower than students during their midcareer assessment ($M = 29.8$, $SD = 6.12$) during Spring 2006, $t(888) = 5.51$, $p < .001$. This increase in critical thinking scores may be attributed to the coursework students have completed since beginning JMU. The Center for Assessment and Research Studies have shared the data with the faculty who teach the critical thinking classes, along with more detailed analyses suggesting where students may need more help or where the curriculum could be adjusted to better address core concepts in critical thinking.

In addition to Cluster One data, we also benefit from Cluster Three (Natural World) data collected by our colleagues. It is our position that critical thinking and scientific reasoning are at least related, that improvements in scientific reasoning constitute to some extent improvements in critical thinking, and that measures of our students' scientific reasoning can inform us about their critical thinking. In particular with respect to training psychology majors at JMU, we believe that our students' critical thinking is enhanced as a result not only of general education coursework designed to address knowledge, skills, and abilities (KSAs) related to critical thinking specifically (i.e., Cluster One, Skills for the 21st Century), but also as a result of coursework designed to address KSAs related to scientific reasoning (i.e., Cluster Three, the Natural World). From this argument, it follows that we also can use measures to assess scientific reasoning as a measure of our students' critical thinking.

The Cluster Three (Natural World) requirements include a math course and science courses to establish quantitative and scientific literacy. The general education program is intended to provide all students with foundational KSAs on which they can build more specialized KSAs from their majors, minors, and preprofessional programs.

The Natural World (NW) assessment instrument consists of 50 objective answer questions. Reliability has steadily improved with each revision of the instrument. Our assessment specialists selected the best items from earlier administrations to form the fifth version, NW–5. The NW–5 showed the best reliability to date, with $\alpha = .67$ for the freshmen and $\alpha = .75$ for sophomores (Horst, Lottridge, Hoole, Sundre, & Murphy, 2005).

To examine scientific thinking in our psychology majors, we examined how psychology majors performed on the NW–5 during two test administrations: Fall 2001 and Spring 2003. Forty-one psychology majors completed the NW–5 testing during Fall 2001, and 70 psychology majors completed the NW–5 during Spring 2003. Of these two groups, 22 overlapped, so we were able to look at independent as well as dependent group differences over time.

Figure 7.1 shows the summary data for performance on the NW–5 test. Because each correct answer on the 50-item test was awarded 2 points, students could obtain a score

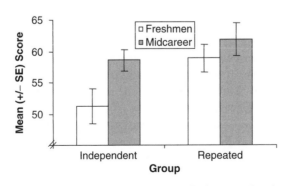

Figure 7.1. Mean (±SE) NW–5 scores for incoming freshman and mid-career students.

from 0 to 100. The bars on the left represent the mean (±SE) test score for independent groups of psychology majors who took the test before beginning classes or during their midcareer assessment (summarizing independent group differences), and the bars on the right represent scores for students who took the test both as incoming freshmen and as midcareer students (summarizing dependent group differences). In both cases, the midcareer psychology students performed better than the incoming psychology students. This difference in performance was confirmed by an independent-samples t test for the independent groups, $t(65) = -2.49$, $p = .015$, $d = .68$, but for the smaller subset of students in which we could link scores over time a dependent-samples t test failed to confirm a statistically significance difference for the repeated group, $t(21) = -.99$, $p = .33$, $d = .25$.

The significantly higher scores of midcareer students are consistent with an increase in scientific reasoning among our psychology majors over their first two years at JMU. However, there are several caveats. First, this difference was significant only for the independent groups; data from the repeated group, which represents actual growth over time for a group of students, failed to reach statistical significance (although this could be a function of the small sample size, $n = 22$). Second, there are a number of reasons that midcareer students may do better that are not specific to scientific reasoning skills (e.g., student maturation, number of courses completed, the loss from the university of those students with the lowest aptitude for science and mathematics).

We did not confirm a statistically significant amount of improvement within the small group of individuals who repeated the test. However, the fact that scores for the dependent group changed in a positive direction and the fact that the scores for midcareer students in the independent group were statistically higher than those of the freshmen is support for the hypothesis that our psychology majors' scientific reasoning does improve over their first years at JMU, and this effect ranges from small ($d = .25$) to moderate ($d = .68$). Furthermore, to the extent that scientific reasoning is related to critical thinking, these data support the assertion that our students' critical thinking skills improve over that time.

Like the data from the CTCT, faculty who teach courses in Cluster Three of the general education program receive data from the NW assessment, and they have used this information to make changes in coursework to better address students' needs in this area. Additionally, faculty have continued to improve the assessment instrument used to assess scientific reasoning; faculty currently administer version 8 of the NW test.

Overall, the current data are encouraging, and we view these assessments from our general education program as informative. Critical thinking is not the province of psychology alone, and to the extent that other sectors of our university curriculum address these issues, using assessments of those experiences can provide us meaningful data. By looking beyond our specific psychology curriculum we get a more complete picture of our psychology students' KSAs. Furthermore, it may be possible to use these more general tests to examine specific components of the psychology curriculum. For example, the NW test may be an appropriate tool for assessing our students' skills before and after completing our statistics and research methods course sequence. Thus, although designed to assess more general skills, these instruments may have utility that is specific to the psychology major.

Assessing Critical Thinking in the Psychology Major

In addition to assessing critical thinking of our psychology students engaged in general education coursework, we also test critical thinking during the end of our students' undergraduate careers. These senior assessments focus on the KSAs of the psychology major. The instruments we use for these assessments focus on critical thinking as well as other important learning goals and outcomes for the psychology major (see Halonen et al., 2002).

Assessment of Critical Thinking Using Behavioral Checklists

The Academic Skills-Experience Inventory (ASI; Kruger & Zechmeister, 2001) measures 10 skill areas relevant to the goals of a psychology major and liberal arts education. Each skill area has 9 questions, so the entire scale consists of 90 questions. Each question describes a specific behavior, and the student must select either "applies to me" or "does not apply to me." Although this 90-item scale is long, students are able to fill it out quickly because they are making only a dichotomous choice for each item.

One of the 10 skill areas is critical thinking/problem solving. The critical thinking component has 3 sections: evaluating research studies, evaluating costs/benefits, and taking human biases into account when making decisions. Each of these sections has 3 items. For example, one of the items relevant to evaluating research studies is "I have written a critique of a published research study." The possible range on this scale is 0–9 with higher numbers reflecting that the student has engaged in more of these activities. Kruger and Zechmeister (2001) reported that seniors scored significantly higher on the critical thinking items than first-year students as a result of their educational experiences.

We have found this instrument helpful for measuring critical thinking for several reasons. First, we are able to compare the critical thinking scores of our seniors to students from other schools. Based on Kruger and Zechmeister's (2001) article, we know that psychology seniors at JMU (M = 4.91, SD = 1.67) report similar critical thinking experiences as the students at Loyola University of Chicago (M = 4.59, SD = 2.06), $t(232)$ = .41, p > .05. Second, we are able to measure whether changes to our major will have an impact on the critical thinking scores. We have recently modified our psychology curriculum. Because we have been using the ASI for several years, we will be able to determine if these changes to our program impact students' critical thinking scores. Because this is just the first year of the new major, it is too early to tell if the new curriculum will increase students' critical thinking experiences. However, we do have an assessment strategy in place to measure any changes that may occur.

Assessment of Critical Thinking Using Student Reflections

In 2002, the Task Force on Undergraduate Psychology Major Competencies appointed by the Board of Educational Affairs of the American Psychological Association published their recommendations for a guiding list of learning goals and outcomes for an under-graduate psychology major (Halonen et al., 2002). Specifically, the Task Force proposed a list of 10 goals to reflect the learning expectations that students should achieve by the completion of an undergraduate degree in psychology. Most notable for the current chapter was the inclusion of Goal 3 (Critical Thinking) as one of the important 10 goals to promote in our undergraduate training.

Jane Halonen, who served as both the chair of the Task Force on Undergraduate Psychology Major Competencies and the chair of JMU's psychology department, chal-lenged and partnered with our assessment committee to develop an assessment tool to measure student growth on all 10 goals. This challenge led to the development of an APA undergraduate learning goal self-reflection exercise that incorporated a mixed-method approach (Creswell, 2002), enabling us to collect quantitative and qualitative data on each of the 10 goals. We provided students a brief definition of each goal and a list of example learning outcomes associated with that goal. Then to obtain quantitative data, students rated how strongly they agreed that they had achieved each goal and rated how strongly they thought JMU's undergraduate psychology program provided opportunities to achieve each goal. Next, to obtain qualitative data, we asked students to offer open-ended feed-back explaining their quantitative ratings for each goal and to list particular experiences or recommendations that they had to help achieve this goal. (See Appendix 1 for the general directions for the APA goal self-reflection exercise and Appendix 2 for how the critical thinking goal was presented to participants.)

Based on the quantitative data from the self-assessment, students agreed that they had achieved Goal 3 (Critical Thinking). Specifically, students in 2004 (M = 4.38, SD = .76) and in 2005 (M = 4.19, SD = .77) rated their agreement with the first question ("I think that I achieved this goal") quite high. Similarly, an inspection of students' responses to the second statement ("JMU's psychology program provided opportunities to achieve this goal") revealed a similar pattern. Students in 2004 (M = 4.17, SD = .95) and in 2005 (M = 4.10, SD = .85) rated strong agreement with this statement.

We should note that our students did not rate all 10 goals as favorably as Goal 3 (Critical Thinking). As a result, we used students' lower ratings on other goals to motivate a number of changes to our undergraduate program. Specifically, we added new courses to our cur-riculum to help students achieve the goals that they rated low. In addition to highlighting which areas of our curriculum are in need of improvement, another benefit to assessing the self-reflection exercise on APA goals each year is that we can use the quantitative data to track whether changes to the program are having the intended impact of increasing students' ratings in subsequent years.

In addition, the qualitative data for the APA self-reflection exercise have provided us great insight into understanding how our curriculum impacts learning on each goal, like Goal 3 (Critical Thinking). When coding the open-ended data, we followed Creswell's (2002) recommendations of first reading through the text, dividing the text into more meaningful segments, labeling each text segment with a one or two word code, and reduc-ing the number of codes into overarching themes. In our first pass through the Goal 3 (Critical Thinking) data, we noticed a general trend where students' comments were positive, negative, or mixed about our department's ability to promote critical thinking. For example,

- Positive – "I really think JMU always kept you thinking. There were so many times when you had to present your own ideas. I think the research projects in 211 are a great example. I also loved my 400 level classes! My 497 really allowed me to think outside the norm, and share my ideas with the rest of the class."
- Negative – "These issues didn't come up very often in the curriculum I chose. I didn't have very many classes where there was a need to think creatively, and I don't feel that criticizing arguments was ever encouraged."
- Mixed – "Some classes were helpful with this and some required me to do very little critical thinking (it was more straight memorization to get a good grade)."

To provide a measure of effect size for qualitative data, we examined the frequency for the three categories of responses. In 2004, 67% of the responses were positive, 9% were negative, and 24% were mixed. In 2005, this breakdown remained unchanged with 66% of the responses positive, 10% negative, and 24% mixed.

Next, we looked at the more detailed list of codes and overarching themes for the qualitative data. A clear pattern of seven overarching themes emerged from students' open-ended responses revealing when critical thinking was likely and not likely to occur in our major and at JMU. These themes were specific psychology classes (e.g., research methods), specific class formats (e.g., discussion), specific class assignments/activities (e.g., writing/lab projects), specific professors, psychology classes in general, other nonpsychology classes (e.g., philosophy), or lack of opportunities. The frequency with which each of these themes occurred in our 2004 and 2005 samples appears in Table 7.1. The most frequently cited themes linked to promoting critical thinking were specific classes and specific class assignments. In terms of specific psychology classes that promoted critical thinking, it is helpful to know that JMU's psychology curriculum is based on the St. Mary's Model (Brewer et al., 1993), where students progress through the curriculum starting with foundational coursework in introductory psychology, followed by methodology coursework in statistics and research design, followed by specific content coursework, and ending with a senior capstone experience. Although students mentioned that faculty promoted critical thinking at all levels of our curriculum, the two areas that stood out were methodology courses and capstone courses (see Table 7.2). Also noteworthy, but not surprising, was the mention of

Table 7.1. Coding Frequency of Overarching Themes Linked to Critical Thinking in Open-Ended Data

	2004	2005
Specific psychology classes	28%	26%
Specific class formats	12%	13%
Specific assignments/activities	17%	27%
Specific professors	9%	10%
Psychology classes in general	14%	15%
Other nonpsychology classes	12%	2%
Lack of opportunities	9%	6%

Table 7.2. Coding Frequency of Specific Classes Linked
to Critical Thinking in Open-Ended Data

	2004	2005
Lower level electives	0%	8%
Methods	31%	30%
Area courses	14%	16%
Upper level electives	24%	11%
Capstone	31%	35%

specific class formats where students noted the most benefit to develop critical thinking in discussion-based classes over lecture-based classes. For example, one student noted:

> I don't feel I took a lot of classes where there was an opportunity to think critically. A lot of classes were just, sit in a lecture hall, take notes, and take a multiple choice test. However, I really like my senior capstone seminar now because we get to discuss and express our thoughts and ideas.

And finally, to confirm the importance of using data from general education coursework as a source of critical thinking, a number of students highlighted their coursework outside of psychology (specifically in philosophy and Cluster One of general education) as key in promoting their critical thinking skills.

We also uncovered a number of unexpected and interesting findings in students' open-ended comments. For example, students often focused on creative thinking in open-ended responses. Although we first thought students misread Goal 3 and confused the labels creative and critical, we quickly realized that the APA Goal 3 definition does emphasize both critical and creative thinking (see Appendix 2) and that our students were carefully attending to the definitions provided in our assessment. However, as we debate what critical thinking is (and is not), we need to consider carefully whether our measures align with APA's critical thinking learning goal or if the APA learning goal definition for critical thinking will need to be revised to align with best practice to assess critical thinking. Another interesting finding was a student who noted, "I am told to think critically, but not told how," revealing that our teaching may be too abstract or focused on the jargon of critical thinking rather than the practice of critical thinking. Finally, we were intrigued to find that a number of students mentioned needing coursework to be more demanding and challenging in order to promote critical thinking.

In summary, our open-ended, qualitative data offer a "recipe" for promoting critical thinking in psychology coursework that appears to be relatively straightforward:

- Make classes discussion-based (rather than lecture)
- Make classes activity-based with writing, group projects, and critiquing research (rather than multiple-choice exams)
- Model critical thinking as professor and demand it of your students.

However, a number of these practices take time, resources, and training. How do we balance our faculty roles and still promote critical thinking? One final purpose in identifying and assessing the 10 APA learning goals proposed by the Task Force on Undergraduate Psychology Major Competencies was to appeal to administration for more resources that are necessary for quality education and reaching each of the 10 goals.

Suggestions For Assessing Critical Thinking

At JMU, we assess critical thinking through a variety of measures. Faculty outside of psychology are responsible for assessing critical thinking skills from the general education courses, but by sharing data at JMU, we are able to benefit from other perspectives trying to measure the same construct. Perhaps faculty from other institutions can incorporate how other departments at their institution assess critical thinking into their programmatic strategy.

Even within our department assessments, we assess critical thinking with multiple measures. We have obtained useful information in both a behavior checklist and a self-reflection exercise. These assessment tools are easy to administer. An institution without a formalized assessment day could embed these instruments in a senior-level course.

Although our approach is multifaceted, we realize that it is limited. We could evaluate critical thinking in the psychology classroom. Many of our colleagues use writing assignments, exam questions, and projects that assess one or more critical thinking skills. We could select a random sample of assignments and projects and review the products for evidence of critical thinking. Another strategy would be to have a specific critical thinking writing activity that all students complete as a part of assessment day activities. On paper these approaches seem promising, but in reality they can be problematic. Finding faculty to review and evaluate these products can be a challenge.

Another strategy worthy of consideration for future assessment plans might be a standardized critical thinking test not specific to major content. There are a variety of tests suitable for college students, and each covers different critical thinking skills. Some tests are multiple choice only, and others include an essay component (see Norris & Ennis, 1989). A limitation of this approach for our department would be the cost of these assessment instruments. We currently graduate approximately 225 students each year, and paying for an assessment instrument would be costly. We encourage readers to weigh the pros and cons of each of these strategies and to review additional resources available on the Web, like the Assessment CyberGuide for Learning Goals and Outcomes in the Undergraduate Psychology Major, at APA's Educational Directorate (http://www.apa.org/ed/guidehomepage.html) and through other readings (such as Halonen et al., 2003).

Conclusions

Unlike the men in the parable that introduced our chapter, we are not blind to the majesty of the elephant. Our approaches to assess critical thinking examine only limited components, but we do not conclude in haste that we have fully defined or captured all facets of critical thinking. Instead, we use our limited but valuable information to inform faculty and administration about the strengths and shortcomings of our program, and assessment information provides key evidence that helps our department head argue for additional funding and resources. We also use our knowledge of student responses to discuss with current students the value of specific types of courses as well as inform them about the APA's 10 learning goals. Our assessment plan is dynamic and constantly shaped by department needs as well as cost of materials, size of student body, and faculty energy. Assessing critical thinking is not easy, but we enjoy the challenge of trying to measure the construct.

References

Brewer, C. L., Hopkins, J. R., Kimble, G. A., Matlin, M. W., McCann, L. I., McNeil, O. V., et al. (1993). In T. V. McGovern (Ed.), *Handbook for enhancing undergraduate education in psychology* (pp. 161–182). Washington, DC: American Psychological Association.

Campbell, D. T., & Fiske, D. W. (1959). Convergent and discriminant validation by the multitrait-multimethod matrix. *Psychological Bulletin, 47*, 15–38.

Creswell, J. W. (2002). *Educational research: Planning, conducting, and evaluating quantitative and qualitative research.* Upper Saddle River, NJ: Merrill/Pearson.

The Critical Thinking Company. (n.d.). *Cornell Critical Thinking Test Level Z Software.* Retrieved July 27, 2007, from http://www.criticalthinking.com/getProductDetails.do?code=c&id=05511

Halonen, J. S., Appleby, D. C., Brewer, C. L., Buskist, W., Gillem, A. R., Halpern, D., et al. (Eds.). (2002). *Undergraduate major learning goals and outcomes: A report.* Washington, DC: American Psychological Association. Retrieved May 1, 2005, from http://www.apa.org/ed/pcue/taskforcereport2.pdf

Halonen, J. S., Bosack, T., Clay, S., & McCarthy, M. (with Dunn, D. S., Hill IV, G. W., et al.). (2003). A rubric for learning, teaching, and assessing scientific inquiry in psychology. *Teaching of Psychology, 30*, 196–208.

Horst, S. J., Lottridge, S., Hoole, E., Sundre, D. L., & Murphy, K. (2005). *Spring 2003 cluster 3 assessment report.* Harrisonburg, VA: James Madison University, Center for Assessment and Research Studies.

James Madison University, Center for Assessment and Research Studies. (2006). *Spring 2006 cluster 1 assessment report.* Harrisonburg, VA: James Madison University, Center for Assessment and Research Studies.

Kruger, D. J., & Zechmeister, E. B. (2001). A skills-experience inventory for the undergraduate psychology major. *Teaching of Psychology, 28*, 249–253.

Norris, S. P., & Ennis, R. H. (1989). *Evaluating critical thinking.* Pacific Grove, CA: Midwest Publications.

Saxe, J. G. (1878). The blind men and the elephant. In W. J. Linton (Ed.), *Poetry of America: Selections from one hundred American poets from 1776 to 1876* (pp. 150–152). London: George Bell & Sons.

Stoloff, M., Apple, K. J., Barron, K. E., Reis-Bergen, M. J., & Sundre, D. A. (2004). Seven goals for effective program assessment. In D. Dunn, C. Mehrotra, & J. Halonen (Eds.), *Measuring up: Assessment challenges and practices for psychology* (pp. 29–46). Washington, DC: American Psychological Association.

Appendix 1: Directions for Self-Reflection Exercise on APA's Learning Goals for the Psychology Major

Self-Reflection Exercise on American Psychology Association's (APA) Learning Goals for the Psychology Major

Directions

In this assessment, the Undergraduate Psychology Program asks you to reflect on your experiences in the psychology major at JMU for two purposes:

1   To provide honest feedback to the psychology program to assist us to improve the program for future students, and
2   To give you the opportunity to integrate your learning experiences into a meaningful whole before your graduation.

Specifically, we want you to make judgments on each of the 10 learning goals for undergraduate psychology recently identified by the American Psychological Association (APA). For each learning goal, you will see a short definition followed by a list of ways that students can fulfill meeting this goal. Then, we are asking you to:

1   Judge whether or not you think that you have achieved this goal.
2   Judge whether or not you think that JMU's undergraduate psychology program provided opportunities for you to achieve this goal.
3   Provide open-ended feedback explaining your first two ratings.

In your open-ended feedback, express what you think has been most meaningful to you, whether positive or negative. You can also provide recommendations to help the program be more successful in meeting this goal for future students.

Appendix 2: Example of Goal 3 and Quantitative and Qualitative Questions Assessed

Goal 3 Critical Thinking Skills in Psychology

Students will respect and use critical and creative thinking, skeptical inquiry, and, when possible, the scientific approach to solve problems related to behavior and mental processes. For example, a student meeting this goal should be able to:

* Use critical thinking effectively.
* Engage in creative thinking.
* Use reasoning to recognize, develop, defend, and criticize arguments and other persuasive appeals.
* Approach problems effectively.

	Strongly Disagree	Strongly Agree

1 I think that I achieved this goal.   1—2—3—4—5

2 JMU's psychology program provided   1—2—3—4—5
opportunities to achieve this goal.

3 In the space below, provide your rationale for your two ratings above. For example, list the particular experiences that helped you achieve this goal, and offer any recommendations to the department to improve our ability to help students meet this goal.

Author Notes

We thank Kara Makara and Shannon Willison for their help with data analyses. We also thank Donna Sundre, Sue Lottridge, and Amy Thelk from the JMU Center for Assessment and Research for their help with assessment data related to general education. We are also grateful for Jane Halonen's support on this project.

Address correspondence to Kevin J. Apple, Department of Psychology, MSC 7404, James Madison University, Harrisonburg, VA 22807; e-mail: applekj@jmu.edu.

Chapter 8

A Process Approach to Thinking Critically About Complex Concepts

Stacie M. Spencer and Marin Gillis

As instructors, we spend considerable time defining concepts and discussing how everyday words are used to represent complex concepts within our discipline. Students are good at memorizing definitions for exams, and many can generate examples of concepts from their own experiences; however, students struggle when asked to apply new concepts, and through application exercises, it becomes clear that the understanding of concepts is superficial. One of the challenges of teaching psychological concepts is that many of the concepts we use in psychology are used differently in everyday language. Another challenge is that in the psychology literature a concept may have multiple definitions or, in many cases, may be used without being defined. In order for students to learn a new concept in psychology, it is essential that they understand how that concept is used by the instructor and incorporate that definition into their concept schemas. The purpose of this chapter is to describe a methodology that we have found to be successful in overcoming these challenges and in developing critical thinking skills. Our methodology employs concept measurement as the vehicle through which students develop deeper comprehension of a concept as well as develop the cognitive skills of a critical thinker.

Like many of the concepts we teach in psychology, critical thinking can be understood in a variety of ways (Appleby, 2006; Halonen, 1995). For the purposes of this discussion, Appleby's definition of critical thinking, which focuses on the cognitive skills used to make decisions, will be employed (Appleby, 2006). Appleby's six skills of a critical thinker are based on the Cognitive Domain of Bloom's Taxonomy of Educational Objectives (as cited in Appleby, 2006) and comprise retention (the ability to remember), comprehension (the ability to understand meaning), application (the ability to solve problems with the information learned), analysis (the ability to examine and understand the organization of the component parts of a whole), synthesis (the ability to create new wholes using separate component parts), and evaluation (the ability to critique information in order to assess validity), which reflect a progression of skills that move from a superficial to a deep level of thinking and knowledge.

Stacie M. Spencer & Marin Gillis

A Process Approach to Teaching Critical Thinking Skills

Table 8.1 summarizes a process approach to teaching concepts that can be used specifically to increase depth of understanding but can also be used to teach transferable critical thinking skills. In this approach, students systematically progress through Appleby's six skills by engaging in the process of developing an instrument to measure a specific concept. The use of instrument development has been used successfully in test and measurement courses (Hynan & Foster, 1997), and the evaluation of existing measures has been used successfully in a variety of undergraduate and graduate courses to teach the importance of precise construct

Table 8.1. Process Steps for Teaching Concept Definitions through Instrument Development

Step 1. Concept Definitions
Discussion Topic: Concept definitions

Individual Assessment: Exam items that require students to define and compare/contrast multiple definitions of the same concept.

Critical Thinking Skills: *Retention* and *Comprehension*

Step 2. Instrument Components
Discussion Topic: Components of a measurement instrument

Group Activity: Creation of a new instrument to measure the concept

Individual Assignment: Reaction paper that identifies the definition of the concept that was used to design the instrument and describes the decisions that were made to design the instrument.

Critical Thinking Skills: *Application*

Step 3. Reliability and Validity Concepts
Discussion Topic: Reliability and validity

Group Activity: Peer evaluation and feedback of group instruments

Critical Thinking Skills: *Analysis* and *Synthesis*

Step 4. Evaluation of Existing Measurement Instruments
Discussion Topic: Differences between professional and lay instruments

Group Activity: Comparison of new instrument to established professional measures

Individual Assignment: Identification of a lay instrument online or in a magazine; reaction paper that evaluates the strengths/weaknesses of a specific professional and specific lay instrument and identifies how these instruments differ from one another and from the new instrument.

Critical Thinking Skill: *Evaluation*

Step 5. Final Project
Group Activity: Discussion of evaluation assignments; Revise original group instrument
Individual Assignment: Reaction paper that provides the concept definition that the new instrument best reflects, provides a rationale for each component of the instrument, describes changes made in the revision process, and indicates the sources for those changes (peer feedback, sample lay instrument, sample professional instrument).

Critical Thinking Skills: *Retention, Comprehension, Application, Analysis, Synthesis, and Evaluation* conceptualization, the use of multiple methods of construct measurement, and the importance of matching measurement to concept definitions (Brockway & Bryant, 1998).

The approach presented here is exemplified using the concept of stress (as taught in a Stress and Illness course), although this approach could be used for any concept in any course. Stress is an excellent example of a concept in psychology that is used differently in everyday language, has multiple definitions within the psychology literature, and is often used in the literature without definition. For example, stress is used frequently in everyday conversation as an indication of how we feel ("I'm so stressed out"), of the demands in our lives ("This job is so stressful"), or as an explanation for someone else's behavior ("She snapped at you because she is under a lot of stress"). Within the literature, two common ways to define stress are as (a) the events in our lives that cause psychological or physical threat (stressors), or as (b) a change in physiological activity in response to a stressor (strain; Sarafino, 2002, p. 71). The differences in these definitions are significant, especially if stress is being discussed as a predictor of illness.

Step 1. Concept Definitions

The first step in this process resembles the typical approach to teaching concepts. The instructor conducts a class discussion of stress. Before providing any definitions, the instructor asks students to take a moment to write down what they believe stress is. Students then share their definitions with the class, and the instructor writes them on the board so that similar definitions are grouped together. The instructor informs students that there are several definitions of stress found in the literature, two of which are (a) stress as an accumulation of events in our lives (stressors) and (b) stress as a physiological response (strain; Sarafino, 2002). Further, stressors are commonly categorized as (a) catastrophic (e.g., hurricanes, tornadoes), (b) major life events (e.g., loss of a loved one, divorce, retirement from work), and (c) daily hassles (e.g., waiting for a late bus, standing in a long line to buy movie tickets; Sarafino, 2002, p. 71). Strain is typically reflected in changes in sympathetic activity (increased heart rate, respiration, and sweating, pupil dilation, and slowed digestion), endocrine activity (increased cortisol levels), and immune functioning (decreases in circulating lymphocytes, increased inflammation; Kemeny, 2003). Students are asked to generate lists of examples of stressors that fall under each category and to provide examples of situations in which they have experienced physiological changes that would indicate strain.

The first two of Appleby's critical thinking skills, *retention* and *comprehension*, are easily assessed after this type of discussion. In order to demonstrate *retention*, students must be able to remember specific information such as the different definitions of stress used in psychology. This may be assessed, for example, through exam items that require students to match concepts to definitions (stressor versus strain); match examples to concepts (death of a loved one, getting married, and starting a new job are stressors; increased blood pressure, pupil dilation, and sweating indicate strain); or to simply write out the definitions for stressors, catastrophic events, major life events, daily hassles, and strain, sympathetic change, endocrine change, and changes in immune functioning.

In order to demonstrate *comprehension*, students must be able to go beyond retaining the definitions that have been provided; they must be able to demonstrate an understanding of the *meaning* of stress. Like retention, comprehension may be assessed through exam items. Comprehension exam items could require students to compare and contrast stressors and strain or major life events and daily hassles. Comprehension exam items could also require students to explain why it is important to know whether a researcher defines stress as stressors or as strain.

Step 2. Instrument Components

The second step in this process focuses on the elements that must be included in an instrument designed to measure stress. The instructor provides a general overview of the decisions that must be made when creating an instrument. In addition to determining items (including item content, valence, and wording), these decisions include identifying the population for which the measure is intended (e.g., children, adolescents, adults, students, athletes, employees); the time frame respondents will use when considering the items (e.g., the past week, month, three months, year); the response format that will be used (e.g., frequency of stressor or strain, yes/no, Likert scale to indicate impact or intensity, predetermined item values); how the responses will be scored (e.g., by summing the values selected, counting the yes responses, multiplying frequency by impact/intensity); and directions that will be provided so that the respondents will know what to do.

After each instrument component is listed on the board and described, students count off to form five-member groups. Once in their groups, students prepare a list of group member responsibilities for the instructor. For example, groups identify which member will lead the discussion, who will type the measure, and who will post the measure to the virtual learning environment (e.g., Blackboard and WebCT). Although they are given an hour to create the measure, most groups need more time to finish generating items and might assign additional responsibilities such as generating items or editing the typed measure before it is posted.

Appleby's third critical thinking skill, *application*, is assessed through this task. In order to demonstrate application, each student must submit a reaction paper that identifies the definition of stress that is reflected in their instrument and describes the decisions made in the process of creating the stress instrument.

Step 3. Reliability and Validity Concepts and Biopsychosocial Model

The third step in this process introduces the concepts of reliability and validity as well as the concept of the biopsychosocial model (an approach to medicine that includes an evaluation of biological, psychological, and social influences on illness and the development of a comprehensive treatment plan that addresses all three factors). In this step, students generate definitions of these concepts based on what they have learned in other courses (e.g., Statistics, Research Methods, Biology, Chemistry, Health Psychology). The instructor provides definitions for specific types of reliability (e.g., test–retest, split-half, and interrater) and specific types of construct and criterion validity (e.g., face, content, convergent, discriminant, predictive, concurrent). Students also provide examples of each of the three components (biological, psychological, social) of the biopsychosocial model.

Prior to this class meeting each student prints out and completes all of the instruments designed to measure stress that have been created by each group in the class. After the class discussion on reliability, validity, and the biopsychosocial model, students meet with their original groups and pair up with another group to discuss these concepts and to provide feedback on their instruments. Students are instructed to verify the definition of stress reflected in their respective instruments, ask the other group for clarification where needed, and offer suggestions for how to improve directions, items, and response format. Students are also instructed to give reasons for how the different definitions of stress fit within the three components of the biopsychosocial model (e.g., an instrument that measures strain reflects the biological component), and to predict the reliability and validity of their instruments.

Appleby's fourth and fifth critical thinking skills, *analysis* and *synthesis*, are developed through these tasks. In order to develop analysis, students must be able to discuss how the different definitions of stress fit within the three components of the biopsychosocial model. In order to demonstrate synthesis, students must be able to explain why reliability and validity, concepts learned in other courses, are relevant to defining and measuring stress.

Step 4. Evaluation of Existing Measurement Instruments

The fourth step in this process highlights the differences between instruments designed to measure the same concept. In this step, the instructor discusses the differences between instruments that are developed systematically by professionals for research or clinical purposes (professional measures) and instruments that are created out of interest or for entertainment purposes (lay measures). Sample professional and lay measures are distributed to highlight differences in population, item content/structure, response formats, scoring, and directions.

After this discussion, students meet with their groups to evaluate the sample professional and lay stress measures and to discuss what similarities and differences exist between their instrument and each of the samples. Students are instructed to consider each of the components of instrumentation that were presented in Step 2 as well as the concepts of reliability and validity that were presented in Step 3. Students also determine which of the instruments (including their own) they think is the best measure of stress and create a list of reasons to support their decision.

Appleby's sixth critical thinking skill, *evaluation*, is developed through these tasks. In order to demonstrate evaluation, each student submits a reaction paper that includes an evaluation of one professional measure of stress and one lay measure of stress (that they find on their own from a magazine or the Internet), a discussion of the similarities and differences between the measures, and a discussion of which measure was identified as the best overall stress measure.

Step 5. Final Project

The fifth and final step in this process is a culmination of all that has been discussed and developed over the first four steps. Students meet in their groups to share the lay measures they discussed in their respective reaction papers and to use the information they have collected from the peer evaluations of their measure and from evaluating other stress measures to revise their original instrument. Revised instruments are posted to the virtual learning environment (Blackboard and WebCT).

All of Appleby's six critical thinking skills (retention, comprehension, application, analysis, synthesis, and evaluation) are assessed through the final project. After students revise and post their original stress measures, they print and complete each group's newly revised stress measures. They then write reaction papers that describe the changes made to their measure; indicate the reason for each change (better understanding of reliability and validity, peer feedback, reflects one of the sample lay or professional stress measures); and identify the specific definition of stress that is reflected in the revised stress measure.

Evaluation of the Process

This approach to teaching the concept of stress was evaluated using a supplemental teaching evaluation form that specifically addressed the steps described previously. Feedback collected from 62 students (from two sections of the course) indicated that the approach was successful in moving students from a superficial level of understanding to a deeper level that included all six of Appleby's skills of a critical thinker.

Students were asked to describe what they learned about stress and measurement by going through this process. Comments reflected three general themes. Students spontaneously indicated that these activities helped them (a) learn that there are different definitions of stress; (b) understand the importance of the distinction between stress and other concepts such as coping, anxiety, and depression; and (c) understand that a good instrument takes time to develop and should demonstrate reliability and validity.

Students were also asked to indicate whether or not they recommended these activities be used in future Stress and Illness courses. Only 3 out of 62 students indicated that they did not recommend these activities be used again. Of these three, two indicated that they did not believe the process helped them learn about stress, and one student commented that too many points (toward the final grade) were given to the process. In contrast, the remaining 59 students indicated that the process engaged them in the material and helped them understand and apply the material better because it required them to think. Students also commented that the process included a welcome variety of class discussion (lecturing) and activity and indicated that working as a group allowed them to benefit from others' perspectives and knowledge and provided the added benefit of pooling ideas.

Discussion

This approach has been used successfully over several semesters and across several sections of a Stress and Illness course, a course that is primarily enrolled with nonpsychology majors and with students from different levels of academic development (freshman through advanced undergraduates). This approach is learner-centered and is designed to foster the *development* rather than the *demonstration* of skills. In order to develop skills, students need opportunities to practice, to receive feedback (from peers and instructors), and to assimilate feedback. This requires multiple discussions, activities, and assignments that build on one another and yield a culminating product.

This approach could be used to teach any concept in psychology, in any course. In the example provided in this chapter, all students worked on the same concept because it was central to the course; however, groups could work on different concepts and still progress through the same process, including the paired-group feedback sessions and discussions. For example, in a Personality course, each group could focus on a different characteristic (optimism, neuroticism, extraversion); in an Abnormal Psychology course, each group could focus on a different type of disorder (depression, anxiety, schizophrenia); and in an Introduction to Psychology course, groups could, in addition to those listed previously, select from a variety of concepts that represent each of the topical areas discussed (perception, sleep, addiction, intelligence, motivation, attitudes, conformity).

As described here, this approach takes place over several weeks and requires five to six class meetings. Because students submit assignments for each of the steps, class meetings devoted to this process do not occur consecutively; other course material is covered between each step. Although the content communicated by the instructor (definitions of stress, the components of a stress measure, distinctions between reliability and validity, the relationship between stress definitions and the biopsychosocial model, and the differences between lay and professional stress measures) could be covered in one or two lectures, we maintain that condensing the material to two lectures would result in critical thinking that is limited to retention and comprehension, Appleby's first two skills.

In addition to developing a deeper understanding of a specific concept (stress), this approach includes a variety of techniques such as reflective writing (Rickabaugh, 1993) and collaboration (Cooper, 1995) that have been demonstrated to enhance the development of critical thinking skills. Although students work through the content of their reaction papers in groups, each student is required to write his or her own reaction paper. Reaction papers provide a basis for students to elaborate on ideas discussed in the group, to assess their knowledge and skills, and to develop written communication skills (Rickabaugh, 1993).

Although this approach could be modified from a group process to a set of individual activities, the collaborative aspect is believed to be essential in the development of deeper concept mastery and the development of critical thinking skills. According to Cooper (1995), working in heterogeneous groups to solve a common problem leads to the development of divergent thinking and to the discovery of the steps that lead to the end products that are typically the focus of lectures; the "model–practice–feedback" loop involves interactions between students and interactions between students and instructor that support the active learning and critical thinking of each student. Group discussions provide opportunities for students to model critical thinking, to develop interpersonal communication skills such as listening to others' ideas and providing constructive feedback, and to develop the ability to communicate complex ideas.

Similarly, discussions between the instructor and the group provide opportunities for the instructor to model critical thinking, a technique that Gray (1993) referred to as "instructor as thinker" (p. 70) and argued is essential to successfully teach critical thinking. For example, a group might be struggling to determine if their measure of college students' major life events should include exam taking or if exam taking is a daily hassle. The instructor could talk through the process of comparing the definitions of major life events and daily hassles, considering the nature of the other items in the measure, and thinking about the item in the context of the response format and time frame (e.g., does the measure ask the respondent to indicate the number of times the event has happened over the past 12 months?). By thinking aloud, the instructor demonstrates one way to solve the problem.

And finally, this approach results in the development of skills that can be transferred to evaluating information obtained through the Internet and nonprofessional sources. By directly comparing professional and lay measures, students learn that while both are easily accessed through the Internet, they differ in important ways. Connor-Greene and Greene (2002) provided evidence to support the value in teaching analytical and evaluative skills by having students compare sources of information available through the Internet.

In conclusion, it is clear that there is a relationship between conceptual understanding and critical thinking in that one cannot learn a concept by memorizing the definition; one must learn the concept through the process of thinking critically. The skills that must be taught for students to understand concepts are multidimensional and are best taught through a variety of methods including didactic instruction, group activities, and individual writing assignments. Although this approach seems organizationally intensive for the instructor, it is flexible and is easily adapted to other courses that include conceptual understanding and critical thinking objectives. Students seem not only to like this approach but also to develop skills that can be transferred to other courses and will serve as basic tools for lifelong learning.

References

Appleby, D. C. (2006). Defining, teaching, and assessing critical thinking in Introductory Psychology. In D. S. Dunn & S. L. Chew (Eds.), *Best practices for teaching introduction to psychology* (pp. 57–69). Mahwah, NJ: Lawrence Erlbaum Associates.

Brockway, J. H., & Bryant, F. B. (1998). You can't judge a measure by its label: Teaching the process of instrumentation. *Teaching of Psychology, 25*, 121–123.

Connor-Greene, P. A., & Greene, D. J. (2002). Science or snake oil? Teaching critical evaluation of "research" reports on the Internet. *Teaching of Psychology, 29*, 321–324.

Cooper, J. L. (1995). Cooperative learning and critical thinking. *Teaching of Psychology, 22*, 7–9.

Gray, P. (1993). Engaging students' intellects: The immersion approach to critical thinking in psychology instruction. *Teaching of Psychology, 20*, 68–74.

Halonen, J. S. (1995). Demystifying critical thinking. *Teaching of Psychology, 22*, 75–81.

Hynan, L. S., & Foster, B. M. (1997). A project for developing tests in a psychological testing and measurement course. *Teaching of Psychology, 24*, 52–54.

Kemeny, M. E. (2003). The psychobiology of stress. *Current Directions in Psychological Science, 12*, 124–129.

Rickabaugh, C. A. (1993). The psychology portfolio: Promoting writing and critical thinking about psychology. *Teaching of Psychology, 20*, 170–172.

Sarafino, E. P. (2002). *Health psychology: Biopsychosocial interactions* (4th ed.). Hoboken, NJ: John Wiley & Sons.

Author Notes

Please send correspondence regarding this chapter to Stacie M. Spencer, Associate Professor of Psychology, Director, Health Psychology Program, School of Arts and Sciences, Massachusetts College of Pharmacy and Health Sciences, 179 Longwood Avenue, Boston, MA 02115. Phone: 617.732.2946; e-mail: stacie.spencer@mcphs.edu

or to

Marin Gillis, Director of Medical Humanities and Ethics, University of Nevada School of Medicine, Mail Stop 342, 1664 N. Virginia Street, Reno, NV 89557. Phone: 775-682-7725 (PT); e-mail: mgillis@medicine.nevada.edu

Part III

Critical Thinking in Critical Psychology Courses

Chapter 9

Integrating Critical Thinking with Course Content

David W. Carroll, Allen H. Keniston, and Blaine F. Peden

In this chapter we explain some ways to integrate critical thinking into course content. Our target audience is teachers of psychology who want to take this step but are unsure how to do so. We offer concrete examples about how novices can devise and implement critical thinking activities in their courses. For seasoned veterans who already teach their students to think critically (Gross, this volume; Stanovich, 2007), we present an approach that may lead them to see their efforts in a different light.

We define critical thinking as "reasonable reflective thinking focused on deciding what to believe or do" (Ennis, 1986, p. 12). This definition encompasses skills such as assessing evidence for an assertion (Browne & Keeley, 1986), applying concepts to new examples (Halpern, 1998), recognizing gaps in knowledge (Gray, 1993), and recognizing fallacies in arguments (Browne & Keeley, 1986).

The desire to teach critical thinking in our courses raises the issue of how to combine course content with critical thinking. On the one hand, covering all the material in a course could consume the entire term, leaving no time for critical inquiry. On the other hand, critical thinking requires thinking about something, and thus has to be introduced in terms of appropriate content. We believe that a balance between teaching course content and exercising critical thinking can be achieved without compromising either goal.

This chapter consists of three sections. In the first section, we examine activities suitable for a variety of psychology classes. We describe activities potentially useful to instructors interested in incorporating critical thinking into their classes but not inclined to completely reorganize their courses from a critical thinking perspective. In the second section, we discuss how critical thinking may be infused throughout a course by presenting course case studies for cognitive psychology and the history and systems of psychology. We believe this section should interest instructors who already incorporate critical thinking activities in their courses on a limited basis and wish to integrate thinking activities more fully throughout their courses. In the final section we present our conclusions, discuss principles for the construction or selection of good critical thinking activities, and identify some remaining issues.

Activities that Integrate Critical Thinking with Course Content

In this section, we examine a short list of activities that promote both critical thinking about and understanding of course content potentially useful in most psychology classes. These techniques allow instructors to implement critical thinking to enhance and deepen content learning rather than to interfere with presentation and retention of material. Our list comprises (a) critical thinking exercises, (b) ignorance questions, (c) debates, (d) self-assessment assignments, (e) audiovisual media assignments, and (f) Internet assignments.

Critical Thinking Exercises

Peden and Keniston (1991) developed a series of activities designed to teach students about observations, inferences, and assumptions. Each exercise was a multiple-choice essay question with five alternatives. The stem instructed students to identify and label each alternative as an assumption, inference, or observation and then explain their labels in a paragraph. Some stems asked "Which of the following is an assumption as opposed to an inference or an observation?" whereas stems for other questions asked "Which of the following is an observation as opposed to an assumption or inference?" Here is an example edited for clarity:

> In "Football, Fast Cars, and Cheerleading: Adolescent Gender Norms, 1978–1989," Suitor and Reavis (1995) compare college students' reports about sources of prestige for male and female high school students across the span of a decade. Which of the following statements represents an assumption by the authors that makes this work interesting and important to them? Which of the other statements are inferences the authors make? Which are observations? Circle the letter of the statement that is the assumption and explain why it is the assumption; then indicate and explain whether each other statement is an inference or an observation.
>
> A.   Adolescents are the harbingers of gender roles in the coming decades.
>
> B.   American adolescents entered the 1980s with relatively traditional gender roles.
>
> C.   There were substantial differences in most of the avenues by which boys and girls acquired prestige in high school in the early 1980s.
>
> D.   The overall change in prestige girls acquired through participation in sports was due to changes in the *boys'* perceptions.
>
> E.   There was relatively little change in gender norms among high school students between the early and late 1980s.

Keniston and Peden (1992) used the same format to engage students in other types of critical thinking as well. An introductory psychology textbook by Wade and Tavris (1987) provided guidelines for critical thinking that helped Keniston and Peden create critical thinking exercises. They also used the approach two other ways. On one hand, they devised critical thinking exercises for Stanovich's *How to Think Straight about Psychology* (2007), and on the other hand, they implemented critical thinking in activities for quantitative reasoning and the analysis of ideas. Peden and Keniston (1992) showed that scores on the assignments improved continuously during a school term.

Ignorance Questions

Instructors teach what we know about a discipline; however, experts understand what we do not know as well as what we do know. To encourage students to be curious (a critical thinking disposition according to Wade and Tavris, 1987), Peden and Keniston (1991) devised ignorance question exercises. Ignorance questions are stimulated but not answered by either textbook or class lecture. For example, a student who read a chapter on cross-cultural similarities in basic emotions might offer an appropriate ignorance question such as "If all humans express emotions with the same facial expressions, then why does so much distrust and misunderstanding exist between cultures?"

There are different ways to implement this activity (Carroll, 2001; Peden & Keniston, 1991). Instructors can require students to write ignorance questions about lectures, readings, or both. We have used different options for grading ignorance questions. Sometimes we graded ignorance question assignments and other times we graded ignorance questions only on exams. We have even simply given students extra credit for ignorance questions. The following five-point grading scale may be used for ignorance questions:

5   good ignorance question
4   potentially a good ignorance question, but not entirely clear
3   question answered in the text
2   question irrelevant to course content under study
1   joke

Questions scored as 2 or 3 may be appropriate questions, but not good ignorance questions.

In general, ignorance question exercises lead to a classroom ambience that promotes active learning, curiosity, and critical thinking by students. Peden and Keniston (1991) also demonstrated that students' ignorance question scores improved from the beginning to the end of a term. Qualitatively, some students regularly submitted good ignorance questions and most students produced at least one good question in a semester. Furthermore, students consistently rated the activity favorably.

Debates

Instructors have required student debates in a variety of classes (e.g., Bauer & Wachowiak, 1977; Elliot, 1993; Moeller, 1985). Students regard debates as interesting, involving, and "live" in ways that other class presentations are not. Although students often are anxious about debating in class, typically they rate the activity favorably.

The critical thinking goal for debates is to view issues from multiple perspectives. Several studies reported that debates moderate preexisting student attitudes (Budesheim & Lundquist, 1999; Carroll, 2006; Finken, 2003). For example, students who debated contraception in a human sexuality class subsequently expressed less extreme views on the topic (Finken, 2003). In other words, debating a topic may engender a critical disposition to tolerating uncertainty (Wade & Tavris, 1987).

Self-Assessment Assignments

Carroll and Peden (2007) employed self-assessment assignments as a critical thinking tool. At the end of a term, our students assessed how well they met course goals by completing a three to five-page paper. Self-assessments by students in three classes (perception, ethics, and history and systems) at two universities revealed that students use different language in self-assessment assignments than in traditional academic assignments (e.g., term papers, take-home exams). Self-assessments contain more first-person singular pronouns, more emotion words (particularly positive emotion words), and more cognitive words than traditional assignments.

The use of cognitive words (think, discover, and believe) is particularly relevant to critical thinking. The incidence of cognitive words in essays increases when individuals experience emotional upheaval (Pennebaker, Mehl, & Niederhoffer, 2003). Reviewing one's performance in a class increases both the emotionality and the thoughtfulness of essays.

Moreover, our preliminary data suggest that self-assessments differ from other "personal" assignments, such as an autobiography, in number of cognitive words. Although autobiographies contain more first-person and emotion words than traditional academic assignments, they contain fewer cognitive words than self-assessments. We believe self-assessments encourage students to think about their academic performance. Casual conversations with students about the self-assessment assignments reveal that they have to employ a rather different strategy from the more common "cramming for the final" approach. That is, students must review and think about the content of the course and their effort and accomplishment regarding their mastery of content and development of skills.

Audiovisual Assignments for Television and Films

Many instructors have used television and movies to teach critical thinking about psychological concepts. Schwarzmueller's (2006) forensic psychology students developed multimedia presentations from movies and television shows. Students identified clips related to course content and critiqued media portrayal of these concepts. Students strongly agreed that the assignment encouraged them to think about how entertainment media portray forensic work.

Similarly, Kelley and Calkins (2006) found that study of popular portrayals of memory in films fostered students' critical thinking. Their students wrote reports that compared the film's portrayal of memory with evidence discussed in class using an adaptation of the critical thinking rubric developed at Washington State University. The rubric was revised in 2006 as "The Guide to Rating Critical and Integrative Thinking" and placed online. Students made progress toward a variety of critical thinking goals, such as identifying the main question, assessing supporting evidence, and considering other positions. Informally, we have observed similar effects using the film *Memento* (Nolan, 2000).

A strong study by Hall and Seery (2006) reported a group activity to help students evaluate media reports of psychological research. Students read about research in an online newspaper and in a scholarly journal. They then responded to questions about what kinds of information are most likely to be included in a media report of psychological research, how newspaper headlines may be misleading, and why it is important to know about the study itself. Compared to a group that did not engage in the group activity, the treatment group's scores on the three questions were much higher.

These audiovisual assignments illustrate how to integrate critical thinking and course content. The assignments support learning because students must learn the name and definition of a psychological construct and also must identify an example of the concept in the media to evaluate the accuracy of the portrayal. Thus students engaged in critical thinking at the same time they learned course content.

Internet Assignments

Several instructors have created critical thinking assignments that employ the Internet. Sung, Lin, Lee, and Chang (2003) used the Internet for a peer critique program in an experimental psychology course. Students submitted research proposals on the Web, received peer feedback, and revised their proposals. Instructors familiar with course content blindly rated the proposals before and after peer discussion. Ratings of proposals after peer evaluation were higher than before evaluation.

Other assignments require students to critique information found on the Internet. For example, Miserandino (2006) found that an Internet-based ice cream personality test promoted student learning about the role of reliability and validity in test design. Similarly, Connor-Greene and Greene (2002) developed an assignment in which students read an Internet article about the dangers of aspartame and wrote individual reactions to it. The students subsequently worked in groups to answer a series of questions regarding the nature and quality of the evidence in the article. In contrast to their initial reactions as individuals, the discussion groups noted and described multiple limitations of the article. These examples illustrate ways to promote critical thinking about information on the Internet.

Course Case Studies in Integrating Critical Thinking into Upper Level Courses

The previous section of the chapter described activities that promote critical thinking while teaching course content. All the activities are discrete and represent ways to focus on specific critical thinking objectives. However, some instructors may want to infuse critical thinking across assignments. In this approach critical thinking becomes a feature of learning all aspects of course material. In this section we illustrate a way to integrate critical thinking with course content by weaving critical thinking objectives into the fabric of a course. We illustrate this tapestry approach to critical thinking with case studies of a cognitive psychology course and a history and systems of psychology course.

Our general approach identifies the critical thinking opportunities inherent in the course content and course resources. For example, Wade and Tavris's (1987) general psychology textbook presented 10 guidelines that students should apply when thinking critically about psychology. In addition to modeling critical thinking throughout the text, Wade and Tavris integrated the guidelines into their book. Thus students learned to think critically as a process of acquiring and mastering content in an introductory course. The important point is that critical thinking was woven into the content rather than presented as a study aid or an incidental learning feature.

In applying the Wade and Tavris (1987) tapestry approach to content and critical thinking, we identify points of contention, evidentiary issues, and intellectual problems endemic to content of one's course. The tapestry approach is not burdensome either to students or instructors because content and critical thinking are part of the same package.

Cognitive Psychology

Cognitive psychology is a large domain that presents many teaching challenges and opportunities. Instructors of the course know that teaching and learning issues begin with the selection of a textbook. In contrast to other areas of psychology (e.g., child psychology) there is no real "canon" that governs either the content or the order of topics in a textbook. From the start, the instructor exercises critical thinking capacities by choosing the text that defines and orders the content.

The diverse topics, theories, and methodologies pose a challenge for instructors and students alike, who sometimes regard these diversities as alternatives, or more intensely, as rivals for correct understanding of a problem. The material demands active, reflective, evaluative involvement if it is to result in more than a rote recitation of the list of things a student needs for examinations.

In teaching cognitive psychology Keniston explicitly lectures about the critical thinking threads early in the course (i.e., after teaching about the first topic, perception) and then revisits the threads or guidelines in subsequent lectures, discussion, assignments, and examinations. Keniston emphasizes the following problems in his cognitive psychology course:

- *Inference*: How do we study what we cannot "see" directly?
- *Circular reasoning*: How do we avoid tautologies in our definitions or explanations?
- *Causality*: How do we draw appropriate conclusions from correlational and experimental data?
- *Multiple perspectives*: Whose ideas are right? What is the best solution?
- *False dichotomies*: How do we learn that two ideas, apparently mutually contradictory, actually are complementary parts of the solution to a puzzle?

- *Complexity*: When does an explanation grow too complex? When does it involve so much qualification or "patching up" that it ceases to be effective?
- *Unit of analysis*: What is the basic element in any given system of thought? How much reduction is necessary to arrive at the fundamental atom of cognition?
- *Hypothesis testing*: How do we learn to rely on disconfirmatory rather than confirmatory evidence?
- *Physiological substrates*: How do we know when physiological data provide proof of a concept or theory about cognitive function?

The list is not exhaustive, but it provides ample opportunities for critical thinking exploration, application, and "teachable moments" throughout the course. Generating this kind of list can inspire instructors to develop lectures, devise counterparts to the activities described in the previous section, develop guidelines for longer papers (reviews, proposals, research projects), and write examination questions. As students practice and master the ability to recognize these problems in their course study materials, they may spontaneously implement them in class. For example, students sometimes use a guideline to question one of the instructor's own ideas or criticize the teacher's presentation! Rather than rely completely on such spontaneous occurrences of critical thinking, we recommend that instructors implement these guidelines regularly. Each day, for example, instructors can challenge the class to name a flaw in the readings or in a presentation and explain why there is a flaw and how it might be overcome.

Our list of critical thinking guidelines may be idiosyncratic, but clearly relates to cognitive psychology course content and resources. Teachers in other content areas can generate similar lists of critical thinking threads to weave into the tapestry of their course. The second case study presents different and more detailed opportunities to infuse critical thinking into another course.

History of Psychology

Courses in history and systems of psychology offer numerous opportunities for teaching and learning critical thinking. Contemporary textbooks (e.g., Goodwin, 2004; Schulz & Schulz, 2004; Wertheimer, 2000) illustrate that history in general requires constant vigilance concerning its data, historians' agendas and viewpoints, and its methods.

Each of the "problems of history" provides instructors with opportunities to elaborate the list of problems. By way of example, there are many problems with historical data. Such data may:

- have been collected prior to posing the research questions
- not have been carefully collected
- not have been collected at all
- be scattered, incomplete, or distorted
- not be replicable
- not allow assessment of reliability and validity.

In addition to teaching students to think critically about the data of history, instructors can encourage critical thinking about other problematic aspects of course material: (a) how to do history despite the problems with data, (b) how to decide when the history of psychology begins, and (c) the problem of why we study history at all. Another opportunity for critical thinking in the history of psychology is how to understand the many schools and systems of psychology.

Robert Watson's Prescriptions

Robert Watson (1967) made a contribution toward understanding schools and systems of psychology in a classic paper on psychological prescriptions. Watson's work influenced the scholarship and teaching of the history of psychology and also provided a way to construct a new, critical history of psychology (e.g., Brennan, 2003). Watson argued that psychology is a preparadigmatic science because the competing schools and systems differ dramatically in terms of what psychologists should study and how psychologists should conduct research. Watson made this point forcefully by comparing and contrasting schools and systems in terms of 18 prescriptions displayed in the table in Appendix 1 as polar adjective with explanations. The 18 prescriptions address four aspects of a psychological system:

- Content (e.g., conscious mentalism vs. unconscious mentalism)
- Method (e.g., quantitativism vs. qualitativism)
- Philosophy (determinism vs. indeterminism), and
- Orientation (e.g., functionalism vs. structuralism).

One can characterize a school or system in terms of its positions on the 18 prescriptions. Keniston uses Watson's (1967) prescriptions to teach students how to thinking critically about historical psychological perspectives. Different assignments require students to (a) characterize the key issues addressed by systems of psychology; (b) compare and contrast systems, (c) derive a sense of psychology's core purpose and unity, and (d) identify students' convictions about the subjects and methods of psychology. The prescriptions provide one way to infuse critical thinking into the tapestry of a history and systems course.

Survey. Keniston uses Watson's (1967) prescriptions in a pretest and posttest survey. On the survey students indicate their views on a four-point scale for each of the 18 dichotomous prescriptions starting with (conscious mentalism–unconscious mentalism) and ending with (staticism–dynamicism). At the start of the course the instructor distributes the pretest survey to students who indicate their position on each prescription once they understand the meaning of the terms. After the pretest, the instructor informs the class that they will use the prescriptions to learn about course content and to compare and contrast the schools and systems of psychology throughout the course. In other words the prescriptions will be part and parcel of the entire course. Near the end of the semester student complete the posttest. Use of a posttest survey provides a way to study changes in students' thinking over the course of the semester (Chang, Wojtanowicz, & Keniston, 2005; Vitulli, 1995).

Lectures. Instructors can use the prescriptions to organize lectures about major figures and systems of psychology. For example, Keniston gives an introductory lecture entitled "Wundt's Prescription for Psychology" that uses the prescriptions to lay out the main features of Wundt's system of psychology. There are two goals: (a) focus on the prescriptions and (b) compact treatment of Wundt's work that sets students up for further reading in their textbook and articles. Similar lectures about every major figure or system can employ Watson's (1967) prescriptions. However, we suggest encouraging students to learn from and apply the framework presented by the instructor's lecture on Wundt.

Tests. Keniston uses the prescriptions for questions on tests. Here is an example of a multiple choice question:

> One of the philosophical foundations of modern psychology is scientific materialism, or mechanism. This strain of thought makes specific prescriptions about how we should understand human mind and behavior. Here are eight of the prescriptions that Robert Watson contends define the issues we study in psychology. Which four of these are the "prescriptions of scientific materialism?"

Vitalism	Determinism	Naturalism	Dualism
Monism	Purism	Theism	Methodological Objectivism

Here is an example of an essay question in which students summarize a historical figure's ideas in terms of Watson's (1967) prescriptions:

> Write Freud's prescription for psychology. Use Watson's prescriptions as indicated in the survey that I used at the beginning of the semester; you could fill the form out as you imagine Freud would. Then write a paragraph in which you highlight the distinguishing characteristics of the prescription.

How the Prescriptions Infuse Course Content with Critical Thinking

Watson's (1967) prescriptions allow instructors to infuse critical thinking into a history and systems of psychology course by providing a framework for teaching as well as a vehicle for thinking about course content. As a framework, the prescriptions help an instructor to achieve perspective, integrity, and unity in a discipline that often seems fragmented and haphazard. As a vehicle, the prescriptions carry students repeatedly through exercises that keep them thinking about what they are learning and that prompt them to construct their own understanding of psychological systems.

Learning about the prescriptions affords multiple critical thinking opportunities. At heart they expose the assumptions inherent in psychological systems. Identifying prescriptions requires students to discover and explain the positions various systems take on the same set of prescriptions. Identifying a system's prescriptions prepares students for a comprehensive comparison and contrast among systems. Doing this may also encourage students to examine their stereotypes about schools. For example, they may learn that Freudian psychology is not as irrational or ill-conceived as some claim. In a different vein, analyzing systems of ideas leads students to see patterns in the values, theoretical orientations, and preferred methodologies characteristic of types of systems, as well as attuning them to variations within broad categories of systems. For example, the exercise makes students aware of the basics of and variations among behaviorist systems.

As students repeatedly use the prescriptions to understand course content and answer questions on tests and assignments, they acquire a critical sense of psychology as a discipline grappling with a diverse but finite set of issues. They consider how capable men and women could take diametrically opposed positions on central issues like the value of consciousness to understanding human behavior. The effort can stimulate the gamut of critical thinking skills and dispositions (Wade & Tavris, 1987).

The result of working repeatedly and systematically with the prescriptions is, we hope, a cherished goal for anyone teaching critical thinking: Students begin to define their beliefs concerning psychology. The prescriptions become a practiced vocabulary for naming and integrating the important dimensions of students' convictions about how to study, test, and apply what they have learned about the history and systems of psychology.

Evidence that the Prescriptions Enhance Student Learning

We have not formally evaluated whether use of Watson's prescriptions promotes critical and reflective thinking by students. But we do have a surprising affirmation of their value in the history and systems course from spontaneous student endorsements.

At the end of the course, students write two short essays they choose from a menu. One question asks them to identify "the five most important 'things' [they] learned from studying the history of psychology." Perhaps because the question seems easy, many students choose it. At the end of the spring 2005 semester, 47 of 75 (63%) answered this question by listing 67 different topics. Although most topics were unique, the most common answers included (a) the concept of Zeitgeist (49%), (b) understanding the problems of history (43%), and (c) Watson's prescriptions (32%). All three choices endorse critical thinking. The critical thinking dimension of the course was salient to and valued by many students.

General Conclusion

We have described critical thinking activities appropriate for many psychology courses. We also have described two course case studies that illustrate how to weave critical thinking into the fabric of the course. In this last section we present conclusions, discuss principles for constructing or selecting critical thinking activities, and identify some remaining issues.

Our critical thinking activities and course case studies illustrate that instructors can promote critical thinking and mastery of course content without impeding either. In addition, these techniques comply with best practices for undergraduate education (Chickering & Gamson, 1987). These practices include active learning, respecting diverse talents and ways of learning, and communicating high expectations.

Considerable research indicates that students learn more when actively engaged in exercises and assignments. We have reviewed many activities that require students to plan, organize, and direct a project. For example, students who critique media presentations of psychological concepts must identify examples of concepts and include them in the class project. Moreover, successful group projects require students to divide responsibilities and also meet individual obligations to the group. Engagement in an activity produces deeper and more permanent learning.

Regarding diverse talents and ways of learning, instructors who employ critical thinking techniques respect individual differences among students. Students appreciate the opportunity to create their own questions or conduct debates as a counterpoint to the lecture–exam structure typical of many college classes. Anecdotal experience indicates that students who struggle to learn in traditional formats thrive in assignments that permit personal involvement and creativity. In addition, instructors who employ critical thinking activities tap into the diversity of the students in a class. For example, when students write ignorance questions on a textbook chapter or research article, the questions may be quite diverse. Ignorance questions thus provide an easy way to incorporate attention to diversity issues within a class.

Also, an emphasis on critical thinking communicates high expectations to students. Instructors who teach critical thinking want students to master the concepts in a particular field of study, but also be able to critique, integrate, and apply this information.

We illustrated that general principles underlie ways to teach both critical thinking and course content, but some problems remain. Although many of the studies provided evidence of improved thinking or improved retention, we do not know whether these improvements are fleeting or permanent. In addition, we do not know whether the skills acquired in one class will transfer to other classes or situations (but see Halpern, 1998 for suggestions on how to promote transfer). Thus we have made progress in the implementation and study of critical thinking; however, instructors still have mountains to climb.

In this chapter we described ways to incorporate critical thinking goals into objectives of our courses in a way that integrates them with teaching course content. Our basic strategy identifies the important elements of critical thinking inherent to skilled understanding and mastery of the methods, facts, and ideas of the disciplinary subfield. Subsequently, we either construct or we search the teaching literature for lectures, demonstrations, and activities that exercise those elements of critical thinking. Readers of our chapter should find material that they can immediately put to use in their teaching. We also hope that our readers will create their own ways to infuse critical thinking in their courses by drawing on their expertise and passion to do more than "get through the syllabus."

References

Bauer, G., & Wachowiak, D. (1977). The home-court advantage: A debate format for the teaching of personality. *Teaching of Psychology, 4,* 190–192.

Brennan, J. B. (2003). *History and systems of psychology* (6th ed.). Upper Saddle River, NJ: Prentice Hall.

Browne, M. N., & Keeley, S. M. (1986). *Asking the right questions: A guide to critical thinking* (2nd ed.). Englewood Cliffs, NJ: Prentice-Hall.

Budesheim, T. L., & Lundquist, A. R. (1999). Consider the opposite: Opening minds through in-class debates on course-related controversies. *Teaching of Psychology, 26,* 106–110.

Carroll, D. W. (2001). Using ignorance questions to promote thinking skills. *Teaching of Psychology, 28,* 98–100.

Carroll, D. W. (2006). Thinking about historical issues: Debates in the history and systems class. *Teaching of Psychology, 33,* 131–134.

Carroll, D. W., & Peden, B. F. (2007, February). *Assessing self-assessment: Linguistic analysis of reflective versus other student papers.* Poster presented at Innovations in the Scholarship of Teaching and Learning at the Liberal Arts Colleges, Northfield, MN.

Chang, L., Wojtanowicz, M., & Keniston, A. H. (2005). *Basic tenets of psychology students' beliefs about psychology from the first to the fourth year.* Paper presented at the annual meeting of the Midwestern division of the Council of Teachers of Undergraduate Psychology, Chicago, IL.

Chickering, A. W., & Gamson, Z. F. (1987). Seven principles of good practice in undergraduate education. *AAHE Bulletin, 39,* 3–7.

Connor-Greene, P. A., & Greene, D. J. (2002). Science or snake oil? Teaching critical evaluation of "research" reports on the Internet. *Teaching of Psychology, 29,* 321–324.

Elliot, L. B. (1993). Using debates to teach the psychology of women. *Teaching of Psychology, 20,* 35–38.

Ennis, R. H. (1986). A taxonomy of critical thinking dispositions and abilities. In J. B. Baron & R. S. Sternberg (Eds.), *Teaching thinking skills: Theory and practice* (pp. 9–26). New York: Freeman.

Finken, L. L. (2003). The complexity of student responses to in-class debates in a human sexuality course. *Teaching of Psychology, 30,* 263–265.

Gray, P. (1993). Engaging students' intellects: The immersion approach to critical thinking in psychology instruction. *Teaching of Psychology, 20,* 68–74.

Goodwin, C. J. (2004). *A history of modern psychology* (2nd ed.). New York: John Wiley.

Hall, S. S., & Seery, B. L. (2006). Behind the facts: Helping students evaluate media reports of psychological research. *Teaching of Psychology, 33,* 101–104.

Halpern, D. F. (1998). Teaching critical thinking for transfer across domains. *American Psychologist, 53,* 449–455.

Kelley, M. R., & Calkins, S. (2006). Evaluating popular portrayals of memory in film. *Teaching of Psychology, 33,* 191–194.

Keniston, A. H., & Peden, B. F. (1992, Spring). Infusing critical thinking into college courses. *Issues in Teaching and Learning, 7*–12.

Miserandino, M. (2006). I scream, you scream: Teaching validity and reliability via the Ice Cream Personality Test. *Teaching of Psychology, 33,* 265–268.

Moeller, T. G. (1985). Using classroom debates in teaching developmental psychology. *Teaching of Psychology, 12,* 207–209.

Nolan, C. (Director). (2000). *Memento* [Motion picture]. United States: Newmarket Films.

Peden, B. F., & Keniston, A. H. (1991). Methods of promoting critical thinking by general psychology students. *The Wisconsin Dialogue, 11,* 12–34.

Peden, B. F., & Keniston, A. H. (1992). Critical thinking exercises: A preliminary report about two forms of a critical thinking exercise for introductory psychology students. In D. J. Stroup & R. P. Allen (Eds.), *Critical thinking: A collection of readings* (pp. 43–48). Dubuque, IA: Wm C. Brown.

Pennebaker, J. W., Mehl, M. R., & Niederhoffer, K. G. (2003). Psychological aspects of natural language use: Our words, our selves. *Annual Review of Psychology, 54*, 547–577.

Schulz, D. P., & Schulz, S. E. (2004). *A history of modern psychology* (8th ed.). Belmont, CA: Thompson/Wadsworth.

Schwarzmueller, A. (2006). Critiquing media depictions of forensic professionals: A project for students. *Teaching of Psychology, 33*, 204–207.

Stanovich, K. E. (2007). *How to think straight about psychology* (8th ed.). New York: Allyn & Bacon.

Suitor, J. J., & Reavis, R. (1995). Football, fast cars, and cheerleading: Adolescent gender norms, 1978–1989. *Adolescence, 30*, 265–272.

Sung, Y.-T., Lin, C.-S., Lee, C.-L., & Chang, K.-E. (2003). Evaluating proposals for experiments: An application of Web-based self-assessment and peer-assessment. *Teaching of Psychology, 30*, 331–334.

Vitulli, W. F. (1995). Contributions to the history of psychology: CII. Attitudinal shifts in responses to "psychological prescriptions" among undergraduate students in a "systems of psychology" course. *Psychological Reports, 77*, 840–842.

Wade, C., & Tavris, C. (1987). *Psychology*. New York: Harper & Row.

Washington State University Center for Teaching, Learning, & Technology. (2006). *The guide to rating critical and integrative thinking*. Retrieved March 19, 2008 from http://wsuctprojectdev. wsu.edu/ctr_docs/CIT%20Rubric%202006.pdf

Watson, R. (1967). Psychology: A prescriptive science. *American Psychologist, 22*, 435–443.

Wertheimer, M. (2000). *A brief history of psychology* (4th ed.). Belmont, CA: Wadsworth.

Appendix 1: Robert Watson's (1967) Contrasting Prescriptions of Psychology

Prescriptions	Definitions
Conscious mentalism–Unconscious mentalism	The study of mind should focus on conscious mental processes or structures versus a focus on unconscious mental processes or structures.
Contentual objectivism–Contentual subjectivism	The proper focus of psychology is behavior versus mental processes or structures.
Determinism–Indeterminism	Human behavior or events can be explained entirely in terms of what led to them versus they can only partly be explained by what led up to them.
Empiricism–Rationalism	Human knowledge is acquired by experience versus human knowledge is acquired by reasoning guided by innate mental abilities.

Prescriptions	Definitions
Functionalism–Structuralism	The proper focus of psychology is on activities/processes of mind or behavior versus the proper focus of psychology is on structures/contents of mind or behavior.
Inductivism–Deductivism	Research should begin in observations versus research should begin with a set of claims assumed to be true.
Mechanism–Vitalism	We understand behavior entirely in terms of physical, biological, and chemical structures and processes versus we understand behavior as the outcome of a special life force unique to living things.
Methodological objectivism–Methodological subjectivism	The primary data of psychology should be observations every one can make versus the primary data of psychology should be our own personal, subjective experiences.
Molecularism–Molarism	Psychologists should break phenomena into the small units that build our behavior and minds versus psychologists should identify large units that organize our behavior and minds.
Monism–Dualism	Mind and matter are fundamentally the same thing versus mind and matter are fundamentally different things.
Naturalism–Supernaturalism	We can understand nature by discovering the laws that govern it versus we must understand that forces outside of nature (that exist separately from nature) guide it.
Nomotheticism–Idiographicism	Psychology should focus on finding a few general laws that explain everything versus psychology should uncover the rules that explain particular events or people.
Peripheralism–Centralism	Psychology should focus on external aspects of behavior versus psychology should focus on the internal aspects of behavior.
Purism–Utilitarianism	We should seek knowledge for its own sake versus we should seek knowledge we can use for other purposes (e.g., to solve human problems).
Quantitativism–Qualitativism	We should strive to define what we know in terms of measures and amounts versus we

	should strive to define what we know in terms of kinds or types.
Rationalism–Irrationalism	Human behavior should be understood in terms of rational, intelligent mental and behavioral processes versus human behavior should be understood in terms of emotions and their impact on mental and behavioral processes.
Staticism–Developmentalism	Psychologists should focus on a particular period in the life of individuals versus psychologists should focus on how people change over time.
Staticism–Dynamicism	Psychologists should focus on what is constant in mind and behavior versus psychologists should focus on what changes and what causes change.

Chapter 10

Critical Thinking on Contemporary Issues

Susan L. O'Donnell, Alisha L. Francis,
and Sherrie L. Mahurin

Critical thinking, also known as scientific thinking, involves a willingness to consider evidence and alternative sources of information before drawing conclusions (Wade & Tavris, 2005). This form of thinking presents both a challenge and an opportunity for psychology instructors. The challenge arises with the realization that critical thinking is not a natural ability for every student. Halonen and colleagues (2003) referred to this initial developmental level as "untrained" (p. 198). However, the challenge of an untrained thinker becomes an opportunity, given that as faculty we can teach the ability to think critically with explicit, systematic instruction related to the process of gathering and evaluating information (Halonen et al., 2003).

Teaching the introductory psychology course provides a venue in which we can take advantage of that opportunity. In many cases, students in this course are in their first year of college and, as such, we have the opportunity to introduce fundamental thinking skills early in their academic career. Students who are still exploring potential majors may benefit from the accompanying emphasis on the science of psychology. In addition, the inclusion of introductory psychology as a general education requirement at many schools also means that students have the opportunity to delve into critical thinking across disciplines.

This chapter focuses on one possible strategy for explicit, systematic instruction related to critical thinking. It centers on the progressive application of nine critical thinking guidelines to assist students in evaluating information about personally salient issues. We have applied the strategy to integrate in-class lecture or discussion with out-of-class assignments related to both content-based and critical thinking objectives. Our strategy is consistent with the Elaboration Likelihood Model (ELM), which suggests that students are motivated to examine arguments more carefully when issues are important to them (Cook, Moore, & Steel, 2004). Furthermore, Cook et al. believe students are guided by an intrinsic need to be correct, which may result in a level of defensiveness regarding preexisting beliefs when they encounter traditional attempts to persuade. We hope to capitalize on this need for a subjective feeling of correctness without invoking defensiveness by encouraging skills directly related to the central route to persuasion. ELM suggests a link between student motivation, willingness to apply effort, and personal relevance. Our strategy for teaching critical thinking requires students to analyze material that is relevant to their lives in order to maximize motivation and effort. Given their life experiences, it is likely that issues that are personally relevant to college students include the effects of parental divorce and maternal employment, violent video games or pornography, and attention deficit hyperactivity disorder (ADHD).

Objectives associated with this approach are consistent with the developmental rubric for scientific inquiry articulated by Halonen et al. (2003). More specifically, the following discussion outlines a process that uses personally salient issues to assist students in moving from the "before training" category to the "basic" level on the rubric (p. 198). The issues are drawn from *Taking Sides: Clashing Views on Psychological Issues* (Slife, 2006), a volume in the extensive "Taking Sides" series published by McGraw-Hill.

Progressive "Stair-Steps" to Development

As a beginning teacher, one of us (SO'D) provided students with various issues from the Slife (2006) book with instructions to read the entries and write a response, confidently expecting high-level, integrative responses. The other author (AF) handed students a lengthy list of critical thinking guidelines with instructions to "apply them in analyzing an issue related to psychology." In retrospect, both realize the naïveté of these approaches – we were each surprised with the low quality of the students' responses and devastated at our perceived "failure" to teach them such an important skill.

Literature regarding teaching and critical thinking suggests that a progressive, "stair-stepped" approach, consistent with Halonen et al.'s (2003) developmental rubric, is more effective at helping students develop thinking skills. Teachers can use the guidelines discussed in the following section in such a manner, allowing students to establish a foundation of fundamental skills and then practice those skills in conjunction with more advanced critical thinking. We begin by introducing students to a basic question that encourages critical thinking, such as "What is fact and what is opinion?" Then we provide instruction on related procedures, such as fact-checking, source identification, or logical analysis. Introducing each of the nine questions and their associated procedures one by one allows students to build skills in critical thinking piece by piece, without being overwhelmed. At the same time, there is a natural accumulation of skills, creating a stair-stepped approach. This progression allows for an additional advantage in that we can integrate the focus of each step into the various content areas commonly included in the introductory psychology course.

Guidelines for Thinking Critically

In formulating a strategy for teaching critical thinking, one author (AF) began by reviewing the critical thinking objectives noted in various teaching tools in psychology (e.g. Using

Taking Sides, n.d; Wade & Tavris, 2005). Triangulating information from various sources resulted in a list of "Nine Important Questions to Ask When Thinking Critically." The nine questions focus on both the source of information and the presentation of information. More specifically, the questions are:

1 What is fact and what is opinion?
2 Where do the facts come from?
3 What cause/effect relationships are proposed?
4 Are there faulty generalizations?
5 Is the issue oversimplified?
6 Is propaganda being used?
7 Is the information distorted?
8 Is deception being used?
9 Is stereotyping or ethnocentric thinking being employed?

We discuss each question in more detail in the following pages, including associated objectives and related content areas as well as examples of the ways in which we can use the *Taking Sides* book in practicing the related critical thinking skills.

Question #1: What is Fact and What is Opinion?

In this phase of critical thinking development, the objective is for students to develop the ability to distinguish between an assertion based on fact and an assertion based on opinion. A fact is a piece of information supported by evidence and linked to empirical data. We then incorporate this association between facts and empirical data into a lecture on psychological science and the use of the empirical method, typically in the first week of class.

The *Taking Sides* Issue #8 discussion of divorce and its impact on children (Hetherington & Kelly, 2006; Wallerstein & Lewis, 2006) brings a discussion to life while introducing important issues related to facts, opinions, and empirical evidence. We assign the task of reading both perspectives and then instruct students to find information on the Internet regarding each of the lead authors, Judith Wallerstein and E. Mavis Hetherington. Inevitably several students come back with the information that Wallerstein is the foremost authority on divorce in this country. When asked the source of this claim, students credit a Web site listed on the first page of results from a Google search of her name—a Web site duplicating the inside cover of her book jacket (Wallerstein, Lewis, & Blakeslee, 2002). This observation leads to a natural discussion of the difference between fact and opinion. The recognition that all opinions are not equally valid is an important first step for students who are still learning to think scientifically (Ruggiero, 2006).

Question #2: Where do the Facts Come From?

Having established the difference between facts and opinion, the next task is to differentiate between diverse sources of empirical information. The objective at this stage is for students to be able to identify strengths and weaknesses of information sources. This objective is directly linked to issues addressed in discussions of the various research methods employed by psychological researchers.

Taking Sides Issue #5 on ADHD addresses this objective, while giving students exposure to the PsycINFO database and introducing the biological perspective on behavior. In light of a growing number of children being diagnosed with ADHD, students find this issue interesting. The two papers on this issue discuss the use of behavior genetics research (twin and adoption studies) to determine genetic explanations for ADHD. In the process, students tend to ask which method of research is "right." These inquiries allow for a class discussion on using different research techniques to triangulate toward "truth," rather than simply looking at an issue in black-and-white terms.

Issue #7 in *Taking Sides*, which focuses on the topic of maternal employment, also provides a reference for discussing the sources of information. Noting that the authors of the articles are from different disciplines (developmental psychology and sociology/anthropology) provides for a discussion of the usefulness of cross-disciplinary study and the value in terms of breadth of understanding.

Another approach to understanding the nature of specific facts allows students to examine research findings from a different perspective. Returning to the *Taking Sides* issue on divorce (Issue #8), we assign students to look up information about the two different research samples used by Wallerstein and Hetherington. The findings reported in the two articles are quite different, which can be traced to the study populations—the sources of their facts. Wallerstein's study is based on a clinical sample, whereas Hetherington's is a normative sample. Both sets of findings are certainly "facts," but are they both equally helpful for understanding the impact of divorce on children? Rather than a simple "yes" or "no" response, this discussion requires in-depth thinking about how each set of findings illuminates different types of influences and how both conclusions can contribute to the understanding of an issue. Such a discussion can be beneficial for introducing the notion that even conclusions that appear to contradict each other can be valid in helping us to understand human behavior from a psychological perspective, what Halonen et al. (2003) referred to as interpretation within the descriptive skills domain.

Question #3: What Cause/Effect Relationships are Proposed?

In psychology, despite the reality that much of the research on interesting social conditions tends to be limited by correlational data, findings are often condensed into sound bites that make it seem as if the research is causal in nature. The objective of this step is not only to remind students that "correlation does not equal causation," but also to think critically about assertions of causal relationships presented in various contexts. Lecture, discussion, and textbook readings support this objective by delineating the characteristics of experimental research compared with correlational designs. In class, we address causality using multiple issues. First, we return to Issue #8 on divorce. We create a list of the negative outcomes that Wallerstein and Lewis (2006) credit as effects of divorce, such as anger, or fear of intimate relationships. Then we brainstorm as many other possible causes of those outcomes as we can think of, such as poor parenting or peer relationships. This activity serves to illustrate the idea that outcomes are often multidetermined and complicated. We ask students whether it is reasonable to assume that divorce is the sole cause of all these different outcomes or if some of them might occur in individuals who are from nondivorced homes. Their writing assignment requires them to review several different papers on the effects of divorce and describe whether any of the data are actually causal.

The *Taking Sides* issue of video games and violence (Issue #16) provides another engaging topic for practice. Gentile and Anderson (2006) produce correlational data that they believe suggests that violent games cause violence in children; Olsen (2006) contends that the data are not conclusive in terms of causation. Gentile and Anderson include a paragraph in their paper discussing how developmental science is producing a body of work that allows for causal conclusions despite the lack of experimental data. We have students respond to that assertion in writing. These issues allow students to discuss the idea of whether correlational data can ever "prove" causation, such as the data the American Academy of Pediatrics (AAP) used when it declared in a 2000 joint statement with five other medical groups that television violence causes aggression in children (AAP, 2000). Issue #18, whether pornography is harmful, centers on the same argument that there is no actual causal evidence that the use of pornography leads to rape. Both video games and pornography are salient issues, drawing a great deal of student interest, and men in particular are motivated to believe that these are harmless pastimes, thus making for a lively set of papers. For both topics, a key component of this assignment is to require the PsycINFO search to cover both sides of the issue in order to prevent students from submitting only literature reviews that support their preexisting views.

Question #4: Are there Faulty Generalizations?

With this question, we progress from identifying and critiquing the sources of information to introducing a more detailed analysis of both the source and the use of the information. The objective is for students to learn to identify situations in which information presented as fact is taken out of the context within which it was initially generated. In our experience, students often have an initial bias that all research should apply to all people. We would like to help them understand that research targeting a specific population is valuable, but the conclusions then need to be limited to that population. This is a difficult idea, so we bring back a familiar topic—Issue #8 (on divorce)—and revisit the idea that Hetherington and Kelly's (2006) and Wallerstein and Lewis's (2006) findings are not wrong, merely specific to their particular study populations. We move to Issue #7 and consider the generalizability of the research on maternal employment in both papers. We have them look at sample characteristics and determine to whom the results apply, revisiting the idea that one author is writing about children and the other is writing about adolescents. Again, not wrong, but different. The presentation of antidepressant use and suicide (Issue #12) is particularly useful for identifying generalizations. An initial step is to analyze the characteristics of the samples used for the referenced research and determine to whom the results apply, pointing out the section in the Healy and Whitaker (2006) paper referring to epidemiological studies. We then use this topic as a reference point for teaching about "representative" samples, including discussion of the difference between a representative sample and a targeted sample. We also discuss samples of convenience, highlighting the amount of research carried out on college students, linking back with earlier discussions of research methods. One author (SO'D) used to do this exercise discussing representative samples before targeted samples, but found that students found this approach more difficult. Our guess is that beginning the discussion with generalizable research, as is implied by the representative sample, serves to confirm students' initial bias, making it more difficult to eventually dislodge from their thinking.

Question #5: Is the Issue Oversimplified?

As students become more experienced in analyzing the data used to support an assertion, it is also important to encourage them to consider ideas that are "watered down" in order to make them more accessible to nonscientists. The objective at this stage is to improve students' ability to identify alternative explanations or contrasting perspectives on an issue. Multiple intelligences (Issue #10) provides an opportunity for structured practice related to this objective. Having heard a simplistic form of the theory of multiple intelligences in school and other venues (e.g., a warm-fuzzy "we're all intelligent in different ways" idea), students frequently indicate their support, thinking they understand it. Reading these chapters often leads to the discovery that their understanding was superficial at best. Gardner (2006) presents a strong, multidisciplinary set of scientific criteria by which he determines whether a characteristic can be considered an intelligence (e.g., specific structures in the brain or effects of brain damage). Gottfredson (2006) reports equally scientific findings that support the presence of a generalized factor, or "g," that underlies other specific characteristics (e.g., verbal fluency or mathematics). As students are focusing on attempting to decide which view is *correct*, we often need to remind them that even the scientific community is split and perhaps they are not really qualified to draw a conclusion. We can then turn the discussion around to usefulness, considering ways in which each view of intelligence can help us to understand human behavior. Students resist being told that they are not qualified to make a judgment on an issue, but learning when it is appropriate to rely on experts is an important part of critical thinking.

Question #6: Is Propaganda Being Used?

Considering generalization and simplification encourages students to focus on the presentation of information. Questioning the uses of propaganda introduces another dimension in considering the intent of the presenter or author. By this point, students are well versed in the idea that, in psychology, facts come from empirical research (which tends to exclude propaganda, we hope!). Realistically, however, students obtain information from a wide range of nonacademic publications. The objective is not to encourage students to view all attempts at persuasion as negative, rather to increase students' ability to recognize when propaganda is being used in order to allow them to evaluate an assertion independent of peripheral attempts to persuade and influence. In other words, the objective is to increase ability to evaluate the content of the argument rather than, or in spite of, the presentation.

We revisit the various perspectives on ADHD (Issue #5) to provide practice related to this objective while reinforcing learning related to identifying the sources of facts. After reviewing the earlier discussion, students are asked to analyze Internet sites discussing the disorder and possible treatments. This analysis includes identifying forms of propaganda used in the text, such as whether specific studies are cited, balance in the presentation of the effectiveness of various treatments, and locating funding sources for studies. Issue #11, which addresses the question of whether ADHD even exists, provides another resource for practicing this objective, as Timimi, Moncrieff, Jureidini, et al. (2006) argue that the diagnosis is merely an attempt to sell medications.

Question #7: Is the Information Distorted?

Distortion results from the presenter's attempt to influence or persuade the audience. The objective at this stage is to encourage additional critical thinking about factual information. More specifically, the objective is for students to increase their ability to identify potential biases represented by a presenter's selection of data sources. This objective offers students a new perspective on course content as they use their newfound knowledge of psychology to analyze various representations of psychological information and theory in popular culture. We return to the familiar topic of divorce (Issue #8) to introduce this critical thinking question. In previous discussions, we noted that the two studies used for the issue draw on very different populations (clinical-only compared to a normative sample). Additional analysis of the study populations used for these studies generates discussion regarding the distortions in understanding that can result from these population differences. For example, students are asked to consider how their opinions might change if they only read one of these two articles, pointing out the value of multiple sources in detecting distortions.

Issue #7, focused on the topic of maternal employment, also provides a reference for discussion of information distortion—this time in the context of the editor's choice of articles. Brooks-Gunn, Han, and Waldfogel (2006) wrote about children in the preschool stage, whereas Vander Ven, Cullen, Carrozza, and Wright (2006) wrote about adolescents. On the surface, these two papers appear to be addressing the same issue, but in reality they are comparing apples to oranges. Assigning students to write about the issue can lead to independent discovery of the discrepancy. One author's (SO'D) experience has been that students, when looking for articles to support each argument, independently come to the conclusion that the two articles aren't really comparable. Finally, we have students note that the Gentile and Anderson (2006) paper is condensed from their book and, therefore, is not a peer-reviewed article. We discuss the importance of the peer-review process and assign them to look up the sources from the book to see whether empirical research correctly supports the authors' suggestions (we have to provide a copy of the book because the references were omitted from *Taking Sides*).

Question #8: Is Deception Being Used?

The previous discussion of the presentation of material and use of influence tactics assumes an attempt to persuade but not to deceive. Realistically, students must also learn to identify indications of deception in the presentation of information. The objective at this stage is to encourage skeptical evaluation of material, using critical thinking skills related to faulty generalization, oversimplification, and propaganda to identify potentially fraudulent uses of information. This objective dovetails with students' continued tendency to apply their knowledge of psychology to analyze the world around them. Given that one aspect of the debate in Issue #5, genetic explanations of ADHD, revolves around Faraone and Biederman's (2006) claim that Joseph (2006) neglected to cite relevant research, we show students how to use PsycINFO to investigate this assertion. Conclusions from this activity, as well as those accompanying previous critical thinking questions, can provide a spring-board for discussion of deception. This discussion is particularly relevant to Halonen et al.'s (2003) ethics domain where, before training, students tend to believe that most researchers are unethical: willing to falsify or twist their research in order to "prove" their theories. We also take this opportunity to talk about the many ways researchers attempt to maintain objectivity.

Question #9: Is Stereotyping or Ethnocentric Thinking Being Employed?

In considering stereotyping and ethnocentric thinking, the critical thinking guidelines transition again to question potential influences on the ways in which information is presented. This phase generates two interrelated objectives. One objective is to improve students' ability to identify assumptions about particular groups or stereotypes that individuals use in making assertions about behavior. A second, somewhat more person-ally threatening, objective is to encourage students to question the degree to which they use the standards of their nationality, religions, and cultural traditions to judge others. One approach to addressing these objectives is to present students with systematic, empirical information related to topics that represent alternatives to their reality. For example, one author (SO'D) works with a student population that is overwhelmingly homogenous: White, middle-class, and evangelical Christian. Although the University encourages critical thinking and acceptance, students' relative lack of experience with individuals from different cultures leads to high levels of ethnocentric thinking. Issues such as "Is drug addiction a choice?" (Issue #13), "Is treating homosexuality ethical?" (Issue #15), and "Is pornography harmful?" (Issue #18) typically require them to think about things outside their normal daily lives. Researching supporting and contradictory information in PsycINFO assures students that the articles were not cherry-picked for their sensationalism, exposing students to sources and topics with which they might not otherwise be engaging.

Assessment

Given the investment of time and energy required by this approach, the importance of assessment of learning outcomes is magnified. One assessment strategy is to require a written response related to each activity from the *Taking Sides* book. Because each student is at a different level of thinking, applying the standards from the basic level of Halonen et al.'s (2003) rubric will ensure minimum competence and provide feedback designed to stimulate a higher level of thinking than currently presented. Given those standards, we grade papers for the individual writing assignments at a "check, check-plus, check-minus" level. This pedagogical strategy parallels suggestions from Dunn (2006) regarding the need to increase the amount of writing assigned in psychology classes while not making the instructor's workload too onerous. A final written assignment assesses comprehensive critical thinking ability, applying a standard grading rubric including information about evidence of critical thinking along with other content areas. The task for that final paper can again draw upon the *Taking Sides* book, requiring students to select one issue, gather outside sources, and write a paper describing the evidence on each side of the issue and then, optionally, drawing conclusions.

Conclusion

Critical thinking is not a natural ability for every student, which creates both a challenge and an opportunity for psychology instructors. The Elaboration Likelihood Model (ELM) suggests that we can better position ourselves to take advantage of that opportunity by applying critical thinking skills to understand issues that are relevant to students' lives. Similarly, we can reduce the likelihood that we will overwhelm our students by utilizing a progressive strategy. The implementation discussed in this chapter is only one approach. Examples can be tailored to specific classes or psychological content areas, including using different volumes in the *Taking Sides* series or primary sources. The questions can be re-arranged and modified to fit an individual instructor's personal preferences. Assignments can be modified given the resources of individual instructors. Our approach is offered for inspiration, given our common interest in improving students' critical thinking skills.

References

American Academy of Pediatrics. (2000). *Joint statement on the impact of entertainment violence on children.* Congressional Public Health Summit, July 26, 2000. Retrieved 20 May, 2007, from http://www.aap.org/advocacy/releases/jstmtevc.htm

Brooks-Gunn, J., Han, W., & Waldfogel, J. (2006). Maternal employment and child cognitive outcomes in the first three years of life. In B. Slife (Ed.), *Taking sides: Clashing views on psychological issues* (14th ed., pp. 124–131). Dubuque, IA: McGraw-Hill.

Cook, A. J., Moore, K., & Steel, G. D. (2004). The taking of a position: A reinterpretation of the elaboration likelihood model. *Journal for the Theory of Social Behaviour, 34,* 315–331.

Dunn, D. S. (2006, January). *Teaching writing: Exercises and assessment methods for use across the psychology curriculum.* Presentation from 28th Annual National Institute on the Teaching of Psychology, St. Petersburg Beach, FL.

Faraone, S. V., & Biederman, J. (2006). Nature, nurture, and attention deficit hyperactivity disorder. In B. Slife (Ed.), *Taking sides: Clashing views on psychological issues* (14th ed., pp. 91–103). Dubuque, IA: McGraw-Hill.

Gardner, H. (2006). A multiplicity of intelligences. In B. Slife (Ed.), *Taking sides: Clashing views on psychological issues* (14th ed., pp. 184–190). Dubuque, IA: McGraw-Hill.

Gentile, D. A., & Anderson, C. A. (2006). Violent video games: The newest media violence hazard. In B. Slife (Ed.), *Taking sides: Clashing views on psychological issues* (14th ed., pp. 300–308). Dubuque, IA: McGraw-Hill.

Gottfredson, L. S. (2006). The general intelligence factor. In B. Slife (Ed.), *Taking sides: Clashing views on psychological issues* (14th ed., pp. 191–200). Dubuque, IA: McGraw-Hill.

Halonen, J. S., Bosack, T., Clay, S., & McCarthy M. (with Dunn, D. S., Hill, IV, G. W., et al.). (2003). A rubric for authentically learning, teaching, and assessing scientific reasoning in psychology. *Teaching of Psychology, 30,* 196–208.

Healy, D., & Whitaker, C. (2006). Antidepressants and suicide: Risk–benefit conundrums. In B. Slife (Ed.), *Taking sides: Clashing views on psychological issues* (14th ed., pp. 217–224). Dubuque, IA: McGraw-Hill.

Hetherington, E. M., & Kelly, J. (2006). For better or for worse. In B. Slife (Ed.), *Taking sides: Clashing views on psychological issues* (14th ed., pp. 149–154). Dubuque, IA: McGraw-Hill.

Joseph, J. (2006). Not in their genes: A critical view of the genetics of attention-deficit hyperactivity disorder. In B. Slife (Ed.), *Taking sides: Clashing views on psychological issues* (14th ed., pp. 77–90). Dubuque, IA: McGraw-Hill.

Olsen, C. K. (2006). Media violence research and youth violence data: Why do they conflict? In B. Slife (Ed.), *Taking sides: Clashing views on psychological issues* (14th ed., pp. 309–316). Dubuque, IA: McGraw-Hill.

Ruggiero, V. R. (2006). *Becoming a critical thinker* (5th ed.). Boston: Houghton Mifflin.

Slife, B. (Ed.). (2006). *Taking sides: Clashing views on psychological issues* (14th ed.). Dubuque, IA: McGraw-Hill.

Timimi, S., Moncrieff, J, Jureidini, J. et al. (2006). A critique of the international consensus statement. In B. Slife (Ed.), *Taking sides: Clashing views on psychological issues* (14th ed., pp. 210–213). Dubuque, IA: McGraw-Hill.

Using *Taking Sides*: Questions to ask when examining a position. (n.d.). Retrieved May 30, 2007, from http://www.dushkin.com/usingts/guide/ho01.mhtml

Vander Ven, T. M., Cullen, F. T., Carrozza, M. A., & Wright, J. P. (2006). Home alone: The impact of maternal employment on delinquency. In B. Slife (Ed.), *Taking sides: Clashing views on psychological issues* (14th ed., pp. 132–138). Dubuque, IA: McGraw-Hill.

Wade, C., & Tavris, C. (2005). *Invitation to psychology* (3rd ed.). Upper Saddle River, NJ: Pearson Education.

Wallerstein, J. S., & Lewis, J. M. (2006). The unexpected legacy of divorce: Report of a 25-year study. In B. Slife (Ed.), *Taking sides: Clashing views on psychological issues* (14th ed., pp. 142–148). Dubuque, IA: McGraw-Hill.

Wallerstein, J. S., Lewis, J. M., & Blakeslee, S. (2002). About the author. *The unexpected legacy of divorce: A 25-year landmark study.* Retrieved 19 April, 2007, from http://www.webheights.net/dividedheart/waller/uld.htm

Author Note

Correspondence concerning this chapter should be addressed to Susan L. O'Donnell, Department of Psychology, George Fox University, 414 N. Meridian St., #6155, Newberg, OR 97132. E-mail: sodonnell@georgefox.edu

Chapter 11

The Repertory Grid as a Heuristic Tool in Teaching Undergraduate Psychology

Joseph A. Mayo

Teaching courses in undergraduate psychology presents special challenges to even the most experienced educators. In addition to concerted efforts to cover a wide array of information in an organized and comprehensible fashion, instructors continually search for ways to promote higher-level learning while stimulating students' classroom participation and enthusiasm for the subject matter. As a vehicle for accomplishing these educational aims in the undergraduate psychology classroom, I use an innovative pedagogical strategy that effectively highlights dichotomous meaning dimensions within the parameters of George A. Kelly's (1955) *personal construct theory* (PCT) of personality. Kelly began his career as an engineer before becoming a clinical psychologist. Partly due to the fact that Kelly was not an eager self-publicist, his theory rarely qualifies as required reading outside of classes in both history and systems of psychology and personality theories. Although prominent psychological contemporaries, including Jerome Bruner (1956) and Carl Rogers (1956), have favorably reviewed Kelly's work, many general readers misinterpret the core features and direction of PCT and thereby offer conflicting interpretations of Kelly's work (Kenny, 1984). Biographical notes on Kelly's life and the underpinnings of his theory can be found in a collection of his papers edited by Maher (1969).

The basic tenet of PCT is that every human being acts as a "personal scientist" who anticipates and predicts events through unique psychological processes (Kelly, 1955). Paramount to these processes is a system of *personal constructs*, which Kelly defined as hierarchically linked sets of bipolar meaning dimensions (e.g., good–bad, easy–difficult, and relevant–irrelevant) that each person uses to organize and interpret the world. From his theory, Kelly derived a psychotherapeutic interview strategy called the *repertory grid technique* (RGT)—originally named the *role construct repertory test*—as an instrument for uncovering a patient's personal constructs with a minimum of therapist intervention and bias. In this method, the therapist functions as a facilitator who permits the patient to discover his or her own personal constructs. For example, using the RGT to explore a patient's personal relationships, Kelly might have focused attention on the self and "significant others" (e.g., family and friends) as elements (persons, objects, events, or problems that you wish to explore). Kelly would have then asked the patient to pair two of these elements in contrast with the third (e.g., "My friends and I are open to new challenges, whereas my parents are closed-minded people."). This process of triadic comparison and contrast leads the patient to elicit a bipolar construct (i.e., open to experience–closed to experience) without interference from the therapist.

Although Kelly initially formulated the RGT to elicit personal constructs in clinical settings, adaptations and applications of this technique have also been observed in classroom environments (e.g., Tobacyk, 1987). Not only are bipolar constructs an integral component of various texts that may be used in undergraduate psychology courses (see Lundin, 1996; Santrock, 2002), but it is also readily possible for instructors to formulate such meaning dimensions on their own. For example, in teaching abnormal psychology an instructor may introduce the following bipolar constructs to help students understand the definition of abnormal behavior: typicality–atypicality, functionality–dysfunctionality, social acceptability–social unacceptability, and cultural universality–cultural variability.

Drawing both from meaning dimensions embodied in the thematic content of textbooks and from self-generated bipolar constructs, I have used the RGT to facilitate learning in my undergraduate psychology classes. Although the RGT exists in various formats, one that I have found particularly useful involves a rating grid in which students rate each element via a Likert-type scale anchored by two construct poles. Based on previously published reports in which I systematically validated the pedagogical efficacy of RGT (Mayo, 2004a, 2004b), I will summarize the instructional methodology that I used in teaching both introductory life span development and history of psychology.

Life Span Developmental Psychology

In teaching life span development, I selected 10 leading representatives of 7 major developmental theories as the elements on which to focus my instruction (Mayo, 2004b). As selection criteria, I relied on key contributors to theoretical perspectives commonly identified across various life span development textbooks. The theories and corresponding contributors were ethological (Konrad Lorenz), contextual (Urie Bronfenbrenner), psychodynamic (Sigmund Freud and Erik Erikson), learning (B. F. Skinner and Albert Bandura), humanistic (Abraham Maslow), cognitive (Jean Piaget and Lawrence Kohlberg), and sociocultural (Lev Vygotsky). Applying the RGT, I devised bipolar constructs relative to important developmental issues: heredity–environment, continuity–discontinuity, stability–change, internality–externality, unidimensionality–multidimensionality, and testability–lack of testability. I lectured on these constructs at the start of the course and revisited them intermittently throughout the remainder of the semester. I obtained the first three constructs from developmental issues presented in Santrock's (2002) text, whereas I created the final three constructs on my own.

I instructed students to rate separately the positions of each developmental theorist on each bipolar construct. Employing a series of 7-point rating scales, students printed an

Table 11.1. Sample of a Student-Completed Grid

	Theorist: Sigmund Freud							
	Ratings							
	1	2	3	4	5	6	7	
1. heredity	–	X	–	–	–	–	–	environment
2. continuity	–	–	–	–	–	X	–	discontinuity
3. stability	X	–	–	–	–	–	–	change
4. internality	–	X	–	–	–	–	–	externality
5. unidimensionality	X	–	–	–	–	–	–	multidimensionality
6. testability	–	–	–	–	–	–	X	lack of testability

X on the corresponding line within each rating continuum that best matches the corresponding theorist's view. See Table 11.1 for a sample, student-completed grid pertaining to Sigmund Freud.

After completing a rating grid for each developmental theorist, I asked students to summarize the aggregate results of their rating-grid assignments by compiling a comprehensive matrix that categorized the perspectives of all 10 theorists. See Table 11.2 for a student-completed, comprehensive matrix.

I assigned both the individual ratings and the comprehensive matrix as take-home, paper-and-pencil assignments to be completed independently by each student. I then used the comprehensive matrices as focal points for a 75-minute, whole-class discussion at the conclusion of the semester. This discussion served to prepare students for success on a comprehensive final examination that emphasized salient similarities and differences among the targeted developmental theorists. To minimize the possibility of experimenter effects in composing and grading the final examination, I selected 50 multiple-choice questions from factually and conceptually based test-bank items, with greater emphasis on the latter.

History and Systems of Psychology

In reviewing the relevant literature, I uncovered a single anecdotal report on the application of the RGT in teaching history and systems of psychology. Tobacyk (1987) provided students with names of great figures throughout the history of psychology (elements that comprise the columns of the grid) and a teacher-generated list of bipolar meaning dimensions (constructs that comprise the rows of the grid) that he used to organize course content (e.g., conscious vs. unconscious). Afterward, he required students to evaluate each great figure with each bipolar construct in working, row-by-row, through the grid.

Borrowing from Tobacyk's (1987) prior classroom application of the RGT, I adapted his approach to teaching an introductory-level, historical foundations of psychology course offered in the form of a special-topics colloquium that met weekly for two, 50-min sessions

Table 11.2. Sample of a Student-Completed, Repertory Grid Matrix with Six, 7-Point Construct Continua

	Ratings							
	1	2	3	4	5	6	7	
1. heredity	L	F		M	P	E	Ba, Br, K, S	environment
2. continuity	Ba, L, S, V				M	E, F, K, P		discontinuity
3. stability	F, L						Ba, Br, E, K M, P, S, V	change
4. internality	K, L	F, P	M		Ba	E	Br, S, V	externality
5. unidimensionality	F, L, S	Br, K	P	E, M	Ba, V			multidimensionality
6. testability	Ba, L, S	Br, V	K, P				F, M	lack of testability

Note: Ba = Bandura, Br = Bronfenbrenner, E = Erikson, F = Freud, K = Kohlberg, L = Lorenz, M = Maslow, P = Piaget, S = Skinner, V = Vygotsky.

(Mayo, 2004a). Dividing the course into three instructional units, I generated a list of bipolar constructs on which students rated the positions of 24 preselected contributors (8 per unit) to philosophical/prescientific psychology (e.g., Aristotle, René Descartes, John Locke, and Immanuel Kant); the early years of scientific psychology (e.g., Wilhelm Wundt, William James, Sigmund Freud, and John B. Watson); and the chronological development of psychology's principal specialty areas over the past century (e.g., Kurt Lewin, Gordon Allport, Noam Chomsky, and Carl Rogers). Using Lundin's (1996) text as a frame of reference, I selected the first six constructs to represent deep-rooted issues in the intellectual history of psychology: mind–body, nature–nurture, subjectivism–objectivism, holism–elementalism, free will–determinism, and utility–purity. In contrast, I designed the final two constructs (verity–falsity and major contribution–minor contribution) in an attempt to ascertain students' subjective views of each contributor's work. In rating the degree of perceived truth embodied in each contributor's perspective, I asked students to consider the sociohistorical factors in which each contribution was made. In the case of major versus minor contribution, I asked students to assess each contributor's legacy to the historical evolution of psychology.

I asked students to rate the intellectual, philosophical, or theoretical stance of each contributor as take-home, paper-and-pencil assignments in each unit of the course. I employed a series of 11-point rating scales to allow students a wide range of variability in their rating choices. I required that students work independently in completing each assignment. In recording their construct-specific ratings on each grid, I asked students to print an X on the appropriate line within each rating continuum—somewhere between lines 1 and 11—that most closely approximates the perspective of each contributor.

Different from the more traditional application of the RGT as I described earlier in my life span development course, I also asked students to provide written justification for each of their construct ratings. In offering supporting rationale for their ratings, students became increasingly aware of the value of evidence-based conclusions over unsubstantiated opinions. Moreover, I allotted 30–45 mins for whole-class discussion immediately after students completed each of the three rating-grid assignments. During these discussions, students shared their analyses and critiqued their classmates' expressed views.

Implications for the Undergraduate Psychology Curriculum

Altogether, the learning outcomes that I have observed in my own undergraduate psychology classes (Mayo, 2004a, 2004b) suggest that the RGT, as the centerpiece of assessment in Kelly's PCT, is a practicable pedagogical strategy. Of benefit to both teachers and students, the RGT affords an overall framework from which to organize course content. Consistent with Tobacyk's (1987) conclusions in evaluating the instructional value of the RGT, the use of bipolar constructs "helps in achieving a more sophisticated level of understanding than that obtained by the mere memorization of material" (p. 111). In particular, the RGT encourages students to evaluate, compare, and contrast competing intellectual perspectives. When conjoined with opportunities for classroom discussion, the RGT also invites active participation in the learning process.

The broad range of bipolar meaning dimensions inherent in the subject matter of other psychology courses makes the RGT a promising heuristic tool across the undergraduate psychology curriculum. Repertory grid is especially well suited to those undergraduate courses, such as personality theories, where a list of bipolar constructs (e.g., rationality–irrationality and proactivity–reactivity) forms an integral part of available texts (e.g., Hjelle & Ziegler, 1992) and/or may be easily formulated by instructors, students, or both.

Accurately assessing students' conceptual systems is often difficult, time-consuming, and limited in scope (Fetherstonhaugh & Treagust, 1992). As a means for teachers to address these concerns, a well-conceived rubric built around the RGT can effectively communicate assessment criteria to students. A teacher can use such a rubric to more clearly articulate behavioral expectations, formative feedback, and the strengths and weaknesses of students' work (Allen, 2004).

Computer applications of the RGT are also available for classroom use in eliciting and assessing students' rating grids. After teaching students how to enter their own rating-grid data by means of user-friendly computer programs, computerized grid analysis may be used by teachers and learners alike to gain additional insights into students' conceptual systems—particularly in the absence of written and/or oral justifications of construct ratings. One such computer program is WebGrid III (Gaines & Shaw, 2005), a cost-free, web-based implementation of the RGT. Using a sample grid associated with contributors to the early decades of scientific psychology (completed for extra credit by a student in my historical foundations of psychology colloquium), I will demonstrate the outcomes of webGrid III grid elicitation and interpretation. Since this example involves eight bipolar constructs on which eight contributors (elements) are rated on 11-point continua, Figure 11.1 illustrates an 8 × 8 × 11 rating-grid display.

Using the data set depicted in Figure 11.1, WebGrid III permits different grid-analysis possibilities, obtained from both cluster analysis and principal-components analysis procedures. As shown in Figure 11.2, the cluster-analysis technique (named FOCUS

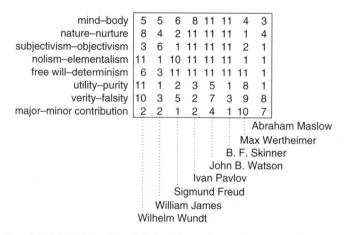

mind–body	5	5	6	8	11	11	4	3
nature–nurture	8	4	2	11	11	11	1	4
subjectivism–objectivism	3	6	1	11	11	11	2	1
nolism–elementalism	11	1	10	11	11	11	1	1
free will–determinism	6	3	11	11	11	11	11	1
utility–purity	11	1	2	3	5	1	8	1
verity–falsity	10	3	5	2	7	3	9	8
major–minor contribution	2	2	1	2	4	1	10	7

Abraham Maslow
Max Wertheimer
B. F. Skinner
John B. Watson
Ivan Pavlov
Sigmund Freud
William James
Wilhelm Wundt

Figure 11.1. Sample WebGrid III Data Display. From Gaines, B. R., & Shaw, M. L. G. (2005). WebGrid III [Computer program]. Alberta, Canada: Knowledge Science Institute. Available at the following URL: http://tiger.cpsc.ucalgary.ca/.

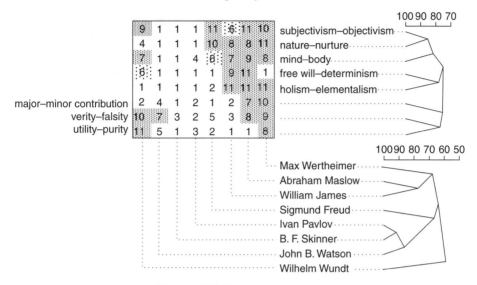

Figure 11.2. Sample WebGrid III FOCUS Clustering. From Gaines, B. R., & Shaw, M. L. G. (2005). WebGrid III [Computer program]. Alberta, Canada: Knowledge Science Institute. Available at the following URL: http://tiger.cpsc.ucalgary.ca/.

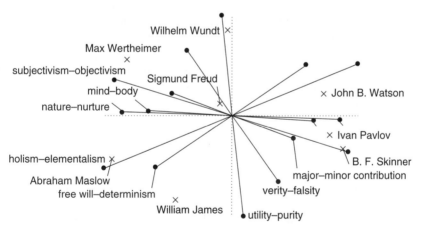

Figure 11.3. Sample WebGrid III PrinCom Map. From Gaines, B. R., & Shaw, M. L. G. (2005). WebGrid III [Computer program]. Alberta, Canada: Knowledge Science Institute. Available at the following URL: http://tiger.cpsc.ucalgary.ca/.

Clustering) not only permits inferences to be drawn on whether two constructs are applied similarly to different elements, but it also compares how different elements are rated on the same constructs.

Figure 11.3 shows the results of a principal components analysis (called PrinCom Map), which plots the constructs and elements in providing a visual overview of how they relate to one other.

As a versatile assessment tool, the RGT can be used not only to "provide snapshots of construct systems at a given point in time" (Winer & Vazquez-Abad, 1997, p. 366), but also to assess changes in dynamically evolving conceptions across time. In examining evidence of students' conceptual change, it may prove useful to link this information to Carey's (1985) distinction between *weak restructuring* and *strong restructuring* of a person's conceptual systems over time. In weak restructuring, students make new connections between/among new concepts that already exist in their long-term memories. In contrast, students change their core conceptions when engaging in strong restructuring.

It is also possible for teachers to vary intended learning outcomes through variations in the adopted RGT format. In place of a *provided construct form* of the grid, where the teacher supplies students with a list of bipolar constructs on which to rate predetermined elements, educators may choose to employ an *elicited construct form* of the RGT (Bannister & Mair, 1968), in which students themselves generate and apply constructs, with or without instructor prompting. For instance, students may begin by assessing the perspective of a single psychological contributor for whom they have generated a series of constructs in the form of short-phrase descriptions (*emergent poles*) and their bipolar opposites (*implicit poles*). By repeating this process with other contributors, students can create an anchoring point from which to compare and contrast the views of an increasingly wider range of individuals. This RGT strategy resembles the concept known as *laddering*, which is a platform for deeper construct elicitation involving the evaluation, modification, and interconnection of ideas. Depending on an instructor's preferences, students can work through this process either individually or in small groups, subsequently submitting their responses to the entire class for peer feedback. As Tobacyk (1987) noted in using the elicited construct form of the RGT in teaching history and systems of psychology, this strategy assumes greater student familiarity with course content. This approach can also help students to develop creative and evaluative skills that can generalize beyond the confines of the course assignment in question.

References

Allen, M. J. (2004). *The use of scoring rubrics for assessment and teaching*. Available from Mary J. Allen, Director, Institute for Teaching and Learning, California State University, 401 Golden Shore, 6th Floor, Long Beach, CA 90802-4210.

Bannister, D., & Mair, J. M. M. (1968). *The evaluation of personal constructs*. London: Academic Press.

Bruner, J. S. (1956). A cognitive theory of personality: You are your constructs. *Contemporary Psychology, 1*, 355–357.

Carey, S. (1985). *Conceptual change in children*. Cambridge, MA: MIT Press.

Fetherstonhaugh, T., & Treagust, D. F. (1992). Students' understanding of light and its properties: Teaching to engender conceptual change. *Science Education, 76*, 653–672.

Gaines, B. R., & Shaw, M. L. G. (2005). WebGrid III [Computer program]. Alberta, Canada: Knowledge Science Institute. Retrieved December 7, 2007, from http://tiger.cpsc.ucalgary.ca/

Hjelle, L. A., & Ziegler, D. J. (1992). *Personality theories: Basic assumptions, research, and applications* (3rd ed.). New York: McGraw-Hill.

Kelly, G. A. (1955). *The psychology of personal constructs* (Vols. 1–2). New York: Norton.

Kenny, V. (1984). An introduction to the personal construct theory of George A. Kelly. *Irish Journal of Psychotherapy, 3*, 24–32.

Lundin, R. W. (1996). *Theories and systems of psychology* (5th ed.). Lexington, MA: Heath.

Maher, B. (Ed.). (1969). *Clinical psychology and personality: The selected papers of George Kelly.* New York: Wiley.

Mayo, J. A. (2004a). A pilot investigation of the repertory grid as a heuristic tool in teaching historical foundations of psychology. *Constructivism in the Human Sciences, 9*, 31–41.

Mayo, J. A. (2004b). Repertory grid technique as a means of comparing and contrasting developmental theories. *Teaching of Psychology, 31*, 178–180.

Rogers, C. R. (1956). Intellectual psychotherapy. *Contemporary Psychology, 1*, 357–358.

Santrock, J. W. (2002). *Life-span development* (8th ed.). Boston: McGraw-Hill.

Tobacyk, J. J. (1987). Using personal construct theory in teaching history and systems of psychology. *Teaching of Psychology, 14*, 111–112.

Winer, L. R., & Vazquez-Abad, J. (1997). Repertory grid technique in the diagnosis of learner difficulties and the assessment of conceptual change in physics. *Journal of Constructivist Psychology, 10*, 363–386.

Author Note

Send correspondence to Joseph A. Mayo, Professor of Psychology, Division of Business and Social Science, Gordon College, 419 College Drive, Barnesville, GA 30204; e-mail: joe_m@gdn.edu; telephone: 770-358-5004.

Chapter 12

Critical Thinking in Critical Courses: Principles and Applications

Janet E. Kuebli, Richard D. Harvey, and James H. Korn

Becoming a critical thinker is no simple task. It does not happen in a flash, overnight, or even in a 15-week semester. A college diploma does not guarantee that its bearer became a good critical thinker. Certainly, particular habits of mind or dispositions may enable some people to become critical thinkers more readily than others. In most cases, however, learning critical thinking takes time, practice, and deliberate effort from both students and their teachers. Nevertheless, most people agree that critical thinking (CT) is an essential educational objective for all students, beginning in the primary grades through the college years and beyond. If you are reading this book you probably also agree that fostering CT in your classroom is worthwhile.

Despite the widespread and positive buzz among educators, employers, and policy makers about the merits of CT, college students often fail even to recognize when they are engaging in CT. One of us (Kuebli) asked psychology majors in a capstone course to define CT. Many of them defined it as any kind of thinking that required effort. One student described using CT in the split second it took him to brake before slamming into the car ahead of him. Several students reported doing CT while walking to class or on their cell phones. Another student commented that she was usually "in bed either right before I fall asleep or when I wake up and don't have to get out of bed. Also in class especially if I'm not interested in the class." For the most part, these psychology majors did not understand CT as a complex construct that includes examining multiple perspectives, reasoning logically, and evaluating evidence about ideas or claims for the purpose of changing beliefs or taking actions.

Certainly there is more than one way to provide CT instruction. Two general approaches are implicit and explicit (Gray, 1993). More implicit approaches guide students through discussions and activities that are designed to infuse and elicit critical thinking without drawing attention to the thinking processes themselves. The Socratic method of questioning, for example, could be used in this way. More explicit approaches add instruction about CT itself, and support students' metacognitive awareness and monitoring of their own thinking processes. A basic premise of this chapter is that explicit teaching about CT can help college students to become better critical thinkers. By focusing directly on CT, teachers help students to clarify their naïve misconceptions about CT and enhance transfer of CT to endeavors outside the classroom. To that end, we present a framework to help instructors achieve these goals.

At the college level, we also recommend that programs intentionally distribute CT instruction across the psychology major curriculum. Teaching CT in general psychology can provide a foundation upon which students progressively build these skills as they work through their courses, culminating in capstone courses. We provide some illustrations of this strategy as employed at our own institution in psychology courses taken at different points in our curriculum.

Learning to teach CT is also challenging. This book provides many examples of activities that involve students in CT, ways to assess that thinking, and programs to encourage it. Instructors often learn to teach this skill by reading, planning, attending teaching workshops, and by trial-and-error in the classroom. But are there better ways whereby teachers can learn to teach critical thinking? We begin by describing a graduate course on the teaching of psychology that strives to achieve this, followed by a description of a framework for teaching CT. Although our experiences are as teachers of undergraduate and graduate students, we believe that the principle of helping students to become more aware of when they are thinking critically may also be extended to primary and secondary classrooms. Finally, we describe several CT assignments we have used successfully in different college classes we teach.

Learning to Teach Critical Thinking

One of us (Korn) has taught many aspiring college teachers about the art and science of teaching psychology for over 35 years. In his course—The Teaching of Psychology—the first major activity is the writing of a teaching philosophy (Korn, 2004). Students write a series of drafts, with peer review, and continue to revise the statement as the class works on other elements of teaching. In many such statements, students write something like: "I want my students to think critically about psychology."

Next students work on developing a syllabus for a course they expect to teach. The selected course may be general psychology, more intermediate courses like social psychology or child development, or a more advanced topical seminar or capstone course. The most challenging part of this activity is stating the course objectives in a way that will be useful for deciding what methods to use and how to assess learning. And again, "think critically about psychology" appears often as an objective.

Then students look at how the design will be implemented in the teaching methods and assessment. Here new teachers often talk about the style and content of their lectures, but all of us know that lectures are not as effective as other methods for promoting thinking (Bligh, 2000). How can we do better to achieve the objective of helping beginning teachers learn to teach CT? We can start by providing thought-provoking readings and opportunities to practice critical thinking, and through modeling.

Reading

There are several good textbooks for the beginning teacher of psychology. Forsyth's *The Professor's Guide to Teaching* (2003) is one that we recommend. A quick survey of eight books on teaching psychology showed how their authors addressed CT. All these books recommended involving students using discussion, writing, and other methods. Two books had separate chapters on teaching thinking; four books had sections on thinking in various places in their texts. There are also entire books on CT, including those by Halpern (1996) and Smith (2002). Especially impressive is a book by Svinicki (2004), *Learning and Motivation in the Post-Secondary Classroom,* which provides an extensive application of cognitive psychology principles to student learning with clear, useful examples. Many experts on CT have also written articles on the topic.

Thinking

Class discussions of assigned readings about critical thinking are a starting point for demystifying this otherwise fuzzy concept that people endorse readily yet so superficially. Good discussion will also get aspiring teachers to think critically about their philosophy and course design. These must be considered together because the course design is the philosophy one puts into practice. "What do you mean when you say that you want your students to think critically about psychology?" is the stimulus question. This is an old question for some readers, but new to beginning teachers. Generating their own preliminary definitions of CT is a useful early group activity. Students can usually produce something similar to the definitions they will read more about later. These aspiring student teachers thus also practice critical thinking about CT. This technique is used throughout the course in order to develop teachers who can critically evaluate perspectives and empirical evidence on CT teaching strategies.

Next, this definition gets translated into course objectives, and eventually into objectives for individual units of the course. Student teachers learn about the cognitive taxonomy, originally outlined by Bloom, Engelhart, Furst, Hill, and Krathwohl (1956). Bloom et al.'s well-known Taxonomy of Educational Objectives included a hierarchy of thinking processes. Three lower level thinking skills—knowing, comprehending, and applying—formed the foundation for three higher level skills: analyzing, synthesizing, and evaluating. In recent years, Bloom's model has been revised by Anderson and Krathwohl (2001). Bloom's work also underlies the framework we will present shortly. One of the interesting things that student teachers discover is that critical thinking is not a formal item in most taxonomies, although the elements are certainly there. That means teachers must synthesize the individual elements into something that fulfills their own definitions of critical thinking before they can specify course and unit objectives.

The true test for students who aspire to teach CT comes when they actually teach. During our Teaching of Psychology course, each student is required to "guest teach" two class periods in a regularly scheduled course, usually one offered by their teaching mentor. They design a teaching module that includes objectives for those two classes. If CT is an objective, as is so often the case, then we want to see critical thinking happening, for example in small group discussion or in-class writing.

Modeling

Another assignment is to have students observe experienced teachers, and talk with those teachers about their philosophy and practice. Observation of experienced teachers, whether good or poor in terms of teaching critical thinkers, helps the aspiring teacher ask whether CT was a course objective and, if so, how it was accomplished and assessed. Not all teachers have good answers to those questions. One need not be a graduate student in a teaching of psychology class to use these strategies. Experienced teachers who want to develop and/or improve their teaching of CT also can use reading, thinking, and modeling.

Barriers

There are several barriers that must be overcome if one is to be a teacher of critical thinking. Three of these are the lecture habit, cognitive laziness, and the curse of covering. Many teachers think of teaching as lecturing, so that is what they do. However, a large body of research (Bligh, 2000) shows that other methods are better than lecturing for teaching thinking, including the specific skills that constitute critical thinking. According to Bligh, teaching students to think requires that students be put in situations where they have to answer questions, analyze and critique perspectives, and solve problems. Compared to lecture, other methods such as discussion give students considerably more practice in the testing of their own thoughts which is essential for the development of CT.

Teachers also need to resist their students' natural tendencies toward cognitive laziness. Most students expect teachers to give them facts and entertain them, and do not at first like thinking activities. Critical thinking, as already noted, is hard work. Helping students understand what distinguishes CT from other kinds of thinking can help justify the hard work we seek from them.

Finally, many teachers feel compelled to "cover content." Teaching critical thinking can be more time-consuming than other teaching techniques. It takes time to explore with students multiple perspectives on a topic, to comprehend evidence for and against claims and to critically evaluate those claims, or to creatively synthesize evidence to formulate novel insights or implications. Since a semester is finite, teaching always involves trade-offs. The curse of covering all the textbook chapters can steer instructors away from teaching CT. Alternatively, if we take time to help students learn to think critically, we may have to forego the chapter on psychotherapies or on social development.

The Critical Thinking Pedagogical Framework

Given its status as a "mystified" concept (Halonen, 1995), CT means different things to different people. Despite considerable similarity and overlap among experts, different definitions abound (see Table 12.1). What matters most is that instructors individually and collectively grapple with the concept of CT. Each of us is a better teacher when we engage in a critically informed process of understanding different views of what constitutes CT and how to teach it. The Critical Thinking Pedagogical Framework described next is the product of such thinking by one of us (Harvey).

The CT Pedagogical Framework, shown in Table 12.2, illustrates the relationships between three pedagogical elements: academic skills, critical thinking abilities, and instructional methodologies across the curriculum. *Academic skills* are listening, reading, writing, and speaking. These skills coincide with the work output that is normally required for the assessment of student learning (e.g., assignment, exams).

Table 12.1. Defining Critical Thinking

Many writers have proposed their own definitions of critical thinking (CT). A sampling includes the following:

Smith (2002, p. 2): "a logical and rational process of avoiding one's preconceptions by gathering evidence, contemplating and evaluating alternatives, and coming to a conclusion."

Bensley (1998, p. 5): "reflective thinking involving the evaluation of evidence relevant to some claim so that a sound conclusion can be drawn about the claim."

Ennis (1989, p. 4): "reasonable, reflective thinking that is focused on deciding what to believe or do."

Halpern (1996, p. 5): "the use of those cognitive skills or strategies that increase the probability of a desirable outcome. It is used to describe thinking that is purposeful, reasoned, and goal-directed—the kind of thinking involved in solving problems, formulating inferences, calculating likelihoods, and making decisions when the thinker is using skills that are thoughtful and effective for the particular context and type of thinking tasks."

Simon & Kaplan (as cited in Halpern, 1996, p. 5): "the formation of logical inferences."

Stahl & Stahl (as cited in Halpern, 1996, p. 5): "the development of cohesive and logical reasoning patterns."

Moore & Parker (as cited in Halpern, 1996, p. 5): "the careful and deliberate determination of whether to accept, reject or suspend judgment."

McPeck (1981, p. 8): "a propensity and skill to engage in an activity with reflective skepticism."

Jakoubek (1995, p. 57): "an active and systematic attempt to understand and validate arguments."

Kurfiss (1988, p. 2): "an investigation whose purpose is to explore a situation, phenomenon, question, or problem to arrive at a hypothesis or conclusion about it that integrates all available information and that can therefore be convincingly justified. In critical thinking, all assumptions are open to question, divergent views are aggressively sought, and the inquiry is not biased in favor of a particular outcome."

Brookfield (1987, p. 1): "calling into question the assumptions underlying our customary, habitual ways of thinking and acting and then being ready to think and act differently on the basis of this critical questioning."

Apps (1985, p. 151): "emancipatory learning ... that which frees people for personal, institutional, or environmental forces that prevent them from seeing new directions, from gaining control of their lives, their society and their world."

Table 12.2. The Critical Thinking Pedagogical Framework

Academic skills	Critical thinking abilities	Instructional methodologies
Listening	Remembering	Defining concepts
Reading	Analysis	Reasoning elements
Writing	Comprehension	Concept mapping
Speaking	Application	Systems thinking
	Inferring	
	Evaluation	
	Synthesizing	

Critical thinking abilities refer to the person's thinking competencies. These abilities correspond closely to what Bloom and others consider CT skills, although the order in which we present them is not identical. *Remembering* refers to basic abilities of recognition and recall memory. *Comprehension* goes beyond remembering since it entails summarizing or restating others' ideas in one's own words, thus implying a deeper and more personalized state of knowledge. As in most CT models, *application* ranges from simply using existing knowledge in familiar situations to recognizing when prior knowledge can be used in a novel situation. *Analysis* requires taking ideas or claims apart, examining the individual components, and understanding their relationship to each other and to other ideas. In our model, we add the ability to *infer*, which entails reasoning in order to draw meaning or conclusions from evidence. *Evaluation* means that claims or ideas are appraised in light of evidence of some sort. *Synthesizing* is the highest ability in our framework, which Anderson and Krathwohl (2001) refer to as the ability to "create." When we synthesize, we reorganize or refashion the knowledge we start with into something novel and fresh.

Instructional methodologies are the strategies, tools, and techniques that instructors use to increase students' capacities for critical thought. These are the tools and techniques that students must be taught to use. They must be illustrated and modeled by instructors both during lectures and in class discussions. Furthermore, students must be held accountable for using them in both in-class and out-of-class assignments. Such methodologies should entail both discipline-specific and more generic universal techniques. For example, encouraging students to speculate on how dispositional and situational factors interact to determine behavior across all theories would be an example of a more discipline-specific (i.e., social psychology) technique. Requiring students to produce argument analyses would be an example of a generic universal technique that could be used regardless of course content. Some more generic universal examples are listed in Table 12.2, but certainly many more methods would qualify.

This framework illustrates the interdependencies between instructional methods, critical thinking, and skill assessments. At the classroom level, the framework can be used as a pedagogical tool for the instructor and as a metacognitive "map" for the student. To use it as a pedagogical tool requires the instructor to think first about the level of critical thinking appropriate for the course. The instructor must then choose those instructional methods and tools that will develop the students' capacity for critical thinking *at that level*. Finally, the instructor chooses course activities, assignments, and exam formats that will engage the student in listening, reading, writing, and speaking, and also allow for assessment of the desired level of critical thought demonstrated by these skills.

Providing the framework to students will make salient the CT abilities that the course seeks to help them develop and help them better understand the reasons they are asked to demonstrate particular academic skills. Students generally expect their courses to require listening, reading, writing, and occasionally, speaking. However, they are not generally aware of the degree to which these skills *reflect* the capacity for critical thought. The framework can be used to explicitly point out the connection between the instructional methods of the course and the development of these important critical thinking abilities. Furthermore, it can help students see the connection between these critical thinking abilities and the various activities and skill assessments of the course. Thus the framework can support students' navigation between the instruction and the assessment in the course.

At the program level, various courses can be ordered according to the level of critical thinking abilities that are emphasized. Typically, lower level courses in the program, which emphasize breadth of exposure, tend to require one or more basic levels of critical thinking abilities (e.g., remembering, comprehension). In general psychology, for example, simply introducing the critical thinking abilities, thereby giving students a vocabulary for thinking about critical thinking, may be the essential objective. Teachers may then inform students that their job is to demonstrate their ability to recall and comprehend each of the critical thinking abilities. Assignments in courses immediately following general psychology may emphasize developing students' capacities for a single critical thinking ability (e.g., analysis or inferring). The highest level courses, which typically emphasize depth, can require relatively more complex and sophisticated critical thinking abilities (e.g., evaluation, synthesis), often in combination.

Curriculum-mapping techniques (e.g., Harden, 2001) help track critical thinking instruction across classes in the major. Courses can be programmed according to the complexity of critical thought involved and assessed. Programmatically mapping CT in this way has multiple advantages. First, CT instruction can be deliberately sequenced in a more developmentally meaningful and appropriate fashion. For example, we put the cart before the horse if we direct students to evaluate and synthesize knowledge claims before they are able to comprehend or analyze those same claims. Mapping also reveals gaps and duplications in CT instruction across courses. Thus instructors who require critical analysis and inference may mistakenly assume that their colleagues are teaching the other critical thinking abilities of evaluation and synthesis. In the absence of programmatic assessment of CT, we may not recognize that certain critical thinking abilities are neglected in our curriculum. Coordinating CT instruction across classes can also permit instructors to reinforce each other's teaching. We can help students understand how CT exercises in lower level classes were designed to transfer to or contribute to more demanding assignments in higher level classes.

Ideas for CT Teaching in Two Different Kinds of Courses

Teaching CT in Social Psychology

Social psychology is a mid-level course within the psychology curriculum at our institution and regularly taught by one of us (Harvey). Right from the start, students are explicitly told that the objective of the course is twofold: (a) to introduce them to the various topics of social psychology, and (b) teach them how to think critically about those topics. Students are handed the framework (see Table 12.2) on the first or second day of class. The course actually involves some of all the levels of critical thinking; but those CT abilities most emphasized are comprehension, application, and analysis. To begin the process of meta-reflection, the instructor uses the framework to review how the various critical thinking tools that will be used through the semester should enhance the student's capacity for comprehension, application, and analysis of the material. The instructor also reviews how activities, assignments, and exams will involve and assess students' capacity for the three critical thinking abilities.

Specific examples of some of the "tools" used to develop students' ability to engage in analysis and comprehension include Paul and Elder's (2001) "Eight Elements of Reasoning" and Harvey's (2004) "Four Ways of Defining a Construct." These tools are both integrated into the classroom lectures of the instructor and required in assignments. An important tool that emphasizes application requires students to complete and reflect on scales used by social psychologists (e.g., self-esteem, sex role attitudes). Another important application tool requires students to work in groups to design a persuasive advertisement (or political campaign) based around what is perhaps the most famous model of attitudes and persuasion (i.e., "The Elaboration Likelihood Model"; see Petty & Cacioppo, 1984). In lieu of a lecture, the students wrestle with understanding the contingencies of the persuasion model, so as to be able to apply it. Finally, the class votes on the best presentation when teams present their advertisement or campaign to the class. Thus a variety of tools exercise the CT abilities highlighted in the class.

Students are explicitly told which CT abilities are involved in the assessments (i.e., assignments and exams). Each assignment includes an explicit statement of which CT abilities are involved. Also, the complexity of the CT abilities assessed in the exams progresses over the semester. That is, the first exams focus primarily on recalling concepts, whereas later exams focus primarily on applying and analyzing the concepts.

Teaching CT in a Capstone Course

In architectural circles, "capstone" refers to the top stone that completes a building. Capstone courses are usually designed to top off and integrate psychology majors' course-work. The capacity to engage in effective and more or less independent critical thinking in a capstone course should be the "crowning achievement" of students' studies as psychology majors.

Perlman and McCann, in a 1999 survey of undergraduate psychology departments, reported that 63% had a capstone requirement. At some colleges, capstones are advanced psychology senior seminars. These are often "issues-based" capstones in which readings and discussions cut across typical course boundaries. Other programs strive for integration through study of the history of psychology, with student research projects, or through field practica or internships. Presumably all of these capstones can be taught so as to nurture CT.

One of us (Kuebli) teaches a different kind of capstone course called Critical Thinking About Psychology. The class typically enrolls seniors whose plans do not include becoming a psychologist. Instead, some aspire to careers in law, medicine, social work, education, or business while for others the Bachelor's degree will be their first and last stop in postsecondary education. Many express academic burnout and the fervent desire to "get on with it," by which they mean their real lives. Usually, the students are as bright as (or brighter than) the majors going on to graduate programs in psychology. However, teaching this group poses unique challenges because they do not automatically see how psychology figures in their future endeavors. These considerations influenced the aims of the course.

The course has two main elements. About one-third of the course is devoted to lectures, readings, and class discussions related to what psychologists think about critical thinking. Thus the class takes an explicit approach to CT instruction. Students first contrast their preconceptions about CT with experts' definitions (see Table 12.1). We also contrast CT with other related constructs, including wisdom, common-sense, and street smarts. They generate their own lists of people they admire as critical thinkers and justify their selections in terms of the individual abilities that constitute critical thinking. We discuss different perspectives on the development of CT (e.g., trait vs. habit), including Perry's (1970) stage theory of reflective thinking, which students find thought-provoking. They also review psychological evidence pertaining to the implications of language use and memory for critical thought. Additionally, we examine psychological explanations for a variety of critical thinking errors and fallacies (e.g., fundamental attribution error, intervention-causation fallacy; see Ross, 1977). Students practice identifying fallacies and pseudoscience in newspaper articles and on Internet sites. Ideally, this explicit focus on CT reinforces critical thinking lessons in prior courses. This instruction further serves as a backdrop for the remaining two-thirds of the course which emphasizes application of critical thinking to team projects involving problem-solving.

The project problems are of the sort students may encounter after graduation in the so-called "real world"—on the job, in their communities, or in their personal relationships. Durso (1997) described projects in which students applied psychological theory and methods to real problems generated by local businesses. Similarly, this class requires that students assemble the distinct CT skills acquired in prior courses—such as the social psychology course described above—in the service of a complex problem in the world. According to Halpern (1998), CT learning does not readily transfer to new tasks and situations, especially when taught more implicitly. Reminding students that they are applying what they are learning about doing CT to real-world problems helps them to practice transferring those abilities to contexts outside the classroom. Additionally, the use of real-world problems helps students connect psychology in the classroom with the field's potential to help solve problems they may encounter after graduation.

Specifically, their projects must target ill-defined problems, those for which "correct answers" are not immediately discernable. Moreover, the problems must involve prescriptive issues. Prescriptive issues can often be stated in terms of a "Should we do x or should we do y?" question. In past semesters, for example, students critically examined whether or not the legal age of driving should be increased to 18 and whether recess should be eliminated in elementary schools. Prescriptive issues are characterized by competing values and multiple stakeholders, and therefore lend themselves to more than one solution (Browne & Keeley, 2007). Solutions to the project problems therefore typically "depend" on a host of factors. The primary task for students is to seek out and comprehend multiple perspectives on a prescriptive issue, and to identify and weigh relevant empirical evidence in the psychological literature that can inform their understanding of the problem and its possible solutions. Finally, students are charged with the task of generating their own "best" collective solution.

In this class, it is important that the project is an active, inquiry-style group learning activity in order to challenge students' assumptions that CT is always a solitary thinking endeavor. Since the projects call for collaborative CT, we take class time to discuss their group project gripes and techniques for more effective teamwork. We also review strategies for building critically informed and reasoned consensus, such as discussing roles, permitting everyone to express their view, checking for consensus, listening, and using conflict resolution techniques.

A brief overview of the capstone project follows. Students begin by individually finding newspaper articles on prescriptive psychology-related topics and issues (e.g., whether or not personality tests should be used in personnel hiring decisions, or whether high impact sports should be encouraged or discouraged in youth). Students assigned to teams then pool articles, select topics, and get instructor approval before proceeding. The next step is to demonstrate comprehension of the core issue by writing a problem statement abstract. The team then gathers empirical evidence related to the problem, thus ensuring that students can link their topic to psychology. This important step also orients them to the objective of recommending scientifically informed solutions.

Teams also conduct interviews with people from the community who are affected by the problem or involved in its solutions. This activity increases the likelihood that students will encounter perspectives other than their own and usually awakens them to the true complexity of the issue at hand. After analyzing and evaluating the evidence they have collected from the empirical literature and their interviews, students form inferences, apply knowledge, synthesize new solutions, and reach consensus about the wisest solution or course of action. Specifically, at the end of the semester, they formulate a scientifically grounded action plan. They produce a team poster summarizing the problem and their recommendations. These posters are proudly displayed at our annual departmental undergraduate symposium, and symposium judges' ratings become part of our annual departmental assessment. Students also submit an individually written report that is assessed in terms of its demonstration of their ability to consider multiple perspectives and detect fallacies in those perspectives, to think logically and use evidence, to synthesize novel solutions, and to communicate clearly.

The role of the capstone instructor is that of facilitator, consultant, and cheerleader. Essentially, the instructor serves as "metacognitive" ally and coach. This is appropriate in a capstone course where students' own active learning efforts should be center stage. Typically, the challenges of teaching include managing senior burnout, countering passive learning habits, helping teams make their projects more concrete, empowering students to be more resourceful, and managing team dynamics. By the end of the semester, students comment on how their initial assumptions about their topics were challenged and how dramatically their thinking has changed.

This capstone experience presents students with complex situations in which they must actively contribute to teaching themselves as well as others about how to create practical solutions to novel, real-world problems. The project strives to exercise and showcase critical thinking abilities first acquired and later fine-tuned in lessons from prior classes. The instructor, critically informed about critical thinking, scaffolds the entire project, but then stands back to await (and hopefully applaud) the final products of everyone's hard work.

Conclusions

We presented a framework for how critical thinking can be taught across the psychology curriculum. We have argued, perhaps implicitly, that teachers of critical thinking must first be taught to be critical thinkers themselves. Furthermore, they should be taught how to teach the subject. To assist in this latter endeavor, we have provided the Critical Thinking Pedagogical Framework as a potential guide for structuring instruction in critical thinking. Finally, we illustrated how critical thinking instruction might progress from lower level to higher-level critical core courses across the psychology curriculum. We argue that critical thinking is an essential mediator between what teachers do in the classroom and true academic achievement on the part of students. Thus seeing the connection between instructional methodologies and critical thinking competencies should be of paramount importance for teachers.

References

Anderson, L. W., & Krathwohl, D. R. (2001). *A taxonomy for learning, teaching, and assessing: A revision of Bloom's taxonomy of educational objectives.* New York: Longman.

Apps, J. W. (1985). *Improving practice in continuing education: Modern approaches for understanding the field and determining priorities.* San Francisco: Jossey-Bass.

Bensley, D. A. (1998). *Critical thinking in psychology: A unified skills approach.* Belmont, CA: Thomson Brooks/Cole Publishing Co.

Bligh, D. A. (2000). *What's the use of lectures?* San Francisco: Jossey-Bass.

Bloom, B. S. (Ed.), Engelhart, M. D., Furst, E. J., Hill, W. H., & Krathwohl, D. R. (1956). *Taxonomy of educational objectives: Handbook I: Cognitive domain.* New York: David McKay.

Brookfield, S. D. (1987). *Developing critical thinkers: Challenging adults to explore alternative ways of thinking and acting.* San Francisco: Jossey-Bass.

Browne, N., & Keeley, S. (2007). *Asking the right questions: A guide to critical thinking.* Upper Saddle River, NJ: Prentice Hall.

Durso, F. T. (1997). Corporate-sponsored undergraduate research as a capstone experience. *Teaching of Psychology, 24,* 54–56.

Ennis, R. H. (1989). Critical thinking and subject specificity: Clarification and needed research. *Educational Researcher, 18,* 13–16.

Forsyth, D. R. (2003). *The professor's guide to teaching: Psychological principles and practices.* Washington, DC: American Psychological Association.

Gray, P. (1993). Engaging students' intellects: The immersion approach to critical thinking in psychology instruction. *Teaching of Psychology, 20,* 68–74.

Halonen, J. S. (1995). Demystifying critical thinking. *Teaching of Psychology, 22,* 75–81.

Halpern, D. F. (1996). *Thought and knowledge: An introduction to critical thinking* (3rd ed.). Mahwah, NJ: Erlbaum.

Halpern, D. F. (1998). Teaching critical thinking for transfer across domains: Dispositions, skills, structure training, and metacognitive monitoring. *American Psychologist, 53,* 449–455.

Harden, R. M. (2001). Curriculum mapping: A tool for transparent and authentic teaching and learning. (AMEE Guide No. 21). *Medical Teacher, 23*(2), 123–137.

Harvey, R. D. (2004). *Four ways to define anything.* Unpublished manuscript, Department of Psychology, Saint Louis University, Saint Louis, MO.

Jakoubek, J. (1995). Developing critical-thinking skills in psychology content courses. *Teaching of Psychology, 22*(1), 57–59.

Korn, J. H. (2004). Writing a philosophy of teaching. In W. Buskist, V. W. Hevern, B. K. Saville, & T. Zinn (Eds.), *Essays from e-xcellence in teaching, 2003* (Chap. 7). Retrieved November 28, 2007 from the Society for the Teaching of Psychology Web site, http://teachpsych.org/resources/e-books/eit2003/eit03-07.pdf

Kurfiss, J. G. (1988). *Critical thinking: Theory, research, practice and possibilities* (ASHE-ERIC Higher Education Report No. 2) Washington, DC: Association for the Study of Higher Education.

McPeck, J. E. (1981). *Critical thinking and education.* New York: St. Martin's Press.

Paul, R., & Elder, L. (2001). *Critical thinking.* Upper Saddle River, NJ: Pearson Education, Inc.

Perlman, B., & McCann, L. I. (1999). The structure of the psychology undergraduate curriculum. *Teaching of Psychology, 26*(3), 171–176.

Perry, W. G. (1970). *Forms of intellectual and ethical developments in the college years: A scheme.* New York: Holt, Rinehart & Winston.

Petty, R. E., & Cacioppo, J. T. (1984). The effects of involvement on responses to argument quantity and quality: Central and peripheral routes to persuasion. *Journal of Personality and Social Psychology, 46,* 69–81.

Ross, L. (1977). The intuitive psychologist and his shortcomings. In L. Berkowitz (Ed.), *Advances in experimental social psychology* (Vol. 10, pp. 173–220). New York: Academic Press.

Smith, R. A. (2002). *Challenging your preconceptions: Thinking critically about psychology* (2nd ed.). Belmont, CA: Wadsworth.

Svinicki, M. D. (2004). *Learning and motivation in the post-secondary classroom.* Bolton, MA: Anker Publishing Company, Inc.

Author Note

Correspondence concerning this chapter should be addressed to Janet E. Kuebli, Department of Psychology, Saint Louis University, and 3511 Laclede Avenue, St. Louis, Missouri, 63103. E-mail: kueblije@slu.edu

Chapter 13

Teaching Critical Thinking in Statistics and Research Methods

Bryan K. Saville, Tracy E. Zinn, Natalie Kerr Lawrence, Kenneth E. Barron, and Jeffrey Andre

Statistics and research methods courses are constants in psychology curricula (Perlman & McCann, 2005; Stoloff, Sanders, & McCarthy, 2005) because they function as the glue that binds together other areas of psychology (Stanovich, 2007) and serve as the building blocks on which psychologists construct, verify, and extend what they know about psychological phenomena. The American Psychological Association (APA) Task Force on Psychology Major Competencies echoed this sentiment, listing knowledge of science in general and research methods in particular as primary goals for undergraduate education (APA, 2007). In fact, some psychologists have even argued that *the* primary goal of undergraduate education in psychology is to teach students to think like scientists (e.g., Brewer et al., 1993).

Many statistics and research methods instructors also strive to teach critical thinking, which APA lists as one of its primary goals for undergraduate education as well (APA, 2007). However, although most faculty would vigorously endorse statistics and research methods as courses that help promote these goals, we would be remiss if we did not recognize that students often fail to appreciate what they can learn in these courses. For example, it is not uncommon for students in these courses to "go through the motions," learning course content—or at least retaining it long enough to do well on an exam—but failing to see how knowledge of statistics and research methods can make them better consumers of information or better decision makers once they leave the classroom. Similarly, many students, especially those whose interests lie in the area of applied psychology (e.g., clinical psychology, industrial/organizational psychology), fail to comprehend how knowledge of statistics and research methods will make them better practitioners. In essence, students who take statistics and research methods often do not think critically about the information they encounter in these courses. As a result, although they may have a basic understanding of statistical and methodological concepts, they fail to grasp how thinking critically about this information can, at the least, make them better consumers of information and maybe even better psychologists. Thus the primary purpose of the present chapter is to discuss ways that statistics and research methods instructors can teach their students to think critically. First, however, we briefly discuss what critical thinking entails along with barriers that statistics and research methods instructors may encounter on their way to reaching this important goal.

What is "Critical Thinking"?

Although instructors often speak freely of "critical thinking," this concept is not easy to define. Halonen (1995), for example, defined critical thinking as "the propensity and skills to engage in activity with reflective skepticism focused on deciding what to believe or do" (p. 76), but she also stated: "Ask 12 psychology faculty members to define the term *critical thinking*, and you may receive 12 overlapping but distinct definitions" (p. 75). Nonetheless, psychologists have made progress in identifying certain behaviors that are indicative of critical thinking. In their report on learning outcomes and goals for undergraduate psychology education, APA's Task Force on Psychology Major Competencies (2007) listed the following, among others, as characteristics of critical thinking: (a) examining the quality of information (e.g., making a distinction between empirical evidence and speculation); (b) analyzing media reports of psychological research; (c) tolerating ambiguity; (d) recognizing poorly defined and well-defined problems; and (e) evaluating the quality of a particular solution and revising it if needed.

Despite disagreements about the definition of critical thinking, there is relative consensus among educators that critical thinking is an essential skill that students should acquire (e.g., Appleby, 2005). Furthermore, given that much of the material in statistics and research methods courses lends itself nicely to critical thinking—one characteristic of which is using a scientific approach when problem solving (APA, 2007)—these courses provide a prime context in which to teach this important skill. In fact, to teach statistics and research methods without a focus on critical thinking would, in our opinion, be a mistake. Before statistics and research methods instructors dive headfirst into this task, however, they should be aware of barriers that may stand in the way of their ability to teach their students to think critically about the material they encounter.

Barriers to Addressing Critical Thinking

By most accounts, teaching students to think critically is an important goal that many statistics and research methods instructors attempt to accomplish during their courses. Furthermore, because critical thinking is often a skill that takes time for students to learn, many statistics and research methods instructors tackle the issue right off the bat, addressing these skills in one form or another from the first day of class onward. However, just as teaching other topics in psychology often requires instructors first to consider barriers that may impede students' ability to grasp certain concepts—for example, the notion that humans only use 10% of their brains (see Chew, 2005)—so too must statistics and research methods instructors consider barriers that may preclude their students from learning how to think critically about the information they encounter in their courses and beyond. Below we discuss some of the more prominent barriers that may make it especially difficult to teach critical thinking in statistics and research methods.

Required Courses

Quite often, students view statistics and research methods as necessary evils rather than as courses that are valuable in their own right—they are prerequisites they *must* take before they can move on to other "real" psychology courses. Consequently, students who think they have no say in their decision to take these courses may not be motivated to learn, or think critically, about course content.

Students Dislike "Math"

Another barrier to teaching critical thinking is students' self-reported dislike of math. However, most understand that it is their duty to forge through an anxiety-provoking semester of statistics, so they can take other, more "interesting" psychology courses. Unfortunately, many are disappointed to find that their research methods courses contain considerable discussion of these much-maligned topics (Saville, 2008). Consequently, the "math phobia" that often grips students in their statistics courses sometimes carries over into their research methods courses, again providing a barrier that teachers must overcome in hopes of getting their students to think critically about statistics and research methods.

Misconceptions About, and Dislike of, Science

Ask students to state what they know about the particulars of science, and one may come to realize that (a) students often possess misconceptions about science in general and about psychology as a science in particular; and (b) students tend not to have positive views of science or, if they are indifferent toward it, tend to state that science is something in which they are not that interested. For example, there is a common notion that psychology is one of the humanities and consists of topics that researchers cannot study scientifically (Saville, 2008). Similarly, although most people have positive views of psychology, some tend to hold negative views of science (Webb & Speer, 1985; Wood, Jones, & Benjamin, 1986), suggesting that there is a disconnection between what people know about psychology and what they know about science. How students acquire these misconceptions and dislikes is beyond the focus of this chapter (see Chew, 2005; Taylor & Kowalski, 2004). Nevertheless, misconceptions about science often make it difficult for teachers to get their students to think critically about course material, especially when the material seems to many students to be more scientific—and thus less interesting—than some of the material they encounter in their other courses.

Real-World Connections are not Obvious

Considerable research suggests that students view "real-world relevance" as important to learning course material (e.g., Buskist, Sikorski, Buckley, & Saville, 2002). However, whereas students quickly identify the importance of such topics as memory and motivation, few initially see how *t* tests and threats to internal validity, for example, are relevant to their lives. Consequently, many students—especially those whose future plans do not include graduate school—often wonder what statistics and research methods can provide for them. Only when students see the relevance of the material they learn in these courses can teachers begin to break through the walls that stand in the way of their students' ability to think critically.

Students Do Not See the Inherent Value in These Courses

Quite possibly the greatest barrier to teaching critical thinking in statistics and research methods is that most students become psychology majors in the hope of pursuing careers as practitioners. Because many students are under the mistaken impression that careers in counseling, for example, will not require them to know about statistics and research methods, they often do not see the value in taking such courses. Instead, they think they would be better served by focusing on courses such as abnormal psychology and personality (Johanson & Fried, 2002). Until students understand the importance of these courses with regard to their futures (e.g., Grocer & Kohout, 1997; Keith-Spiegel, Tabachnick, & Spiegel, 1994), they may not see the value in thinking critically about course material.

Teaching Content Versus Critical Thinking

As psychology has evolved over the past century, so too have the statistical analyses and research methods that psychologists use. This new information has made its way into statistics and research methods textbooks, with the expectation that instructors will spend time discussing these important topics. With an increased number of topics to cover—and no concurrent increase in the number of days in which to cover them—many teachers believe that they should spend the majority of their time focusing on course content and less time focusing on critical thinking skills—skills that also take time to teach.

Becoming aware of these and other possible barriers to critical thinking may make it easier for statistics and research methods instructors to address them if—or, maybe more accurately, *when*—they arise. Next, we discuss some ways to address these barriers to critical thinking.

Addressing these Barriers to Critical Thinking

Each of the barriers mentioned above presents a challenge for instructors who want to teach critical thinking in statistics and research methods courses. Fortunately, there are ways to circumnavigate these barriers. Below we provide a variety of strategies—from specific class activities to course- or system-wide changes—that can help remove one or more of these barriers.

Course Activities

There is a bevy of activities that instructors can incorporate into their statistics and research methods courses to help foster students' critical thinking. One way to spark interest in these required courses is to make connections between course content and students' own lives. For example, instructors can administer a survey on the first day of class to learn more about their students (e.g., interests, hobbies) and use this information to tailor examples, demonstrations, and exam questions to match students' experiences. Another activity that can help connect students to the material entails having them create individual course portfolios (Sciutto, 2002). These portfolios, which reflect students' personalized approach to understanding course material, enhance learning by having students compile and integrate course material (e.g., notes, assignments) into an easily accessible resource they can use when they discuss statistics and research methods in subsequent psychology courses.

It is also important to confront students' math anxiety and "statisticophobia" in these courses (Dillon, 1982). One way to do this might be to have students read sections from the book *Innumeracy: Mathematical Illiteracy and its Consequences*, in which Paulos (2001) addresses misconceptions about math and the importance of understanding probability theory (see also Paulos, 1995). For example, one frequently held misconception concerns the "hot-handed" basketball player who has made several shots in a row. When asked to state the probability that this player will make the next shot, students often give a greater-than-chance answer (i.e., the probability is greater than 50%, even though one shot is independent of the next). Paulos devoted a portion of his book to refuting the myth of "streaks" and discussed how knowledge of probability theory can provide insight into such occurrences. We have found that students respond positively to this book and enjoy confronting many of the misconceptions they hold. In addition, allowing students to repeat exams (Friedman, 1987) when they perform poorly, or using self-correcting exams (Montepare, 2005), can help alleviate students' anxiety about poor course performance. Either way, by confronting issues of math anxiety and statisticophobia early on and repeatedly, instructors may ultimately have more time to focus on critical thinking skills.

Critiquing journal articles and research reports published in the popular media is another useful technique for highlighting real-world applications of statistics and research methods (e.g., Connor-Greene & Greene, 2002; Hall & Seery, 2006). For example, by evaluating certain claims made by advertisers, students gain an appreciation for the relevance of statistics and research methods (Beins, 1985). Instructors can also bring in real-world examples of course material (e.g., newspaper articles) and link these examples to students' interests.

Although some instructors prefer to use "canned" data sets in their courses, a potentially better way to "bring the data to life" is to have students (a) construct their own studies (e.g., Lutsky, 1993; Thompson, 1994), or (b) replicate classic psychology experiments, and then analyze the results (e.g., Stedman, 1993). For example, students might conduct an experiment on counterfactual thinking in which they imagine that they had recently taken an exam in one of their courses (see Medvec & Savitsky, 1997) and that they had either just made a B+ or just missed an A–. Typically, students who imagine that they just missed an A– are less satisfied with their grade than those who imagine that they just made a B+. Students then analyze their data using a *t* test or analysis of variance (ANOVA), which tends to make the experiment and the statistical analysis more relevant and gives them a "legitimate feeling of ownership for the data" (Thompson, 1994, p. 41). Moreover, these types of activity help students understand how statistics and research methods are closely linked.

Course Format Changes

As most psychology teachers will agree, unfamiliarity with course material can hinder critical thinking in any class, a notion that might be especially true in statistics and research methods courses. For instance, in statistics courses, the use of complex mathematical equations, which can be daunting even for the "math-oriented," may exacerbate students' feelings of unfamiliarity—especially when instructors focus on computational equations. To illustrate, consider the computational formula for the Pearson product-moment correlation:

$$r = \frac{N \sum XY - \sum X \sum Y}{\sqrt{N \sum X^2 - \left(\sum X\right)^2} \sqrt{N \sum Y^2 - \left(\sum Y\right)^2}}$$

This formula is familiar to statistics instructors, but does it really make students think critically about correlation? Probably not. More than likely, using this formula to discuss correlations becomes an exercise in calculator work. In such cases, simple "one-shot" course activities, like the kind we discussed in the previous section, may do little to assuage our students' fear of math or increase the likelihood that they will think critically about what a correlation is. Instead, statistics instructors could alter the format of their courses. Rather than using computational formulas to teach students about statistics, we suggest focusing on conceptual formulas. For example, because a correlation refers to a *relation* between two variables, instructors could focus on getting students to think conceptually about correlations. To do so, instructors could instead use the following conceptual formula, which is based on *z*-scores:

$$r = \frac{\sum Z_X Z_Y}{N}$$

With this equation, students begin to see that "correlation" refers to the average relation between an individual's scores on two different variables. When *z*-scores are plotted in a scatter plot, the negative and positive product quadrants become more obvious.

Because students rarely hand-calculate statistics once they complete these courses, taking a more conceptual approach will likely get them to think critically about the course material they encounter in their statistics and research methods courses.

Using Alternative Teaching Methods

Another potential way to increase the likelihood that your students will think critically about course material is to use alternative teaching methods that force students to examine the material in a fashion that deviates from more traditional teaching methods. Although there are numerous alternative teaching methods that statistics and research methods instructors can use in their classrooms, the following methods seems especially promising in their ability to promote enhanced learning as well as critical thinking.

Interteaching.   Interteaching is a new method of classroom instruction that has its roots in B. F. Skinner's operant psychology (Boyce & Hineline, 2002). Although earlier behavioral teaching methods (e.g., Keller, 1968), which focused on modifying the teaching environment and increasing reinforcement for desired behaviors, have produced outcomes superior to more traditional methods of instruction, college and university instructors have failed to adopt these methods for a number of reasons (see Buskist, Cush, & DeGrandpre, 1991). Interteaching is based on the same tenets as earlier behavioral teaching methods but is more amenable to classroom adoption. In essence, interteaching entails a "mutually probing, mutually informing conversation between two people" (Boyce & Hineline, 2002, p. 220) that allows both students and teacher continually to interact with one another and reinforce some of the behaviors that teachers hope to see in their students (e.g., discussion of course material, asking questions when material is confusing). Because others have described interteaching in more detail elsewhere (see Barron, Benedict, Saville, Serdikoff, & Zinn, 2007; Boyce & Hineline, 2002; Saville, Zinn, Neef, Van Norman, & Ferreri, 2006), we will not discuss the particulars of the method here. Instead, we will focus on how the use of interteaching seems to have a positive effect on critical thinking.

Although interteaching is relatively new, a mounting number of studies suggest that it may lead to higher exam scores than more traditional methods of classroom instruction (see Barron et al., 2007; Saville, Zinn, & Elliott, 2005; Saville et al., 2006). In addition, evidence from our classrooms suggests that interteaching may lead to increases in the behaviors associated with critical thinking. Saville and Zinn conducted a study in which they alternated interteaching and lecture several times throughout the course of a semester. To provide partial controls for possible confounds, they counterbalanced the order of teaching method across two sections of an undergraduate research methods course (i.e., one class participated in interteaching while the other class heard a lecture over the same material; see Saville et al., 2006, Study 2, for a description of this method). At the end of the semester, students completed Ferrett's (1997) "attributes of a critical thinker" inventory, which asks respondents to self-report how often they engaged in certain behaviors that are associated with critical thinking (e.g., asks relevant questions, admits lack of understanding, changes one's mind when learning new facts). Specifically, students reported whether they were more likely to engage in each of these behaviors with interteaching or with lecture.

Of the 15 attributes/behaviors contained on Ferrett's inventory, students in both sections reported engaging in 10 of them more often with interteaching. For three of the attributes (evaluating statements and arguments from readings and class, examining one's own assumptions and opinions about course material, and looking for supporting evidence for problems), students in both sections reported that they did so equally with interteaching and lecture. Finally, there were section differences for two of the attributes: For being "curious about course material," one section reported doing so more with interteaching, whereas the other section reported doing so more during lectures; for "evaluating knowledge of course material," one section reported doing so more with interteaching, whereas the other section reported doing so equally with interteaching and lecture.

Overall, these results suggest that interteaching may produce increases in the behaviors that are indicative of critical thinking. Clearly, this is not to say that lecture-based courses, when constructed correctly, cannot (and will not) lead to increases in critical thinking (McKeachie, 2002). However, the very nature of interteaching—with its focus on student discussion, peer-to-peer teaching, and frequent feedback—may be more likely to provide a context in which students engage in these highly desired behaviors.

An integrated statistics–research methods course.   Recently, Dunn, Smith, and Beins (2007) edited the volume *Best Practices for Teaching Statistics and Research Methods in the Behavioral Sciences.* Interestingly, their title reflects two ways in which instructors typically approach their statistics and research methods courses. First, the title separates statistics and research methods. Likewise, most instructors view statistics and research methods as distinct courses—hence the reason they commonly appear in our psychology curriculum as such. Second, the title places statistics before research methods, reflecting another common pedagogical practice: teaching statistics before research methods. Indeed, at our university, we have followed this approach for some time. Students take Psychological Measurement and Statistics (Psyc 210), and then they take Psychological Research Methods (Psyc 211).

Although the logic for this two-semester sequence is grounded in wanting students to learn basic statistical concepts that they can later apply in their research methods course, a critique of this approach suggests that it may not provide a context in which students can appreciate why they are taking statistics (Barron et al., 2007; Christopher, Walter, Horton, & Marek, 2007). Failure to provide context for learning can severely impact student motivation (Lepper & Henderlong, 2000) and comprehension (Bransford & Johnson, 1972). Thus, teaching statistics before research methods is akin to "putting the cart before the horse." Does it really make sense to spend a great deal of time teaching students about specific tools they will use to analyze data before teaching them why we conduct research in the first place? Should we then be surprised when students have trouble comprehending the information they encounter in their statistics courses? And should we be surprised that we have to spend time in our research methods courses revisiting ideas they covered in statistics?

In addition to teaching two separate courses, we are now offering a new year-long, integrated version of these courses. Specifically, students shift in and out of units on statistics and research methods each semester. Our goal is to provide students with better context in which they can learn about the different methodological approaches and statistical tools that psychological researchers use to build a valid body of knowledge. To correct the "horse before the cart" problem we mentioned earlier, students first learn about a particular research method (e.g., descriptive research methods) and what types of question researchers can answer with it (e.g., prevalence rates of different psychological disorders). Students then learn about the statistical tools that researchers use to analyze data and draw conclusions from a particular research method. Next, students complete a hands-on research project that immediately allows them to use both the method and its accompanying statistical tools. Finally, students discuss the strengths and limitations of adopting a particular research method, and the need to adopt other methods and statistics in order to answer other types of research questions, which starts the process over again. The goal of this new format is simple: to provide students with better context in which they can appreciate why different research methods and statistical tools are necessary for psychology and necessary for us to be better researchers.

Taking this more elaborate approach in a normal semester course would drastically limit the number of methodological and statistical techniques that instructors could introduce. But with a year-long, two-semester sequence, we are in a position to teach the same content that we normally teach in our regular semester-long courses. In Psychological Research Methods and Data Analysis I (Psyc 212), students learn the history and use of science in psychology, along with two of the four major research methods used in psychology: descriptive and correlational approaches. We also cover the statistical tools associated with these methods (descriptive statistics, correlation and regression, and the basics of inferential statistics). In Psychological Research Methods and Data Analysis II (Psyc 213), students learn the other major research approaches used in our field—experimental and quasi-experimental designs—and the statistical tools associated with these approaches (*t* tests and ANOVAs). After completing this two-semester sequence, students can appreciate how researchers are motivated by different research goals, how answering a particular research question requires the use of a particular research method, and how using a particular research method requires the use of a particular statistical tool (see Figure 13.1).

As instructors, few of us would say that we were inherently excited to learn about the differences between one-sample, independent-sample, and dependent-sample *t* tests, let alone how to calculate the formulas by hand. However, when reframed first and foremost

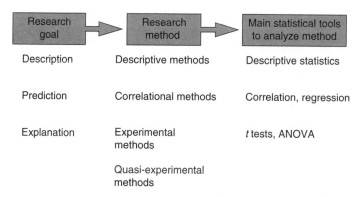

Figure 13.1. Organizational framework for providing context in an integrated research methods and statistics course.

as a question we have about psychology, then knowing that we have a particular strategy we need to adopt to answer that question becomes more valuable and worthwhile to learn. Although the progression of teaching many of our statistical concepts makes sense to us as instructors (e.g., moving from one-sample *t* tests to dependent- and independent-samples *t* tests), we always need to keep in mind what it is like to be a student, especially if we want them to think deeply and critically about what we are teaching.

Conclusion

Statistics and research methods are arguably two of the most important—if not *the* most important—courses in traditional psychology curricula, simply because they serve as the cornerstone on which students subsequently build knowledge of other psychological phenomena. In addition, statistics and research methods are ideal courses in which instructors can begin to teach their students how to think critically about information they encounter both in and out of the classroom. In fact, Barron and Halonen (2005) found that psychology majors reported engaging in critical thinking more in their statistics and research methods courses than they did in their other psychology courses. However, because of the nature of these courses, instructors will likely encounter several barriers that may preclude them, at least initially, from teaching their students important critical thinking skills. Thus instructors should not attempt to teach these skills until they have addressed the barriers that may interfere with their ability to do so effectively. We hope that some of the ideas contained in the present chapter will help statistics and research methods instructors to sidestep some of the roadblocks they may encounter on their way to teaching their students to think critically. In time, your students will not only become better at thinking critically about the information they encounter in their psychology courses, but maybe even more importantly, they will become better at thinking critically about the information they encounter as they step outside the hallowed halls of academia.

References

American Psychological Association, Task Force on Psychology Major Competencies. (2007). *APA guidelines for the undergraduate psychology major*. Washington, DC: Author.

Appleby, D. C. (2005). Defining, teaching, and assessing critical thinking in introductory psychology. In D. S. Dunn & S. L. Chew (Eds.), *Best practices for teaching introduction to psychology* (pp. 57–69). Mahwah, NJ: Erlbaum.

Barron, K. E., Benedict, J. O., Saville, B. K., Serdikoff, S. L., & Zinn, T. E. (2007). Innovative approaches to teaching statistics and research methods: Just-in-Time Teaching, Interteaching, and Learning Communities. In D. S. Dunn, R. A. Smith, & B. C. Beins (Eds.), *Best practices for teaching statistics and research methods in the behavioral sciences* (pp. 143–158). Mahwah, NJ: Erlbaum.

Barron, K. E., & Halonen, J. (2005, September). *Programmatic assessment of critical thinking*. Paper presented at Engaging Minds: Best Practices in Teaching Critical Thinking Across the Psychology Curriculum conference, Atlanta, GA.

Beins, B. C. (1985). Teaching the relevance of statistics through consumer-oriented research. *Teaching of Psychology, 12,* 168–169.

Boyce, T. E., & Hineline, P. N. (2002). Interteaching: A strategy for enhancing the user-friendliness of behavioral arrangements in the college classroom. *The Behavior Analyst, 25,* 215–226.

Bransford, J. D., & Johnson, M. K. (1972). Contextual prerequisites for understanding: Some investigations of comprehension and recall. *Journal of Verbal Learning and Verbal Behavior, 11,* 717–726.

Brewer, C. L., Hopkins, J. R., Kimble, G. A., Matlin, M. W., McCann, L. I., McNeil, O. V., et al. (1993). Curriculum. In T. V. McGovern (Ed.), *Handbook for enhancing undergraduate education in psychology* (pp. 161–182). Washington, DC: American Psychological Association.

Buskist, W., Cush, D., & DeGrandpre, R. J. (1991). The life and times of PSI. *Journal of Behavioral Education, 1,* 215–234.

Buskist, W., Sikorski, J., Buckley, T., & Saville, B. K. (2002). Elements of master teaching. In S. F. Davis & W. Buskist (Eds.), *The teaching of psychology: Essays in honor of Wilbert J. McKeachie and Charles L. Brewer* (pp. 27–39). Mahwah, NJ: Erlbaum.

Chew, S. L. (2005). Seldom in doubt but often wrong: Addressing tenacious student misconceptions. In D. S. Dunn & S. L. Chew (Eds.), *Best practices for teaching introduction to psychology* (pp. 211–223). Mahwah, NJ: Erlbaum.

Christopher, A. N., Walter, M. I., Horton, R. S., & Marek, P. (2007). Benefits and detriments of integrating statistics and research methods. In D. S. Dunn, R. A. Smith, & B. C. Beins (Eds.), *Best practices for teaching statistics and research methods in the behavioral sciences* (pp. 187–202). Mahwah, NJ: Erlbaum.

Connor-Greene, P. A., & Greene, D. J. (2002). Science or snake oil? Teaching critical evaluation of "research" reports on the Internet. *Teaching of Psychology, 29,* 321–324.

Dillon, K. M. (1982). Statisticophobia. *Teaching of Psychology, 9,* 117.

Dunn, D. S., Smith, R. A., & Beins, B. C. (Eds.). (2007). *Best practices for teaching statistics and research methods in the behavioral sciences.* Mahwah, NJ: Erlbaum.

Ferrett, S. K. (1997). *Peak performance: Success in college and beyond* (2nd ed.). New York: McGraw-Hill.

Friedman, H. (1987). Repeat examinations in introductory statistics courses. *Teaching of Psychology, 14,* 20–23.

Grocer, S., & Kohout, J. (1997). *The 1995 APA survey of 1992 psychology baccalaureate recipients.* Retrieved May 15, 2007, from http://research.apa.org/95survey/homepage.html

Hall, S. S., & Seery, B. L. (2006). Behind the facts: Helping students evaluate media reports of psychological research. *Teaching of Psychology, 33,* 101–104.

Halonen, J. S. (1995). Demystifying critical thinking. *Teaching of Psychology, 22,* 75–81.

Johanson, J. C., & Fried, C. B. (2002). Job training versus graduate school preparation: Are separate educational tracks warranted? *Teaching of Psychology, 29,* 241–243.

Keith-Spiegel, P., Tabachnick, B. G., & Spiegel, G. B. (1994). When demand exceeds supply: Second-order criteria used by graduate school selection committees. *Teaching of Psychology, 21,* 79–81.

Keller, F. S. (1968). Good-bye teacher … *Journal of Applied Behavior Analysis, 1,* 79–89.

Lepper, M. R., & Henderlong, J. (2000). Turning "play" into "work" and "work" into "play": 25 years of research on intrinsic versus extrinsic motivation. In C. Sansone & J. M. Harackiewicz (Eds.), *Intrinsic and extrinsic motivation: The search for optimal motivation and performance* (pp. 257–307). San Diego: Academic Press.

Lutsky, N. (1993). A scheme and variations for studies of social influence in an experimental social psychology laboratory. *Teaching of Psychology, 20,* 105–107.

McKeachie, W. J. (2002). *McKeachie's teaching tips: Strategies, research, and theory for college and university teachers* (11th ed.). Boston: Houghton Mifflin.

Medvec, V. H., & Savitsky, K. (1997). When doing better means feeling worse: The effects of categorical cutoff points on counterfactual thinking and satisfaction. *Journal of Personality and Social Psychology, 72,* 1284–1296.

Montepare, J. M. (2005). A self-correcting approach to multiple choice tests. *APS Observer, 18*(10), 35–36, 43–44.

Paulos, J. A. (1995). *A mathematician reads the newspaper.* New York: Anchor Books.

Paulos, J. A. (2001). *Innumeracy: Mathematical illiteracy and its consequences* (2nd ed.). New York: Hill and Wang.

Perlman, B., & McCann, L. I. (2005). Undergraduate research experiences in psychology: A national study of courses and curricula. *Teaching of Psychology, 32,* 5–14.

Saville, B. K. (2008). *A guide to teaching research methods in psychology.* Malden, MA: Blackwell.

Saville, B. K., Zinn, T. E., & Elliott, M. P. (2005). Interteaching vs. traditional methods of instruction: A preliminary analysis. *Teaching of Psychology, 32,* 161–163.

Saville, B. K., Zinn, T. E., Neef, N. A., Van Norman, R., & Ferreri, S. J. (2006). A comparison of interteaching and lecture in the college classroom. *Journal of Applied Behavior Analysis, 39,* 49–61.

Sciutto, M. J. (2002). The methods and statistics portfolio: A resource for the introductory course and beyond. *Teaching of Psychology, 29,* 213–215.

Stanovich, K. E. (2007). *How to think straight about psychology* (8th ed.). Boston: Allyn & Bacon.

Stedman, M. E. (1993). Statistical pedagogy: Employing student-generated data sets in introductory statistics. *Psychological Reports, 72,* 1036–1038.

Stoloff, M., Sanders, N., & McCarthy, M. (2005). Profiles of undergraduate programs in psychology. Retrieved May 10, 2007, from http://www.apa.org/ed/pcue/profiles_intro.html

Taylor, A. K., & Kowalski, P. (2004). Naïve psychological science: The prevalence, strength, and sources of misconceptions. *The Psychological Record, 54,* 15–25.

Thompson, W. B. (1994). Making data analysis realistic: Incorporating research into statistics courses. *Teaching of Psychology, 21,* 41–43.

Webb, A. R., & Speer, J. R. (1985). The public image of psychologists. *American Psychologist, 40,* 1063–1064.

Wood, W., Jones, M., & Benjamin, L. T., Jr. (1986). Surveying psychology's public image. *American Psychologist, 41,* 947–953.

Part IV

Integrating Critical Thinking Across the Psychology Curriculum

Chapter 14

Writing as Critical Thinking

Dana S. Dunn and Randolph A. Smith

Critical thinking is not one strategy, but many strategies. It involves the exercise and development of various skills aimed at bridging the gap between a current and a desired state (Halonen & Gray, 2000; Sternberg, Roediger, & Halpern, 2007). In psychology, the aim of teaching critical thinking is often to refine students' abilities to describe, predict, explain, and control behavior. But what about writing? How do psychology students' abilities to express themselves in text form represent critical thinking? Writing is similar to critical thinking in that it requires the integration and execution of various skills, including argument, organization, and planning, as well as a working comprehension of grammar and punctuation rules. Some authors even claim that writing is a form of problem solving (Flower, 1998; see also Hayes, 2006; Hayes & Flower, 1980), one of the tools in the critical thinking arsenal.

We believe that writing is simply another form of critical thinking, perhaps a higher form, because most writers in psychology—both students and professionals—write with the goal of sharing their ideas with others. That is, they export the transactional nature of their critical thinking beyond themselves to others. To inform others effectively, writers must transform their thoughts into prose form, a process requiring not only the aforementioned skills but a bit of social intelligence, notably the ability to adopt readers' perspectives to anticipate their questions as well as learning needs.

When developing course activities and assignments, we urge teachers to consider the scientific reasoning level of their students: An introductory psychology student has a different understanding of the discipline than one enrolled in research methods or an advanced topical seminar (Halonen et al., 2003). The same holds true for the effective teaching and learning of discipline-related writing skills. Writing activities for first-year students in psychology should be more expressive and exploratory, whereas those aimed at advanced undergraduates, most often majors, can be more transactional and scientifically grounded.

Our goal in this chapter is to offer a point of view on writing as critical thinking. To do so, we will discuss the role of critical reading in writing, identify some practical writing activities that promote critical thinking, and consider the unique role of American Psychological Association (APA) style (APA, 2001) as a method for teaching and learning critical thinking in psychology.

Critical Reading for Critical Writing

Students need to read *and* write, and so do faculty. We believe that learning to write critically in psychology goes hand in hand with learning to read critically. We like to expose our students to high quality readings from psychology and the wider social science literature. The goal of such exposure is to teach them to evaluate both the quantitative and the qualitative nature of experimental and nonexperimental research.

The term "evaluate" can be a loaded one for students as they often assume that published ideas are not only already vetted by experts (which is often true, at least where publications in top-flight journals are concerned) but that their content is also somehow sacred and not to be challenged (which is patently untrue, as knowledge evolves through replication, revision, and refinement). Critical evaluation of the psychological literature depends on a working understanding of the scientific method, familiarity with data analysis and statistical inference, and exposure to particular research methods used within the discipline. Our assumption, then, is that students should take—or be enrolled in—some sequence of courses in research methods and statistics (e.g., Brewer et al., 1993; Dunn, Smith, & Beins, 2007). Beyond teaching these basic skills to students or presuming they already have them, teachers must ensure that students can search the literature, interpret claims and arguments, learn from exemplars, and evaluate what they read by writing about it. We begin with literature searches.

Searching the Literature

Learning to search the psychological literature—online databases (e.g., PsycINFO), online library catalogs, and printed periodicals, among other sources—is an excellent way for students to develop an analytical perspective on research. In research methods classes and topical seminars, for example, faculty members can point to strengths, weaknesses, shortcomings, and unknowns in available research. The best learning is associated with the virtual and physical search of resources, tracking them down, and carefully reading them to learn what was done, why, and what was found. Faculty guidance is important here, if only to teach students about the nature of primary and secondary sources, why journals are important to the discipline, and how to evaluate quality therein (e.g., Dunn, 2008).

We also believe that students stand to learn a great deal when they work closely with reference library professionals, either by seeking the help of a librarian to track down pertinent information or through a tutorial designed to reveal a library's resources. If nothing else, such collaborations can help students learn to discern science from pseudoscience as they sort through sources (e.g., Toedter & Glew, 2007). Many students do not take advantage of their local resources because they remain unaware of their existence or because they do not know how to locate and use them. Thus we believe that an essential component of critical reading and writing is learning to use a library's reference resources, periodicals, and book holdings effectively.

Interpreting Claims

Ultimately, writing in psychology is about persuasion, convincing readers that some particular hypothesis and its supporting data suggest that people act, think, or feel one way for a discernible reason. Building a case for a psychological theory involves rallying supporting evidence in the form of experiments and their results. Findings from earlier studies guide the design and execution of subsequent research efforts in an ongoing cycle. The foundation of this empirical process lies in the claims author-researchers offer, the arguments for or against a particular rationale for the occurrence of behavior. Written claims and arguments in psychology are about advocating and presenting ideas to persuade, surprise, intrigue, co-opt, or even excite an audience of readers (e.g., Spellman, DeLoache, & Bjork, 2007).

Written arguments come in three basic types: emotional (*pathos*), ethical (*ethos*), and logical (*logos*). Arguments from the heart have no place in science; thus students need to recognize emotional tugs, appeals that lack solid empirical support (e.g., "Women are better primary caregivers of children than men because they are naturally nurturing"). Ethical arguments are character-based and often involve authority relationships or touch on matters of trust, integrity, or credibility. Ethics is certainly an important part of psychological research, notably in the relationship between researcher and research participant, but arguments in psychology should be authoritative in the sense of reliability and credibility, not mere source (e.g., "IQ results obtained in an Ivy League lab are apt to be more trustworthy than those found in a research center at an underfunded public university").

Naturally, scientific claims in psychology should be logical and based on facts and reason. Such claims should be based on clear, testable hypotheses and supported by peer-reviewed evidence found in the existing psychological literature. The purpose of most claims or arguments is to persuade, preferably with supporting evidence (i.e., empirical data, citations). Few, if any, ideas in psychology do not have some grounding in prior research. Spellman and her colleagues (2007), for example, identified five categories of frequent claims in psychology (see Table 14.1).

Any classroom discussion of research claims should evaluate them from a variety of perspectives. When reading an argument, students should consider the claim's author, that is, by asking about the researcher's intention. Additionally, students should reflect on the intended audience. Who are they? Why should they be interested in the findings? These and related questions are obvious to instructors, less so to students. We believe that students will benefit from learning to recognize these claim types as they learn to navigate the psychological literature. In turn, they can use the categories shown in Table 14.1 to craft their own claims in lab reports, review papers, and other writing exercises (see also Spellman et al., 2007; Stoloff & Rogers, 2002).

Table 14.1. Claims Categorized: Some Typical Types of Arguments Offered in Psychology

---

Theory advancement or modification – claims made to extend or revise what is known (e.g., "Our findings qualify the role of some automatic processes in working memory.").

New ideas or improvements – claims that share novel approaches (e.g., "We developed a new paper and pencil measure for assessing implicit attitudes.").

Challenges to prevailing assumptions – claims aimed at overturning existing theories explanations of results (e.g., "The results from our studies confirm that positive emotions elicit distinct and different behavioral responses compared to negative emotions.").

Utility and application of results – claims indicating that results can be used to address some problem constructively (e.g., "We found that academic intrinsic motivation can be encouraged among elementary schoolchildren who are at risk for learning delays.").

Contesting established judgment – claims offered to counter expectations or assumptions with supporting evidence (e.g., "Despite the ubiquity of media advertising, our series of studies reveals that the connection between persuasive messages and actual purchase is extremely limited.").

Source: Adapted from Spellman et al. (2007).

Learning from Exemplars

How can students be taught to discern logical, evidence-based psychological research from poorly designed or flawed efforts? The best course is to have them read high quality exemplars from the literature. We will expose psychology majors, of course, to a variety of high quality examples through class work, library research, and the discipline-based textbooks they read. Teachers can supplement these examples by intentionally presenting the details of high quality studies to students. Presenting inconclusive, questionable, or hard-to-interpret studies or descriptive (i.e., noncausal) findings is also a good idea so that students can learn to distinguish the reliable, scientific wheat from the chaff. Fine books that promote this sort of approach to critical thinking are available (e.g., Marton, 2006; Meltzoff, 1998; Stanovich, 2007).

Alternatively, students can learn from one another by reading and critiquing work produced by other students. Various undergraduate journals exist, and the material published in them is readily understood by undergraduate students (Ware, Badura, & Davis, 2002). More to the point, evaluating the strengths and weaknesses of such work can be a more gentle entry into critical reading than immediately tackling the work of professional psychologists, especially famous ones.

Evaluating Reading Through Writing

For students, a typical part of evaluating what they read involves taking notes about it, whether on index cards or in a notebook (paper or computer). This general activity can be improved upon by having students create a "reader's guide" concerning whatever topic they are researching (Henderson, 2000). This guide is a topical précis containing a content outline (e.g., history of topic, major topics, theories and methods), a list of key researchers and theorists, main issues, current research foci, and essential sources (e.g., books, handbooks, articles). Preparing a reader's guide is a relatively painless way to read and review the relevant literature concerning a topic in advance of conducting an empirical study or writing a more narrow research paper (for specific guidelines, see Henderson, 2000).

Writing Activities Promoting Critical Thinking

We believe that students need to develop a critical acumen where writing is concerned. How can they do so? Writing in psychology is not a spectator sport: Students must become engaged with the material by performing basic tasks associated with designing and executing an experiment or other study. We suggest that three categories of writing activities—basic tasks, process issues, and outcomes—can link critical thinking to writing. Table 14.2 lists sample writing activities within each of the three categories. We encourage readers to think of additional writing activities that fall under the categories. We now briefly discuss each category in turn.

Basic Tasks

Basic tasks constitute the "bricks and mortar" writing activities in the psychology classroom. Most of these activities are associated with the teaching and learning of research methods and experimentation in psychology. After conducting an experiment—often but not always one determined by an instructor—students must learn to encapsulate the main

Table 14.2. Illustrative Writing Activities for Teaching Critical Thinking

Basic tasks
- Summarizing the literature
- Writing hypotheses
- Putting results into prose form (i.e., translating data analyses into text)
- Writing about tables and figures

Process issues
- Expressive versus transactional writing
- Anticipating audience needs
- Drafting, revising, refining
- Critiquing their own writing (revising and editing as both critical reflection and self-regulation)
- Seeking peer as well as instructor comments on papers
- Critiquing peer writing

Outcomes
- Informal papers (in-class writing, reaction papers)
- Formal papers (lab reports, literature review papers)
- Portfolios
- Posters

points of existing research, to describe the question being tested by their research (highlighting the manipulation of independent variables and the measurement of a dependent variable), to translate statistical findings into declarative statements, and to lead readers through tabular or graphic data displays (see the top section of Table 14.2). All of these tasks require student writers to convey the meaning of relatively complex information (e.g., defining and operationalizing variables, relationships among variables, statistical results) in the clearest, most concise manner possible. Learning to do so requires patience, tenacity, (usually repeated) experiences, good models to work from, and mastery-oriented feedback from an instructor. Until they gain sufficient research experience and acquire feedback following trial and error, most students will not view conducting empirical research and writing about it as complementary exercises. A variety of other writing activities—some of the basic tasks—pertaining to research methods and statistics courses can be found in Schmidt and Dunn (2007).

Process Issues

As noted earlier, the writing process involves a certain degree of social intelligence on the part of writers, namely, making themselves understood by and communicating with others (see the middle section of Table 14.2). The *expressive or exploratory writing* (i.e., free writing) movement in higher education has been helpful in this vein (e.g., Elbow & Belanoff, 1989; see also LePore & Smyth, 2002). Students quickly produce writing, which means they then have something to work with and to learn from (e.g., Dunn, 1994). Learning to make such beginning efforts understandable to others involves increasingly *transactional writing*; that is, learning to write for a particular audience. In practice, the audience is an audience of one, a student's instructor, but in theory, the audience is a professional one, other students of psychology.

Critical thinking is also part of the drafting, revising, and refining side of writing. As a paper is shaped through several iterations (i.e., free writing to rough draft to polished paper), students should be learning to ask themselves questions that refine the text for readers—from word choice to grammar and punctuation. Part of drafting and revising is learning to critique one's own writing, which promotes the beneficial critical thinking of ongoing self-assessment (Have I satisfied the assignment's requirements? Will others understand it?; Dunn, McEntarffer, & Halonen, 2004). Self-regulation skills—learning to know when to keep revising, when to seek feedback from others, or when to quit writing—are also important because they compel student writers to reexamine and rethink what they have already produced (see the middle section of Table 14.2). For instance, in a workshop-oriented classroom, students become used to reading and commenting on one another's work with regularity throughout the writing process (e.g., Dunn, 1994, 2008; Elbow & Belanoff, 1989).

Outcomes

Ultimately, most students and many faculty view writing as being about outcomes, essentially the papers produced after conducting, thinking about, or discussing research (see the bottom section of Table 14.2). Such outcomes are important, but we do not want to dilute the importance of basic writing tasks and process issues—we view these categories of writing activities as being on the same level of importance as finished formal papers. We hasten to add that informal writing activities, such as in-class writing, short reaction papers, or even the creation of poster summaries of research, also constitute valuable, if circumscribed, writing experiences. The importance of helping students learn to offer written comments quickly and efficiently should not be underestimated, especially because most of the budding writers in our classes will not become psychologists. Nonetheless, we have an obligation to refine their writing abilities within our sphere of disciplinary influence.

Following Rickabaugh (1993), we believe that students benefit from maintaining an ongoing portfolio of the writing they do in and for psychology classes. Such a portfolio contains the incidental as well as major writing assignments they do for work in the major. Routine examination of the portfolio's contents can demonstrate developmental progress and allow students to examine outcomes from the past to avoid repeating writing errors (e.g., passive voice, formatting problems, ill-conceived research claims). Faculty, too, can consult these writing portfolios as a periodic check of formative assessment or a summative evaluation measure of a department's focus on teaching writing as a form of critical thinking.

Writing in APA Style as a Mode of Critical Thinking

Writing APA-Style Papers

Madigan, Johnson, and Linton (1995) conceptualized APA style as epistemology, a point with which we largely agree. As such, learning APA style goes far beyond a set of rules for writing and actually helps students learn how psychologists think; ideally, students begin thinking in the same manner themselves, a process that Madigan et al. referred to as "paradigmatic thinking" (p. 249). In this manner, students gain some ability to think critically through the writing process because they learn to think in the paradigm that psychologists use.

Writing each section of an APA-style report forces students to learn to apply different types of critical thinking skills. For example, the Abstract requires students to discern the most important elements of their study and report only those—all within a 120-word limit. The introduction requires several critical thinking skills. Students must perform a critical literature search; although it may be simple to find many studies related to their topic, they must sift among those many to find the truly important ones. Next, they must arrange these studies in a logical progression—although chronological order may seem logical, it may not be the best way to tell the "story" leading to their study. Finally, they must learn to piece the story together so that the reader can see that their experiment is the next logical step in the progression of research. The Method section forces students to think critically about how to actually test the hypothesis that they have developed, as well as how to report what they have done so that the picture is complete for the reader.

The Results section requires that students think critically about the type of data they have collected, the experimental design they have used, and how to communicate clearly what they have found to the reader. Finally, the Discussion makes students think about the place of their study in the "big picture"—how does their study add to psychology's body of knowledge? What questions does their study answer, what questions does it leave unanswered, what new questions does it reveal? Virtually all of these types of thinking are new for students, and they do not come easily. Given that any psychologist has read a variety of published experimental reports that have fallen short on some (or many) of these counts, these types of thinking are not necessarily easy even for professionals.

Story schemas.   In addition to viewing APA style as epistemological, Madigan et al. (1995) likened the format for empirical reports (introduction, Method, Results, Discussion sections) to the schema for a story with characteristics that psychology and psychologists value. The story schema is consistent with the schema of the scientific process, which is "all about" critical thinking. By following the outline of an APA-format report during the research process, students learn first to review relevant empirical literature to develop a research question. Deriving a research question from a literature search involving many research articles certainly involves critical thinking. After developing the research question, students must think critically to develop the methodology required to answer the research question. After conducting the experiment, gathering the data, and analyzing the data, students must use their critical thinking abilities to interpret the results of the analyses. Finally, students must use their critical thinking skills to determine the "big picture" of the research: What do the results mean in terms of the previous literature, and what are the overall conclusions from the study?

Hedging conclusions.   Madigan et al. (1995) also pointed out that it is important for psychology students to learn about hedging conclusions. As we have taught students to write research reports over nearly 50 years of teaching, we have often seen students who are writing their first research report use the words "prove" or "proven" in their conclusions (e.g., "These data prove that …"). No psychologist who is well versed in APA writing style would make this type of mistake. It seems that critical thinking is necessary to note and understand the shortcomings of one's own research study. Reading and writing in APA style helps to develop this type of critical thinking, which Madigan et al. termed important to students learning about psychology's culture.

APA-style writing.   Madigan et al. (1995) also emphasized that the approach to writing is different in APA style compared to what students have previously learned. For example, in English composition classes, students have learned to focus on language as the product (Madigan et al.). In other words, in composition writing, the focus is on the writing itself. Students have learned about various linguistic devices and writing styles that embellish the writing; readers read for entertainment value or to appreciate the good writing. On the other hand, Madigan et al. (1995, p. 433) referred to "language as medium" in APA-style writing. In other words, the goal of the language in scientific reports is not to entertain, but to inform. This approach is foreign to most students and may account for the great difficulty that students have in both writing and reading APA-style empirical reports. They may claim that such writing is "dry" or "dull." Although APA-style writing is not meant to be boring, the fact that it is devoid of the literary conventions of fiction writing may predispose students to find it boring. However, in trying to extract critical information or details from a research report, flowery language would simply be extraneous and, perhaps, distracting. It takes critical thinking on the part of students to learn the importance of precise scientific writing. Practice in using APA-style writing helps students learn and incorporate this lesson.

Reading and Critiquing APA-Style Papers

Related to making gains in critical thinking by writing in APA style is gaining the ability to use critical thinking in reading APA-style reports. When students first encounter such a report to read, they are often overwhelmed by the different types of writing in the various sections and may simply maintain that they cannot make any sense of the report. However, after learning about how psychologists write the various sections, students often begin gaining a measure of critical thinking in reading, and even critiquing, research reports.

In much the same way that they must think critically about each section when writing a research report, students should use a critical eye in conducting a literature search and in reading those sections. For example, in reading the Abstract, students must be able to apply critical analysis skills to determine whether an article is likely to be related to their research topic or area. This type of skill is crucial in using time effectively in a literature search. With the introduction, students should read with a critical eye toward the author developing a research hypothesis. Does each study add to the progression of thought that leads to the hypothesis? Has the author summarized each study accurately? Is there an alternative interpretation of any study that the author has missed (or simply ignored) in deriving the hypothesis? The Results section requires students to apply their critical thinking skills about the data and analysis. Is the analysis appropriate for the type of data that the author reported? Does the author provide all the necessary information for the analysis (or analyses) used (e.g., is there an interaction term/finding for a design with two independent variables?)? Finally, in reading the Discussion section, students must critically analyze the author's conclusions to determine whether they are appropriate. Also, critical thinking about the Discussion section can lead a student to develop an idea for a new research project that is an outgrowth of the one the student is reading. Thus reading and critiquing research reports provide ample opportunities for students to develop and use their critical thinking skills.

As an example of such reading and critical thinking, Gareis (1995) had introductory psychology students read and critique articles cited in their textbook. Rather than simply summarizing the articles, students described study variables, hypothesis, operational definitions, and method plus results. In addition, they critically evaluated the study, discussed how the article demonstrated concepts from the course, and compared the actual article to its description in the text. In their evaluation of the assignment, students reported that it helped them to "think critically about research" (p. 234). Of course, student reports are not necessarily the same as actual outcomes. On the other hand, students *were* able to spot inconsistencies between their text and the actual research. Although some of the inconsistencies were minor (e.g., number of participants in a group), some were much more important (e.g., describing a within-subjects design as a between-subjects design).

Given how hesitant students in research methods classes are to critique published articles, this achievement in introductory students is most impressive.

Closing Comment: The Teacher's Role in Writing as Critical Thinking

We want to close this chapter with encouragement tempered by reality: Teaching writing requires time, effort, and a willingness to be candid with students. You will often feel overworked and pressured by papers to read and return, and you will necessarily need to develop a thick skin when meeting with students who claim they know how to write and, what's more, already write well (if only in their opinion). Your own experience with the peer review process of publishing in the discipline of psychology can help (i.e., your skin may have been thickened by past skirmishes with reviewers and editors), but so does explaining—not pleading—your case to students early on. You must explain to them why writing is an essential and all too often neglected aspect of practically everyone's educational experience. Your goal is to improve on what they already know how to do by helping them to become more critical—constructive as well as decisive—about their work.

References

American Psychological Association. (2001). *Publication manual of the American Psychological Association* (5th ed.). Washington, DC: Author.

Brewer, C. L., Hopkins, J. R., Kimble, G. A., Matlin, M. W., McCann, L. I., McNeil, O. V., et al. (1993). Curriculum. In T. V. McGovern (Ed.), *Handbook for enhancing undergraduate education in psychology* (pp. 161–182). Washington, DC: American Psychological Association.

Dunn, D. S. (1994). Lessons learned from an interdisciplinary writing course: Implications for student writing in psychology. *Teaching of Psychology, 21,* 223–227.

Dunn, D. S. (2008). *A short guide to writing about psychology* (2nd ed.). New York: Longman.

Dunn, D. S., McEntarffer, R., & Halonen, J. S. (2004). Empowering psychology students through self-assessment. In D. S. Dunn, C. M. Mehrotra, & J. S. Halonen (Eds.), *Measuring up: Assessment challenges and practices for psychology* (pp. 171–186). Washington, DC: American Psychological Association.

Dunn, D. S., Smith, R. A., & Beins, B. C. (Eds.). (2007). *Best practices for teaching statistics and research methods in the behavioral sciences.* Mahwah, NJ: Erlbaum.

Elbow, P., & Belanoff, P. (1989). *A community of writers: A workshop course in writing.* New York: McGraw-Hill.

Flower, L. (1998). *Problem-solving strategies for writing in college and community.* Fort Worth, TX: Harcourt Brace College Publishers.

Gareis, K. C. (1995). Critiquing articles cited in the introductory textbook: A writing assignment. *Teaching of Psychology, 22,* 233–235.

Halonen, J. S., Bosack, T., Clay, S., & McCarthy, M. (with Dunn, D. S., Hill, G. W. IV., et al.). (2003). A rubric for authentically learning, teaching, and assessing scientific reasoning in psychology. *Teaching of Psychology, 30,* 196–208.

Halonen, J., & Gray, C. (2000). *The critical thinking companion for introductory psychology* (2nd ed.). New York: Worth.

Hayes, J. R. (2006). New directions in writing theory. In C. A. MacArthur, S. Graham, & J. Fitzgerald (Eds.), *New directions in writing theory* (pp. 28–40). New York: Guilford.

Hayes, J. R., & Flower, L. S. (1980). Identifying the organization of writing processes. In L. Gregg & E. Steinberg (Eds.), *Cognitive processes in writing* (pp. 3–30). Hillsdale, NJ: Erlbaum.

Henderson, B. B. (2000). The reader's guide as an integrative writing experience. *Teaching of Psychology, 28,* 257–259.

LePore, S. J., & Smyth, J. M. (Eds.). (2002). *The writing cure: How expressive writing promotes health and well-being.* Washington, DC: American Psychological Association.

Madigan, R., Johnson, S., & Linton, P. (1995). The language of psychology: APA style as epistemology. *American Psychologist, 50,* 428–436.

Marton, J. (2006). *Fables for developing skeptical and critical thinking in psychology.* Victoria, BC: Trafford.

Meltzoff, J. (1998). *Critical thinking about research: Psychology and related fields.* Washington, DC: American Psychological Association.

Rickabaugh, C. A. (1993). The psychology portfolio: Promoting writing and critical thinking about psychology. *Teaching of Psychology, 20,* 170–172.

Schmidt, M. E., & Dunn, D. S. (2007). Teaching writing in statistics and research methods: Addressing objectives, intensive issues, and style. In D. S. Dunn, R. A. Smith, & B. C. Beins (Eds.), *Best practices for teaching statistics and research methods in the behavioral sciences* (pp. 257–273). Mahwah, NJ: Erlbaum.

Spellman, B. A., DeLoache, J., & Bjork, R. A. (2007). Making claims in papers and talks. In R. J. Sternberg, H. L. Roediger III, & D. F. Halpern (Eds.), *Critical thinking in psychology* (pp. 177–195). New York: Cambridge University Press.

Stanovich, K. E. (2007). *How to think straight about psychology* (8th ed.). Boston: Allyn & Bacon.

Sternberg, R. J., Roediger, H. L., III, & Halpern, D. F. (2007). *Critical thinking in psychology.* New York: Cambridge University Press.

Stoloff, M. L., & Rogers, S. (2002). Understanding psychology deeply through thinking, doing, and writing. *APS Observer, 15*(8), 21–22, 31–32.

Toedter, L. J., & Glew, D. F. (2007). Is it science or pseudoscience? An inquiry-based exploration of science gone astray. In T. E. Jacobsen & T. P. Mackey (Eds.), *Information literacy collaborations that work* (pp. 161–176). New York: Neal-Schuman Publishers.

Ware, M. E., Badura, A. S., & Davis, S. F. (2002). Using student scholarship to develop student research and writing skills. *Teaching of Psychology, 29,* 151–154.

Author Note

Send correspondence concerning this chapter to either author: Dana S. Dunn, Department of Psychology, Moravian College, 1200 Main Street, Bethlehem, PA 18018-6650; e-mail: dunn@moravian.edu; Randolph A. Smith, Department of Psychology, PO Box 10036, Lamar University, Beaumont, TX 77710; e-mail: randolph.smith@lamar.edu.

Chapter 15

Using Service Learning to Promote Critical Thinking in the Psychology Curriculum

Elizabeth Yost Hammer

When considering learning objectives, most psychology faculty want their students to develop critical thinking skills and see the relevance of course material in addition to learning basic concepts and theories of the field. With these goals in mind, service learning (i.e., learning course concepts through active service in the community) is an excellent pedagogical tool that encourages students to construct knowledge as opposed to simply receiving it, and in doing so fosters both motivation to learn and critical thinking skills (Beckman, 1997; Klinger, 1999). By providing powerful, real-world opportunities to discuss and analyze course material, service learning not only enhances students' understanding of course material, but also increases awareness of and involvement with the community, self-awareness, and sensitivity to diversity (Gelmon, Holland, Driscoll, Spring, & Kerrigan, 2001). Unlike many other tools, service learning has multiple benefits to the institution and the community as well, including building positive, reciprocal partnerships between the two (Roschelle, Turpin, & Elias, 2000; Valerius & Hamilton, 2001).

For service learning to be successful in developing critical thinking skills and fostering student learning, it must include community activity that (a) addresses specific learning objectives for the course, (b) targets a community need, and (c) is seamlessly and consistently integrated into the course (Ozorak, 2004). These characteristics are what distinguish service learning from volunteerism (another worthwhile endeavor), where students engage in the community without a direct link back to academic content. It is the academic objective of service learning that makes it distinct.

Heffernan (2001) described several ways that service learning is typically integrated into the college curriculum, including discipline-based service-learning courses, capstone courses, and service internships. This chapter focuses on discipline-based service learning where students engage in community service throughout the semester and integrate their experiences into the coverage of course content. Further, I present some of the service-learning assignments that I have used in psychology courses to promote critical thinking and provide some tips for getting started and maximizing the effectiveness of service learning.

Elizabeth Yost Hammer

Service-Learning Assignments

Service learning cuts across all disciplines and, when innovative faculty are creative with assignments, it can be effective in any field. Psychology, with its emphasis on human behavior, is an obvious choice for this pedagogy (Ozorak, 2004). In studying human behavior, psychologists can use community interactions to illustrate theories and provide opportunities for concepts to come to life more easily than can professors in many other fields. Courses such as developmental psychology and social psychology are easily applied to community sites serving a wide array of populations. In fact, most social psychology courses have a unit on prosocial behavior—and what better way to illuminate theories of helping behavior than to have students engage in community service? Therefore, to encourage students to apply social psychological constructs to real-world situations and to develop their critical thinking skills, I have incorporated service-learning assignments into the course.

I invite three to five site supervisors to come to class to make presentations about their sites and recruit students in the first week of the semester. I typically require students to complete a minimum of 16 hours at the site of their choice; 8 hours must be completed by midterm with the final 8 completed by the end of the semester. Students have time sheets for their supervisors to sign. Depending on practical issues (e.g., course load or class size), I alternate between two types of assignments: maintaining a service-learning journal and a more traditional paper.

For the journal assignment, students maintain a structured social psychology journal throughout the semester. For each chapter, students write two or three pages on a specific topic. Table 15.1 provides examples of typical writing assignments. Students turn in their journals seven times over the course of the semester (approximately every 2 weeks), and the overall journal grade is the same percentage of the final grade as an exam (usually about 15%).

For the more traditional paper assignment, students write a midterm and a final paper integrating course material into their experiences at the sites. For the midterm paper, I give students the following guidelines.

Table 15.1. Sample of Chapter Entries for Service-Learning Journal Assignment in Social Psychology

Chapter on Prosocial Behavior
Service learning is a situation where you are engaging in helping behavior. Using this experience, describe some motivational factors, situational factors, personal influences, and interpersonal influences that have come into play. Be clear and specific by only picking a handful of memorable factors or influences.

Chapter on Social Cognition
Discuss schemas. What are some schemas that have influenced your behavior or the behavior of others at your service-learning site? Apply research evidence presented in Chapter 3, using it as support for your personal observations.

Analyze your service-learning experience using two distinct theories from the first half of the course. This assignment requires you to go beyond mere application of theory in that your analysis should demonstrate how the course material has enhanced or influenced your experience. For example, how has knowledge of a specific theory changed the way you interpreted an interaction or made you behave differently than you would have without that knowledge?

The instructions for the final paper are identical except that students must use one theory from the first half of the semester and two from the second half. (See Appendix for an excerpt from a sample student paper.)

To promote critical thinking, I wrote the paper assignment in a way that requires students to go beyond simply applying the course material, a task many (though admittedly not all) students can easily do. Instead, the assignment asks students to critique their behavior using the knowledge they have gained from the course. This process is a bit more difficult for students, and it challenges them to use the course material to think critically about their experiences. For instance, in a recent semester, a student worked with Hunger Relief, an organization that provides meals to the homeless. In her paper she chose to examine the psychological concept of schemas, mental units of organized knowledge about objects or events in our social world (Fiske & Taylor, 1991). She mentioned that her schemas for the homeless were incorrect because many of the people she talked with were not lazy or choosing to remain homeless; instead, many were actively seeking employment and trying to improve their situations. She pointed out that she had fallen prey to the fundamental attribution error (Ross, 1977) by making internal attributions about homeless people in general (i.e., all homeless people are lazy). Up to this point in her paper, the student had only *applied* the material, yet the assignment challenged her to go one step further. That is, how did knowing about the fundamental attribution error *change* her while she was there? At first, all she could come up with was "Being aware of this bias will help me avoid it in the future." Through class discussion and stretching her critical thinking skills, she was able to come to the realization that recognizing the error in her schema allowed her to feel that she had more in common with the people she was feeding than she had thought, which in turn made her feel less timid and afraid around them and more likely to engage with them. By struggling through this thought process, the student became aware not only of the power of social cognition, but also of opportunities to think critically about her social world.

There are pros and cons to each of these assignments. A major benefit of the journal assignment is that it keeps students thinking about their service-learning experiences throughout the course. By writing entries every two weeks, students are continuously integrating their work at the site into the course material (as opposed to only doing this twice a semester). Also, having an entry for each chapter ensures that students apply a broader array of theories and topics to their experiences. Conversely, the traditional papers allow for more depth. It goes without saying that a shortcoming of the journal approach is that it generates a great deal of writing for the instructor to review and grade. In contrast to the midterm and final paper, students turn in the journals every two weeks, so faculty must be diligent in responding to assignments and getting them back to the students promptly. Instructors can vary these assignments (e.g., reflections could be done in a blog or discussion board). Like any assignment, it should be selected to meet the objectives for the course.

In-Class Uses of Service Learning

For service learning to effectively encourage critical thinking, it must be an important component of the course and not merely tacked on. It is a common rookie mistake (indeed one that I made myself) simply to add a service-learning assignment to a course without altering the presentation of course material or integrating it into the course. In this case, students quickly perceive it as "busy work" and treat it as such. Further, without being carefully incorporated into the course, service learning can become mere "feel-good" activities" (Valerius & Hamilton, 2001, p. 339). In contrast, when faculty seamlessly integrate service learning into the overall class structure and reflect it in the course grading, students will perceive it as an important component and attend to it as they would a more traditional assignment. Therefore, it is useful to incorporate students' service experiences into the course above and beyond the actual assignment.

One simple way to include service learning in class time is to call regularly for examples from service learning during class discussion. For example, after discussing the research on self-fulfilling prophecies (Rosenthal & Jacobsen, 1968), I ask students to reflect on ways that this theory might factor into their site interactions. Another method is to incorporate service learning into in-class group work. Because I use collaborative learning techniques in my course (see Giordano & Hammer, 1999, for a review), I am able to insert students' experiences into their activities. For example, after lecturing on theories of helping behavior, I have students (in their in-class groups) critique each theory using their own motives at the service-learning site. This activity typically stimulates an interesting discussion of intrinsic versus extrinsic motivation for the students (i.e., are they motivated by the helping experience or the grade?) that brings the theories to life in a way that a hypothetical situation could not. I also include in exams service-learning reflective questions that reinforce the idea that this is an important and valuable component of the course: An example might be "Distinguish between normative and informational social influence. Provide a clear example of each from your service-learning experience." Finally, I incorporate service learning by using classroom assessment techniques such as a minute paper (see Angelo & Cross, 1993). Using service learning in these ways keeps the students' community experiences in the forefront of the course and encourages them to apply their experiences to course content continuously throughout the semester.

Student Evaluation Data

I gathered data over several semesters (Spring 2002–Fall 2003) for Social Psychology classes, a second-semester, freshman course.[1] When asked to respond to "The service aspect of this course helped me to understand better the required lectures and readings," 59% to 71% responded "Agree" or "Strongly agree."[2] When presented with "The service aspect of this course helped me see how the subject matter I learned can be used in everyday life," 71% to 83% responded "Agree" or "Strongly agree." For "The service aspect of this course made me aware of some of my own biases or prejudices," 77% to 92% responded "Agree" or "Strongly agree." When asked to identify positive aspects of the service-learning experience, students' responses included "The opportunity to get out of my comfort zone and grow more as a person," "A better understanding of how social psychology relates to everyday life," "Made the theory we learned in class more realistic," "Gave me personal satisfaction," and "Chance to help in the community." When asked to identify negative aspects of the service-learning experience, students responses included "Time-consuming," "Hard to fit in schedule," and "Transportation was an issue."

Tips for Getting Started and Maximizing Your Success

Like any tool, successful service learning requires that faculty carefully match the pedagogy to student learning outcomes (Valerius & Hamilton, 2001). So the first place to start is to carefully *consider your course objectives*. What do you hope to accomplish from the assignment, and how can you meet this goal?

If possible, *work with your service-learning office*. If your campus has an office, the staff can help you match your course objectives to appropriate sites, to make contact with site supervisors and facilitate communication, and to advise and negotiate should any problems arise at a site. If your university does not have a specific office set aside for service learning, you need to make contact with community sites yourself. Look to local organizations with which you are familiar or have contacts. Keep in mind that there might be staff on campus who can help facilitate these community contacts. For instance, someone in student affairs or campus ministry who organizes student volunteers can be a valuable resource for identifying community needs and establishing contacts.

It is very important to *develop meaningful assignments* around service learning. Although the service-learning site itself is an important factor (e.g., students get a very different experience tutoring school children versus gutting a flooded home), the actual assignment that focuses the service-learning experience on the course content is crucial in meeting course objectives. I have worked closely with the Writing Across the Curriculum director over the semesters to refine the quality of my writing assignments, and as a result they have changed significantly from when I began incorporating service learning.

Pick a variety of sites. Students have different interests and career goals, so it is nice to offer them an array of site options from which to choose. I usually work with three to five sites. I have found that fewer limits students' options whereas more makes oversight unwieldy. I make an effort to have variety in the sites in terms of location (e.g., walking distance to campus, on a public transportation line, requiring a car), services needed (e.g., tutoring, physical labor, art skills), required schedule (e.g., 2 hours a week, a one-shot all-day commitment), and population served (e.g., kids, elderly, disabled) Note that students typically like working with children, and the one semester I did not offer a site that served children I heard many complaints.

I caution against absolutely requiring service learning, having done this my first semester. Not all students in your class will be ready to engage in the community. The reasons can range from explanations such as personal stress or trauma to scheduling or time conflicts; whatever the reason, forcing a student into the community does not benefit the student or the site. As a result, it is important to *provide alternatives to service learning*. In developing an alternative, it is essential to make it equivalent in terms of time commitment and difficulty level. In my course, students have an option to read and critique a novel as opposed to a community site. The time it takes to read the novel is comparable to that required of service learners, and the paper (or journal) assignments are identical with the exception of what students critique (i.e., service site interaction versus character interactions). Incidentally, very few students chose this alternative option.

Visit sites whenever possible. Obviously it is not always possible to visit every site with every student. However, I cannot emphasize enough the extent to which visiting the site gives you insight into the experience of the student and allows you to more skillfully integrate it into class. Further, it allows you to integrate course content on the spot in interacting with students. Due to the hectic pace of faculty life, visiting sites is difficult to do, yet I have found it to be an invaluable experience for both myself and my students.

Service learning takes energy and effort from the professor. *Beware of burnout.* I do not use service learning in every class each semester. Instead I pick one class in which to use it. Like anything we do in class (e.g., lectures, assignments), doing the same thing over and over becomes stale. Rotating which of my courses uses service learning allows me to work with it within different content areas, student levels, and the like. It keeps me fresh by challenging me to find new ways to incorporate the service into course content.

Finally, *be flexible.* One of the benefits of service learning is that it takes learning out of the classroom and out of the hands of faculty; one of the intimidating aspects of service learning is that it takes learning out of the classroom and out of the hands of faculty. However, true experiential learning requires faculty to turn over control of the classroom and empower students to take charge of their own learning. Service learning epitomizes this approach and can be an exceptional way to enhance student learning of course content, expand their perspectives of their communities and the social world, and increase their critical thinking skills. In addition, it can enrich your teaching, encourage your involvement in the community, and add a new dimension to your class. As Ozorak (2004, p. 138) asked: What are we waiting for?

Notes

1 During this time I was a faculty member in the Department of Psychology at Loyola University, New Orleans.

2 The lower percentages reflect a semester where there was difficulty with one particular service-learning site. As a result, I dropped that site midsemester, and students made alternative arrangements. Interestingly, in my 10 semesters of using service learning, this was the only semester I had to discontinue a site midsemester.

References

Angelo, T. A., & Cross, K. P. (1993). *Classroom assessment techniques: A handbook for college teachers* (2nd ed.). San Francisco, CA: Jossey-Bass.

Beckman, M. (1997). Learning in action. *College Teaching, 45,* 72–75.

Fiske, S. T., & Taylor, S. E. (1991). *Social cognition.* New York: McGraw-Hill.

Gelmon, S. B., Holland, B. A., Driscoll, A., Spring, A., & Kerrigan, S. (2001). *Assessing service learning and civic engagement.* Providence, RI: Campus Compact.

Giordano, P. J., & Hammer, E. Y. (1999). In-class collaborative learning: Practical suggestions from the teaching trenches. *Teaching of Psychology, 26,* 42–44.

Heffernan, K. (2001). *Fundamentals of service-learning course construction.* Providence, RI: Campus Compact.

Klinger, T. (1999). Applying sociocultural psychology to the service-learning experience: Service-learning as a pedagogical tool for developing critical thinking in college students. *Korean Journal of Thinking and Problem Solving, 9,* 25–37.

Ozorak, E. W. (2004). Integrating service-learning into psychology courses. In B. Perlman, L. I. McCann, & S. H. McFadden (Eds.), *Lessons learned: Vol. 2. Practical advice for the teaching of psychology* (pp. 137–146). Washington, DC: American Psychological Society.

Roschelle, A. R., Turpin, J., & Elias, R. (2000). Who learns from service learning? *American Behavioral Scientist, 43,* 839–847.

Rosenthal, R., & Jacobsen, L. F. (1968). *Pygmalion in the classroom.* New York: Holt, Rinehart, & Winston.

Ross, L. (1977). The intuitive psychologist and his shortcomings: Distortions in the attribution process. In L. Berkowitz (Ed.), *Advances in experimental social psychology* (Vol. 10. pp. 174–221). New York: Academic Press.

Valerius, L., & Hamilton, M. L. (2001). The community classroom: Serving to learn and learning to serve. *College Student Journal, 35,* 339–344.

Appendix: Excerpt from a Sample Student Paper

My experience tutoring underprivileged children through the "Children Are Reason Enough" (CARE) program exposed me to the problems of poor societies and the impact of proactive social organizations in impeding the cyclic outcome of an impoverished society. In addition, an understanding of various psychological studies was influential in my understanding of social variables and personal perceptions.

My mindset throughout my first afternoon at CARE proved the influence of the Fundamental Attribution Error. Having grown up in New Orleans, I had presupposed ideas of what "type" of people to expect from public schools. My presumption undoubtedly guided me to pick out examples of what I expected and, throughout the afternoon, I became increasingly peeved at children who would not try or who told me to do their homework. I am ashamed to admit it, but I found myself thinking these children were unmotivated and lazy. I continued making these personality assumptions until the end of the session when I had a chance to talk to some of the volunteers not from New Orleans. One said, "I wonder what goes on in that little girl's home life." At that point I realized how biased I was to making generalities based on my assumptions. I also realized how psychology class was going to fit into my service-learning experience by examining situations as opposed to personalities.

My initial generalization of the students' behavior was based on my opinion of their personalities. I deemed the children unproductive because they were lazy and uncooperative. In retrospect, I realize that by shifting my focus to the situation I was able to change my outlook and interpretation of their outward personalities. The children might be acting lazy because they were participating in an after school program until six at night after a full day at school. By evaluating the situation more closely, I came to view most of the children as considerably resilient in light of their situation. I also appreciated the CARE program's role in improving the situations for these kids.

Author Note

I am indebted to Dr. Carol Jeandrone who gave me the green light on service learning and Dr. Melanie McKay who was instrumental in changing my assignments for the better. I also appreciate Rebecca Gonzales for fully engaging in her community site. Finally, I am grateful to the editors of this volume for their helpful comments on an earlier version of this chapter.

Chapter 16

Beyond Standard Lectures: Supporting the Development of Critical Thinking in Cognitive Psychology Courses

Jordan P. Lippman, Trina C. Kershaw,
James W. Pellegrino, and Stellan Ohlsson

As cognitive psychologists, we have a keen interest in understanding how people learn. We also love teaching, as well as thinking and studying about how best to educate people. We believe that student learning is best facilitated through the careful and principled design of learning environments that foster the development of discipline-specific knowledge and skill, that increase student interest and motivation to study the discipline, and that support the development of lifelong learning skills and critical thinking. We base design decisions on principles of learning and cognition and by co-ordinating teaching strategies (i.e., pedagogy), domain content (e.g., memory and cognition), and assessment techniques.

The cognitive literature indicates that students learn best when they are motivated, interested in the content, and challenged (e.g., Donovan, Bransford, & Pellegrino, 1999). To make content meaningful, faculty should also challenge students to relate class material to their lives and experiences. They should learn to think critically and evaluate claims made by professors, scientists, textbooks, and the media. To succeed, students must take responsibility for their education and learn to approach academic tasks strategically. Effective students are aware of the strategies they use and the extent to which they have understood material that they have just learned, listened to, or read. Research on memory and cognition has shown that effective learning occurs when people:

- build new understanding by adding onto and revising pre-existing knowledge
- distribute study over longer durations of time (instead of cramming the night before an exam, for instance)
- revisit the same material multiple times and from multiple perspectives
- analyze new knowledge for meaning and relevance
- link abstract concepts to concrete examples and experiences
- reflect on their thinking and learning and attempt to try new learning strategies.

It is often a challenge to incorporate theory-based principles of learning, instruction, and assessment into the design of higher education courses, because any such design activity involves simultaneous consideration of sets of environmental constraints on what is feasible. In our case, the issues and constraints are significant. The University of Illinois at Chicago (UIC) has a diverse student population, many of whom work part- or full-time in addition to commuting to school while pursuing a full class load. The courses we teach typically involve 2nd to 4th-year students who have taken prerequisite courses such as introductory psychology and research methods before taking our course in Cognition and Memory. We are typically constrained to offering our courses in large lecture-style classrooms, with twice weekly class meetings of 75 mins, with no separate scheduled discussion sections and with limited teaching assistant support. We believe that even under such circumstances it is feasible to incorporate theory-driven activities designed to enhance student learning outcomes.

To understand aspects of what we do to enhance student learning we need to be clear about what we consider important in our field. The primary object of study in cognitive psychology is the mind. The mind, however, is not directly observable, and cognitive psychologists make inferences about the properties of the mind based on indirect observations of how people perform on carefully designed tasks. To properly evaluate claims about mental structures and processes, and to put them in perspective, students of cognitive psychology must understand the research methods and logic used to reach conclusions. Much of what we expect students to learn in the courses we teach is not "fact" in the traditional sense of the word. All theories and conclusions are provisional in the sense that they are the best explanations of experimental observations we have to date. However, they are not set in stone, and often there are multiple competing explanations of cognitive phenomena. Theories are evaluated based not on who believes them but how well they can explain the outcomes of various observations. Theories are also evaluated in terms of explanatory power, usefulness for promoting research, applicability, and evolutionary significance.

We designed the activities discussed in this chapter to promote the development of scientific thinking skills and learning regarding important content in cognitive psychology. All three activities are consistent with the design principles noted previously; they ask students to consider the relationship between theory and evidence, which we consider to be at the core of critical thinking in science. Although they differ in the type of evidence and method of analysis, they all promote critical evaluation of this relationship. We believe these activities also promote active engagement and interest in the material. Some ask students to reflect on the scientific process, whereas others encourage students to integrate class material with knowledge and experiences outside of class. We chose activities for different reasons and implemented them in a variety of ways depending on class size and other factors.

In the remainder of this chapter we describe a set of different types of activities that we have used—including some variations—to accomplish the goals described previously. In each case, we describe the activity and how one or more of us has implemented it, provide evidence for its effectiveness at increasing critical thinking skills, including student evaluations and performance data when possible, and describe ways to adapt the activity to other contexts.

Participation in Experiments and Reflection on the Meaning of the Data

We give students firsthand experiences with cognitive phenomena discussed in the text and class meetings by having them participate in online and in-class experiments. Participating online prior to class provides concrete experiences of phenomena before discussing them, thereby enhancing meaning and retention of the material, whereas participating during class accomplishes the same thing while increasing interest and engagement. In both cases, students are acutely interested to see how the results came out. The main benefit of these activities, however, is promoting the development of critical thinking by getting students to make predictions and interpret the results once they are presented in class. In this section, we review the types of experiments used for out-of-class experiences and in-class demonstrations and illustrate how we make use of the data to enhance critical thinking in class.

Implementation of Activity

For online activities, students either participate in selected experiments from the commercially available CogLab 2.0 (Wadsworth, n.d.) or in tasks we have created and hosted ourselves. Access to Wadsworth's online CogLab can be purchased individually, or it can be bundled with various textbooks at a reduced cost (e.g., Goldstein, 2005, which we have used on more than one occasion). The CogLab Web site lists individual labs by topic, and Goldstein's text indicates relevant labs for different topics. Most of the labs relate to basic cognitive phenomena (e.g., perception, imagery, episodic memory, simple verbal reasoning) so we have created our own lab exercises to demonstrate more complex cognitive phenomena not covered by CogLab, such as nonverbal reasoning, text comprehension, and skill learning. Table 16.1 presents a sample list of topics, the relevant labs, and their relative popularity; both Wadsworth and locally developed labs are listed. To promote critical thinking, we introduce the paradigm and theoretical background for a particular experiment and then ask students to make predictions about the results. After presenting the results, we interactively discuss their interpretation in light of typical, sometimes competing theories. The Deese–Roediger–McDermott (DRM) false-memory paradigm (Deese, 1959; Roediger & McDermott, 1995) and the Stroop (1935) task are two classic cognitive situations we have effectively used as online CogLabs as well as in-class demonstrations.

False memories come in various shapes and sizes, but in all cases they are recollections of experiences that never happened. Properties of the memory system that make it extremely powerful, enabling quick interpretation and storage of events and efficient recollection of memories for distant and previously irrelevant experiences, also make it susceptible to distortions of various kinds. Theorists argue that schemas serve to help with the interpretation and storage of experienced events as well as subsequent reconstruction of memories of those events when they are "retrieved." These properties and mechanisms are easily demonstrated using the DRM paradigm, which is based on Roediger and McDermott's (1995)

Table 16.1. List of Sample CogLabs from Pellegrino's Class by Topic and Popularity

Topic	CogLabs[a]	Popularity[b]
Mental imagery and visual processing	Mental Rotation	13%
	Mental Scanning	7%
Semantic memory: organization and processing	Prototypes	8%
	Lexical Decision	6%
	Implicit Learning	5%
Sensory memory	Partial Report	3%
Short-term and working memory	Memory Span	34%
	Brown–Peterson	13%
	Operation Span	8%
	Sternberg Search	3%
Episodic memory: Storage & retrieval	Encoding Specificity	12%
	Levels of Processing	7%
Episodic memory: Forgetting & false memories	False Memory	36%
	Forgot-it-all-Along	17%
	Remember/Know	15%
Introduction to language	Word Superiority	21%
	Stroop	13%
Comprehension	(Vocabulary & comprehension)	5%
Problem solving and decision making	Risky Decisions	21%
	Monty Hall	15%
	Wason Selection Task	9%
	Typical Reasoning	9%
Intelligence	(Nonverbal reasoning)	12%

[a] "Home-grown" labs are listed in parentheses. The rest are part of the Wadsworth CogLab Package.
[b] Percentage of students who chose each as one of their three favorite labs.

replication of Deese's (1959) classic study: A list of target words (e.g., *sour, candy, sugar, bitter, good, taste*, etc.) is presented, and then participants immediately categorize a new list of words as either present or not present in the originally experienced list. Because words in the original list all tend to activate the "sweet" schema, this critical lure is inevitably "remembered" as being on the target list whereas unrelated distractors in the new list are appropriately rejected. Students are often surprised that, even when aware of the effect ahead of time, they cannot prevent these false memories from appearing. This simple and robust effect can be demonstrated with visual or auditory stimuli and with recognition or recall tests. In class, the instructor can present the list of target words visually or orally and the number of people who recognize each word can be recorded.

To promote critical thinking about the nature of the episodic memory process, we introduce the paradigm and then ask students to make predictions about the results (even though they can access their results and that of the larger group online, many do not make use of this feature of CogLab). Figure 16.1 presents a graph of the results from the Wadsworth CogLab for Ohlsson's Spring 2005 class showing accurate recognition of original target words, accurate recognition of unrelated distractor or lure words, and a

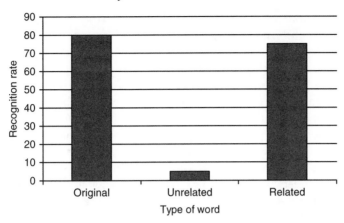

Figure 16.1. Data from the False Memory Wadsworth CogLab. Wadsworth CogLab 2.0 Cognitive Psychology Online Laboratory Web site. (n.d.). Retrieved April 24, 2007, from http://coglab. wadsworth.com/

high false recognition rate for the "false memory lure." Once we present the results, a fruitful discussion can ensue in which students think critically about the mechanisms responsible for the results and what this demonstration reveals about an important principle related to the accuracy of episodic memory.

The Stroop (1935) effect is a simple and very robust demonstration of processing automaticity. Lists of color words are either presented in a matching condition with the ink color identical to the color name (e.g., *black* printed in black ink) or in a mismatch condition with a different ink color than the color name (e.g., *red* printed in black). In Wadsworth's online version, students must categorize the print color of words as quickly as possible. In class, the instructor can present words in various ways and students can be asked to respond aloud together. A very effective approach is to have one person volunteer to be the test participant who reads aloud, have another serve as timer, and have everyone else perform the same task as the volunteer participant but do so silently. Students find the matching condition very easy but will experience considerable interference in the mismatch condition and slow down their response rate as well as make mistakes. We present the Stroop paradigm in the same manner as the DRM: Students make predictions, we reveal the results, and then we discuss and interpret the results.

The Stroop (1935) effect allows students to think about the differences between highly skilled automatic processing situations and slower, more effortful controlled processing situations. In addition, this activity can prompt discussion about when and how a controlled process becomes automatic. For example, if you do the Stroop task in the mismatch condition several times, will it become easier? What if a person who did not know English as well as the typical college students tried the Stroop task? What would happen in that condition? What about children who are learning to read? This type of discussion allows for introduction of ideas relating to the effects of individual differences, learning, and practice—thus going beyond a simple discussion of the distinction between automatic and controlled processes.

Personal response systems (PRS). Pellegrino and Lippman have also engaged students during class by using handheld personal response system (PRS) units and the associated data capture and presentation software (Interwrite Learning Personal Response System, n.d.). Such systems allow for display of multiple-choice or true–false questions with immediate capture and display of aggregate student responses. In Pellegrino's classes, each student was assigned a PRS unit at the start of the semester, which was then brought to class and used to earn daily class participation points. We required them to return the unit (or pay for its replacement) before a final grade in the class would be posted. Students may also purchase a PRS unit and then sell the units to future students; in some cases the units can be bundled with the text and sold through the bookstore. PRS units are particularly useful in large classes where it is otherwise difficult to gain the attention of all students and to gauge the distribution of their responses to questions. Because students can respond anonymously, there is little reluctance to respond to challenging queries and no concern about publicly embarrassing oneself if it turns out your response to a query is not "correct." Often students see that they are not alone in responding in a particular way and feel less concerned about spontaneously explaining why they may have made the choice they did.

We have used PRS to elicit student misconceptions and preconceptions regarding key concepts and topic areas such as how memory works or the nature of intelligence, to demonstrate phenomena like false memory, and in the prediction and interpretation of data from online CogLab experiments. After describing the theory and design of a study (an online CogLab, class demonstration, or other described study) we might display a set of possible predictions and then ask students to select one. After displaying a graph of the distribution of their responses, we ask one or more students to volunteer and explain their responses. Finally, we present the actual results. Alternatively, we have presented the design and results of a study and then used PRS to elicit student endorsements for potential interpretations of the data. Thus, PRS allows us to engage all students in a large lecture in the critical thinking involved in making predictions and interpreting results. It also provides us with a means of collecting immediate formative assessment information regarding students' understanding of critical aspects of the material (Wiliam, 2007) with the opportunity to immediately address misunderstandings rather than simply move on.

Analysis of Activity

In volunteer end-of-term evaluations in Pellegrino's classes, we ask students about their favorite parts of the class. Students consistently rate the online CogLab and lecture as their first or second favorite. We coded students' open-ended explanations of why they selected CogLab as their favorite component of the class as well as responses to an open-ended request for comments about the activity. In both cases, the most common comments indicated that students liked the CogLabs because they were concrete, easy to do, interesting, interactive, and fun. The following comments illustrate why students liked the CogLab assignments:

- "The best part was that the labs were fun and interesting. It was interesting to see how my results came out."

- "I think they were a great interactive way to get personally involved in the cognitive difficulties we were learning about in class."
- "CogLab was easy to do and interesting because it provided concrete demonstrations of phenomena discussed in class."

Although a majority of students liked the CogLabs, a number also indicated that we may have assigned too many of them or that it was too difficult to initially set up their CogLab accounts. Our experience is that the latter issue results from students failing to read and follow the instructions carefully, so instructors need to be prepared for such concerns.

Kershaw's Summer 2005 class ($n = 50$) rated the demonstrations used in class. Two of their favorites were the Stroop (1935) effect and a demonstration of false memory (rating = 4.4/5 for each activity). Finally, students tend to think that PRS is an effective way to engage with some of the course material. In fact, roughly 75% of students in Pellegrino's classes thought that we used PRS the right amount each class period and on the right number of days in the semester.

Conclusions and Applications to Other Courses

Actively engaging students in the process of generating data and predicting and interpreting results is an effective way to promote critical thinking about constructs that are often otherwise abstract. Students can complete online CogLabs prior to class or engage in in-class activities through demonstrations or the use of the personal response units. Students then become more engaged with the course material by actually experiencing the cognitive phenomena they would otherwise only read or hear about. They gain experience in scientific reasoning by making predictions and evaluating the possible meaning of results.

In addition to the learning benefits gained by students via these activities, instructors benefit as well. From an instructor's perspective, the activities are generally easy to incorporate into the normal flow of the class, especially once one has some experience doing so. Some materials such as the Wadsworth CogLab system or PRS units can be bundled with textbooks. Other materials, such as the in-class demonstrations, take minimal resources. We have used these activities in cognitive psychology classes ranging from 25 to 150 students. In addition, activities such as these are easy to implement in other courses. For instance, Wadsworth and other publishers now offer online laboratories in many disciplines. Materials aside, we believe the critical thinking benefit of such activities is creating an environment conducive for students to connect personal experience with data and theory and providing them with the opportunity to discuss and reflect on their interconnections.

Analysis of Empirical Articles and Connection to Class Content

One activity we use in our cognition courses to promote critical thinking asks students to analyze empirical journal articles and think about how they connect to course content.

In Kershaw's classes, articles are the primary reading materials; for each article students complete a required activity developed by Kershaw and Lippman (under review). In Pellegrino's classes, this activity was an extra-credit assignment. We developed this activity to enhance students' critical thinking and reading skills and to provide an opportunity to engage in an authentic activity. In addition, students are introduced to the way psychological data is reported in the scientific community.

Implementation of Activity

Kershaw selected one article for every major subject area in cognitive psychology according to the following criteria: (a) the article had to present original experimental results; it could not be a review article; (b) the article had to be relatively short in length, approximately 10 pages or less; and (c) the article had to cover an aspect of the particular cognitive psychology topic that Kershaw judged as being relevant to the students' lives (see Table 16.2 for a sample list of articles by course topic).

Students read each article before coming to class and turned in a reading worksheet that asked several standard questions and a unique question for each article. Students engaged in scientific practice and further honed their scientific and critical thinking skills by analyzing the articles for methodological or interpretation issues and by suggesting additional manipulations that could enhance the research. The unique discussion question for each reading asked students to consider real-world applications of the research or to make connections to other articles or research covered in class. To introduce this activity, we have them read a sample article and try to answer the questions themselves but we then answer the questions together in a class discussion of how to dissect a journal article.

We will illustrate this technique based on an article by Strayer and Johnston (2001), who conducted a study about driving and talking on a cell phone. Kershaw has used this article as a reading about attention because it is about the impact of divided attention on performance but also illustrates the selective and divided attention experimental paradigms and introduces issues related to automaticity and individual differences. Students identify the purpose of the research (e.g., to study the impact of divided attention on driving performance), succinctly explain the method by identifying the independent variable (e.g., concurrent distraction vs. no distraction conditions) and dependent variable (e.g., performance on a secondary tracking task) and the results (e.g., performance is lower in the concurrent distraction condition). Students then connect the implications of the results in terms of the goals of the article (e.g., Experiment 1 showed participation in a conversation can impact performance using a hand-held or hands-free device). Students critique the research and suggest changes to increase external validity (e.g., suggesting the simulated driving tasks were not realistic and suggesting alternatives) or internal validity (e.g., suggesting having an additional condition where other people in the car talked in the background). For this article, the unique question was: "On July 8, 2006, it became illegal to use a handheld cell phone while driving in Chicago. Based on the results of the article, as well as your own opinion, is this an appropriate ban? Why or why not?" In answering this question for this article, students linked the findings to larger social and political issues, giving them practice in critical thinking and helping them see the relevance of class content.

Table 16.2. List of Journal Articles Assigned by Topic

Topic	Articles Used
Perception	McCarley, J. S., Kramer, A. F., Wickens, C. D., Vidoni, E. D., & Boot, W. R. (2004). Visual skills in airport-security screening. *Psychological Science, 15*, 302–306.[b]
Divided attention	Strayer, D. L., & Johnston, W. A. (2001). Driven to distraction: Dual-task studies of simulated driving and conversing on a cellular telephone. *Psychological Science, 12*, 462–466.[b]
Working memory	Conway, A. R. A., Cowan, N. A., & Bunting, M. F. (2001). The cocktail party phenomenon revisited: The importance of working memory capacity. *Psychonomic Bulletin and Review, 8*, 331–335.[a]
	Beilock, S. L., & Carr, T. H. (2005). When high-powered people fail: Working memory and "choking under pressure" in math. *Psychological Science, 16*, 101–105.[c]
Episodic memory	Lewandowsky, S., Stritzke, W. G. K., Oberauer, K., & Morales, M. (2005). Memory for fact, fiction, and misinformation: The Iraq war 2003. *Psychological Science, 16*, 190–195.[c]
Cognitive aging	Ryan, L., Hatfield, C., & Hofstetter, M. (2002). Caffeine reduces time-of-day effects on memory performance in older adults. *Psychological Science, 13*, 68–71.[b]
Language	Boroditsky, L. (2001). Does language shape thought?: Mandarin and English speakers' conceptions of time. *Cognitive Psychology, 43*, 1–22.[c]
Problem solving	German, T. P., & Barrett, H. C. (2005). Functional fixedness in a technologically sparse culture. *Psychological Science, 16*, 1–5.[b]
Creativity	Ward, T. B., & Sifonis, C. M. (1997). Task demands and generative thinking: What changes and what remains the same? Journal of *Creative Behavior, 31*, 245–259.[a]

[a] This article was used during the Summer 2004 semester only.
[b] This article was used during the Summer 2004 and 2005 semesters only.
[c] This article has been used since the Summer 2005 semester.

Analysis of Activity

Kershaw assessed this technique by comparing two undergraduate cognitive psychology classes she taught at UIC during the Spring 2003 ($n = 23$) and Summer 2004 ($n = 35$) semesters. The courses covered the same information and used several of the same assignments. The primary difference between the courses was that the Spring 2003 class used a textbook (Ashcraft, 2002), and the Summer 2004 class used journal articles.

The classes were compared on the overall points and common assignments that were unrelated to article content. The students who used a textbook and the students who used articles did not differ in the total number of points or on their scores on one assignment, but students who had the textbook outperformed those who used journal articles on the other assignment. Comparisons of student ratings on a standard UIC student government course evaluation did not differ except for ratings on the following items: "The required readings were valuable" and "You have learned and understood the subject materials in this course." Ratings on both of these questions were higher in the articles-only class.

Students offered comments about the best and worst aspects of the required readings and reading worksheet activities. Student reaction to using journal articles in lieu of a textbook for the Summer 2004 class was mixed but generally positive. For example, one student noted: "I liked the fact that there was no textbook, because we were exposed to more actual experiments and case studies that people did than would probably be possible from a textbook." However, some students noted that some articles were too long or hard to understand; for example, one student said: "Some of the reading assignments were a little hard to read. It was hard to determine what the results were and what they meant." Overall, though, the general consensus of students seemed to be that although the articles were interesting and helped them to learn the concepts in class, it would have been useful to have a textbook to which they could refer. As one student noted: "I happen to like using the articles instead of a textbook. ... Only thing is when sometimes I have questions and I do not have a textbook to refer back to for clarification."

Conclusions and Applications to Other Courses

Students in undergraduate psychology classes can learn critical subject matter equally well with primary source readings or with textbooks. As suggested by Levine (2001), the use of journal articles can promote critical thinking and understanding of the psychological research process. In addition, reflection on and analysis of journal articles helps students to develop scientific reasoning skills, such as making predictions and evaluating results, while integrating their prior knowledge with course content.

The applicability and feasibility of using journal articles as the primary reading materials for undergraduate psychology courses may be limited by class format and characteristics. For example, both classes in this comparison were small by UIC standards. Practicalities of grading with limited teaching assistant support and engaging all students in discussions of the articles may limit the effectiveness of this technique in large classes. However, Kershaw has used a modification of this technique in introduction to psychology courses at the University of Massachusetts Dartmouth, which average 65–75 students. The articles chosen for the latter class tend to be easier and more general than the articles used for the cognitive psychology course. In addition, instead of using a standard reading worksheet that emphasizes methodology and theory, Kershaw created reading worksheets for each article that directed students to particular sections in their book to help them answer questions.

Cognition in Daily Life Exercise

We created the cognition in daily life exercise to help students think critically about psychological theories by getting them to analyze their daily experiences in light of them.

This activity helps students think about how the phenomena discussed in class play out in their daily lives (i.e., by engaging in processes of generalization and application of the scientific knowledge). We believe this activity helps improve critical thinking skills, increases interest in the subject, and enhances comprehension and retention of course content. The activity increases students' retention of content because linking theories with memories of daily experiences elaborates and strengthens memory traces of the theories. It increases the likelihood that students will use concepts to interpret future behavior because theories are stored with links to many different contexts, which increases the probability of retrieval and successful transfer.

Implementation of Activity

We have used this activity in three main ways: Diary of Memory Failures (Ohlsson, Pellegrino, and Kershaw), Cognition in Daily Life Report (Pellegrino), and Dear Grandma Letter (Pellegrino). In each case, students recorded events from their lives and, in a final report, interpreted them using course concepts. Breadth and depth of the content covered, logistics of recording and reporting events, and final report style differed for each assignment. The Diary of Memory Failures focused students exclusively on situations involving episodic long-term memory malfunction whereas the Cognition in Daily Life Report and Dear Grandma Letter assignments asked students to reflect on the generalizability of three different course themes. We asked students to submit periodic diary updates or to save their journal entries until it was time to write one final report. We have also asked students to submit a report relating to each major unit shortly after it concluded (e.g., semantic memory, episodic memory, higher-order cognition). The Diary of Memory Failures and Cognition in Daily Life Reports are formal reports of the events followed by theoretical interpretation, but the Dear Grandma Letter asks students to write about the events and theories in a conversational manner that their grandparents could understand.

Student examples. Student examples of a reported memory failure from Cognition in Daily Life Report and an example relating to problem solving from a Dear Grandma Letter helps illustrate how these assignments can differ in flavor but still promote critical thinking.

Example 1: Memory Failure from a Cognition in Daily Life Report

It was a Sunday afternoon around 1:30pm, and I was driving after a stressful weekend of working my second job with the Chicago Tribune. On my way home, I passed by a post office and realized that I had completely forgotten to mail out a very important document for work. Luckily, the sight of the post office cued my memory into recalling that I was supposed to do something before it was too late.

This relates to memory failure and the cue-dependent nature of memory. Seeing the post office as I was driving was a visual cue. It reminded me that there was something I needed to do, and right away I associated the post office with the Chicago Tribune, which I then associated with my document. ... This illustrates the close link between how information is encoded and retrieved and that retrieval cues can be very context-specific. Proactive interference may have also had a role. Every weekend on Sunday, I need to mail out the same documents with updated information. Memories about all the previous weeks may have prevented me from remembering that I had not yet mailed out my documents on that particular weekend.

Example 2: Problem Solving from a Dear Grandma Letter

Dear Nanna,

In my cognitive psychology class we recently discussed some interesting theories about how we solve problems. ... Apparently we aren't as efficient at these things as you'd think. For example, we tend to approach problem solving in a familiar, expected way, even if it's better to "break set," or break from the obvious approach. The word used to describe sticking to a familiar, but less effective routine is "einstellung," which you should understand, being German! ... I was heading downtown (south) to meet a friend for dinner. Even though temperatures were sub-zero, I waited for a bus because I didn't want to splurge on a cab. After about 15 minutes, by which time my feet had frozen, I saw a northbound bus approaching. ... It stopped long enough to for me to catch it but I resisted going in the opposite direction. ...

This reminds me of a "problem" we discussed in class that requires "backtracking" at one point [to solve it]. Most people resist this decision, because it appears to move them away from the desired goal. If I hadn't resisted the idea of backtracking, and instead broke set, I'd have spared my feet! As it turned out, I had to wait for that bus to turn around and head southbound. Stay warm!

Although the styles of these two student responses differ greatly, they both show that the students were trying to apply the concepts from the course to make sense of the cognitive mechanisms responsible for their own, everyday behavior.

Analysis of Activity

We coded open-ended responses on an end-of-term evaluation item that asked students from Pellegrino's classes to offer comments about the best and worst aspects of the Cognition in Daily Life Report assignment from three semesters (Spring 2004, Fall 2004, and Spring 2006). Reactions were mixed, with a majority being positive; the most frequent comments related to how the task helped students learn the content and see how it related to their daily lives. For example, one student wrote, "Even after the assignment was turned in, I continued to think about things in my life that pertain to class." Negative comments were mostly about task logistics such as difficulty associated with keeping track of the diary entries and complaints about the complexities of having to write about three events relating to each of two or three themes. For example, one student wrote, "Many of the cognitive events that I observed weren't related and this made it very difficult to combine them when writing the paper." Ratings on two questions that asked students to rate how much they learned from and enjoyed the assignment on a 5-point Likert scale were consistently above 3.5, suggesting people enjoy and learn from these assignments.

To simplify the report and task of keeping track of diary entries, we changed the activity into the Dear Grandma Letter.

We asked students from Pellegrino's courses what their favorite component of the course was in Fall 2006; their two favorite components were the online CogLabs and Dear Grandma Letter assignments, and no student indicated that the Dear Grandma assignment was their least favorite assignment. We coded students' explanations of why this component was their favorite. In order of decreasing frequency the reasons were that it was easy and enjoyable, they thought linking class content to real life helped them learn the concepts, and they liked the informal and simple style of writing a letter instead of a report.

Conclusions and Applications to Other Courses

The cognition in daily life assignments have students think critically about how theories can (or cannot) explain their daily cognitive experiences. Having students evaluate their experiences in terms of theories from class leads to increased appreciation of the pervasiveness of cognitive phenomena as well as retention and comprehension of the scientific principles and content.

In terms of practical use of these assignments, we believe it is important to make clear your expectations of what students are to write, and to simplify as much as possible the logistics of keeping track of diary entries. Overall, students like the assignment because it helps them learn the content and think about its relevance to their lives.

This type of assignment could be readily implemented in other courses. Kershaw has used a shortened version of the memory diary in her introductory psychology course (n = 75 students). As an additional application, students in a social psychology course could keep a diary of their attribution or stereotyping experiences.

General Discussion

Everyone agrees that students learn best when they are active. After a century of research into learning, cognitive psychologists have developed an appreciation for the types of mental activities particularly supportive of effective learning. The challenge is implementation: How do you engage students in active learning and critical thinking when the setting is a lecture hall with one professor and 100–200 students meeting for 60–75 mins twice a week? It requires considerable creativity on the part of the instructor to design activities that can be effectively implemented within this standard undergraduate course format.

The examples summarized exemplify some tricks of the trade we have found useful. One of these approaches involves creative use of homework activities to promote critical thinking. The various diary activities engage students and focus their attention on critically evaluating their daily experiences. The online demonstration experiments support the class presentation of particular phenomena, but they also support a semester-long attention to the methodology of psychological experimentation. The main benefit of these activities comes from discussion of meaning of the design and results during in-class discussions.

Another trick involves turning the classroom itself into an occasion for student activity. Classroom discussions are of course desirable, but not every issue lends itself to discussion, and students might find it futile to come up with positions on their own for issues where they know that the instructor has the right answer "hidden up his or her sleeve" already. Assigning original articles opens up a space for discussion, because students can challenge the instructor's interpretation of the conclusions. Precisely because the article is written by somebody other than the instructor, the latter's opinion about it need not be normative for the class, and students can feel free to deviate from the instructor without thereby demonstrating ignorance or risking their grade. It helps if the topic is interesting in itself and if the discussion is structured.

Technology enables activities of this sort. The personal response system lets the instructor take input from the students, which in turn forces them to make up their minds about the issues at hand. Also, it enables in-class demonstrations of basic effects. Although technology is a help, it is not a necessity. We have frequently implemented in-class activities where the students respond by raising their hands, a very cheap and accessible personal response system.

Activity-based lecture classes require more effort and innovation on the part of the instructor in the planning and preparation stage. Once designed and fine-tuned, however, the actual teaching of a course is easier and more relaxed for both students and instructor, perhaps because less is now riding on the lectures. It also fits the mindset of the current generation of American students. They are more used to interactive scenarios than scenarios requiring sustained but passive attention. These advantages translate into higher student evaluations, greater quality learning, and enhanced critical thinking. Although we do not have objective evidence as yet to support this claim, we believe that the critical thinking skills learned though these activities transfers readily to other areas of students' academic and personal lives. At the very least, we have created some of the critical conditions for such transfer to occur.

References

Ashcraft, M. H. (2002). *Cognition* (3rd ed.). Upper Saddle River, NJ: Prentice Hall.

Deese, J. (1959). On the prediction of occurrence of particular verbal instructions in immediate recall. *Journal of Experimental Psychology, 58,* 17–22.

Donovan, M. S., Bransford, J., & Pellegrino, J. W. (1999). *How people learn: Bridging research and practice.* Washington, DC: National Academy Press.

Goldstein, E. B. (2005). *Cognitive psychology: Connecting mind, research, and everyday experience.* Belmont, CA: Wadsworth.

Interwrite Learning Personal Response System. (n.d). Retrieved April 24, 2007, from http://www. interwritelearning.com/products/prs/index.html

Kershaw, T. C., & Lippman, J. P. (under review). Using empirical journal articles as primary reading material in undergraduate cognitive psychology courses. *Teaching of Psychology.*

Levine, E. (2001). Reading your way to scientific literacy. *Journal of College Science Teaching, 31,* 122–125.

Roediger, H. L., III, & McDermott, K. B. (1995). Creating false memories: Remembering words not presented in lists. *Journal of Experimental Psychology: Learning, Memory, and Cognition, 21,* 803–814.

Strayer, D. L., & Johnston, W. A. (2001). Driven to distraction: Dual-task studies of simulated driving and conversing on a cellular telephone. *Psychological Science, 12,* 462–466.

Stroop, J. R. (1935). Studies of interference in serial verbal reactions. *Journal of Experimental Psychology, 28,* 643–662.

Wadsworth CogLab 2.0 Cognitive Psychology Online Laboratory Web site. (n.d.). Retrieved April 24, 2007, from http://coglab.wadsworth.com/

Wiliam, D. (2007). Keeping learning on track: Formative assessment and the regulation of learning. In F. K. Lester Jr. (Ed.), *Second handbook of mathematics teaching and learning* (pp. 1053–1098). Greenwich, CT: Information Age Publishing.

Chapter 17

Why We Believe: Fostering Critical Thought and Scientific Literacy in Research Methods

Bernard C. Beins

Critical Thinking

People know what they believe, and they believe what they know. And, in some cases, they are wrong. For example, many people believe that good students are socially inept loners, even though ample research has shown that good students display a wide range of desirable social traits (Stanovich, 2004). And simply providing new information is often ineffective in changing people's minds (Anderson, Lepper, & Ross, 1980). Thus it would behoove students to generate habits of critical thinking about how they acquire and update what they know. The research methods course is an ideal venue for enhancing such thought.

Critical thinking comprises formulating questions clearly and precisely, gathering and testing relevant information, recognizing our (and others') assumptions and perspectives, and communicating effectively to develop solutions (Scriven & Paul, 2007), all goals associated with conducting research.

Further, students must learn to differentiate between knowledge that they can trust and that they cannot. Unfortunately, there is no certain algorithm for such decision making; there are, at best, tentative heuristics, and critical thinkers must identify their own and others' biases and assumptions (Smith, 2002).

As teachers work to engender critical thinking in students, psychology teachers work toward a particular type of critical thinking: scientific thinking. Recent research indicates a relatively poor incidence of scientific literacy in the populace, roughly 28%. Surprisingly, this low value actually represents an increase from 10% since 1988 (Miller, 2007).

Miller's assessments actually reflect what Maienschein and students (1998) referred to as *science literacy*, which is knowledge of scientific material. This type of knowledge differs from *scientific literacy*, which is oriented toward process and context, rather than content. In a broad sense, scientific literacy involves knowledge and understanding of scientific concepts and processes required for personal decision making and civic involvement

(National Science Education Standards, 1995). These are desirable outcomes; the important question is whether learning the process of research fosters scientific literacy.

Does Psychology Promote Scientific Literacy?

Scientific literacy relates to one's ability to describe, explain, and predict natural phenomena. Using the National Science Education Standards (1995), it is easy to see how psychology promotes scientific literacy, as shown in Table 17.1.

If one regards scientific literacy as a variation on general critical thinking ability, there is evidence that psychology promotes such habits of thought, at least at the graduate level (Lehman, Lempert, & Nisbett, 1988). Psychology graduate students in the social science domains showed improvements in both statistical and methodological reasoning and in conditional reasoning as applied to everyday life. After three years in graduate school, students in the natural science areas of psychology and students in chemistry showed non-significant declines. All three cohorts were initially comparable on the measures.

One implication of the Lehman et al. (1988) study is that the type of training accorded psychology graduate students in the social areas promotes what the National Academy of Sciences refers to as scientific literacy. One further question is whether the trend toward greater critical thought at the graduate level might exist at the undergraduate level. There is some preliminary evidence that it can (Holmes & Beins, 2008): As students progressed through a highly empirical psychology curriculum, their level of scientific literacy increased, and their patterns of interest converged on those seen among graduate students.

The development of science literacy (i.e., factual knowledge) is less obvious. Clearly, psychology students learn the science of behavior. With courses in neuroscience, sensation,

Table 17.1. The Ways Psychology Promotes Scientific Literacy

Component of scientific literacy	How psychology research methods courses address the component
Asking questions about everyday occurrences and finding answers to the questions	Developing research questions to identify factors related to behaviors of interest
Describing, explaining, and predicting natural phenomena	Creating well-specified variables associated with behaviors, then using those factors to develop knowledge about the behaviors
Reading scientific articles in the popular media with enough understanding to engage in discussion of the article	Bringing examples of research reported in the press and discussing strengths and limitations
Evaluating the quality of scientific information	Learning to spot confounds and to generate alternate explanations for research findings
Posing and evaluating arguments based on evidence	Writing the results discussion of research projects; writing balanced literature reviews on controversial issues

and perception, psychology students develop science literacy that extends into the natural and physical sciences. But their knowledge of areas in physics, chemistry, and biology can remain limited, just as physics students might not show a great deal of science literacy in the behavioral sciences or in the other life sciences. As Lehman et al. (1988) have shown, however, exposure to the social areas of psychology exert a more general, positive effect on students' reasoning abilities for situations that are not psychological in nature.

A sophisticated approach to answering complex questions about issues in everyday life should not be surprising. Psychology deals with complex systems in which multiple co-occurring variables influence or are associated with behaviors. Disentangling these variables and their effects is difficult. Psychological explanations tend to involve hedging, at least in part due to the complexities of behavior. Madigan, Johnson, and Linton (1995) noted that writing in psychology reveals the complexity and the discipline's phenomena, hence their conclusions:

> Hedge words implicitly recognize the uncertain flow of the ongoing stream of empirical studies investigating complex phenomena. New findings can and do cause old conclusions to be abandoned. Hedge words also convey an impression that theories are more tenuous and less permanent than the data that generate them, an idea that has characterized empirical disciplines since the time of Bacon. (Madigan et al., 1995, p. 428)

Such hedge words include "tend" or "suggest," which imply tentativeness. Hedging also occurs in phrases, such as "does not rule out" rather than "the results point to" (Madigan et al., 1995, pp. 431–432).

Examples of Different Modes of Belief

Students coming into the research methods course may not have a good sense of the different ways that they hold knowledge or, as Charles Peirce might have expressed it, fix their beliefs. To understand the strength of the scientific approach, students will benefit from understanding other modes of knowing. Peirce included four ways of knowing: tenacity, authority, the *a priori* method, and the scientific method (Peirce, 1877). These ways of knowing are useful for introducing students to a new way of thinking about their knowledge, at the beginning of a course.

Tenacity

Sometimes people simply adopt beliefs, according to Peirce (1877), then refuse to consider any alternate idea, even in the face of contrary facts. Why might this obstinacy take place? Peirce suggested that, "in many cases it may very well be that the pleasure he derives from his calm faith overbalances any inconveniences resulting from its deceptive character" (¶ 23).

In discussing this way of believing, one can give students an example that represents the limitations of tenacity. For instance, what do students (and the populace in general) know about lemmings? The modal "fact" about lemmings is that they commit suicide en masse.

Unfortunately for students' knowledge (but fortunately for lemmings), these rodents do not commit suicide, either individually or in groups.

The myth of lemming suicide seems to have gained permanence in our culture on the basis of the 1958 Disney movie, *White Wilderness*, in which the movie makers ostensibly caught lemmings leaping to their deaths (Snopes, 2007; Woodford, 2003). So strong was the belief that lemmings committed suicide that, because the film makers could not induce a single lemming to commit suicide, they herded the rodents and threw a number into the water to depict what the animals would not do. The makers of the movie held the belief of lemming suicide, contrary to all evidence.

As Peirce (1877) noted, "a man may go through life, systematically keeping out of view all that might cause a change in his opinions" (§ 23). Peirce recognized the limitations to this method of fixing beliefs, including the fact that, eventually, one's beliefs would be at variance with reality. He noted that some people, but not all, recognize the weaknesses of tenacity and manage to overcome the tendency to fix ideas this way.

Authority

A second way of fixing beliefs is by virtue of someone's status as an authority. Peirce (1877) discussed authority in terms of an imposition of beliefs to control behavior, but the reliance on authority need not be associated with societal control. Contemporary discussions of authority easily relate to scientific pronouncements of the ubiquitous "experts."

The problem with relying on authority for knowledge is that the authorities may make pronouncements that do not represent reality. For instance, some people believe in creationism or its cousin, intelligent design, because of statements of religious authorities. The scientific evidence favors the theory of evolution (APA Online, 2007).

One persistent myth that relies on authority involves the arguments made in opposition to Christopher Columbus's proposal to sail west from Europe to reach India. According to lore, the dogmatists in the court of King Ferdinand and Queen Isabella argued that the earth was flat, so such a trip would be impossible; Columbus, in his wisdom, argued otherwise.

This scenario has appeared in countless textbooks. It has the disadvantage of being untrue, however (Gould, 1994). According to Gould, one of the founders of Cornell University concocted the myth as part of a plan to drive a wedge between religious and scientific communities: Religious dogmatists spouted the party line, but the ostensibly scientific and empirical Columbus knew the truth. In reality, Gould reported, educated people had known since the time of the ancient Greeks that the world is round. In reality, those who opposed Columbus's expedition correctly argued that the world was too big and that Columbus and his crews would perish before reaching India. The explorers were lucky to have bumped into an unknown continent, which saved them.

A more recent, and more damaging, reliance on authority concerned the so-called "refrigerator mothers" of autistic children. The term originated with the psychiatrist Leo Kanner in the 1940s and was promoted by Bruno Bettelheim (Laidler, 2004). According to Kanner's hypothesis, a mother's emotional coldness and withdrawal from a child was responsible for autism. This hypothesis caused notable guilt in mothers. There seems never to have been any empirical support for the hypothesis; those who fell prey to it did so because of the pronouncements of authorities. This type of material is useful when students learn about the development of theory and the need to base it on empirical data.

According to Peirce (1877), astute thinkers and observers can go beyond using authority to fix their beliefs. Such people "cannot help seeing that it is the mere accident of their having been taught as they have, and of their having been surrounded with the manners and associations they have, that has caused them to believe as they do and not far differently" (¶ 28).

The a Priori *Method*

Sometimes people establish beliefs because those beliefs seem to make the most sense or are "agreeable to reason." Unfortunately, as Peirce (1877) pointed out, the beliefs arise in the absence of fact. The fixing of such belief leads to induction, but at its basis, its assumptions are based on convention or on the current fashion of thought. As such, Peirce said, this method resembles that of authority, although perhaps without the forced compliance.

One example involves the question of why people catch colds. The popular belief is that exposure to cold weather causes colds; the scientific view is that viruses are to blame. Classic research has shown no link between temperature and colds (e.g., Douglas, Lindgren, & Couch, 1968), and medical personnel appear confident that exposure to the cold does not lead to colds: "That question has been answered many times. Chilling does not hinder your immunity as long as you aren't so cold that your body defenses are destroyed" (Mirkin, 2007, ¶ 3).

Some recent research (Johnson & Eccles, 2005) has suggested a link between having one's feet chilled in cold water and catching a cold, but those who developed colds reported catching more colds to begin with, so it is not clear whether the cold water was instrumental in their development of symptoms. Based on the published evidence, there seems to be as much evidence against the cold–cold link as for it.

In fact, a good critical thinking question involves why there is so little evidence for a link between temperature and catching a cold if there is, in fact, a connection. Several studies show no association; they could be victims of Type II errors—if an analysis has insufficient power, for instance, a valid association may not be apparent. The one study that shows the link may have arisen due to a Type I error—for unknown reasons, the participants in the chilled group may simply have caught colds. Given the so-called file drawer problem (Rosenthal, 1979), wherein researchers put nonsignificant results away in their file drawers because of the publication bias toward significant effects, there may be any number of studies that failed to find a cold–cold link.

The beliefs may be based on currently fashionable ideas and may show a degree of consistency. But the *a priori* method is an insufficient basis for holding one's knowledge.

The Scientific Method

Ultimately, the best approach to critical thought, at least as most psychologists suppose, is the scientific method in which fact and evidence dominate. As Peirce (1877) described it, "I may start with known and observed facts to proceed to the unknown (¶ 33)."

As all researchers know, not every question is amenable to an empirical, scientific approach. If one cannot develop a reliable measurement of an idea, one cannot test it scientifically. Thus one might best address questions of morality and religion nonscientifically, even if one could scientifically study behavioral elements of religiosity.

For example, Galton's (1872) study of the efficacy of prayer investigated a religious topic: Do people who are the recipients of prayer (e.g., the Royal Family) live longer than others who are not so fortunate (e.g., lawyers)? Was his research scientific? It met the four criteria for science: objective, data-driven, public, and verifiable. So one must conclude it was scientific. It clearly was not perfect, but perfection is not one of the characteristics of science. On the other hand, the question of whether a particular behavior is moral or ethical is not one that lends itself to a scientific approach. This is a particularly useful exercise when discussing the difference between science and pseudoscience.

How can one know whether one's beliefs are veridical? Unfortunately, because knowledge is always provisional on the emergence of new information, it is difficult to know. And, in science, truth is an elusive concept, one that researchers have essentially replaced with the concept of level of confidence in a finding (Salsburg, 2002).

Supreme Court Justice Stephen Breyer (1998) recognized the difficulty of knowing what to believe. His contribution to the discussion of belief, in the context of scientific literacy, was to opine that knowing how to choose experts and to understand their limitations and biases does not require knowledge of science itself. His approach reflects a useful version of scientific literacy. It differs from blind reliance on authority because there is a recognition of limitations and the need to identify sources in whom one can have a high level of confidence.

How should students approach a decision on what to believe? They cannot possibly read everything relevant to a topic or conduct their own studies, so they are often reliant on professors or other authority figures. But the students have to decide, in general, which authority has greatest credibility. A type of meta-knowledge is important: knowledge of sources of knowledge.

Peirce's (1877) scientific approach, as powerful as it is, still poses limitations. His assumption that "it is necessary that a method should be found by which our beliefs may be determined by nothing human, but by some external permanency—by something upon which our thinking has no effect" (¶ 31) fails to recognize that one's assumptions and theoretical perspectives render facts contingent and, potentially, impermanent. One might gain great confidence in each individual datum, but the data that lead to an emergent theory can be replaced by other facts, leading to other theories.

The Popular Media

The popular media provide a stream of stories about scientific findings, including those in psychology. Journalists are not scientists, though, so one must consider the degree to which their reporting accurately reflects research findings. By the same token, scientists are not journalists; they may fail to communicate effectively with nonscientists.

Clearly, the problem of comprehensible and accurate presentation of research results is not always the result only of journalistic flaws. It is no secret that researchers often write in ways incomprehensible to outsiders. It is also no secret that researchers are sometimes simply poor writers. As Bruner (1942) wrote, with tongue only partially in her cheek, "I have even succumbed to a conviction that authors are engaged wilfully and with malice in suppressing every vestige of spontaneity and emphasis in what they are writing" (p. 53), including "the tortured circumlocutions of the passive voice" (p. 55). Ferreting through turgid prose undoubtedly contributes to many journalistic missteps.

Questioning the Conclusions

In one example, several newspapers reported that African-Americans received certain heart-related treatments only 60% as often as White men. In reality, referrals for Black men did not differ from those of White men, and Black women were referred 87% as often as White men. The problem is that journalists misinterpreted a technical term and misunderstood the research results. As a result, *The New York Times*, *The Washington Post*, and *USA Today* all misreported the results (Greenstein, 1999).

Because of the different goals of scientific and journalistic writing, readers need to be aware that the issues that are important to scientists differ from those of journalists. Journalists look for captivating stories and are probably less interested in the caveats that researchers think are important. This type of material is useful for students who are learning how to write their results in either technical or nontechnical format, the demands of which differ.

As an example, reporter Jim Dyer wrote about the so-called "Monster Study" in which a researcher conditioned children to stutter, some of them experiencing lifelong distress because of it (Dyer, 2001). Although it was a captivating, if horrific story, researchers subsequently called into question the claims that Dyer made (Ambrose & Yairi, 2002). For instance, one woman who had participated in the study as a child asserted that her life was ruined because of her stuttering. It appears that, subsequent to the study, she did not stutter for the next six decades, beginning to do so only when she met her husband (Owen, 2003b) or when he died (Owen 2003a), depending on the account.

There was further misinformation in *The Village Voice* (Collins, 2006), the implication appearing that the researchers unsuccessfully attempted to reverse the stuttering they had induced. The actual data from the study indicated no increase in stuttering in the groups that were supposedly conditioned to stutter (Ambrose & Yairi, 2002).

A number of legitimate journalistic sources picked up the story. Unfortunately, the more scholarly research in a professional journal did not attract much attention. A juicy controversy is always better copy than a sober counterargument. It would behoove students to learn that news reports about research are always simpler than the actual research and that it is not wise, particularly with controversial research, to take a news report at face value.

Questioning the Data

Sometimes one can question not only the conclusions that appear in popular sources but also the data that writers adduce to support their arguments. Best (2001, 2004) has documented cases of "mutant statistics" in the popular press. These are statistics that are transformed from the original into variants that lack validity.

Best (2001) referred to "The Worst Social Statistic Ever" (pp. 1–4). A writer claimed that the number of children killed by guns had doubled every year since 1950. This assertion is patently false because, if true, it would imply that by the turn of the century, a quadrillion children would have been shot in a single year. The actual statistic, cited by the Children's Defense Fund, was that since 1950, the number of children killed by guns had doubled, a very different figure.

Another instance of ostensible data that has circulated involves the incidence of spousal abuse on Super Bowl Sunday. Since 1993, an urban legend has spread that there is a notable increase in abuse on that day (Snopes, 2005). Fortunately for the sake of women, there appears to be no support for the extravagant claims of abuse on game day. According to the Snopes urban legends Web site (2005), one organization even mailed letters to women, advising them not to stay in the same house as their husbands during the football game. (A less well publicized, but accurate, Super Bowl statistic involves higher traffic fatalities following the Super Bowl in the state of the game's loser; Redelmeier & Steward, 2005.)

Another controversial statistic is the claim that 4 million adolescents (children aged 12 to 17) in the United States smoke (Kovar, 2000). This claim by a former Surgeon General of the United States has many negative implications. However, there are some important elements that need to be understood in context. For example, almost all of the smoking took place among the older adolescents, not entirely reassuring, but better than the thought that many 12 and 13-year olds are smoking. Furthermore, what does it mean to be a *smoker*? The researchers categorized anybody who took even one puff in the past 30 days as a smoker. In truth, 41% had smoked one to five cigarettes on the infrequently occurring days they smoked. In addition, 31% had smoked less than one cigarette, and that often meant sharing that single cigarette with friends (Kovar, 2000). Without looking past the initial data, the situation seems bleak. For the 25% of adolescents who are already addicted, it is bleak. But for the majority of the "smokers," the problem is potentially manageable. Students benefit from considering these problems when learning about operational definitions and methods of measurement.

Assessment

Helping students develop the habit of critical thinking and of developing scientific literacy is an important task that teachers face. A significant component of the teaching process is assessment as to whether students are developing as hoped. In this section, there are several activities that can guide the assessment process.

Modes of Belief

After students learn about Peirce's (1877) different modes of fixing beliefs, they should be able to generate examples from their own lives to characterize tenacity, authority, the *a priori* method, and the scientific method. That is, what do they know that arises from each of the modes of fixing beliefs? And why does the belief fall into that category?

The students should recognize that tenacity is associated with simply wanting to believe or refusing to consider alternatives. Authority, which in this case can involve either social coercion or simply reliance on an expert, involves acceptance of a pronouncement by virtue of the status of the person who offers it. The *a priori* method relates to the acceptance of certain assumptions that lead to logically induced beliefs, even if those assumptions are not questioned. Finally, the scientific method pertains to the development of so-called permanent facts that exist independently of people and their particular perspectives and beliefs.

Scientific Literacy

A scientifically literate student should be able to question the process by which information develops. For example, for the question of how many adolescents smoke, students can relate how the operational definitions of "smoker" and "adolescent" affect the conclusions drawn by researchers. If asked, students should be able to identify assumptions and biases underlying questions. There are sufficient sources of bad questions on surveys to give students practice on taking apart and reassembling survey items.

Finally, students should know that real-world phenomena are very resistant to easy cause-and-effect explanations. For example, if one examines teen pregnancy rates (The National Campaign, 2002) and temperatures in the 50 states (NOAA Satellite and Information Service, 2007) there is a correlation between the average temperature in a state and the teen birth rate in the state. A simple causal statement about warmth, scant clothing, sex, and pregnancy may come to students' minds. However, there are alternate explanations, including the fact that states with mandated emphasis on abstinence in sex education curricula show the highest average teen pregnancy rates. Here, too, a simple causal model comes to mind: Students who do not learn about contraception end up pregnant. The problem is that the sex education–pregnancy link is just as correlational as the temperature–pregnancy link. Scientifically literate students should be able to generate multiple possible inferences and ways to test the validity of those inferences.

Another facet of scientific literacy is being able to recognize what is scientific and what is not. For instance, the Mozart effect (Rauscher, Shaw, & Ky, 1993, 1995) led to sensational media coverage in the 1990s. The supposed effect involved an increase in intelligence when people listened to Mozart as opposed to stories. Subsequent studies failed to replicate the effect and, in fact, identified some possible confounds (e.g., Steele, Bass, & Brook, 1999; Thompson, Schellenberg, & Hussain, 2001), such as listeners' preference for such music. Students should be able to identify why the research on the so-called Mozart effect was scientific, even though the phenomenon was illusory. Similarly, students should have enough knowledge to assess the claims about facilitated communication (a generally discredited technique for communicating with autistic individuals), or about astrology. The criteria for scientific status are in the process of asking questions, not in the topic of those questions per se.

Bernard C. Beins

Evaluating the Popular Media

Most students who have completed the introductory psychology course have heard of the murder of Kitty Genovese and the research on bystander intervention that it spawned (e.g., Darley & Latané, 1968). As it turns out, the lore of her murder demonstrates bystander intervention too simplistically.

Students should be able to identify the claims made in what has been written, most of which is consistent with portrayals in introductory psychology textbooks (e.g., Dorman, 1998). For instance, how do people know that 38 people witnessed the attack on Genovese and did not intervene? Did they not intervene because they were simply callous, or was it the bystander effect?

DeMay (2006) has evaluated claims that have appeared in the media about the Kitty Genovese murder. Based on his assessment, there are quite a few questionable or outright inaccurate statements. Students can read through a report (such as Dorman's *Newsday* article cited previously) to see what facts are asserted. In addition, they should be able to separate fact from conclusion. They can then read DeMay's criticisms, such as the questionable number of actual eyewitnesses, how much an eyewitness could actually have seen, and others. Furthermore, the site of the murder was near a bar where there was quite often loud commotion, so Genovese's cries for help might have been indistinguishable from the normal sounds associated with people who are inebriated. The iconic story is a good one, but its premises are problematic.

Conclusion

Knowing what to believe is a complicated process. The research methods course is an ideal vehicle for demonstrating to students that they should consider knowledge to be provisional and that they need to assess both how they have fixed their beliefs and the quality of the evidence that relates to what they believe.

Examples from everyday life can generate useful discussions of how to foster critical thinking and scientific literacy. A little knowledge may be a dangerous thing. But a little knowledge of one's knowledge may not be a dangerous thing; rather, it could be a very beneficial thing.

References

Ambrose, N. G., & Yairi, E. (2002). The Tudor study: Data and ethics. *American Journal of Speech-Language Pathology, 11*, 190–203.

Anderson, C. A., Lepper, M. R., & Ross, L. (1980). Perseverance of social theories: The role of explanation in the persistence of discredited information. *Journal of Personality and Social Psychology, 39*, 1037–1049.

APA Online. (2007). *APA adopts policy statement opposing the teaching of intelligent design as scientific theory*. Retrieved March 20, 2007 from http://www.apa.org/releases/design.html

Best, J. (2001). *Damned lies and statistics: Untangling numbers from the media, politicians, and activists.* Berkeley: University of California Press.

Best, J. (2004). *More damned lies and statistics: How numbers confuse public issues.* Berkeley: University of California Press.

Breyer, S. (1998). Science and society: The interdependence of science and law. *Science, 280,* 537–538.

Bruner, K. F. (1942). Of psychological writing: Being some valedictory remarks on style. *Journal of Abnormal and Social Psychology, 37,* 52–70.

Collins, P. (2006, April 10). Monster mash: Uncovering a secret history of stuttering research. *The Village Voice.* Retrieved February 16, 2007 from http://www.villagevoice.com/arts/0615, collins,72806,12.html

Darley, J. M., & Latané, B. (1968). Bystander intervention in emergencies: Diffusion of responsibility. *Journal of Personality and Social Psychology, 8,* 377–383.

DeMay, J. (2006). *Kitty Genovese: The popular account that is mostly wrong.* Retrieved March 13, 2007 from http://www.oldkewgardens.com/ss-nytimes-3.html

Dorman, M. (1998, June 10). The killing of Kitty Genovese. *Newsday.* Retrieved March 31, 2008 from http://www.newsday.com/community/guide/lihistory/ny-history-hs818a,0,7944135.story

Douglas, R. G. J., Lindgren, K. M., & Couch, R. B. (1968). Exposure to cold environment and rhinovirus common cold. Failure to demonstrate effect. *New England Journal of Medicine, 279,* 743.

Dyer, J. (2001, June 10). Orphan experiments come to light: Children were made to stutter, and left with a lifelong burden. *JSOnline.* Retrieved February 16, 2007 from http://www2.jsonline.com/news/nat/jun01/stutter11061001.asp

Galton, F. (1872, August 1). Statistical inquiries into the efficacy of prayer. *Fortnightly Review, 12,* 125–135. Retrieved March 9, 2007 from http://galton.org/essays/1870-1879/galton-1872-fort-rev-prayer.pdf

Gould, S. J. (2004, March). The persistently flat earth. *Natural History, 103,* 12, 14–19.

Greenstein, J. (1999, October). The heart of the matter. *Brill's Content,* 40.

Holmes, J. D., & Beins, B. C. (2008). *Psychology is a science: At least some students think so.* Manuscript submitted for publication.

Johnson, C., & Eccles, R. (2005). Acute cooling of the feet and the onset of common cold symptoms. *Family Practice 22,* 608–613. Retrieved March 9, 2007 from http://fampra.oxfordjournals.org/cgi/content/abstract/22/6/608

Kovar, M. G. (2000). Four million adolescents smoke: Or do they? *Chance, 13,* 10–14.

Laidler, J. R. (2004). *The "Refrigerator Mother" hypothesis of autism.* Retrieved March 12, 2007 from http://www.autism-watch.org/causes/rm.shtml

Lehman, D. R., Lempert, R. O., & Nisbett, R. E. (1988). The effects of graduate training on reasoning: Formal discipline and thinking about everyday-life events. *American Psychologist, 43,* 431–442.

Madigan, R., Johnson, S., & Linton, P. (1995). The language of psychology: APA style as epistemology. *American Psychologist, 50,* 428–436.

Maienschein, J., & students. (1998). Scientific literacy. *Science, 281,* 917. Retrieved March 8, 2007 from http://www.sciencemag.org/cgi/content/summary/281/5379/917

Miller, J. D. (2007, February). *The public understanding of science in Europe and the United States.* Presented at the annual meeting of the American Association for the Advancement of Science, San Francisco, CA.

Mirkin, G. (2007). *Catch a cold.* Retrieved March 9, 2007 from http://www.drmirkin.com/morehealth/9941.html

The National Campaign to Reduce Teen Pregnancy. (2002). *State data.* Retrieved March 8, 2007 from http://www.teenpregnancy.org/america/default.asp

National Science Education Standards. (1995). Retrieved February 28, 2007 from http://books. nap.edu/readingroom/books/nses/

NOAA Satellite and Information Service. (2007, October 5). *U.S. statewide analysis.* Retrieved March 31, 2008 from http://www.ncdc.noaa.gov/oa/climate/research/cag3/state.html

Owen, T. (2003a, July 12). UI professor's son defends him, research. *Gazette Online.* Retrieved February 16, 2007 from http://www.uiowa.edu/~cyberlaw/wj/crg-2-20030713.htm

Owen, T. (2003b, July 12). When words hurt: Stuttering study story missed the mark. *Gazette Online.* Retrieved February 16, 2007 from http://www.uiowa.edu/~cyberlaw/wj/crg-1-20030713.htm

Peirce, C. S. (1877, November). The fixation of belief. *Popular Science Monthly, 12,* 1–15. Retrieved March 9, 2007 from http://www.peirce.org/writings/p107.html

Rauscher, F. H., Shaw, G. L., & Ky, N. (1993). Music and spatial task performance. *Nature, 365,* 611.

Rauscher, F. H., Shaw, G. L., & Ky, N. (1995). Listening to Mozart enhances spatial-temporal reasoning: Towards a neurophysiological basis. *Neuroscience Letters, 185,* 44–47.

Redelmeier, D. A., & Steward, C. L. (2005). Do fatal crashes increase following a Super Bowl telecast? *Chance, 18,* 19–24.

Rosenthal, R. (1979). The "file drawer problem" and tolerance for null results. *Psychological Bulletin, 86,* 638–641.

Salsburg, D. (2002). *The lady tasting tea: How statistics revolutionized science in the twentieth century.* New York: Owl Books.

Scriven, M., & Paul, R. (2007). *Defining critical thinking.* (2004). Retrieved February 28, 2007 from http://www.criticalthinking.org/aboutCT/definingCT.shtml

Smith, R. A. (2002). *Challenging your preconceptions: Thinking critically about psychology* (2nd ed.) Belmont, CA: Wadsworth.

Snopes. (2005). *Super bull Sunday.* Retrieved March 13, 2007 from http://www.snopes.com/crime/ statistics/superbowl.asp

Snopes. (2007). *White Wilderness.* Retrieved March 9, 2007 from http://www.snopes.com/disney/ films/lemmings.htm

Stanovich, K. E. (2004). *How to think straight about psychology* (7th ed.). Boston: Allyn and Bacon.

Steele, K. M., Bass, K. E., & Brook, M. D. (1999). The mystery of the Mozart effect: Failure to replicate. *Psychological Science, 10,* 366–369.

Thompson, W. F., Schellenberg, E. G., & Hussain, G. (2001). Arousal, mood, and the Mozart effect. *Psychological Science, 12,* 248–251.

Woodford, R. (2003). *Lemming suicide myth: Disney film faked bogus behavior.* Retrieved March 9, 2007 from http://www.wildlifenews.alaska.gov/index.cfm?adfg=wildlife_news.view_article& issue_id=6&articles_id=56

Chapter 18

Teaching Critical Thinking About Difficult Topics

Paul C. Smith and Kris Vasquez

Critical thinking is not "content neutral." A number of well-known cognitive and emotional biases influence the ability to evaluate claims (Kahneman, Slovic, & Tversky, 1982). As a result, students' practice of critical thinking is not simply a function of how well they have learned general critical thinking skills. We find that students who can demonstrate solid critical thinking skills predictably fail to use those thinking skills in evaluating certain kinds of beliefs. Some beliefs are "immovable objects": beliefs that we think are the direct result of our personal experiences. Others seem subject to "irresistible forces": biases about our moral values and moral reasoning. In this chapter we will discuss how these beliefs affect the teaching of psychology and give suggestions for coping with issues raised by these beliefs in the classroom.

Immovable Objects

The Persuasive Power of Personal Experience

Consider the following two classroom situations, both familiar to many teachers of psychology:

- A student in the developmental psychology class objects to the textbook's discussion of the effects of corporal punishment in childrearing, using a personal anecdote as support for her argument.
- In an introductory psychology discussion about sleep and dreams, a student asks the instructor how psychologists would explain her precognitive dreams.

At first glance, these two situations may seem to have little in common, as they involve different subject matter, and one involves questions about normal events whereas the other invokes supernatural powers. However, the two situations have an important common element: In each case the student refers to personal experience as support for her belief. In her examination of students' understanding of the purpose of classroom discussion, Trosset (1998) found a "bias in favor of personalized knowledge (as opposed to knowledge accessible to all comers, such as that contained in scholarly writings)" (p. 47). This bias often interferes with students' critical thinking skills in the situations in which we, as faculty, most hope to see those skills applied.

When a student cites personal experiences as support for false beliefs, instructors face a particularly awkward situation, one in which they must balance the need to model open-mindedness about psychological claims with appropriate skepticism about unsupported counterclaims. Of course, it is possible that the student citing personal experience is right and the textbook is wrong, but as anecdotes about personal experiences lack the controls found in even the most basic research, they are only very rarely valid reasons to even suspect that to be the case. Unfortunately, although psychology teachers may be aware of the severe limitations of personal experience as a source of knowledge, students and the lay public generally are not. It is more common to assume that personal experience is a uniquely powerful source of knowledge, one that trumps research and renders critical thinking irrelevant.

Conditionalizing Critical Thinking

Why would students who had developed effective critical thinking skills fail to apply those skills to their personal experience-based beliefs? The failure to apply even well-learned skills is not unusual, and the ability to apply skills and knowledge in appropriate situations is an important factor distinguishing experts from novices in a field (Glaser, 1992; National Research Council, 1999). A student's knowledge is said to be properly "conditionalized" when the student routinely applies that knowledge in the appropriate situations (National Research Council, 1999, p. 31). Unfortunately, the demands of formal education tend to teach students inappropriate methods of conditionalizing their knowledge. When students learning mathematics, for example, learn a new procedure, they may safely assume that they are to use that procedure to solve the homework problems assigned that day. The standard practice of assigning problems related to the day's lesson relieves students of the need to decide whether the newly learned procedure applies to a particular problem. Similarly, the teaching of critical thinking and of psychological research skills may lead students astray in establishing the conditions in which those skills are to be applied. For example, if a teacher focuses exclusively on critiques of media presentations to teach and assess students' critical thinking skills, the students may quite reasonably learn to apply those skills only to media reports. Alternatively, if the examples focus on claims made as a result of motivated biases (e.g., advertisements or intentional scams), the student may learn to think critically only about claims for which a motive for deceit is apparent and to uncritically accept sincere claims.

In general, we can expect that students will learn to apply their critical thinking skills in the contexts in which they learned and practiced those skills. Our main concern is that if the examples used to teach critical thinking skills focus too strongly on evaluations of the findings of formal research, students will learn to apply their critical thinking skills to such evaluations, but not to their other beliefs. In this situation, we will have provided students with a way to reject whatever formal research challenges their unfounded prior beliefs without teaching them to also evaluate those prior beliefs: We will have taught them to defend their personal prejudices against reasonable and well-founded objections.

Whenever we teach students skills, it is important to teach explicitly about the conditions of applicability as well. In the case of critical thinking skills, failure to do so raises the risk of a very undesirable outcome.

Teaching Students to Evaluate Their Personal Experience-Based Beliefs

Including personal experience-based beliefs as targets of critical thinking practice examples does not guarantee that students will apply those skills to their personal experience-based beliefs. Students expect to learn to critique research and the media and are proud to recognize deliberate scams, for example. They may be considerably more resistant to the suggestion that they apply critical thinking skills to their own beliefs, particularly those formed on the basis of personal experience, and they often find ways to avoid changing their beliefs regardless of the amount and quality of evidence presented (Chinn & Brewer, 1993, 1998). Among the factors that determine how strongly people hold and value beliefs is the extent to which those beliefs participate in our explanations of the events we see in the world around us (Anderson, Lepper, & Ross, 1980; Preston & Epley, 2005; Slusher & Anderson, 1996). The belief that personal experience has a special epistemological status is fairly central to how most people understand the world (Trosset, 1998). Furthermore, the belief that personal experience is epistemologically unique is reinforced by cultural norms, and often even by formal education.

Carey and Smith (1993) suggested that the assumption about the unique power of personal experience forms part of a "common-sense epistemology" (p. 237). They propose that persons holding such an epistemology are unaware of the role of theoretically tainted interpretation in the establishment of beliefs and, instead, they "see knowledge arising unproblematically (and directly) from sensory experiences and see knowledge as simply the collection of many true beliefs" (p. 237). If students believe that particular beliefs come directly from sensory experience, they will not consider it necessary to evaluate those beliefs. If we insist that they evaluate those beliefs, we challenge not just the beliefs, but also the students' common-sense epistemology. Making changes to that basic epistemological assumption requires students to make changes to their system of beliefs as a whole.

To what extent is the "common-sense epistemology" correct? Clearly students don't need research or critical thinking to evaluate the beliefs that, for example, they have two children or drive a used car. But they may assume for the same reason—their personal experience—that the belief that they have precognitive dreams is also outside of the domain of research and critical thinking. They may respond to our insistence that they think critically about the evidence for precognitive dreams the same way they would respond if we insisted that they think critically about how many children they have or whether they drive a used car.

What exactly is it that makes some of these beliefs fair game for research and critical thinking although others are not? It is not easy to establish a clear divide: establishing exact conditions of applicability for critical thinking and research raises some epistemological questions that are still unresolved. Critical thinking-minded psychology faculty are fairly good judges of the conditions of applicability of critical thinking and research skills, but paradoxically use a sort of "I know it when I see it" heuristic rather than explicit rules. They often have long experience with false claims and personal experience-based assertions and also have long experience imagining and eliminating alternative explanations. The expertise is in us, but it has not been made explicit. As a result, we do not have a good method of teaching students how to discern between claims that really are supported by certain personal experiences and those that are not. If we expect students to apply their critical thinking skills in everyday life, we need to develop such a method.

Irresistible Forces

Another consistent difficulty in assignments asking for critical thinking from students is that where their values are involved, their ability to think critically seems to be diminished. Students engaging in discussion about a social issue may quickly revert to defensiveness or ad hominem attacks. Although this behavior could be attributed to a lack of background information or analytical skills, it is also possible that the nature of the topic itself impedes critical thinking.

Consider an example assignment from research methods: teaching the distinction between correlation and causation. In this assignment, students are asked to read press coverage of an article discussing cognitive outcomes for children in day care, as well as the original scholarly source (Brooks-Gunn, Han, & Waldfogel, 2002). Though the class has covered extensively the difference between correlation and causation, though the popular press uses the word "cause" in its headline, and though Brooks-Gunn and colleagues explicitly say that their study does not show causal links, the students are often unable to spot the key difference between the original article and the popular press coverage.

In contrast, using Stanovich's (2007) excellent example of the correlation in Taiwan between number of small household electric appliances and use of contraception, the students unfailingly see the folly of drawing causal conclusions from correlational data. Yet somehow when it comes to the question of working mothers, some students appear unable to make this critical distinction. Instead, critical consideration of the validity of the causal conclusions gives way to an emotionally charged voicing of opinions about the economic factors in society that drive women with young children into the workforce, about the sexism inherent in the assumption that mothers are solely responsible for child rearing, and about the selfishness of mothers who won't "do what's right" and stay home with their children.

Similar posturing, without critical thought, can be produced by topics such as the basis of homosexual orientation or the role of evolution in mate selection. It is easy to assume that this lack of rational exchange reflects insufficient reasoning skills.

Listening to the arguments presented certainly provides evidence of poor reasoning. However, recent work in social psychology suggests that touching on moral issues may provoke a predictable set of responses from students that underlies this phenomenon (see subsections "How moral values interfere with critical thinking" and "Motivated irrationality" below).

Morality, in Brief

Moral values are perceived to be universal and obligatory (Turiel, 1983). That is, there is no choice in whether one obeys a moral standard; to violate it is wrong, in the mind of the perceiver, regardless of the actor's culture or circumstances. Moreover, moral values carry with them an affective consequence for violation—an implicit feeling of wrongness (Gibbard, 1990; Rokeach, 1973). These values are not simply choices or social conventions, but rules that contain an implicit directive that all people, everywhere, ought to behave in this way.

In addition, a moral value has an interpersonal focus by definition (Rokeach, 1973), so if, as we argue here, moral values interfere with critical thinking, we should see more of this problem in the social sciences than the physical sciences. That is, a student may argue about whether an object dropped from an airplane at altitude falls straight down or not, but is unlikely to get enraged about whether it ought to do so.

It has long been assumed that moral decisions are based on deliberate reasoning, and increase in sophistication along with general cognitive development (e.g., Kohlberg, 1981). In this model, a person considers the situation, applies the relevant moral rule, and comes to a judgment of whether an action is acceptable or not. And if people do reason in a rational way about moral issues, it should then be possible to address moral questions through evidence and logic. It should be possible to overcome any initial resistance to an argument by an instructor's calm and careful presentation, assuming that students have reached a reasonable level of cognitive development. In practice, however, these possibilities are not always realized.

How Moral Values Interfere with Critical Thinking

Recent research suggests that many moral judgments may not be nearly as rational as traditional models suggest. For instance, Haidt (2001) proposed that moral issues are predominantly informed by affective response, and that any reasoning that occurs takes place after the judgment is made. If Haidt is correct, once students have made their initial, "gut-level" judgments about a topic, they are very unlikely to change their minds in response to factual information. In the case of overwhelming contrary evidence, students will still manage to maintain initial views through selective attention and biased reasoning. This process will look very similar to poor critical thinking that is rooted in other causes, such as a lack of understanding of the evidence. However, if the students have made emotional moral judgments about the topic, providing more evidence will not be effective in promoting critical thinking.

Motivated Irrationality

As teachers, we may hold an implicit assumption that people prefer to hold accurate views about the world over inaccurate views. Though certainly there are situations in all of our lives in which we act mindlessly or behave in ways that cannot be defended on logical premises, those who work as educators may be forgiven for assuming that students would rather learn what the best available evidence says, rather than clinging to erroneous beliefs for their comfort value. The latter behavior is irrational and maladaptive in the classroom and often in other areas of life as well. And yet it is common. Why (we might ask, in frustration) would people prefer irrationality to rationality? What purpose would that serve?

One way that such behavior can be understood is through Tetlock's (2002) social functionalist frameworks. Tetlock's conception of the "intuitive theologian" is particularly useful. An intuitive theologian is a framework that exists to protect sacred values, which are deeply held values endorsed by community consensus. For some people, freedom may be a sacred value; for others, obeying God's laws is one. Belief in these values— which meet the criteria for morality specified earlier—creates a sense of shared identity for the community. Defending the values against attacks supports the individual's need for accountability within the social system. It is important to note that the intuitive theologian is not concerned with the accuracy of the worldview, only that the members of the community act in accordance with it.

As one would expect, given the qualities of moral values, violations are a serious matter to the intuitive theologian. Affectively, the results of a violation are strong and negative (anger, contempt). Behaviorally, violations result in the urge for symbolic acts to demonstrate commitment to the value in question. One remarkable finding from Tetlock and colleagues is that individuals need not act to violate the value; if they even think about violating it, the affective and behavioral consequences are immediate and severe.

This work suggests that once a class discussion has invoked moral values, students will find it almost impossible to consider evidence in a rational way, because they are attending to what are experientially much more pressing demands from their larger social lives. The need to act consistently with personal religious beliefs, for instance, is a central component of identity for many American students. To ask them to entertain, even hypothetically, an argument that they view as a violation of their religious views will leave them angry and more committed than ever to the views you have challenged. If they live lives outside the classroom with commitment to these values, they cannot check them at the door, and would see no value in attempting to do so even if they could. Therefore, critical thinking will not be in evidence.

Too Many Theologians Derail the Discussion

Dealing with one student whose moral judgment has been invoked is challenging. Classroom interaction among students when moral issues are in play is even more so. Skitka, Bauman, and Sargis (2005) found that, compared with students discussing issues without moral content, students discussing moral issues were less co-operative, expressed less goodwill toward partners, were tenser, were more defensive, preferred greater physical and psychological distance, and were less likely to achieve a goal of discussion. Students are aware of the hazards of these discussions: Although many current college students voice strong support for diversity on many dimensions, diversity of moral values is decidedly unwelcome (Haidt, Rosenberg, & Hom, 2003). We feel much more comfortable talking only to those who reaffirm the rightness of what we hold dear.

It is probably not worth trying to point out to students that they behave in this way, either during or after a discussion. In the midst of defending a sacred value, such a critique will be taken as part of the assault and reinvigorate the defenses of the intuitive theologian. And once the discussion has passed, it is unlikely that students will recognize their irrationality. Those who have abandoned evidence to defend a moral value will not recognize that they have done so, because of our cherished belief that we alone are reasonable (see Robinson, Keltner, Ward, & Ross, 1995). We assume that others, even people who share our side of the argument, are biased, and see no reason to find compromise or common ground with someone holding an obviously wrong opinion.

What Happens in the Classroom

Taking all this research into account, we can see that students are set up for a difficult situation—they believe that some questions should never be asked, because just imagining the answer can be a moral violation. And once a moral violation is noted, students are highly motivated to avoid the kind of thinking we are asking them to do, and to restore themselves to their pre-existing state. They are also unable to recognize that any of this is happening.

This process is antithetical to education, but is understandable in light of the multiple goals students are trying to serve. The intuitive theologian framework is functional because it maintains community ties and helps us to navigate social relationships. These goals are important to students and cannot be dismissed just because they are inconvenient to a classroom exercise. Tetlock's research (2002) predicts behavior familiar in the classroom: When faced with an unavoidable contradiction with pre-existing beliefs, an intuitive theologian is motivated to accept facetious arguments or distractions in order to avoid confronting the paradox, or chooses to attack the source of the forbidden cognition. This kind of reasoning is certainly not critical thinking, but should not serve as an indicator that students lack critical thinking skills in general or appropriate evidence on the topic at hand. The intuitive theologian actively undermines skills that the student may be able to demonstrate in other contexts.

Suggestions for Faculty

Students' personal experience-based beliefs and their moral values can get in the way of their application of critical thinking skills. It is very unlikely that this problem can be overcome simply by more teaching of those skills. The problem is not necessarily that the students have insufficient critical thinking skills, but instead that the students are distracted from applying those skills by enthusiasm for the moral aspect of an issue, or that they simply assume that those belief evaluation skills are irrelevant to a situation because they already know the belief to be true. As a result, we believe that instructors need to address the issues of personal experience and morality directly. In this section we will provide a few suggestions for teaching and assessment with respect to this problem.

Assess Critical Thinking in a Variety of Contexts

Are students learning to think critically in general, or are they just learning to defend their uncritical beliefs? If all of our assessments of students' critical thinking skills ask them to evaluate research conclusions, we will never find out whether they have learned to apply those skills outside of that context. Most of our students do not need our urging to be skeptical of science, the media, medicine, or politicians. Assessments focused solely on claims in these areas as the targets of critical thinking risk "letting students off the hook" with respect to thinking critically about their own beliefs. Assessments aimed solely at paranormal beliefs run a similar risk. At a minimum, critical thinking assessments should also explicitly assess students' critical thinking about anecdotes and personal experience-based beliefs: Do they apply their skills as well in those contexts as they do when critiquing research or media claims? It would also be very helpful to know if students understand that a person's certainty about a claim is not evidence for the truth of the claim and that false claims can reflect honest mistakes and not just deliberate deceptions.

Similarly, students should learn explicitly that immediate emotional reactions to highly charged topics are not evidence of the rightness of their judgments. Though it is unrealistic to expect to derail intuitive moral judgment and its emotional correlates, students may, with practice, learn to identify their emotional reactions and take a metaphorical deep breath before considering the content of the argument and the quality of evidence. To assess critical thinking effectively in these contexts we may need to require students to reflect on their thinking and emotional responses in parallel—a challenging task even for the most self-aware among us.

Model Critical Thinking About One's Own Beliefs

Because of the emotional responses evoked by challenges to personal values and to personal experience, it is very important to model critical thinking about one's own beliefs. For example, we might discuss a list of things we do to avoid coming down with a cold, and then point out that because we do many of those things every time we are concerned about getting a cold, we cannot know from our personal experiences which, if any of those things, are effective at warding off a cold. The "Counterattitudinal Advocacy" method (Miller, Wozniak, Rust, Miller, & Slezak, 1996) may also be particularly useful here in helping students come to understand that we want them to think critically about their own beliefs.

Present Research Methods as Methods for Eliminating Particular Biases

It is all too easy for students to mistakenly come to believe that research methods form a set of practices that one follows simply to qualify as a researcher. Students who believe that their personal experience-based beliefs do not need to be evaluated will never consider using those practices to evaluate those beliefs. If research methods are instead presented as a set of methods for eliminating particular reasoning biases, students will be able to understand how those methods might be applied to their experience-based reasoning.

The two best examples of this strategy are probably the evaluation of causal beliefs and the elimination of confirmation bias (Lord, Ross, & Lepper, 1979). The reason that we randomly assign participants to groups in experiments is not that some researchers' code tells us to do so. We do so because we want to be in a position to answer the challenge "How do you know that the groups were not different to begin with?". Similarly, we use blinded measures not because we want to conform to other researchers' behaviors, but because we want our measurements to be free of the effects of confirmation biases.

Be Conscious of the Way Debates Are Framed

The intuitive theologian is especially wary of a trade-off between a sacred moral value and a more mundane concern. It may be more effective for teachers to frame alternative points of view as competing moral values. Politicians are quite aware of this principle, which is why both sides of a political debate are always in favor of cherished values, and neither wants to be accused of opposing a different value. A politician would rather be seen as defending our freedom ("prochoice") or defending the helpless ("prolife") from the opposing side in a debate; in a one-sided debate between values and secular concerns, values will triumph. Teachers should keep in mind, though, that framing presentations in terms of moral values may not increase critical thinking by itself. The best that can be hoped is that engaging the intuitive theologian framework with two contradictory values will reduce the utility of the framework long enough for the professor to model more rational arguments.

Be Aware of Audience Effects

Anything that makes the audience of an argument salient will increase the need for social accountability and thus more firmly engage the intuitive theologian. This is particularly problematic if someone seen as an enforcer of values is part of the audience—students may feel a more pressing need to affirm their values if a representative of those values is watching. Under these conditions it would be normal to see ad hominem attacks on representatives of the counternormative view. Decreasing the salience of the attitude may help to some extent to keep students focused on the critical thinking task at hand.

Keep in mind, though, that even if students can learn important analytical skills on material that is not connected to their moral values, it is not realistic to expect them to transfer these skills smoothly. It is possible that forewarning them, and asking them to adopt an analytical attitude in advance of hearing the argument, may be useful (Pizarro & Bloom, 2003). But if you catch them unprepared, and their first reactions are emotional ones, it will be exceptionally difficult for them to backtrack and consider the arguments in a carefully detached way.

Conclusion

It is ironic that the critical thinking skills we attempt to teach to our students seem to fail where they are needed most, but it is also no accident. Students resist a detached, scientific evaluation of certain beliefs for compelling reasons, including the need to preserve common-sense epistemology and social accountability. We believe that without careful attention to the conditions that promote this resistance, our goal of increasing critical thinking will be difficult to achieve. However, despite the challenges outlined here, we also believe that it is possible to make progress, even in the face of immovable objects and irresistible forces.

References

Anderson, C. A., Lepper, M. R., & Ross, L. (1980). Perseverance of social theories: The role of explanation in the persistence of discredited information. *Journal of Personality and Social Psychology, 39*, 1037–1049.

Brooks-Gunn, J., Han, W.-J., & Waldfogel, J. (2002). Maternal employment and child cognitive outcomes in the first three years of life: The NICHD study of early child care. *Child Development, 73*, 1052–1072.

Carey, S., & Smith, C. (1993). On understanding the nature of scientific knowledge. *Educational Psychologist, 28*, 235–251.

Chinn, C. A., & Brewer, W. F. (1993). The role of anomalous data in knowledge acquisition: A theoretical framework and implications for science instruction. *Review of Educational Research, 63*, 1–49.

Chinn, C. A., & Brewer, W. F. (1998). An empirical test of a taxonomy of responses to anomalous data in science. *Journal of Research in Science Teaching, 35*, 623–654.

Gibbard, A. (1990). *Wise choices and apt feelings.* Cambridge, MA: Harvard University Press.

Glaser, R. (1992). Expert knowledge and the processes of thinking. In D. F. Halpern (Ed.), *Enhancing thinking skills in the sciences and mathematics* (pp. 63–75). Hillsdale, NJ: Erlbaum.

Haidt, J. (2001). The emotional dog and its rational tail: A social intuitionist approach to moral judgment. *Psychological Review, 108*, 814–834.

Haidt, J., Rosenberg, E., & Hom, H. (2003). Differentiating diversities: Moral diversity is not like other kinds. *Journal of Applied Social Psychology, 33*, 1–36.

Kahneman, D., Slovic, P., & Tversky, A. (1982). *Judgment under uncertainty: Heuristics and biases.* Cambridge, UK: Cambridge University Press.

Kohlberg, L. (1981). *The philosophy of moral development: Moral stages and the idea of justice. Vol. 1: Essays on moral development.* San Francisco: Harper & Row.

Lord, C. G., Ross, L., & Lepper, M. R. (1979). Biased assimilation and attitude polarization: The effects of prior theories on subsequently considered evidence. *Journal of Personality and Social Psychology, 37*, 2098–2109.

Miller, R. L., Wozniak, W. J., Rust, M. R., Miller, B. R., & Slezak, J. (1996). Counterattitudinal advocacy as a means of enhancing instructional effectiveness: How to teach students what they do not want to know. *Teaching of Psychology, 23,* 215–219.

National Research Council. (1999). *How students learn: Brain, mind, experience, and school.* Washington, DC: National Academy Press.

Pizarro, D. A., & Bloom, P. (2003). The intelligence of moral intuitions: Comment on Haidt (2001). *Psychological Review, 110,* 193–196.

Preston, J., & Epley, N. (2005). Explanations versus applications: The explanatory power of valuable beliefs. *Psychological Science, 16,* 826–832.

Robinson, R. J., Keltner, D., Ward, A., & Ross, L. (1995). Actual versus assumed differences in construal: "Naïve realism" in intergroup relations. *Journal of Personality and Social Psychology, 68,* 404–417.

Rokeach, M. (1973). *The nature of human values.* New York: The Free Press.

Skitka, L. J., Bauman, C. W., & Sargis, E. G. (2005). Moral conviction: Another contributor to attitude strength, or something more? *Journal of Personality and Social Psychology, 88,* 895–917.

Slusher, M. P., & Anderson, C. A. (1996). Using causal persuasive arguments to change beliefs and teach new information: The mediating role of explanation availability and evaluation bias in the acceptance of knowledge. *Journal of Educational Psychology, 88,* 110–122.

Stanovich, K. E. (2007). *How to think straight about psychology* (8th ed.). Boston: Allyn & Bacon.

Tetlock, P. E. (2002). Social functionalist frameworks for judgment and choice: Intuitive politicians, theologians, and prosecutors. *Psychological Review, 109,* 451–471.

Trosset, C. (1998, September/October). Obstacles to open discussion and critical thinking. *Change,* 44–49.

Turiel, E. (1983). *The development of social knowledge: Morality and convention.* Cambridge, UK: Cambridge University Press.

Part V

Thinking Critical Beyond the Classroom

Chapter 19

Thinking Critically About Careers in Psychology

Deborah S. Briihl, Claudia J. Stanny, Kiersten A. Jarvis, Maria Darcy, and Ronald W. Belter

Critical thinking comprises a variety of academic, decision-making, and problem-solving skills, including skill in information literacy, quantitative reasoning, evaluating competing hypotheses based on evidence, and consideration of multiple perspectives and sources of information when making decisions and solving problems (Halonen & Gray, 2001; Halpern, 2003). The selection of a college major and identification and pursuit of a career in a given discipline are practical forms of problem solving that depend on a variety of critical thinking skills. Effective decision making about careers founded on solid critical thinking and problem-solving skills should help students avoid dissatisfaction with their career choices.

Career decision-making self-efficacy is widely regarded as a key variable in predicting student success. This construct has been linked to enhanced academic and vocational engagement (Betz & Taylor, 2006) and academic persistence (Peterson & del Mas, 2001/2002). The conceptualization of career decision-making self-efficacy integrates self-efficacy theory (Bandura, 1982, 1997) and career maturity theory (Crites, 1978). Bandura (1982, 1997) suggested that self-efficacy beliefs (i.e., people's beliefs regarding their ability to perform a given task successfully) are a major mediator of behavior and behavior change. Low self-efficacy beliefs concerning a particular behavioral domain such as career decision making lead to avoidance of those behaviors, whereas high self-efficacy beliefs regarding career decision making should lead to engagement in those behaviors. Crites (1978) hypothesized that mature career decisions are facilitated by competence in five career choice processes (accurate self-appraisal, gathering occupational information, goal selection, making plans for the future, and problem solving). Betz and Taylor (2006) selected these processes in their conceptualization of the behavioral domains associated with effective career decision making. These processes are also inherently linked to critical thinking competencies.

Career decision-making self-efficacy has been related to students' vocational identity and career exploration (Gushue, Clarke, Pantzer, & Scanlan, 2006). High levels of career decision-making self-efficacy are associated with increased interest and performance in career decision-making tasks and behaviors, whereas low career decision-making self-efficacy is associated with decreased interest and performance in career decision-making tasks and behaviors (Creed, Patton, & Watson, 2002). Reese and Miller (2006) found that students who completed a career development course reported higher levels of career decision-making self-efficacy, specifically in areas related to obtaining occupational information, setting career goals, and career planning. Students who completed a career development course also reported fewer perceived career decision difficulties.

Good arguments can be made about placing a course on careers in psychology at either the beginning of the academic work in the major or as a capstone course. Placing such a course at the start of academic work in the major may enhance students' academic experience by explicitly introducing foundational academic skills and discipline-specific skills. A careers course placed early in the undergraduate program can direct students to resources within the university that they can draw on to facilitate their academic success. Students are encouraged at an early stage in their academic career to clarify their educational and vocational goals and develop a framework to guide their progress toward achieving these goals. The University of West Florida adopted the introductory approach to a careers course whereas Valdosta State University adopted a senior capstone approach. Both courses address issues related to thinking critically about a career in psychology.

Thinking Critically About Careers in Psychology in an Introductory Course

The Careers in Psychology course offered at the University of West Florida is a 1-semester-hour online course. The course consists of a series of modules, each built around specific student learning outcomes. Students earn course grades on a Satisfactory/Unsatisfactory (S/U) basis. Students must achieve mastery in each module to earn a grade of Satisfactory. Some course modules serve an advising function whereas other modules introduce foundational academic skills that students will use and develop in subsequent course work (a complete list of student learning outcomes appears in Table 19.1).

Although the Careers in Psychology course has a number of learning outcomes that are not related to critical thinking, the focus here is on those aspects of the course that directly relate to critical thinking. These aspects include the following modular learning outcomes:

- Identification of the course requirements for completing a degree with a major in psychology
- Information literacy skills (using library databases to identify useful sources; distinguishing between types of arguments made in media sources and scholarly sources; good authorship practices, including paraphrasing skills to prevent problems with plagiarism; introduction to the basic elements of editorial style of the American Psychological Association)

Table 19.1. Student Learning Outcomes for the Modules in the Introductory-Level Careers Course

Module	Student learning outcomes
The Psychology Major	Describe the requirements of the psychology major.
Psychology as a Career	Identify the specializations within the discipline of psychology.
	Describe the career options available to students who complete differing levels of training in psychology (BA, MA, PhD)
Psychology as a Science	Describe the importance of research for the discipline of psychology.
Succeeding as a Psychology Major	Identify effective strategies for learning new information and performing on tests.
	Identify where students can go for help with academic or personal matters.
	Describe how to get research experience as an undergraduate.
Information Literacy: Finding Resources	Use library databases to identify useful sources in the psychological literature for information for a short paper.
Information Literacy: Writing in Psychology	Describe the ethical issues associated with scholarship (authorship, plagiarism).
	Correctly use the basic elements of editorial style of the American Psychological Association when writing.
Ethics in Research and the Practice of Psychology	Describe the ethical issues associated with the profession of psychology, including the ethics of research and the delivery of assessments, treatments, and interventions in psychology.
Graduate School in Psychology	Identify the skills and knowledge expected of successful applicants to graduate programs in psychology.

- Identification of campus resources available to students and recognition of the value of these for success (student services, advising, counseling center, students with disabilities center, etc.)
- Exploration of career options at different levels of education (bachelor's degrees, master's degrees, doctoral degrees)
- Exploration of graduate study in psychology (identification of types of graduate programs, description of admission criteria and materials that must be included in an application).

As part of the advising component of the course, students identify the university requirements for completing a psychology major, identify educational and career options available to psychology majors, and describe the skills expected of competitive candidates for graduate programs in psychology. In identifying the courses required to complete a degree with a major in psychology, students create a clear road map for the courses they should take in the upcoming years of upper division work. Because the decision to major in psychology can be considered as a short-term university career, students identify the skills needed for success as a student majoring in psychology. Students also complete course modules that establish a foundation for thinking skills that they will develop further during completion of the major. These skills include using library databases, evaluating resources in the psychological literature, writing clearly using the rudiments of APA style and the rhetoric of scientific writing (e.g., making arguments based on evidence rather than opinion), and articulating and adhering to ethical behavior both as a student (academic integrity) and in the profession of psychology (research and professional ethics). Students also identify the offices and support services on campus that will assist them in developing these skills. Thus students in this course must evaluate their academic skill in light of the level of skill required for success in the major, identify areas of strengths and deficits for a career in psychology, set goals and plan for the acquisition and development of specific skills, and regulate this process over time.

By establishing basic critical thinking and other academic skills early in the major, students should be better prepared for activities and assignments in advanced courses that will develop and refine these skills. Finally, students should select courses and engage in cocurricular activities that will develop skills important for succeeding as an undergraduate and assist them as they seek employment or admission to a graduate program. Students who are interested in graduate study in psychology should benefit from an early and clear understanding of the skills they ought to master during their undergraduate years and be able to describe how acquiring these skills can impact their potential success beyond their undergraduate years.

Thus the careers course focuses on many student learning outcomes related to critical thinking, self-regulation, and study skills that should contribute to successful completion of the undergraduate major and long-term success in the field of psychology. Improved decision making about the major should be reflected in students making wiser choices when selecting courses and pursuing active engagement in cocurricular experiences to achieve long-term goals such as admission to a graduate program or gaining employment following completion of the bachelor's degree.

Evaluation of the Impact of the Careers in Psychology Course

The course includes a pretest and posttest self-report measure of knowledge of the major requirements and skills associated with the psychology major (Psychology Major Questionnaire, PMQ), a pretest and posttest Career Decision-Making Self-Efficacy Scale Short Form (CDMSE-SF; Betz & Taylor, 2006), and a course evaluation survey. The PMQ is comprised of 25 Likert-style items that request self-reports of skill on student learning outcomes associated with the course and commitment to complete a major in psychology. The PMQ included several items adapted from the self-assessment survey created by Landrum and Davis (2003).

The CDMSE-SF (Betz, Klein, & Taylor, 1996; Betz & Taylor, 2006) consists of 25 self-report items that measure an individual's degree of belief that he or she can successfully complete tasks necessary to making career decisions. Because self-efficacy is defined relative to competence in specific behavioral domains, Betz et al. (1996) used the five career choice competencies identified in Crites's (1978) model to define and operationalize five domains of competent career decision making. Thus the CDMSE-SF includes five subscales (with five items in each subscale) that include self-reports of behaviors pertinent to accurate self-appraisal, gathering occupational information, goal selection, making plans for the future, and problem solving. Responses are obtained using a 5-point confidence scale, ranging from *No Confidence at All* (1) to *Complete Confidence* (5). The CDMSE-SF has satisfactory reliability, with coefficient alpha of .95 (Betz & Taylor, 2006) and 6-week test–retest coefficient of .83 (Luzzo, 1993).

The analysis of PMQ data presented here combines the findings from students enrolled in the first two semesters that the careers course was offered (Fall, 2005 and Spring, 2006). Scores on the PMQ were significantly higher at the end of the term ($M = 110.4$, $SD = 20.4$) than at the beginning of the term ($M = 90.9$, $SD = 13.9$), $t(103) = 8.61$, $p < .001$, suggesting significant improvement in self-reported academic skill and knowledge about the major. Posttest scores on the PMQ were positively related to posttest scores on the CDMSE-SF, $r(85) = .31$, $t(85) = 3.01$, $p < .003$, suggesting that career self-efficacy is significantly related to self-reported knowledge about the major. Analysis of pretest and posttest data on the CDMSE-SF was limited to data obtained during the Spring term because this measure was administered only as a posttest in the Fall term. Scores on the CDMSE-SF were significantly higher at the end of the term ($M = 108.1$, $SD = 5.6$) than at the beginning of the term ($M = 96.5$, $SD = 4.4$), $t(18) = 2.32$, $p < .03$, suggesting significant improvement in self-reported career decision-making self-efficacy.

The instructor modified the course between the Fall and Spring terms to provide students with additional information about the nature of a mastery-model course and emphasize the need to continue taking exams until the mastery criterion score is attained. This modification included a revision of the introductory material in the first module to include a description of characteristics of the course that require students to maintain consistent engagement with the course (e.g., to participate effectively in threaded discussions and contribute to course activities that would be available online for limited time intervals). This information emphasized the need for students to log into the course regularly and monitor their progress throughout the course.

Because the online course system at UWF does not record login data for courses separately, data on student logins specific to this course were not available. However, the system does record combined login data for all courses that include an online component (fully online courses and blended courses) in which a student is enrolled. If we assume that students enrolled in the careers course were comparable in the extent to which online technology was required for their other courses during each of these two semesters, an increase in the frequency of recorded logins might represent the success of these course revisions in promoting increased student engagement and success in the course. The average number of course logins increased from the Fall term ($M = 108.75$, $SD = 70.48$, range = 14 to 453) to the Spring term ($M = 160.3$, $SD = 154.46$, range = 33 to 795).

This difference was statistically reliable, $t(113) = 2.34$, $p = .021$, with students registering on average 47% more logins during the Spring term than in the Fall term.

Although the interpretation of the login data may be ambiguous, the course revision was also associated with a significant increase in the percentage of enrolled students who successfully completed the course (75.8% in Fall 2005; 93.2% in Spring 2006), χ^2 (1, $N = 121$) = 6.64, $p < .01$. Online courses frequently have a serious problem with students who fail to monitor their progress appropriately during the semester, procrastinate, and fall too far behind to complete the course. This finding suggests that a fairly simple intervention can produce a large improvement in successful completion of the course.

In summary, assessment of the careers course suggested that students improved their level of skill in various components of critical thinking. Successful completion of course modules by meeting mastery standards corroborated the students' self-reports of increased competence in these skills. Moreover, these improvements in academic and critical thinking skills were associated with increased levels of reported self-efficacy related to career decision making.

Thinking Critically about Careers in Psychology at the Senior Level

As students prepare to graduate, they need to reflect upon what they have learned in their undergraduate program and how it will apply to their future job choices. Students need to choose a career that will suit them, not a career chosen on the basis of recommendations from friends and family (such as "There are no jobs in that field so you shouldn't do that" or "Gee, you're a really good listener, you should be a therapist") or because it is the hot trend at the moment (such as wanting to be a profiler or start a dot.com business). In order to make a wise career choice, students need to engage in reasonable and reflective thinking. They must gather information about the job that interests them and do a realistic self-assessment of their "fit" for this job. This process is more involved than just identifying what they think they would like to do.

Students need to examine their thinking processes, biases, and assumptions to make the most effective decisions. Students frequently think they have selected the appropriate graduate program and later realize that this program was not where they wanted to be after all. Although many people may believe that career exploration should be a project that students should do early in their major, students should also explore career options again at the end of their major. Students develop cognitively and gain a better understanding of their strengths and weaknesses throughout their undergraduate careers, so it is important to reassess job choices and skills to ensure that their initial choice is still a suitable job choice for them. In the Senior Seminar at Valdosta State University, students develop a job paper project over the semester.

The first part of the job paper project asks students to assess their personality, values, and skills. In the personality section, students must select characteristics that describe them, such as *accurate, creative, empathetic, self-reliant, open-minded, organized, thorough,* and *calm.* In the values section, students select aspects of the job that are important to them, such as *time freedom, change and variety, public contact, helping others, independence,* and *security*. In the skills section, students must determine what they do well, such as *writing, speaking, listening, using computers, data coding, conflict resolution,* and *organization*. This section requires them to identify their strengths and identify their areas of weakness that could cause difficulties. They must discuss five strengths and three weaknesses in their personality and their skills and four values that are important to the job they want and two that are not. Because this activity occurs early in the process, students only briefly discuss how these characteristics relate to their job choice—both their strengths *and* their weaknesses. Students must address not only how their strengths are necessary for the job, but also how their weaknesses might impact their ability to do that job and how they can correct those weaknesses. The assignment stresses honesty in self-evaluation. To increase the quality of the self-evaluation, the assignment instructions encourage students to talk to their family and friends about these characteristics.

Throughout the semester, students assess their knowledge. In general, they evaluate how their experiences in the psychology program helped (or did not help) them develop the knowledge, skills, and abilities needed to be successful in their career choice. To help them complete this analysis, students receive a list of objectives that they should have met by the time they graduate. The department has 14 objectives, and students also use the 10 goals developed by the American Psychological Association Task Force on Psychology Major Competencies (2006). Students rated themselves on a scale from 1 (*Not at all*) to 5 (*Excellent*) to describe how well they feel they met each objective. They also discuss the activities and classes that helped them meet that objective. When completing their self-rating, students should think of the contributions of all courses taken at Valdosta State University, not just the classes within the psychology major. To remind them of which courses they have taken, students print their transcript and complete a course/advisor check sheet, which includes information about the courses they have taken, when they took them, and the grade they obtained.

A representative from the university Career Center comes to class and gives a presentation on how to write a good resume. Students create a resume, which individuals in the Career Center critique. Students should include skills they developed from past work or volunteer experience and education that could be transferable to the job they are interested in. Too often, students do not realize how portable such skills as communication, leadership, ability to use computers, and information gathering actually are in the job market.

Students include information from all of the previously mentioned self-assessments and class assignments in a job paper. In this paper, students include information on training and job description. In the training section, students who plan to attend graduate school must discuss degrees or schooling available (they must look into at least two programs), degree options (e.g., Master's vs. PhD, PhD vs. PsyD), and possible accreditation issues. They must discuss admission standards, including the required GPA (grade point average), minimum GRE (Graduate Record Exam) scores, and other prerequisites such as required courses and research experience that the program may want in successful applicants. They describe the specific coursework that they will complete and describe how the program will suit their needs, because many programs have a particular "slant" to them, such as clinical or industrial/organizational psychology. All students (those who do and do not plan to attend graduate school) must discuss how they can get a particular job (including tests such as the social/civil service exam they may need to take, on-the-job training they will get, etc.).

Students then discuss the job they selected. They give a detailed job description that includes where they would work and what they would do day to day. They must report average pay (including range, starting and median salary, and benefits). If licensing is an issue, they must provide a brief overview of how one earns the required license and what is necessary to maintain that license.

Students need to gather as much information as they can from as many resources as they can (e.g., career centers, Web sites such as the Occupational Outlook Handbook, textbooks, job fairs). They must reference the material throughout the paper and include a reference page. One key aspect to the paper is that they must talk to someone who is either working or teaching in the field to give them a better sense of the area, such as what is necessary to be successful and obstacles they might encounter as they attempt to reach their career goal.

In this paper, they must also include their self-assessment in even more detail (including references as to how they know that certain factors are important to the job). It is important that students not only learn about the job; they must critically evaluate how well they would fit into this career field. Career satisfaction comes from knowing who you are.

Comparing Introductory and Senior Level Careers Courses

Placing a careers course at the start of the major has several advantages. If undergraduate students entering the psychology major become aware of educational and vocational opportunities available at their university, they might capitalize on this knowledge to make better decisions about the kinds of educational experiences in which they participate. When students have a full understanding of the expectations for successful applicants for employment and admission to graduate programs, they may be motivated to take certain required courses more seriously and make better use of their experiences in courses. Such students may be better prepared for the next stage of their adult lives (either employment or graduate school). A more immediate advantage of placing a careers course early in the curriculum is that the course can direct students to resources within the university that they can draw on to facilitate their academic success. This strategy has the potential to improve outcomes related to student retention, student success in the program, and timely graduation rates (Robbins et al., 2004).

On a practical level, an introductory careers course helps students gain a clear understanding of the specific course requirements. Many students do not understand the role played by various required courses in the psychology curriculum and perceive some requirements as arbitrary and unnecessary. This poor understanding is manifested in complaints about certain course requirements ("Why do I have to take statistics? I'm not interested in math!"). The associated procrastination in registering for these courses creates bottlenecks in the curriculum and introduces delays for students trying to meet graduation requirements.

When developing an introductory-level career course, departments should incorporate information about campus resources that promote student success and encourage students to make good use of these resources. Individual faculty members may not be aware of the many offices and services available to assist students who need to improve their skills in writing, library research, or statistical analysis; services for diagnosing and assisting with the accommodation of specific learning disabilities; mental health counseling; career counseling; and volunteer placement. Students learn about many of these offices and services during their undergraduate years, but this learning tends to be a haphazard process. A systematic introduction to the full set of services that contribute to student success might reduce the frequency with which some students get sidetracked in their academic work.

Many students do not fully understand the contribution of cocurricular activities to their education. They may naïvely believe that a college education is composed of the courses that appear on their transcript and any other activities are mere entertainment. Worse, these students may perceive cocurricular activities as distractions that interfere with course work, outside employment, family obligations, or social life. These students fail to engage in these activities and do not gain the full benefit of the educational experiences available at their college or university.

An introductory careers course provides an opportunity to highlight and market cocurricular activities in the department. The course can promote collaborations between students and faculty on research projects by providing information about faculty research interests and encouraging students to identify research projects that are currently under way. Students need to learn about volunteer service and internship opportunities, some of which might be unique to the campus community. They need to know the procedures for obtaining academic credit for these experiences that take place outside the classroom. Students need to be told about the benefits of acculturation to the profession through participation in student organizations and clubs related to psychology. Too often, naïve or introverted students learn about the important benefits of cocurricular activities and discover these resources too late to make full use of them before graduation.

A small number of seniors enrolled in the careers course as an elective. In their written evaluations of the course, they expressed regret that this course did not exist when they were beginning their psychology major. They stated that although they had learned most of the information in the course by the time they enrolled, they believed they would have benefited had they known this information sooner. New majors enrolled in the course wrote comments on course evaluations that expressed appreciation for the information provided in the course and expectations that the course would help them succeed in subsequent courses. Staff in the psychology office commented that students now seem to ask fewer questions about "basic things" when they call the office for help.

Although an introductory careers course might provide students with a road map for their undergraduate activities, a capstone careers course would provide students with a mechanism for integrating their undergraduate experiences. Students need to become more specific about their job choice rather than just have a vague idea of what they would like to do when they graduate. Too often, students enter a graduate program without any idea of the differences between programs, or seek jobs without understanding how the skills they have developed during their undergraduate studies could be applied to the workforce. Because students change in a variety of ways during their undergraduate careers, a careers course offered as a senior capstone course has the advantage of enabling students to explore career options and make career decisions based on their current skills, interests, and abilities. Students in a capstone course should prepare materials that they will immediately use to assist them in achieving the next step in their academic careers as they transition from the college world to the professional world, such as preparing a resume for a job search or writing a letter of intent or personal statement to include in an application for graduate study. Students should learn about the resources available to them to help them prepare these materials, including materials available through the Internet and various campus resources. Students should recap their undergraduate experience by integrating the skills developed through courses taken, projects completed, volunteer work, and extracurricular activities. Students in a capstone course learn how these various experiences translate into transferable skill sets, which they will use when they enter the job market or attend graduate school. Students indicate through course evaluations and alumni surveys that this information was very valuable to them.

References

American Psychological Association, Task Force on Psychology Major Competencies. (2006). *APA guidelines for the undergraduate psychology major*. Washington, DC: Author. Retrieved October 1, 2006 from http://www.apa.org/ed/psymajor_guideline.pdf

Bandura, A. (1982). Self-efficacy mechanism in human agency. *American Psychologist, 37*, 122–147.

Bandura, A. (1997). *Self-efficacy: The exercise of control*. New York: W. J. Freeman.

Betz, N., Klein, K., & Taylor, K. (1996). Evaluation of a short form of the Career Decision-Making Self-Efficacy Scale. *Journal of Career Assessment, 4*, 47–57.

Betz, N., & Taylor, K. (2006). *Manual for the Career Decision-Making Self-Efficacy Scale and the CDMSE-Short Form*. Unpublished test manual. Department of Psychology, Ohio State University.

Creed, P. A., Patton, W., & Watson, M. B. (2002). Cross-cultural equivalence of the Career Decision-Making Self-Efficacy Scale-Short Form: An Australian and South African comparison. *Journal of Career Assessment, 10*, 327–342.

Crites, J. O. (1978). *Career Maturity Inventory*. Monterey, CA: CTB/McGraw-Hill.

Gushue, G. V., Clarke, C. P., Pantzer, K. M., & Scanlan, K. R. L. (2006). Self-efficacy, perceptions of barriers, vocational identity, and the career exploration behavior of Latino/a high school students. *The Career Development Quarterly, 54*, 307–317.

Halonen, J., & Gray, C. (2001). *The critical thinking companion: For introductory psychology* (2nd ed). New York: Worth.

Halpern, D. F. (2003). *Thought and knowledge: An introduction to critical thinking* (4th ed). Mahwah, NJ: Lawrence Erlbaum Associates.

Landrum, R. E., & Davis, S. F. (2003). *The psychology major: Career options and strategies for success* (2nd ed). Upper Saddle River, NJ: Pearson/Prentice Hall.

Luzzo, D. A. (1993). Value of career decision-making self-efficacy in predicting career decision-making attitudes and skills. *Journal of Counseling Psychology, 40*, 194–199.

Peterson, S. L., & del Mas, R. C. (2001/2002). Effects of career decision-making self-efficacy and degree utility on student persistence: A path analytic study. *Journal of College Student Retention, 3*, 285–299.

Reese, R. J., & Miller, D. C. (2006). Effects of a university career development course on career decision-making self-efficacy. *Journal of Career Assessment, 14*, 252–266.

Robbins, S. B., Lauver, K., Le, H., Davis, D., Langley, R., & Carlstrom, A. (2004). Do psychosocial and study skill factors predict college outcomes? A meta-analysis. *Psychological Bulletin, 130*, 261–288.

Part VI

Critical Briefings: Short Reports on Critical Thinking

Report 1

Best and Worst: Learning to Think Like a Psychologist

Dana Gross

Teachers of psychology, like instructors in other fields, endeavor to alter students' patterns of thinking in ways that reflect disciplinary assumptions and emphases (Bransford & Donovan, 2005; Middendorf & Pace, 2004). Compared to students who major in natural sciences and humanities, students in psychology and the social sciences show significantly greater increases in statistical and methodological reasoning (Lehman & Nisbett, 1990). When and how does this cognitive transformation occur? One likely place in the psychology curriculum is a course in research methods that critically evaluates published reports of empirical research (Hubbard & Ritchie, 1999; VanderStoep & Shaughnessy, 1999).

The two-part assignment described in this report engages students' higher order thinking skills by challenging them to evaluate published empirical research at the beginning of a research methods course. In completing the assignment, students articulate an initial set of criteria and, at the end of the course, revisit and reflect on their original answers in light of their experience.

The Assignment: Best and Worst, Part I

The first part of the Best/Worst assignment contains intentionally ambiguous instructions directing students to choose four articles that exemplify the "best" and "worst" problems or research questions and the "best and "worst" research methods. Although students often request specific criteria for each of these categories, the instructor provides no further information, beyond the instruction to find and summarize four articles and provide a rationale for placing each in its particular category.

The next time that the class meets, students discuss their selections and criteria in small groups. Each group then decides which of the entire set of exemplars are the absolute best and worst in each category and shares those choices with the rest of the class by writing them on a white/blackboard. The entire class and instructor look for and discuss similarities and differences among the lists. As a variation of the precourse knowledge questionnaire (Nuhfer, 2004; Wirth & Perkins, 2005), the first part of the Best/Worst assignment helps the instructor gauge students' initial knowledge and assumptions. The whole-class discussion also enables the instructor to preview a range of relevant dimensions and criteria that psychologists use to evaluate research, including the extent to which it is ethical, valid, reliable, systematic, controlled, and unbiased.

At the beginning of the semester, students frequently nominate applied research topics for the "best" problem category and give less positive ("worst") evaluations to basic research topics. Studies of humans are often evaluated more positively than studies of nonhuman animals, especially if the animals are rodents or, even worse, amphibians. Together, these choices suggest that many students are skeptical about the value of animal models and have an initial bias that leads them to believe that research with human participants has a higher likelihood of directly improving people's lives and well-being. In comparison with research problems and questions, students tend to have more difficulty evaluating methods, at least initially. They are also more likely to explain that a method was the "worst" because the article's Method section was difficult for them to understand than because the sample was too small or the measures lacked reliability, validity, or a clear operational definition.

Understanding Students' Thinking about the Best and the Worst

How do beginning research methods students approach the first Best/Worst assignment? Which resources do they tend to use? These questions were explored with a Student Approaches Questionnaire inspired by a well-known rubric for assessing critical thinking (Condon & Kelly-Riley, 2004). Results from several sections of the course indicate that, at the outset, many students selected their four examples by using their own values and personal beliefs more often than they turned to authoritative sources such as the APA ethical principles and code of conduct (American Psychological Association, 2002) or information from their research methods textbook. They rated finding "worst" examples of problems and methods as being more difficult than finding "best" examples. In the follow-up discussion, many students stated that they believed that, by virtue of having been published, articles appearing in journals could not truly belong in the "worst" category. With little personal experience as research participants, let alone as researchers, most students were unable to use their own direct observations as a basis for their answers. Many students drew on previous psychology courses and reported using sources that others (e.g., other instructors or authors of books about "important" studies in psychology) had identified as being valuable or flawed.

Questionnaire responses also indicated that students found the initial Best/Worst class discussion worthwhile and enjoyed the assignment. Representative comments included, "It forced me to think about things like the relevance of articles and the importance of researching problems using ethical/scientific methods" and "Great assignment to get us thinking!" Students said that it was "Interesting to find mistakes in articles, which helps us to edit our own work," and noted that "The vague nature of the assignment was good – we could select anything we wanted—but it also made it difficult to decide what to use."

Best and Worst Revisited: Part II

At the end of the course, students revisit their initial responses to the Best/Worst assignment and reread their explanation for each of their four selections. Then, with the research methods course in mind, they consider (a) whether they would make any additions or subtractions in any of the categories, (b) whether their criteria for evaluating problems and methods have changed, and (c) which specific elements of the course most influenced their thinking about what makes research valuable. Students' responses clearly indicate that they noticed the themes and vocabulary emphasized by the instructor and highlighted in the textbook, but they also reflect a growing awareness of the specificity of their knowledge about disciplinary-relevant dimensions and standards for evaluating empirical research.

Previously chosen "best methods" sometimes turned out to be "packed full of internal validity problems." One student reflected on her greater understanding of the value and necessity of nonexperimental methods: "Now when I look at the method I chose for 'worst method,' it doesn't seem terrible at all … I understand now that there is no other way to investigate this relationship, since running an experiment is unethical." The majority of students noted that they would not change the exemplars they had initially selected, but many recognized that their choices for "best" method contained flaws or were limited in ways that they had not noticed before.

In place of subjective criteria, such as whether the topic was of personal interest, they tended to re-evaluate their initial choices by "taking a more critical look at their methodology and the validity of their experiments." Some students wrote that the course "made me emphasize the importance of having a good procedure and operational definition," while others made observations about external validity, such as: "I never really considered it before this class. I never thought about how far the findings could be generalized and using that as a criteria for a good study." Another common outcome was the realization that inconclusive results are not necessarily a sign of a bad study: "Whether or not a study finds data that is significant or not, if a researcher performs a study correctly, then many things can be learned." One student wrote that the research methods course:

> has given me a rubric to evaluate research, rather than my subjective opinion alone. … What has changed is my ability to articulate why each article is good or bad … Reading back on this now, it is very easy to tell that I am talking about confounding variables … It is these kinds of advances in terms and vocabulary that have really helped me in the clarity and direction of my writing lab reports this semester.

In identifying valuable influences, many students confirmed the value of carrying out their own studies (working in small groups, they carried out a naturalistic observation, developed and administered a survey, and wrote a proposal for a "perfect" experiment—all on the same topic or theme), noting "the aspect that has most influenced my thinking about what makes research worthwhile was that we actually conducted research." One student's post-course self-evaluation embodied many of the points made by other students:

I feel that I'm much more aware of the potential problems and strengths of a study. I feel that with my new knowledge, I'm more qualified to objectively say if a study is good or bad and why. Learning about different study methods and their strengths and weaknesses, ethical limitations, and issues like internal and external validity has allowed me to evaluate studies with the eye of a psychologist, rather than just a student.

Through their postcourse reflections on the initial Best/Worst exemplars and the associated rationales, students demonstrate that they are learning to see—and think—like psychologists.

References

American Psychological Association. (2002). Ethical principles of psychologists and code of conduct. Retrieved June 4, 2007, from http://www.apa.org/ethics/code2002.html

Bransford, J. D., & Donovan, M. S. (2005). Scientific inquiry and how people learn. In M. S. Donovan, & J. D. Bransford (Eds.), *How students learn history, mathematics and science in the classroom* (pp. 397–419). Washington, DC: National Research Council, National Academies Press.

Condon, W., & Kelly-Riley, D. (2004). Assessing and teaching what we value: The relationship between college-level writing and critical thinking abilities. *Assessing Writing, 9,* 56–75.

Hubbard, R. W., & Ritchie, K. L. (1999). The human subjects review procedure: An exercise in critical thinking for undergraduate experimental psychology students. In M. E. Ware & C. L. Brewer (Eds.), *Handbook for teaching statistics and research methods* (2nd ed., pp. 235–236). Mahwah, NJ: Erlbaum.

Lehman, D. R., & Nisbett, R. E. (1990). A longitudinal study of the effects of undergraduate training on reasoning. *Developmental Psychology, 26,* 952–960.

Middendorf, J., & Pace, D. (2004). Decoding the disciplines: A model for helping students learn disciplinary ways of thinking. *New Directions for Teaching and Learning, 98,* 1–12.

Nuhfer, E. B. (2004). Build a knowledge questionnaire for better learning. *Nutshell Notes, 12*(1). Retrieved March 1, 2007, from http://www.isu.edu/ctl/nutshells/nutshell12-1.html

VanderStoep, S. W., & Shaughnessy, J. J. (1999). Taking a course in research methods improves reasoning about real-life events. In M. E. Ware & C. L. Brewer (Eds.), *Handbook for teaching statistics and research methods* (2nd ed., pp. 242–244). Mahwah, NJ: Erlbaum.

Wirth, K., & Perkins, D. (2005). Knowledge surveys: An indispensable course design and assessment tool. *Proceedings: Innovations in the Scholarship of Teaching and Learning Conference.* St. Olaf College/Carleton College. Retrieved March 1, 2007, from http://www.macalester.edu/geology/wirth/WirthPerkinsKS.pdf

Author Notes

Please send correspondence to Dana Gross, St. Olaf College, 1520 St. Olaf Ave., Northfield, MN 55057-1098; email grossd@stolaf.edu

The assignment described in this report was adapted from one the author completed as a graduate student in a research methods course taught by Dr. Anne D. Pick, Institute of Child Development, University of Minnesota. Copies of both parts of the Best/Worst assignment described in this report and the Student Approaches Questionnaire may be obtained by contacting the author.

Report 2

Personal Mission Statements as Tools for Developing Writing and Reflection Skills

Lawrence Benjamin Lewis and Elizabeth Yost Hammer

Researchers and teachers have begun to explore the unique challenges the first year of college presents to students (see Feldman, 2005, for a review). Often driven by hopes of improved retention rates, many universities have responded by creating "first year experience" (FYE) initiatives (Upcraft, Gardner, & Barefoot, 2004). At our university, we collaborated with our Writing Across the Curriculum Program to create an FYE assignment, writing a personal mission statement, aimed at preparing our freshmen to succeed in their first year and in the psychology major.

First-year psychology majors taking introductory psychology in their first semester complete a one-hour "seminar" attached to their intro course. There are many types of writing assignments in psychology classes that encourage personal reflection (e.g., Butler, Phillmann, & Smart, 2001; Connor-Greene, 2000; Fallahi, Wood, Austad, & Fallahi, 2006; Henderson, 2000; Miller, 1997). In this writing-intensive seminar, students work with faculty and (junior or senior level) peer writing assistants to craft a personal mission statement for their time in college.

This writing assignment is due in four stages. First, they write about their academic goals, drawing on the mission and goals of the university for inspiration. Second, they write about career goals, drawing on academic and professional resources. Third, they discuss personal goals including extracurricular activities, community service, and personal development (e.g., life priorities, important core values). Finally, pulling these elements together, they write an integrated, comprehensive personal mission statement.

This assignment allows students to become familiar with the goals and services of the university as well as encouraging them to think critically about their education and life goals. It also provides career advice early in students' undergraduate careers. The use of the mission statement assignment for first-year psychology students has been successful in fostering college-level writing skills and introducing such issues as setting academic goals, career exploration, and personal development in the context of the overall mission and goals of university education.

Lawrence B. Lewis & Elizabeth Yost Hammer

The Personal Mission Statement Writing Assignment

The assigned personal mission statement is a general, comprehensive essay that includes academic, career, and personal goals. The five-page statement includes referenced research. Grades are based on writing style and the manner in which the students present their goals and values as well as the degree of thoughtfulness and reflection. Students are not evaluated on their actual goals and values.

The mission statement addresses three major themes: academic goals, career goals, and personal goals/commitments. As part of preparing the students to write their statements, we include a number of in-class presentations and small-group activities focused around the three themes. For the academic goals section, a university staff member from the academic support center gives a presentation on study skills and time management. We also engage in classroom activities designed to facilitate discussion about the university's mission statement and expected outcomes for graduates. For the career goals section, we invite a panel of professional psychologists to campus to discuss their experiences. In addition, we host a panel of former psychology majors who went on to pursue professions outside the field of psychology (e.g., medicine, law enforcement). Both panels address how their undergraduate psychology training prepared them for their work, and panelists give suggestions to the students on how they could make the best use of time while in college. For the personal values section, we invite faculty and staff affiliated with campus ministry to engage the students in thinking about the role of personal principles and values for their own personal development.

After these introductory experiences addressing academic, career, and personal goals, faculty and peer writing tutors from the university's writing center work with the students on how to translate their ideas into a structured writing assignment. The mission statement assignment is completed in drafts to give students opportunities to improve their writing skills and progressively refine their ideas. (See Table #2.1 for some examples of in-class and brainstorming exercises for each section. Excerpts from a completed mission statement appear in the Appendix.)

Assessing the Outcomes of Writing the Mission Statement

Seventy entering first-year declared psychology majors at a southern Jesuit liberal arts university served as participants. All were traditional-aged students. To examine writing improvement, a sample of 10 students' writing was assessed at three points in time: a prewriting sample before entering the project, a sample at the end of the first semester, and a final sample at the end of the academic year. At the end of the academic year, two English Department faculty members uninvolved with the project independently evaluated each sample using a rubric developed to assess each of the following writing skills, using a 6-point composite scale: the strength of thesis, effectiveness of organization, development of ideas and evidence, strength and clarity of argument, and grammatical and mechanical correctness.

Table #2.1. Examples of In-Class and Brainstorming Exercises for Each Section of the Personal Mission Statement

---

Academic Goals

Why are you in college?
What are your academic goals?
How do the university's stated goals fit with your goals?

Career Goals

What kind of career or job do you imagine yourself getting into?
If you did not have to worry about money, what would you choose to do?
When you think about a career, what is most important to you?
Find two psychology articles that address an issue you might wish explore professionally. What about them interests you?

Personal Goals

List the top five things you want in life.
When you think about your personal life, which activities or people do you consider the most important?
What are the qualities you admire in people and would like to emulate?
As you were growing up, what were the things that motivated you most?

The largest differences were found when comparing students before they completed the project to their final writing assignment at the end of the entire first year experience. The mean score for the prewriting sample was significantly lower ($M = 2.95$) than the final assignment score ($M = 5.25$), $t = -6.41$, $p < .001$. All but one student (who stayed the same) showed improvement from the prewriting assignment to the final assignment.

When looking at the first semester only, seven students showed improvement from the prewriting assignment to the final assignment at the end of the first semester (one decreased, one stayed the same, and one did not have final data). The mean score for the prewriting sample was significantly lower ($M = 2.95$) than that of the final first semester assignment ($M = 4.61$), $t = -3.95$, $p = .004$.

As a measure of carryover from one semester to the next, six students showed improvement from the final assignment in the first semester to the final assignment at the end of the academic year (one decreased, two stayed the same, and one did not have final data). The mean score for the final first semester assignment was lower ($M = 4.61$) than that of the final end-of-year assignment ($M = 5.25$), $t = -2.14$, $p = .065$.

Qualitative reports from students indicated that they developed specific academic, career, and personal goals and that they found the assignment useful. Sample student comments included, "I liked the panelists of psychologists and psychology majors who weren't psychologists," "Writing papers improved critical thinking and APA-style writing," "[The personal values] talk was interesting," and "[A strength was] visualizing your personal values and goals."

Lawrence B. Lewis & Elizabeth Yost Hammer

Benefits of Writing a Personal Mission Statement

As described by Stephen R. Covey in his best-selling book *The Seven Habits of Highly Effective People*, a personal mission statement "focuses on what you want to be (character) and what you want to do (contributions and achievements), and on the values and principles upon which being and doing are based" (Covey, 1989, p. 106). There are a number of long-term benefits that may result from this assignment. This kind of experience provides students with a formal opportunity to examine their lives. It helps them assess their thoughts, feelings, and values, and it provides an opportunity to help students separate their ideas of who they are and what they want from the ideas of others, such as parents and friends. There is a potential for this assignment to provide direction for the student's values and to assist in making long-term goals. We plan to assess students at the end of their college careers to help assess the long-term benefits of this assignment.

Results indicate that the project was successful in helping students write about their goals in progressively more sophisticated ways. In addition to enhanced writing, this assignment also allows for a formal opportunity for students to examine their lives; assess their thoughts, feelings, and values; and make long-term goals. We plan to continue this assignment as part of the psychology first-year experience and to assess the long-term value of the assignment as the students progress through the program.

References

Butler, A., Phillmann, K., & Smart, L. (2001). Active learning within a lecture: Assessing the impact of short, in-class writing exercises. *Teaching of Psychology, 28,* 257–259.

Connor-Greene, P. (2000). Making connections: Evaluating the effectiveness of journal writing in enhancing student learning. *Teaching of Psychology, 27,* 44–46.

Covey, S. (1989). *The seven habits of highly effective people.* New York: Free Press.

Fallahi, C. R., Wood, R. M., Austad, C. S., & Fallahi, H. (2006). A program for improving undergraduate psychology students' basic writing skills. *Teaching of Psychology, 33,* 171–175.

Feldman, R. S. (2005). *Improving the first year of college: Research and practice.* Mahwah, NJ: Erlbaum.

Henderson, B. B. (2000). The reader's guide as an integrative writing experience. *Teaching of Psychology, 27,* 130–132.

Miller, S. (1997). Self-knowledge as an outcome of application journal keeping in social psychology. *Teaching of Psychology, 24,* 124–125.

Upcraft, M. L., Gardner, J., & Barefoot, B. (2004). *Challenging and supporting the first-year student: A handbook for improving the first year of college.* San Francisco, CA: Jossey-Bass.

Appendix: Excerpts From a Sample Mission Statement Paper

As a psychology major, it is hard for me to understand why anyone would choose another major when the study of the human mind has a personal link within all of us. Surprisingly, an important question arose: How would I put my love for sports and medicine together? I have begun to understand the answer, but it still has to develop more fully. Having such high family values, I want to keep my grades and morals high at all times to build my character for the future. Throughout my career, personal, and academic goals I have realized that I want to be successful in sports medicine, have a stress-free life, and follow my religion. I also want to emulate my mother's traits.

First, my aspirations are to be a doctor in the field of sports medicine ...

I plan on receiving a good education at Loyola, which will give me a stable career with less stress on me. For example, while growing up I sometimes saw my parents' friends, who were doctors, flourish and seem to have a great amount of happiness ...

In addition, my religion, Islam, plays a strong role in who I am, and who I want to be ...

Lastly, when looking for a role model, one should look for a few of these traits: trust, love, optimism, unselfishness, and courage. I can only find these traits in one person: my mother ...

In conclusion, being a sports physician will build me a foundation to support a family. I will hopefully be able to supply my family with the essentials it will need, which in turn will make me happy. Following my religion and my mother's ways, I believe it will help me in my future. I feel that I have made the right decision by choosing psychology as my major, and that it will help me in my career of sports medicine.

Report 3

A Module-Based Research Project: Modeling Critical Thinking in Psychology

Nina Lamson and Katherine Kipp

Asking students to do a research paper, even after providing them with lengthy instructions and detailed examples, often can yield disappointing results. It is apparent that the task is overwhelming, partly because a comprehension for the purpose of the process may be lacking. We suggest that, as a foundation for upper division courses, a component of the introductory course explains the research process and how this process forms the basis from which psychology content evolves. We present a sample research project of 10, hands-on, incremental modules designed to model how critical thinking is an integral part of the research process in psychology. Through this process, students gain knowledge in reading research articles and answering pertinent questions that provide the support for an introduction section. They gain an understanding of how to conduct a study by participating in the study, as well as learning how to collect, analyze, and discuss data. The project culminates in a final research paper and an in-class poster session.

Project Overview

The project centers on an experiment investigating the effects of talking on a cell phone while driving, a topic interesting to students and easily adapted for in-class experimentation. The hypothesis investigated is that cell phone conversation would result in slower walking pace on a maze and a decline in accuracy on a cognitive load memory task. Several articles were chosen for the literature review based on their exploration of the effects of cell phone use on driving. For the actual in-class experiment, students acted either as experimenters or as research participants. The basic method involved taking a memory test for a baseline score; then half the participants continued to be tested for memory while they walked a maze in the classroom, and the remaining participants simply listened to random words on the cell phone as they walked the maze. The instructor analyzed and shared the data with the students for inclusion in the Results section and for drawing conclusions in the Discussion section as to how the findings relate to the possible effects of cell phone use while driving.

Steps 1, 2, 3: "Literature Review"

For each of these three steps, students read an article on cell phone use and driving. For each article students then answer 9 to 12 questions pertaining to the goal, methodology, outcome, and conclusions. These modules expose the students to how to investigate a question of interest. In class, lecture and discussions draw parallels between the scientific method and the execution of a research study.

Step 1   *(Strayer & Johnston, 2001) sample questions:* "What are the two hypotheses stated that guide the research on cell phone use and driving? (Hint: they are set in italics in the introduction sections.) What is the focus of each?"

Step 2   *(Spence & Read, 2003) sample question:* "What was considered the single task and what was considered the dual task?"

Step 3   *(Radeborg, Briem, & Hedman, 1999) sample question:* "What was the principal result of the study as presented in the discussion section?"

Steps 4–10: Conducting, Writing, and Presenting the Research

Step 4: The Introduction

Here students use an "introduction template," and they fill in the missing information based on what they learned in Steps 1–3. They also correctly cite the sources, based on provided APA-style examples (American Psychological Association, 2001), and create a title page. This module allows the students to see the type of information included in an introduction, how to write it, and, most importantly, how a hypothesis emerges from exploring the literature.

Step 5: The Method Section

Students write this section after they conduct or participate in the in-class experiment. They learn that the purpose of the Method section is to outline how to test the hypothesis. They learn that it is important to be precise so that another researcher could duplicate the study. To complete this step, students receive guidelines as to what information they should include. They use a diagram of a simplified method section to complete this section.

Step 6: The Results Section

Students receive the instructor-analyzed data from the in-class experiment. They receive information on what it means to find or not find significant results, what interpretations are drawn about the behavior under investigation as a result, and how to report the data. The instructor presents the data in table form to make data incorporation into the appropriate statistical notation easier. Students also receive example "result paragraphs" to use as templates for their writing.

Step 7: The Discussion Section

Similar to the introduction section assignment, students use a discussion template for this module. Here the student learns how to discuss the results in light of the literature and how to consider theoretical and practical implications.

Step 8: Abstract and References

After the research is conducted and written, the students write the Abstract, using a guide for what information to include. For the References, students use an example of formatting references and ordering them on the reference page.

Step 9: Correct and Assembled Final Paper

Students receive the different writing components, marked with corrections from the instructor, and they then correct their first drafts for the final paper and assemble the components as outlined in the assignment. Students submit this final paper with the corrected first drafts so that the instructor can compare the first and final drafts.

The benefit of this module is that the students learn to assemble all the components in a research document, demonstrating to them the investigation, testing, reporting, and discussion of the research question. Their final assembled paper becomes a document they can refer to in the future when having to write other research papers. Most students feel a sense of accomplishment when they view the document in its entirety.

Step 10: The Presentation Poster

Finally, students learn that researchers share their findings with colleagues by presenting a poster at a professional conference. So the final step is for the students to have fun and be creative in providing the findings of this study in a concise, readable, attractive, and informative manner. In a miniconference-style poster session, students are questioned by the instructor about the research to model what occurs in a conference setting.

Nina Lamson & Katherine Kipp

Assessing Critical Thinking

The module-based approach outlined here offers several opportunities for assessing students' critical thinking. First, evaluations of students' initial attempts at critical thinking occur as they turn in drafts of sections and receive those drafts with corrections made by the instructor. Second, evaluation of the content and application of the research methods taught occurs on course exams. Finally, an authentic assessment (Halonen et al., 2003; Palomba & Banta, 1999) of the entire project is possible because the project is a real-world replica of the scientific method in psychology.

Conclusion

The purpose of this project is to familiarize introductory psychology students with the research process by helping them to understand research methods, how research is guided by the scientific method, and how it becomes the basis to the content that is learned in the course. Most importantly, however, this assignment models how critical thinking is an integral part of this process, in that students read, examine, and explore published research, from which a hypothetical question to be tested emerges. Students learn how outcomes can support, modify, or refute a theory, thus demonstrating the dynamics of science.

References

American Psychological Association. (2001). *Publication manual of the American Psychological Association* (5th ed.). Washington, DC: Author.

Halonen, J. S., Bosack, T., Clay, S., & McCarthy, M. (with Dunn, D., Hill IV, G. W., et al.). (2003). A rubric for learning, teaching, and assessing scientific inquiry in psychology. *Teaching of Psychology, 30,* 196–208.

Palomba, C. A., & Banta, R. W. (1999). *Assessment essentials: Planning, implementing, and improving assessment in higher education.* San Francisco: Jossey-Bass.

Radeborg, K., Briem, V., & Hedman, L. R. (1999). The effect of concurrent task difficulty on working memory during stimulated driving. *Ergonomics, 5,* 767–777.

Spence, C., & Read, L. (2003). Speech shadowing while driving: On the difficulty of splitting attention between eye and ear. *Psychological Science, 3,* 251–256.

Strayer, D. L., & Johnston, W. A. (2001). Driven to distraction: Dual-task studies of simulated driving and conversing on a cellular telephone. *Psychological Science, 6,* 462–466.

Report 4

Effectively Using Literature Circles in the Psychology Classroom

Rebecca Wenrich Wheeler

Literature circles function as a multidisciplinary approach that effectively teaches students to think critically about a variety of texts. Although the literature circles format is typically used in English classrooms, I found it can easily be adapted to promote critical thinking in psychology courses. Literature circles enhance students' higher order thinking skills, as students self-direct their learning and interact with other students about a particular writing, as well as foster intellectual curiosity. Lloyd (2004) emphasized that literature circles place greater responsibility on students for their learning in comparison to read-aloud or guided reading tasks. Students use critical reading and questioning strategies to individually prepare for literature circle discussion (Lloyd, 2004). With read-aloud and guided reading, the teacher creates the discussion questions and controls the discussion process. In contrast, the key to a successful literature circle experience comes when the learning is student-centered and the teacher acts as a facilitator.

Origin of Literature Circles

The concept of literature circles gained momentum when Robert Probst's (1994) article "Reader-Response Theory and the English Curriculum" was published in the *English Journal*. In essence, the reader-response theory places the emphasis on the reader and the process of reading (Fischer, 2000; McManus, 1998). This concept works well in psychology classrooms as reader-response theory emphasizes how an individual's assumptions and cultural norms influence readings of texts (McManus, 1998). Implementation of reader-response theory encourages readers to expose gaps and conflicts in texts and raise questions about their own perceptions (Fischer, 2000). Through challenging assumptions, students must evaluate the validity of the sources through which they glean information, thus strengthening their critical thinking skills.

Additionally, the instructor models questioning techniques emphasizing the value of becoming a thoughtful reader (Lloyd, 2004).

Application to the Psychology Classroom

I adapted the literature circles concept to the advanced placement (AP) psychology classroom for three main reasons: to expose students to a variety of psychological topics, to handle a variety of reading levels, and to teach critical thinking and reading skills. First, students experience a variety of topics in a relatively short amount of time, such as the experiences of persons suffering from mental illness or a comparison of learning theories. I provide students with four to eight reading selections from which to choose. I make the selections based on genre, topic, and length, while making allowances for a variety of reading levels. The discussion groups are formed based on book selections, so all students in the group have read the same book. Ideally, the groups will contain four to eight members.

The first literature circle of the semester, I often offer popular nonfiction with high interest, for instance *Reviving Ophelia* (Pipher, 1994), *An Unquiet Mind* (Jamison, 1995), and *Blood Done Sign My Name* (Tyson, 2004). Another variation would be to discuss the psychological concepts present in novels, such as *Catcher in the Rye* (Salinger, 1951) and *Lord of the Flies* (Golding, 1955). In addition, more contemporary novels, such as *The Curious Incident of the Dog in the Night-time* (Haddon, 2004) also function well in the literature circles format. Using popular literature first grabs the students' attention and interests them in reading. Once students become familiar with the literature circle process, the class moves to more challenging pieces, primary documents, and scientific data. In addition, through using popular literature first, I am able to deal with the assumptions students have about psychology early on in the course and move them toward a scientific approach. In a semester, my class typically engages in three literature circle experiences. Through this process the students gain confidence in their own reading and critical thinking skills.

As the semester progresses, I begin to add literature circle texts with meatier psychological concepts, such as Hock's (2004) *Forty Studies that Changed Psychology*. With this text, students choose chapters to read instead of the entire book, allowing the small group to focus deeper on one particular study. I have also used Tim Kasser's (2002) *The High Price of Materialism* and Robert Sternberg's (2004) *The Psychology of Hate*; both provide excellent talking points related to social psychology.

In addition, the literature circles concept helps to manage a variety of reading levels that might exist in an introductory or AP psychology classroom, as the instructor may choose texts on a variety of reading levels. Often "less proficient or inexperienced" readers do not take an active role in reading comprehension and "are less willing to work through their confusion" of the text (Day, Spiegel, McLellan, & Brown, 2002, p. 134); however, through literature circles, reluctant readers gain deeper understanding of readings and learn to work independently (Day et al., 2002). As an instructor, I realize that not all students enter my classroom with the same reading comprehension skills, and therefore I must find ways for all students to access the material. I allow students to look through the books before making their final selection. The students can usually assess if a book is appropriate for their reading level by simply reading the first page.

The literature circle format also provides a vehicle to teach reading and thinking skills. I model for students how to construct quality questions "to clarify meaning, identify confusing vocabulary, and explore the author's intentions" (Lloyd, 2004, p. 118). Students will retain more of what they read if they learn to ask questions while they read. Through small group discussions, students learn how to better articulate their own ideas and value others' perspectives, and become better listeners through engagement in honest conversations with peers (Lin, 2002). Before the small group discussion, students complete a prediscussion handout, which involves choosing passages and topics to discuss and challenging vocabulary. First, the prediscussion handout prompts students to identify three passages noteworthy of discussion and record their reasoning behind choosing each passage. Second, the students must identify and define two psychological terms or difficult vocabulary in each passage. Third, the students must construct five open-ended critical thinking questions related to the reading. I group students with those who read the same work for the discussion.

Student Participation and Assessment

Students must bring their reading materials and prediscussion worksheet on discussion day to participate. Each small group receives a handout with the procedure on conducting the discussion. Each student takes turns leading the group in a discussion of at least one of his or her chosen passages and at least two critical thinking questions. The discussion continues until all students have addressed their passages and questions. During the discussion, the teacher moves around the classroom and listens to the groups' discussions, only interjecting comments when absolutely necessary. The instructor listens to the small group discussions and gathers data to determine which concepts need to be addressed and those the students know well (Day et al., 2002). Day et al. (2002) provide reproducible assessment rubrics to aid teachers when assessing student discussions. For example, a rubric might focus on students' theoretical analysis of passages and whether students provide textual evidence to support opinions (Day et al., 2002). Generally, the discussion averages 40 mins for short pieces and 70 for longer works. A group may move on to the next step when discussion has concluded, whether or not other groups are finished.

Next, as a group, students complete a self-evaluation that prompts them to determine why they discussed certain topics and how the reading might have changed their thinking. In addition, the students choose co-operatively a passage that best exemplifies the purpose of the book, and assess their performance as a group. The group turns in the report sheet with each member's prediscussion worksheet stapled behind it.

The days following the small group meeting, the group completes a postdiscussion activity that connects thematic concepts in a creative format. The postdiscussion activity serves as an assessment, and the product will be shared with the entire class. The type of product varies with the reading's themes and available time. The product possibilities are endless. For example, groups may design and present lesson plans, skits, and commercials or even create board games and comic strips. The product demonstrates that the students understand how to apply the psychological concepts and understand the concepts well enough to teach their peers. One of my favorite postdiscussion activities involved groups creating scale-model laboratories representing significant psychological experiments. When it came time to review for the AP psychology exam, the models provided an excellent visual reminder of the theorists. Who could forget a Ken doll posing as John Watson? Or electrodes attached to a toy cat simulating Hobson and McCarley's (1977) sleep experiments? Appalachian State University student, Courtney Bell (personal communication, June 21, 2007) comments on her AP psychology literature circle experience:

> In small groups, I could hear what others thought about the same material, and often they would bring such different views and thoughts on the material that I got a more clear understanding of the theory. All bring their own experiences and their own insight to each discussion that usually we were able to delve deeper into the material than if we simply read out of the book.

How exciting for a teacher to see students not only reading and enjoying the material but also learning how to articulate their ideas, listen to their classmates, and create memorable products that demonstrate an application of their knowledge.

References

Day, J. P., Spiegel, D. L., McLellan, J., & Brown, V. B. (2002). *Moving forward with literature circles*. New York: Scholastic Professional Books.

Fischer, E. A. (2000). Prescriptions for curing English teacher split personality disorder. *English Journal, 89,* 40–45.

Golding, W. (1955). *Lord of the flies*. New York: Penguin Books.

Haddon, M. (2004). *The curious incident of the dog in the night-time*. New York: Vintage.

Hobson, J. A., & McCarley, R. W. (1977). The brain as a dream-state generator: An activation-synthesis hypothesis of the dream process. *Journal of Psychiatry, 134,* 1335–1348.

Hock, R. (2004). *Forty studies that changed psychology* (5th ed.). Upper Saddle River, NJ: Prentice Hall.

Jamison, K. R. (1995). *An unquiet mind: A memoir of moods and madness*. New York: Vintage.

Kasser, T. (2002). *The high price of materialism*. Cambridge, MA: The MIT Press.

Lin, C. (2002, October). Literature circles. Retrieved April 2, 2008 from http://www.indiana.edu/~reading/ieo/digests/d173.html

Lloyd, S. L. (2004). Using comprehension strategies as a springboard for student talk. *Journal of Adolescent and Adult Literacy, 48,* 114–124.

McManus, B. F. (1998, October). Reader-response criticism. Retrieved June 24, 2007, from http://www.cnr.edu/home/bmcmanus/readercrit.html

Pipher, M. (1994). *Reviving Ophelia: Saving the selves of adolescent girls*. New York: Ballantine Books.

Probst, R. E. (1994). Reader-response theory and the English curriculum. *English Journal, 83,* 37–44.

Salinger, J. D. (1951). *The catcher in the rye*. New York: Little, Brown Books.

Sternberg, R. J. (2004). *The psychology of hate*. Washington, DC: American Psychological Association.

Tyson, T. B. (2004). *Blood done sign my name*. New York: Three Rivers Press.

Author's Note

Special acknowledgement to Tonya Hinton and John Velasquez who assisted in manuscript editing, and Courtney Bell for her student-based insights.

Correspondence concerning this article should be addressed to Rebecca Wenrich Wheeler, Social Studies Department, Southeast Raleigh Magnet High School, Raleigh, North Carolina, 27610. Email: rwheeler1@wcpss.net

Report 5

Introducing Controversial Issues in Psychology Through Debate and Reflection

Sherri B. Lantinga

In the psychology education literature, critical thinking typically refers to students' ability to consider the quality of arguments and their supporting evidence, to define terms, or to examine underlying assumptions (Yanchar & Slife, 2004). To foster such analytical processes, instructors adopt a wide range of pedagogical strategies and assignments. Unfortunately, such assignments are often isolated rather than building on one another, have a single audience (the instructor), and receive only written responses days or even weeks after the students demonstrate their thinking skills. To counter these shortcomings, I developed a set of interrelated assignments to build students' critical thinking abilities, develop their professional communication and information literacy skills, further their understanding of controversies in psychology, and encourage immediate and peer feedback about their thinking (see American Psychological Association, 2007, for national assessment guidelines). I used this project in an introduction to psychological science course, which students normally take after general psychology and concurrently with other foundation courses in the major. This course normally enrolls 15 to 25 freshmen and sophomores who have declared psychology as a major or psychology minors whose majors typically include social work, business, and exercise.

Project Description

The project involves an individual research paper, an in-class group debate/discussion, and individual student responses to the controversial issues. Small groups of two to three students together chose a controversial question from a list I developed from articles in the *Taking Sides* volumes (e.g., Nier, 2005; Slife, 2006). I chose the topics for their ability to engage student interest. The questions focused on research ethics (e.g., use of animals in psychological research) and various mental health issues (e.g., whether religious practice enhances mental health).

Position Paper (Individual)

After choosing their topic, students individually read a related pair of articles from a *Taking Sides* volume, used PsycINFO to locate at least four primary/scholarly references, and wrote a 5-page position paper in which they offered and defended a thesis statement on the issue. I encouraged students to consult with others in their group and to share their references. The grading rubric included seven areas of assessment (thesis, depth of argument, sources, organization, tone, writing style, and conventions) that I scored on three-point scales: excellent, satisfactory, and unsatisfactory. I weighted the first three areas twice as heavily as the other four in determining a final paper grade.

Discussion/Debate (Group)

Shortly after the paper's submission deadline, each group developed and delivered a 10-minute class presentation on their controversial topic. When more than one group had chosen a topic, I assigned them opposite positions for the purposes of class discussion; these groups spent less time on presentation and more time in debate and rebuttal of arguments. After each presentation, the rest of the class asked questions and engaged the presenters in discussion. Each debate/discussion lasted the full class period (50 min) and earned grades based on content, effectiveness of delivery, and ability to answer questions.

Position Paragraphs (Individual)

Prior to the class period in which students presented each issue, I assigned the original pair of controversial articles from *Taking Sides* as reading for the class. Students (all but those who had chosen the issue for their position papers) read both articles and typed a 1–2-paragraph statement that reflected their tentative position on the issue. This assignment ensured a more evenly informed and engaged audience for the presenters. At the end of class debate/discussion for each topic, students individually wrote brief reflections on how the discussion/debate influenced their initial positions. I graded these position paragraphs based on students' ability to support a position with evidence from the readings or other sources and on their ability to articulate how the debate/discussion had influenced their thinking.

Project Assessment

Self-Report Survey

The data described here are from 20 students in my second semester of using the project. A week after the last class presentation, students completed a self-report survey about the project. Nine items assessed improvement in areas related to the project using 4-point

Table #5.1. Self-Report Survey Item Means (Standard Deviations)

The Controversial Issues Research Project...	*M (SD)*
... enhanced my ability to use APA writing style	3.71 (0.56)*
... increased my awareness of various controversies within psychology	3.52 (0.51)*
... improved my ability to consider how defining a term in different ways may change the debate	3.41 (0.66)*
... increased my ability to critically evaluate others' positions on an issue	3.38 (0.58)*
... increased my ability to use evidence to support a position	3.29 (0.64)*
... improved my library/PsycINFO skills	3.14 (0.73)*
... improved my ability to state a thesis	2.95 (0.65)*
... improved my confidence in giving a public presentation	2.93 (0.68)*
... improved my ability to work with others (patience, flexibility, etc.)	2.71 (0.83)

Note: items used 4-point response scales where 1 = *strongly disagree* & 4 = *strongly agree*
*$p < .01$

response scales (1 = *strongly disagree* and 4 = *strongly agree*). Three open-ended items asked students to identify which aspect of the project was most helpful, to describe how the project could be improved, and to offer any other comments. As shown in Table #5.1, students reported the greatest improvements in their use of APA style (APA, 2001) awareness of psychological controversies, and several aspects of critical thinking. Specifically, students indicated deepened understanding of the importance of defining terms, an improved ability to critically evaluate others' positions, and an enhanced ability to use evidence to support arguments. A one-sample *t* test indicated that eight of the nine self-report means were significantly higher than the response scale midpoint of 2.50, *t*s(20) > 2.91, *p*s < .01. In short, students saw themselves as making significant strides in developing their skills, awareness of issues, and critical thinking abilities.

Students' qualitative feedback indicated that many found the position paper to be the most useful, followed by the class discussions/debates. Students reported learning new viewpoints, developing the skill to defend a position publicly, learning how to take a position, and developing clear, logical arguments supported by evidence instead of personal opinion. Some students offered ideas for improving the project, including using "more hard-hitting issues" or requiring an ungraded rough draft. The "other comments" section generated a number of positive comments such as "really opened my eyes to certain issues," and "I loved this project; I think it was helpful in many ways and informational."

Course-Embedded Assessment

To assess students' development as a result of the project, I designed a take-home test with the same format as the position paper. Students read a new pair of controversial articles from a *Taking Sides* volume and wrote a 5-page position paper based on primary/scholarly research articles. I distributed and explained the test on the last day of presentations and gave students 5 days to complete the assignment. I used the same grading rubric for the tests as for the position papers. The position papers averaged 78.90% (SD = 12.80); scores ranged from 40% to 98%. The most significant errors were failure to state a clear thesis, failure to define terms clearly, or failure to defend against counterarguments. Out of a total of 20 papers, only 7 earned a score of "excellent" on the rubric scale "Thesis" and 10 scored "unsatisfactory." In contrast, the take-home test averaged 87.43% (SD = 8.26); scores ranged from 70% to 99%. All but two students scored "excellent" on "Thesis," indicating appreciable improvement in that area.

Improvements

Based on students' and my own assessment of this project, I anticipate making some adjustments in future classes. For example, some of the readings were too difficult for this level of student, so I will seek others that are more appropriate. I will also consider meeting with the groups to further encourage an accountable, team-based approach to the research and preparation for the debate; this would also be a way to check for problems or conflicts ahead of time. Finally, I will give students the option to submit an early draft of their papers a few days ahead of the deadline for formative feedback.

Conclusions

This project was an effective means to develop introductory students' critical thinking and professional skills and to alert students to some controversial issues in psychology. Students learned by finding and reading research, writing cogent arguments to defend a position, preparing a presentation with others, responding to questions and arguments, and hearing others' definitions and arguments about other topics. This project improved students' abilities in ways not possible with a lecture or other instructor-centered format.

References

American Psychological Association. (2001). *Publication manual of the American Psychological Association* (5th ed.). Washington, DC: Author.

American Psychological Association. (2007). *Applying assessment strategies in psychology: Critique of assessment strategies applied to goals and outcomes.* Retrieved March 21, 2007, from http://www.apa.org/ed/critique_study.html

Nier, J. A. (Ed.). (2005). *Taking sides: Clashing views on controversial issues in social psychology.* Dubuque, IA: McGraw-Hill.

Slife, B. (Ed.). (2006). *Taking sides: Clashing views on controversial psychological issues* (14th ed). Guilford, CT: McGraw-Hill/Dushkin.

Yanchar, S. C., & Slife, B. D. (2004). Teaching critical thinking by examining assumptions. *Teaching of Psychology, 31*, 85–90.

Author Note

Please address correspondence concerning this article to Sherri B. Lantinga, Associate Professor of Psychology and Dean of the Social Sciences, Dordt College. E-mail: lantinga@ dordt.edu. 712/722-6038

For assignment details, go to http://homepages.dordt.edu/~lantinga/IPS/index.html

Report 6

The Critical Thinking Lab: Developing Student Skills Through Practical Application

Todd J. Wilkinson, Bryan J. Dik, and Andrew P. Tix

The development of critical thinking skills is widely regarded as a valued outcome of undergraduate learning. Encouraging critical thinking is a particularly important component of teaching an introductory psychology course (e.g., Matlin, 1997; Myers, 1997) and critical thinking skills often are described as highly desirable by potential employers. In short, critical thinking is "worth its weight in gold" (Furedy, 1988, p. 42).

In actual practice, however, the teaching of these skills often is short-changed within traditional curricula (e.g., Barber, 2002). The following in-class experiential exercise represents an explicit effort to facilitate the development of critical thinking skills in an introductory psychology course. The premise of the Critical Thinking Lab, adapted from Fink (2003), emphasizes the development of student skills in analyzing and evaluating course-related content from secondary sources. The primary goal of this exercise is to provide a structured, collaborative learning environment in which students can refine and apply their critical thinking skills by analyzing and evaluating a specific psychological claim. In addition, the exercise provides an opportunity for students to develop their communication skills by working collaboratively toward a shared goal and by orally presenting their evaluation of the claim to the class.

During the week prior to the critical thinking lab, the instructor requires students to find a brief article presented in the news media that presents a specific claim about human behavior or health. Students may find this claim in topical or news magazines, newspapers, or in various online news outlets. On the day of the lab, students bring their articles to class and divide into groups (we recommend a maximum of eight groups total, with five members in each group). Each student briefly presents her or his psychological claim to the group. Each group must then choose one claim to collectively evaluate. The instructor then informs groups that they will be constructing a poster that describes their evaluation of the claim, and that at the end of class, they will briefly present the claim itself, their evaluation of its validity, and their conclusions. Each group works collaboratively to evaluate the claim in a manner that, at minimum, follows these instructions:

1   List all the reasons for believing the claim is true.
2   List all the reasons for questioning the claim or believing it is not true.
3   To what extent is supporting evidence presented in the article?
4   To what extent is this evidence convincing?

In addition, each group forms a consensus conclusion about the claim (e.g., that evidence supports the conclusion that the claim likely is true, or that evidence provided to support the claim is insufficient). As an incentive, the instructor tells students that by virtue of a class vote, members in the group with the best presentation will receive extra credit points.

Materials include butcher paper (or equivalent) and markers. Tape should be available as well for each group to fix their poster to a designated spot along the classroom wall for presentations. Each group has approximately 5 mins (to be adjusted according to how many groups there are and how much time is left before the end of class) to present the claim itself, their evaluation of the claim, and their conclusion. Optimally, the class stands and moves around the classroom as each group presents from their poster location, simulating a poster session at a professional conference. Following the presentation of all posters, each class member receives a sticky note and fixes it to the poster that represents what she or he believes was the best thought-out evaluation (i.e., not simply the flashiest or best designed poster). If preferred, voting also can occur in the form of a secret ballot. After the instructor announces the winning group, discussion ensues (e.g., what makes this poster the best?). The exercise generally takes about 2 hours to complete and works equally well in a single 2-hour time block or spread across two 1-hour class sessions. To help students personalize the learning acquired during the exercise, we incorporated an additional writing assignment with this activity by having students summarize what they learned and demonstrate their critical thinking skills by re-evaluating their group's selected claim in individual papers.

Evaluations and Conclusions

Students (n = 33) completed evaluations of the critical thinking lab at the end of a 15-week semester in which they conducted the lab during the 3rd and 9th weeks. On a Likert-type scale (1 = *no increase*, 3 = *moderate amount*, 5 = *large amount*), students indicated that the lab increased their knowledge and skills related to critical thinking a "moderate to large amount" (M = 3.86, SD = .78). Using items with similar response options, students also rated the exercise as enjoyable (M = 3.98, SD = .8) and useful to them beyond the class (M = 3.79, SD = .87).

The instructor also asked students whether they recommended the critical thinking lab for use with future classes. All but one student recommended using the lab exercise in the future. In addition, students made several positive comments, including that the lab "really helps to see how others extract/critically think about these articles," and "I think it's good practice for critical thinking outside of class." Students suggested that the exercise also was a useful way to promote collaboration and teamwork within the class. Anecdotally, student papers revealed markedly more effective use of critical thinking skills on the second critical thinking paper relative to the first in terms of both content and depth of analysis. Further, students demonstrated enhanced presentation skills, both in their level of confidence in expressing the conclusions reached by their groups and in the clarity with which conclusions were articulated.

This activity represents an enjoyable and useful approach for developing critical thinking skills relevant to evaluating research related to "real life" issues while promoting student collaboration and presentation skills. The method presented here is amenable to modification for fitting differing course structures, schedules, and topic areas, and we encourage readers to do so. Finally, although the paper is an effective tool for students to increase their writing skills while demonstrating critical thinking skills, instructors may omit the assignment to fit the structure of a particular course.

References

Barber, P. (2002). Critical analysis of psychological research: Rationale and design for a proposed course for the undergraduate psychology curriculum. *Psychology Learning and Teaching, 2,* 95–101.

Fink, L. D. (2003). *Creating significant learning experiences: An integrated approach to designing college courses.* San Francisco: Jossey-Bass.

Furedy, J. J. (1988). Teaching critical thinking at the undergraduate level: A golden opportunity worth its weight in gold. In P. J. Woods (Ed.), *Is psychology for them? A guide to undergraduate advising* (pp. 42–48). Washington, DC: American Psychological Association.

Matlin, M. M. (1997). Distilling psychology into 700 pages: Some goals for writing an introductory psychology textbook. In R. J. Sternberg (Ed.), *Teaching introductory psychology: Survival tips from the experts* (pp. 73–90). Washington, DC: American Psychological Association.

Myers, D. G. (1997). Professing psychology with a passion. In R. J. Sternberg (Ed.), *Teaching introductory psychology: Survival tips from the experts* (pp. 107–118).Washington, DC: American Psychological Association.

Report 7

Encouraging Students to Think Critically About Psychotherapy: Overcoming Naïve Realism

Scott O. Lilienfeld, Jeffrey M. Lohr, and Bunmi O. Olatunji

Many students choose to enter the field of psychology because they want to help others. Yet few appreciate the formidable difficulties of determining whether mental health professionals' helping efforts are effective. In particular, many novice psychology students do not recognize the obstacles standing in the way of ascertaining whether a treatment outperforms doing nothing, or of whether a treatment's positive effects exceed those of a myriad of "nonspecific effects" (e.g., placebo effects; see below) shared by many or most therapies (see, e.g., Chambless & Ollendick, 2001, for a review of the movement to develop criteria for, and lists of, empirically supported therapies).

Moreover, many students embark on their coursework holding two key misconceptions about psychotherapy. These misconceptions, we contend, must be addressed before students can learn to think critically about psychological treatment.

Psychotherapy: Two Key Misconceptions

First, many students assume that all of the more than 500 different "brands" of psychotherapy (Eisner, 2000) are effective or at worst harmless. Many believe that "doing something is always better than doing nothing." Yet a growing body of research refutes this assumption (Lilienfeld, 2007; Lilienfeld, Lynn, & Lohr, 2003). For example, research shows that *crisis debriefing*, a treatment that attempts to ward off posttraumatic stress disorder (PTSD) among trauma-exposed victims by urging them to "process" the emotions associated with this trauma, may actually increase individuals' risk of PTSD (McNally, Bryant, & Ehlers, 2002). As a second example, research demonstrates that *facilitated communication*, which purports to enable mute autistic individuals to communicate with the aid of an assistant who guides their hands over a keyboard, is entirely ineffective.

Its seeming effectiveness is due to facilitators' inadvertent control over autistic individuals' hand movements (Jacobson, Mulick, & Schwartz, 1995; Wegner, Fuller, & Sparrow, 2003).

Second, novice students often assume that research designs are not necessary to assess the effectiveness of psychotherapy. To many of them, the fact that "psychotherapy works" seems self-evident. After all, if clients can tell us whether they have improved and therapists can observe clients' improvement across sessions, why the need for complicated research designs?

Naïve Realism

We can answer the question posed above with two words: *naïve realism*. Naïve realism is the erroneous belief that the world is exactly as we see it (Ross & Ward, 1996). The concept of naïve realism is deeply embedded in popular consciousness, as suggested by the ubiquity of such sayings as "seeing is believing" and "what you see is what you get." Most beginning psychology students are naïve realists; they do not realize that (a) their assumptions, expectations, and biases influence their perceptions of the world; and (b) crucial unmeasured variables may account for these perceptions. Segall, Campbell, and Herskovits (1966) referred to this tendency as *phenomenal absolutism* and observed that "The normal observer naively assumes that the world is exactly as he sees it. He accepts the evidence of perception uncritically" (p. 5).

We propose that *naïve realism* is a major, if not *the* major obstacle, to educating students to think critically about psychotherapy. Naïve realism can lead students and therapy trainees to assume incorrectly that they can rely on the raw data of their sensory impressions to gauge therapeutic change. As a result, they can be swayed by their subjective clinical appraisals ("I can see the improvement with my own eyes") and fail to appreciate that apparent client change can be due to a plethora of hidden and often nonintuitive variables. In some cases, they may accurately perceive change, but misunderstand it; in other cases, they may perceive change when it is not present.

Students and trainees may be especially prone to this error when they expect to see change, as is frequently the case following psychotherapy. In such cases, their *confirmation bias*—that this, the tendency to focus on evidence that supports one's hypotheses while ignoring, minimizing, or distorting evidence that does not (Nickerson, 1998)—probably contributes to their perception of change in its absence. Specifically, students' and trainees' propensity to attend to and recall instances of change while discounting and forgetting instances of nonchange can lead them to overestimate the effectiveness of psychotherapy.

Ten Reasons Why Ineffective Psychotherapies Often Seem to Work

Students and trainees often do not appreciate the need for research safeguards against naïve realism, especially randomized controlled designs (RCTs). To become critical consumers of the psychotherapy outcome literature and scientifically informed therapists, students need to understand that RCTs and other research designs help protect against the many rival explanations for apparent change in psychotherapy. Here we outline 10 reasons why naïve realism can fool therapists—and psychotherapy clients—into perceiving therapeutic improvement even when it has not occurred (see also Arkowitz & Lilienfeld, 2006; Beyerstein, 1997). In our view, exposure to these reasons should be de rigueur when teaching undergraduates and graduate students about psychotherapy.

1 *Initial misdiagnosis.* A therapist may misdiagnose a client with an episodic condition, such as bipolar disorder, as having a chronic condition, such as schizophrenia. As a consequence, the therapist may misinterpret naturally occurring change in the client's condition as reflecting treatment effectiveness.

2 *Spontaneous remission.* Many individuals in acute psychological distress improve of their own accord, in part because of their coping mechanisms and in part because they encounter positive life events outside of therapy. As psychoanalyst Karen Horney (1957) observed, "life itself still remains a very effective therapist" (p. 240).

3 *Regression to the mean.* Extreme scores tend to be become less extreme on retesting. This phenomenon is a particular problem when inferring change in psychotherapy because most clients seek therapy when they are at their worst.

4 *Multiple treatment interference.* Many clients in psychotherapy receive other treatments (both psychological and psychopharmacological) at the same time, making it difficult to pinpoint the genuine causes of change (Kendall, Butcher, & Holmbeck, 1999).

5 *Selective attrition.* Clients who drop out of therapy are typically more impaired than those who remain in therapy, resulting in too rosy a picture of treatment effectiveness.

6 *Placebo effects.* Many clients may improve not because of active ingredients in the psychotherapy *per se*, but because they expect to improve. Indeed, research suggests that 40 to 60% of therapy clients report marked improvement between the initial phone call and the first therapy session (Howard, Kopta, Krause, & Orlinsky, 1986), perhaps in part because their moods are buoyed by the anticipation of imminent improvement.

7 *Novelty effects.* People often display an initial positive response to any new intervention that offers the promise of change, although this response tends to wear off rapidly (Shadish, Cook, & Campbell, 2002).

8 *Demand characteristics.* Clients often tell therapists what they think their therapists want to hear, namely that they are getting better.

9 *Effort justification.* Clients may feel a need to justify the energy, expense, and effort of therapy, resulting in reported improvement (Axsom & Cooper, 1985).

10 *Retrospective "rewriting" of one's initial level of functioning.* Research shows that following certain self-improvement programs, such as study skill courses, people do not change on objective measures. Yet they sometimes falsely believe they have improved because they misremember their initial level of functioning as worse than it actually was (Conway & Ross, 1984).

Educational and Assessment Implications

Before introducing students to these 10 reasons, it can be helpful to expose them to optical illusions (e.g., the Muller–Lyer illusion, the Ponzo or railroad tracks illusion) to persuade them that their raw sensory impressions can be deceiving (Hoefler, 1994). Such illusions may help to disabuse them of naïve realism. It may also be helpful to provide them with examples of how naïve realism has led to incorrect beliefs about the natural world, such as the subjectively compelling belief that the world is flat or that the sun revolves around the earth. In both cases, people's raw observations misled them about reality.

Moreover, it may be useful to teach students about the long history of failed treatments in medicine, including psychiatry. Most historians of medicine have argued that prior to 1890, most of the treatments (e.g., bleeding, blistering) that doctors prescribed to patients were either ineffective or harmful (Grove & Meehl, 1996), even though most doctors were persuaded otherwise. Similarly, most early reports of the "effectiveness" of prefrontal lobotomies were based on surgeons' informal observations of improvement. One early proponent of lobotomy wrote that "I am a sensitive observer and my conclusion is that a vast majority of my patients get better as opposed to worse after my treatment" (quoted in Dawes, 1994, p. 48).

To assess whether efforts to teach students about the perils of naïve realism are effective, one can present them with case examples of apparent improvement among clients in psychotherapy, ask them to generate rival explanations for the reported change, and encourage them to develop research strategies that would produce more defensible evidence of treatment effectiveness. If students can accurately identify these explanations and propose ways of controlling for them (e.g., placebo-controlled designs), they are well on their way toward shedding their naïve realism.

References

Arkowitz, H., & Lilienfeld, S. O. (2006, April/May). Psychotherapy on trial. *Scientific American Mind, 2,* 42–49.

Axsom, D., & Cooper, J. (1985). Cognitive dissonance and psychotherapy: The role of effort justification in inducing weight loss. *Journal of Experimental Social Psychology, 21,* 149–160.

Beyerstein, B. L. (1997). Why bogus therapies seem to work. *Skeptical Inquirer, 29,* 29–34.

Chambless, D. L., & Ollendick, T. H. (2001). Empirically supported psychological interventions: Controversies and evidence. *Annual Review of Psychology, 52,* 685–716.

Conway, M., & Ross, M. (1984). Getting what you want by revising what you had. *Journal of Personality and Social Psychology, 47,* 738–748.

Dawes, R. M. (1994). *House of cards: Psychology and psychotherapy built on myth.* New York: Free Press.

Eisner, D. A. (2000). *The death of psychotherapy: From Freud to alien abductions.* Westport, CT: Praeger.

Grove, W. M., & Meehl, P. E. (1996). Comparative efficiency of informal (subjective, impressionistic) and formal (mechanical, algorithmic) prediction procedures: The clinical statistical controversy. *Psychology: Public Policy and Law, 2,* 293–323.

Hoefler, J. M. (1994). Critical thinking and the use of optical illusions. *PS: Political Science and Politics, 2,* 538–545.

Horney, K. (1957). *Our inner conflicts: A constructive theory of neurosis.* London: Routledge & Kegan Paul.

Howard, K. I., Kopta, S. M., Krause, M. S., & Orlinsky, D. E. (1986). The dose–effect relationship in psychotherapy. *American Psychologist, 41,* 159–164.

Jacobson, J. W., Mulick, J. A., & Schwartz, A. A. (1995). A history of facilitated communication: Science, pseudoscience, and antiscience. *American Psychologist, 50,* 750–765.

Kendall, P. C., Butcher, J. N., & Holmbeck, G. N. (Eds.). (1999). *Handbook of research methods in clinical psychology* (2nd ed.) New York: Wiley.

Lilienfeld, S. O. (2007). Psychological treatments that cause harm. *Perspectives in Psychological Science, 2,* 53–70.

Lilienfeld, S. O., Lynn, S. J., & Lohr, J. M. (2003). *Science and pseudoscience in clinical psychology.* New York: Guilford.

McNally, R. J., Bryant, R. A., & Ehlers A. (2003). Does early psychological intervention promote recovery from posttraumatic stress? *Psychological Science in the Public Interest, 4,* 45–79.

Nickerson, R. S. (1998). Confirmation bias: A ubiquitous phenomenon in many guises. *Review of General Psychology, 2,* 175–220.

Ross, L., & Ward, A. (1996). Naïve realism: Implications for social conflict and misunderstanding. In T. Brown, E. Reed, & E. Turiel (Eds.), *Values and knowledge* (pp. 103–135). Hillsdale, NJ: Lawrence Erlbaum Associates.

Segall, M. H., Campbell, D. T., & Herskovits, M. J. (1966). *The influence of culture on visual perception.* Indianapolis, IA: Bobbs-Merrill.

Shadish, W. R., Cook, T. D., & Campbell, D. T. (2002). *Experimental and quasi-experimental designs for generalized causal inference.* Boston: Houghton-Mifflin.

Wegner, D. M., Fuller, V. A., & Sparrow, B. (2003). Clever hands: Uncontrolled intelligence in facilitated communication. *Journal of Personality and Social Psychology, 85,* 5–19.

Author Note

Please address all correspondence to Scott O. Lilienfeld, Ph.D., Professor, Department of Psychology, Room 206, Emory University, 532 Kilgo Circle, Atlanta, Georgia, 30322; email: slilien@emory.edu; fax: 404-727-0372; office phone: 404-727-1125.

Report 8

Effectiveness of a Web-Based Critical Thinking Module

Beth Dietz-Uhler

The importance of understanding critical thinking and the scientific method in psychology courses cannot be overstated (e.g., Nummedal & Halpern, 1995). Not only does recent research suggest that critical thinking is a successful predictor of exam performance (Williams, Oliver, Allin, Winn, & Booher, 2003), but developing critical thinking skills helps students improve their overall thinking skills (Halpern & Nummedal, 1995). Where understanding scientific evidence is concerned, research suggests that students with a science background performed better in introductory psychology courses than students with an arts background (Nathanson, Paulhus, & Williams, 2004). If students approached the study of psychology from a scientific perspective, applying scientific evidence to support their arguments, then it is likely that they would perform better in psychology courses.

How can students develop a scientific perspective? There is evidence to suggest that providing students with beginning-of-the-course experiences to improve their understanding of critical thinking is valuable (e.g., Yanchar & Slife, 2004). Thus it seems that faculty should make efforts to design modules or activities early in the course that promote students' understanding and use of critical thinking. The purpose of this paper is to report the design and assessment of a Web-based, interactive module to improve students' understanding of critical thinking and the scientific method.

Critical Thinking Module

I developed an interactive, Web-based Critical Thinking Module. The module's purpose is to fulfill the goals of promoting students' confidence in using the scientific method and critical thinking and to improve their knowledge of both. The module (Dietz-Uhler, 2005) contains three interactive assignments, one focusing on the scientific method and the other two on critical thinking, although note that only the first two will be discussed in this chapter.

The goal of the first assignment in my introductory psychology course is to understand the scientific method, both in theory and in practice. The module provides basic information about the scientific method, most notably the goals, steps, and data-collection methods. Students then work on an interactive activity requiring them to design (but not carry out) a study using the five steps of the scientific method (formulate a hypothesis, design the study, provide a plan for data collection, provide a plan for data analysis, and indicate likely outlets for reporting the findings). Students type their responses for each of the five steps in a Web-based form which they then submit to me.

The goal of the second assignment is to understand critical thinking. I give students a simple definition of critical thinking as well as the characteristics of critical thinkers (Smith, 1995). Students then engage in an interactive activity in which they consider two arguments. One argument provides scientific evidence to support the author's assertion (e.g., "Evidence shows that people in emergency situations are more likely to receive help if fewer people are available"); the other relies on personal experience (e.g., "Personal experience suggests that the more people available to help in an emergency, the more likely one is to get help"). Students indicate which argument is more convincing to them and state the reason(s) why the argument they chose is more convincing. Students then submit their responses online.

Assessment

To assess the effectiveness of the critical thinking module in improving students' confidence in their use of the scientific method and critical thinking and in their knowledge of both, students completed a brief assessment instrument that relied on the post-then method (Howard, 1980; Howard & Dailey, 1979; Koele & Hoogstraten, 1998). Briefly, in the post-then method (e.g., *How much do you know now?* and *How much did you know then?*), respondents give retrospective pretest ratings. This method eliminates the response-shift bias in pretest/posttest designs because retrospective evaluations are less exaggerated than pretest evaluations. The response-shift bias refers to the tendency for preratings to be elevated, leading to findings of negative, reduced, or nonsignificant treatment effects (Howard, 1980). Using this methodology, students indicated how confident they were that they could use the scientific method, how confident they were that they could use critical thinking, how much they knew about the scientific method, and how much they knew about critical thinking before completing the activity and now using 5-point scales (ranging from 1 = "not very confident/knowledgeable" to 5 = "very confident/knowledgeable").

Students in six different introductory psychology courses ($n = 60$) completed the questionnaire. Analysis of variance showed no significant differences across the six sections (average class size = 10 students) on any of the measures, so the samples were combined. Paired-samples t tests showed significant increases in students' confidence about using the scientific method now ($M = 4.54$, $SD = .57$) compared with before completing the module ($M = 3.68$, $SD = 1.06$), $t(58) = -8.32$, $p < .001$; confidence about using critical thinking now (M = 4.70, SD = .46) compared with before (M = 4.12, SD = .98), $t(59)$ = –5.20, p < .001; knowledge of the scientific method now (M = 4.48, SD = .73) compared with before (M = 3.70, SD = 1.13), $t(59)$ = –7.18, p < .001; and knowledge of critical thinking now (M = 4.77, SD = .43) compared with before (M = 3.85, SD = .94, $t(58)$ = –7.83, p < .001. Thus students reported that their confidence in the use and knowledge of critical thinking and the scientific method was better after than before the module, suggesting that the module was effective in meeting its goals.

Conclusion

The results of this assessment show that students' confidence in the use and knowledge of critical thinking and the scientific method improved as a result of the module. I invite readers to visit the module online and adapt its material and format for their own classroom uses. Of course, these data were self-reported and need to be interpreted as such. Nonetheless, there appear to be significant gains in confidence in the use and knowledge of critical thinking and the scientific method. Future research should focus on the effectiveness of the module in improving students' use of critical thinking in the course.

There is some evidence to show that critical thinking skills can be improved by providing learning experiences about critical thinking early in a course (Nathanson et al., 2004). Coupled with the evidence that students with a science background perform better in an introductory psychology course than students with an arts background (Yanchar & Slife, 2004), it is worthwhile to suggest that modules such as this one be available for students early in the course. Such an activity can, among other things, frame the course for students and instructors and foster the use of critical and scientific thinking.

References

Dietz-Uhler, B. (2005). *Critical thinking module.* Retrieved April 7, 2008, from http://www.users. muohio.edu/uhlerbd/Critical_Thinking_Module.html

Halpern, D. F., & Nummedal, S. G. (1995). Closing thoughts about helping students improve how they think. *Teaching of Psychology, 22,* 82–83.

Howard, G. S. (1980). Response shift bias: A problem in evaluating interventions with pre/post self-reports. *Evaluation Review, 4,* 93–106.

Howard, G. S., & Dailey, P. R. (1979). Response-shift bias: A source of contamination of self-report measures. *Journal of Applied Psychology, 66,* 144–150.

Koele, P., & Hoogstraten, J. (1988). A method for analyzing retrospective pretest/posttest designs: I. Theory. *Bulletin of the Psychonomic Society, 26,* 51–54.

Nathanson, C., Paulhus, D. L., & Williams, K. M. (2004). The challenge to cumulative learning: Do introductory courses actually benefit advanced students? *Teaching of Psychology, 31,* 5–9.

Nummedal, S. G., & Halpern, D. F. (1995). Introduction: Making the case for "psychologists teach critical thinking." *Teaching of Psychology, 22,* 4–5.

Smith, R. A. (1995). *Challenging your preconceptions: Thinking critically about psychology.* Pacific Grove, CA: Brooks/Cole.

Williams, R. L., Oliver, R., Allin, J. L., Winn, B., & Booher, C. S. (2003). Psychological critical thinking as a course predictor and outcome variable. *Teaching of Psychology, 30,* 220–223.

Yanchar, S. C., & Slife, B. D. 2004). Teaching critical thinking by examining assumptions. *Teaching of Psychology, 31,* 85–90.

Author Note

Correspondence concerning this manuscript should be addressed to Beth Dietz-Uhler, Department of Psychology, Miami University, Middletown, OH 45042; e-mail: uhlerbd@muohio.edu; telephone: 513.727.3254.

Report 9

An Introductory Exercise for Promoting Critical Thinking About Psychological Measurement

Jeffrey D. Holmes

Any collection of strategies for teaching critical thinking about psychology should include material addressing psychological testing issues. Measurement topics are particularly important because students are likely to have exaggerated confidence in the validity of test feedback (Beins, 1993). The Internet provides access to an endless collection of psychological measures, but the lack of quality control (Connor-Greene & Greene, 2002) means that cyberspace provides a forum for dissemination of scales and feedback with little or no validity evidence. Surveys of my introductory psychology lab classes revealed that the vast majority of students had completed free access psychological tests online or in magazines and that more than three-quarters of these students believed the results were accurate. Lacking experience with scale construction methods, students may be ill equipped to differentiate well-designed and validated scales from those of dubious quality. This short report presents a manageable exercise to promote critical thinking through greater understanding of complex measurement issues including reliability, validity, statistical error, and construct definition.

Inspired by earlier work on teaching scale construction (Benjamin, 1983), I developed this exercise for a large introductory lab course consisting of 7–10 smaller subsections. The activities, however, are relevant to an array of courses such as research methods, testing, and personality, where instructors can divide large classes into appropriately sized smaller groups. The exercise requires students to construct their own personality scales, collect responses, analyze data, and compare their scales psychometrically to similar and contrasting measures. Implementation of the strategy as described subsequently requires three class sessions, but instructors can simplify the approach. The activity as presented also requires 2–3 hours of simple word processing and data entry that a student assistant could complete.

Session One: Scale Construction

Once the instructor has established small groups (groups of 5–9 students work well), the first session begins with a discussion of commonly researched personality traits and strategies for scale construction. Each of the small groups should research one of three concise personality traits. I use extraversion, openness to experience, and optimism because they are relatively easy for students to grasp. Conversely I avoid assigning clinical symptom constructs, such as anxiety and depression, to prevent student discomfort and the disclosure of information that respondents might later regret. A lab assistant can offer guidance during students' search of Web-based or other literature to better understand and conceptualize their trait.

Following this background research and discussion of the literature, each student produces two or more original items to reflect the target trait. Instructors should provide guidelines for effective item writing such as the importance of clear and concise language, avoiding double negatives, and the advantages of using Likert scales to increase variability (see Clark & Watson, 1995, for a brief review of test construction guidelines). My lab groups initially produce 18–20 items each. The group members then debate the items until they agree on the five that best represent the trait. All groups complete this process independently, resulting in multiple measures of each trait. This procedure permits later analyses of both intertrait and intratrait relationships.

Session Two: Data Collection

Prior to the second session, a student assistant combines each scale into a single instrument for administration (Web-savvy instructors could put the items online to eliminate the need for data entry). The assistant or instructor must maintain an item key to allow for calculation of scale scores later. All students respond to the items written by all groups as well as several online single-trait personality measures. For the latter, I typically use scales measuring perfectionism, locus of control, sensation seeking, and Type A behavior. An instructor might substitute other widely available scales (it would be impractical to list Web sites here because Web addresses change frequently, but a brief search will yield many options). The extra scales add complexity to the activity but could be omitted if necessary. Because students can quickly complete the scales, they spend the remaining class time researching their assigned traits (instructors might also assign this step as a homework activity). Each student should retrieve empirical articles reporting correlations between the assigned trait and other psychological constructs. The students use these sources to generate hypotheses and later to refine their interpretation of the data.

Session Three: Analysis and Interpretation

After students have responded to the scales, an assistant compiles the data and the students perform statistical analyses. The specifics will vary depending on the level and nature of the course. In my introductory courses, I assign descriptive and correlational analyses. Students examine gender differences in trait scores, as well as the interrelations between similar and distinct trait scales. One of the most interesting and pedagogically valuable lessons involves intratrait correlations. Typically these relations are at best moderate, and often similarly intended measures are only weakly correlated. Despite following the same guidelines and having access to the same resources, students in my courses have produced measures that had virtually zero shared variance with measures of the same trait produced by other students. Given the educational goals of this activity, I consider such low correlations a good thing as they provide wonderful fodder for critical thinking. We discuss reliability, validity, and measurement error, as well as how different researchers may conceptualize traits in very different ways. In addition, the intertrait correlations usually are interesting, and students use them to test their *a priori* hypotheses. In my classes, the procedures culminate with each student writing a brief report that includes all elements of an empirical manuscript.

Evaluation and Adaptation to Other Courses

Students have responded favorably to this activity both formally and informally. Hettich (1974) recommended using student-generated data in class activities, and students have reported this aspect of the current exercise to be particularly interesting. Most students thought the activities fulfilled a variety of learning objectives, and most were more aware of the complexity of scale construction following the activity than at the outset. Students also indicated significantly greater agreement with the statement, "Writing a personality test would be an interesting task" at the conclusion of the activity than they had at the beginning.

As noted throughout, one could easily adapt this activity for various courses. Steps might include combining sessions, changing the target traits, or including more sophisticated analyses. For example, instructors could introduce regression by having students examine the incremental prediction of one of the traits using the other two. Further, students could investigate moderating relations by testing whether correlations between traits are moderated by gender. Instructors could introduce more complex measurement issues by including item-total correlations, internal consistency analysis, and even factor analysis to determine how various items fit with intended constructs. To make the activity more practical within a limited time frame, instructors could combine the scale construction and data collection sessions. The students could then analyze the data outside of class and discuss the results during a subsequent class meeting. In conclusion, the flexibility of this exercise permits its use in many different courses to promote critical thinking about psychological measurement.

References

Beins, B. C. (1993). Using the Barnum effect to teach about ethics and deception in research. *Teaching of Psychology, 20*, 33–35.

Benjamin, L. T., Jr. (1983). A class exercise in personality and psychological assessment. *Teaching of Psychology, 10*, 94–95.

Clark, L. E., & Watson, D. (1995). Constructing validity: Basic issues in objective scale development. *Psychological Assessment, 7,* 309–319.

Connor-Greene, P. A., & Greene, D. J. (2002). Science or snake oil? Teaching critical evaluation of "research" reports on the Internet. *Teaching of Psychology, 29,* 321–324.

Hettich, P. H. (1974). The student as data generator. *Teaching of Psychology, 1,* 35–36.

Author Note

Address correspondence to Jeffrey D. Holmes, Department of Psychology, Ithaca College, Ithaca, NY 14850; e-mail: jholmes@ithaca.edu; telephone: (607) 274-7386.

Author Index

Subject Index